Betsy Schwarzentraub skillfully weaves wisdom from the ages, biblical and spiritual guidance, and decades of experience as a stewardship theologian and practitioner into a rich fabric that holds the treasure of the spiritual discipline of faithful generosity. Sit with this book, drink deeply from the knowledge and insights on its pages, and be ready to put into practice its many thoughtful and practical suggestions for growing a generous, grace-filled soul.

MARCIA SHETLER, Executive Director/CEO,
Ecumenical Stewardship Center

This is a blockbuster of a book.... I love its inclusion of the disciplines, the importance of teaching stewardship based on stages of human development, and integrating the teachings of the contemplative movement.... [This] book is invaluable because everything church leaders need to know about the subject is between its two covers.

RODGER R RICE, formerly with Barnabas Foundation

Betsy's wealth of experience as a pastor, teacher and leading voice in the stewardship arena makes *Growing Generous Souls* a critical resource for pastors, and an excellent small group study for churches.... As Betsy articulates so well - living a life of generosity is about so much more than money! In light of God's grace, how can we be anything but generous? *Growing Generous Souls* offers a roadmap for living differently.

REV. DR. CHRISTINE ROUSH, Mission Engagement Specialist for
American Baptist Home Mission Societies; author of *Swimming
Upstream: Reflections on Consumerism and Culture*

*Growing Generous Souls* contains a wealth of wisdom and practical reflections. Betsy Schwarzentraub sets forth an abundance of spiritual and strategic insights for nurturing grateful givers. I recommend it to anyone serving in stewardship space in the geography of the Kingdom.

DR. GARY HOAG, teacher, author,
and spiritual counselor for stewards; founder of *generositymonk.com*

*Growing Generous Souls*...overflows with the author's own spirited enthusiasm and authentic deep love of God. Betsy's latest book is a genuine reflection of her own life and ministry....Reading *Growing Generous Souls* is a joy-filled experience from beginning to end!

SUSAN PETERS, CFRE, Executive Director,
California-Nevada United Methodist Foundation

I thoroughly appreciated Dr. Schwarzentraub's breadth of research and ministry insight....Her Questions for Reflection at the end of each chapter are brilliant, as well as her closing Soul-Making chapter. As a spiritual director, I will undoubtedly refer to her wisdom and applications.

JENNI HOAG, Soulcare anchoress;
founder of *soulcareanchoress.com*

Dr. Betsy gets to the heart of the matter. She helps us focus on where it really counts long term and not simply quick fixes of generosity....It's not enough to do or get with a program; Dr. Betsy challenges us to embrace generous hearts that come directly from the heart of God....

JERRY COLEMAN, Director of Speakers, The Francis Asbury Society;
former Area Director for continental Europe, The Free Methodist Church

Dr. Schwarzentraub has produced an outstanding Stewardship/ Generosity resource that will help grow faithful, generous believers for all generations. *Growing Generous Souls* is a great read for clergy and laity who want to lead and develop cultures of generosity and faithful stewardship in the life of their congregation and community.

REV. MELVIN AMERSON, Resource Specialist,
Texas Methodist Foundation; author of *Celebrating the Offering*,
*Stewardship for African-American Churches: A New Paradigm*, and *Fruit for Celebrating the Offering*

Betsy Schwarzentraub has brought forth a breakthrough resource to undertake a very different course that is not only biblically based and theologically sound, but also scientifically relevant....She creates the opportunities for personal reflection, study group discussions and professional growth that move the reader from simply "doing church" to "being church" wherein all dimensions of generosity combine into life practice.

REV. SANFORD COON, Vice President, Horizons Stewardship;
former President of the New Mexico Conference Methodist Foundation

If you are looking for...a comprehensive collection of ideas about how a person or a church might develop exciting ministries in this area, *Growing Generous Souls* is the book you want....Betsy Schwarzentraub has given the modern Christian church the stewardship equivalent of Calvin's *Institutes* or Thomas Aquinas's *Summa Theologica*.

REV. LYNN MILLER, firstfruits educator;
author of *Firstfruits Living* and *The Power of Enough*

# Growing Generous Souls

## BECOMING GRACE-FILLED STEWARDS

Betsy Schwarzentraub

ISBN 978-1-5323-8868-2
Library of Congress Control Number: 2018915322

For a free small-group study guide, People and Ministries Index, and other resources, go to www.growinggeneroussouls.com.

Generous Stewards Communications
Garden Valley, CA 95633

Edited by Danita K. Moon
Designed by John Reinhardt Book Design
Cover designed by Fred Abbott
Cover photo by Mary Margaret Schwarzentraub
Printed, shipped and distributed by IngramSpark

# Contents

Preface . . . . . . . . . . . . . . . . . . . . . . . . . . . . . . . . ix

1. Compulsive Doing . . . . . . . . . . . . . . . . . . . . . . . . 1
   Doing, Doing, Doing . . . . . . . . . . . . . . . . . . . . . . . 3
   Fragmented Living . . . . . . . . . . . . . . . . . . . . . . . . 6
   "Doing" Church . . . . . . . . . . . . . . . . . . . . . . . . . 10
   Being an Authentic Self . . . . . . . . . . . . . . . . . . . . 13
   Stewardship . . . . . . . . . . . . . . . . . . . . . . . . . . . 15
   Generosity . . . . . . . . . . . . . . . . . . . . . . . . . . . . 16
   Turning Around . . . . . . . . . . . . . . . . . . . . . . . . . 20
   Questions for Reflection . . . . . . . . . . . . . . . . . . . . 25
   Endnotes. . . . . . . . . . . . . . . . . . . . . . . . . . . . . . 25

2. Being and Praise . . . . . . . . . . . . . . . . . . . . . . . . 31
   Who We Are . . . . . . . . . . . . . . . . . . . . . . . . . . . 34
   Identity . . . . . . . . . . . . . . . . . . . . . . . . . . . . . . 44
   Integrity . . . . . . . . . . . . . . . . . . . . . . . . . . . . . . 48
   Being With God . . . . . . . . . . . . . . . . . . . . . . . . . 50
   Singing God's Praise . . . . . . . . . . . . . . . . . . . . . . 51
   Questions for Reflection . . . . . . . . . . . . . . . . . . . . 53
   Endnotes. . . . . . . . . . . . . . . . . . . . . . . . . . . . . . 54

3. Practicing Presence . . . . . . . . . . . . . . . . . . . . . . 59
   Spiritual Disciplines . . . . . . . . . . . . . . . . . . . . . . 59
   Searching the Scriptures. . . . . . . . . . . . . . . . . . . . 60
   Prayer . . . . . . . . . . . . . . . . . . . . . . . . . . . . . . . 66
   Meditation . . . . . . . . . . . . . . . . . . . . . . . . . . . . 70

CONTENTS

Contemplation. . . . . . . . . . . . . . . . . . . . . . . . . . . . . . . . . . . . . . . . .73
Questions for Reflection . . . . . . . . . . . . . . . . . . . . . . . . . . . . . . .75
Endnotes. . . . . . . . . . . . . . . . . . . . . . . . . . . . . . . . . . . . . . . . . . . . .76

4. What Is a Soul? . . . . . . . . . . . . . . . . . . . . . . . . . . . . . . . .79
The Soul and the Bible . . . . . . . . . . . . . . . . . . . . . . . . . . . . . . . .80
Plato . . . . . . . . . . . . . . . . . . . . . . . . . . . . . . . . . . . . . . . . . . . . . . . .82
Aristotle and Plotinus. . . . . . . . . . . . . . . . . . . . . . . . . . . . . . . . .84
Augustine. . . . . . . . . . . . . . . . . . . . . . . . . . . . . . . . . . . . . . . . . . . .87
Other Christian Thinkers. . . . . . . . . . . . . . . . . . . . . . . . . . . . . .88
The True Self . . . . . . . . . . . . . . . . . . . . . . . . . . . . . . . . . . . . . . . . .92
Image of God. . . . . . . . . . . . . . . . . . . . . . . . . . . . . . . . . . . . . . . . .96
Questions for Reflection . . . . . . . . . . . . . . . . . . . . . . . . . . . . . .102
Endnotes. . . . . . . . . . . . . . . . . . . . . . . . . . . . . . . . . . . . . . . . . . . .103

5. Growing as Becoming. . . . . . . . . . . . . . . . . . . . . . . . . . . .III
Growth as Development . . . . . . . . . . . . . . . . . . . . . . . . . . . . . .112
Learning in Families. . . . . . . . . . . . . . . . . . . . . . . . . . . . . . . . . .116
Stages of Faith . . . . . . . . . . . . . . . . . . . . . . . . . . . . . . . . . . . . . .120
Giving and Growth. . . . . . . . . . . . . . . . . . . . . . . . . . . . . . . . . . .125
Building Muscle Memory for Giving. . . . . . . . . . . . . . . . . . . .128
Questions for Reflection . . . . . . . . . . . . . . . . . . . . . . . . . . . . . .133
Endnotes. . . . . . . . . . . . . . . . . . . . . . . . . . . . . . . . . . . . . . . . . . . .133

6. Seasons of the Soul . . . . . . . . . . . . . . . . . . . . . . . . . . . . 139
Planting and Nourishing the Seed . . . . . . . . . . . . . . . . . . . . .139
Flowing Water . . . . . . . . . . . . . . . . . . . . . . . . . . . . . . . . . . . . . . .141
Seasons of Our Lives. . . . . . . . . . . . . . . . . . . . . . . . . . . . . . . . .143
Moving from False Self to True Self. . . . . . . . . . . . . . . . . . . . .144
Growing From the Inside Out. . . . . . . . . . . . . . . . . . . . . . . . . .147
Responding to God's Grace. . . . . . . . . . . . . . . . . . . . . . . . . . . .149
Questions for Reflection . . . . . . . . . . . . . . . . . . . . . . . . . . . . . .151
Endnotes. . . . . . . . . . . . . . . . . . . . . . . . . . . . . . . . . . . . . . . . . . . .152

7. Gratitude. . . . . . . . . . . . . . . . . . . . . . . . . . . . . . . . 153
   The Gratitude Process . . . . . . . . . . . . . . . . . . . . . . . . . 153
   A Joyful Response of Praise. . . . . . . . . . . . . . . . . . . . . . 155
   A Grateful Perspective . . . . . . . . . . . . . . . . . . . . . . . . . 160
   The Benefits of Gratitude. . . . . . . . . . . . . . . . . . . . . . . . 164
   Practicing a Grateful Attitude. . . . . . . . . . . . . . . . . . . . . 168
   The Basis for a Life of Gratitude . . . . . . . . . . . . . . . . . . . 171
   Questions for Reflection . . . . . . . . . . . . . . . . . . . . . . . . 175
   Endnotes. . . . . . . . . . . . . . . . . . . . . . . . . . . . . . . . . . 176

8. Scarcity and the Lure of More . . . . . . . . . . . . . . . . . . 181
   The Lure of More. . . . . . . . . . . . . . . . . . . . . . . . . . . . . 182
   The Rich Fool. . . . . . . . . . . . . . . . . . . . . . . . . . . . . . . 185
   Needs versus Wants . . . . . . . . . . . . . . . . . . . . . . . . . . . 188
   Scarcity Thinking . . . . . . . . . . . . . . . . . . . . . . . . . . . . 190
   Questions for Reflection . . . . . . . . . . . . . . . . . . . . . . . . 194
   Endnotes. . . . . . . . . . . . . . . . . . . . . . . . . . . . . . . . . . 194

9. An Ethic of Enough . . . . . . . . . . . . . . . . . . . . . . . . . 199
   An Abundant Partnership . . . . . . . . . . . . . . . . . . . . . . . 199
   The Problem With Abundance . . . . . . . . . . . . . . . . . . . . 204
   Contentment and an Ethic of Enough . . . . . . . . . . . . . . . . 207
   Simplicity as Freedom . . . . . . . . . . . . . . . . . . . . . . . . . 215
   Questions for Reflection . . . . . . . . . . . . . . . . . . . . . . . . 220
   Endnotes. . . . . . . . . . . . . . . . . . . . . . . . . . . . . . . . . . 221

10. Generosity and Money . . . . . . . . . . . . . . . . . . . . . . . 225
    The Big Taboo . . . . . . . . . . . . . . . . . . . . . . . . . . . . . . 226
    How to Talk About Money in the Church. . . . . . . . . . . . . 228
    A Would-Be God . . . . . . . . . . . . . . . . . . . . . . . . . . . . 231
    Getting Out of Debt . . . . . . . . . . . . . . . . . . . . . . . . . . 233
    A Spiritual Issue . . . . . . . . . . . . . . . . . . . . . . . . . . . . . 235
    Questions for Reflection . . . . . . . . . . . . . . . . . . . . . . . . 240
    Endnotes. . . . . . . . . . . . . . . . . . . . . . . . . . . . . . . . . . 241

CONTENTS

11. Putting God First . . . . . . . . . . . . . . . . . . . . . . . . . . . .245
    Moving Beyond Materialism . . . . . . . . . . . . . . . . . . . . . . .245
    Money and Giving . . . . . . . . . . . . . . . . . . . . . . . . . . . .253
    Ask, Thank, Tell . . . . . . . . . . . . . . . . . . . . . . . . . . . .261
    From Tithing to First Fruits . . . . . . . . . . . . . . . . . . . . . .262
    Questions for Reflection . . . . . . . . . . . . . . . . . . . . . . . .268
    Endnotes . . . . . . . . . . . . . . . . . . . . . . . . . . . . . . . .268

12. The Church and Caring for Souls . . . . . . . . . . . . . . . . . .273
    Shifting the Paradigm . . . . . . . . . . . . . . . . . . . . . . . . .275
    *Koinonia* Community . . . . . . . . . . . . . . . . . . . . . . . . . .281
    *Diakonia* Ministry . . . . . . . . . . . . . . . . . . . . . . . . . .284
    From Tasks to Relationships . . . . . . . . . . . . . . . . . . . . . .285
    Questions for Reflection . . . . . . . . . . . . . . . . . . . . . . . .292
    Endnotes . . . . . . . . . . . . . . . . . . . . . . . . . . . . . . . .293

13. A Renewed Sense of Mission . . . . . . . . . . . . . . . . . . . . .297
    Living in Our Wider Community . . . . . . . . . . . . . . . . . . . . .297
    People in Mission . . . . . . . . . . . . . . . . . . . . . . . . . . .301
    Communities of Gospel Stewards . . . . . . . . . . . . . . . . . . . . .305
    Loving God and Neighbor . . . . . . . . . . . . . . . . . . . . . . . .311
    Questions for Reflection . . . . . . . . . . . . . . . . . . . . . . . .313
    Endnotes . . . . . . . . . . . . . . . . . . . . . . . . . . . . . . . .313

14. Generosity as a Way of Living . . . . . . . . . . . . . . . . . . . .317
    Amazing Grace . . . . . . . . . . . . . . . . . . . . . . . . . . . . .317
    Whole-Life Generosity . . . . . . . . . . . . . . . . . . . . . . . . .320
    Stewards of the Earth . . . . . . . . . . . . . . . . . . . . . . . . .324
    Honoring Ourselves . . . . . . . . . . . . . . . . . . . . . . . . . . .331
    The Art of Forgiving . . . . . . . . . . . . . . . . . . . . . . . . . .336
    Questions for Reflection . . . . . . . . . . . . . . . . . . . . . . . .345
    Endnotes . . . . . . . . . . . . . . . . . . . . . . . . . . . . . . . .345

15. Soul Making . . . . . . . . . . . . . . . . . . . . . . . . . . . . . .351

    Scripture Index . . . . . . . . . . . . . . . . . . . . . . . . . . . .355

# Preface

HOW DO WE grow souls—including our own—in a way that empowers generous attitudes and habits as a way of life? *Growing Generous Souls* arises from my years in ministry. I hope this book will inspire each of us to practice, teach, and model generous living.

Questions and notes following each chapter can spark small-group study, prompt individual reflection, and help the reader locate recommended resources. A Scripture Index will assist Bible study and sermon preparation.

My special thanks and appreciation go out to my designer, John Reinhardt, to my mentor, June Gillam, and especially to Debra Griffin and Peter Stafford, whose critiques and patient persistence helped me shape a rough-and-tumble message into its current form.

This book is dedicated to Ken, my soulmate,
and to Jana, Eric, and Matt,
with all my love.

*Betsy Schwarzentraub*

# Compulsive Doing

"**W**HAT'S THE NEWEST** fundraising program we can use this year?" Yet another call! That made several calls in just one week in which someone asked me that question. They sounded almost as if they were looking for the latest gimmick. Why do they keep asking for programs, I wondered, as if stewardship is just about getting money for the church, or as if we're selling our services, trying to get participants to "buy into" our ministries?

Whatever happened to biblical stewardship, anyway? Even if people aren't sick of being "sold" on financially supporting their congregation (and I bet plenty of them are), I'm sure a lot of leaders are weary of searching for the "magic program" that will turn their church around.

And it's not just a church problem, anyway. How do any of us quit running from one fundraising program to another, and focus instead on developing ourselves and others as stewards of God's grace?

We may recall gatherings where church leaders bragged about their congregations as if their church was constantly growing and filled with miracles. Yes, God is present and beautiful things happen, but that's not the full truth about our lives or what we do. It gets tiring trying to look perfect while hiding our vulnerabilities.

There's another level, as well. What about our own spiritual lives, whether we're religious or not? How do we stop racing from one activity to the next, constantly looking for more? We want to rest in God as our true selves, made in God's image.

And then there's the church culture of doing, doing, doing. It's hard not to feel pressured to join yet another committee or outreach effort to express our faith. Even as pastors, we may struggle to make this week's worship service more inspiring, this year's Easter or Christmas pageant more spectacular, or this season's list of small groups even longer to meet everyone's needs. If some is good, more is better...right?

At this stage in any human endeavor, maybe we feel weary from repeatedly trying to make our mark in the world. Perhaps now, after enduring a major illness, loss, or life-changing experience, we desire a deeper focus.[1] It's not bad to strive to achieve great things: it helps motivate us to improve ourselves and make the world better. But at a certain point, we may want to shift from focusing on accomplishments to something more enduring and tangible, giving greater meaning and sense of legacy.

*Growing Generous Souls* acknowledges the dilemma thousands of us experience with compulsive activity in their personal lives and church involvement. We yearn to taste more fully the freedom of generous-hearted living that Jesus Christ offers us, and to become more joyful stewards of God's grace. This book investigates some core spiritual disciplines to remind us of our identity before God and provides a fuller understanding of our "souls." It describes ways that we, as Christians, can better discover and nourish our true selves, basing our lives in gratitude to God. In challenging the ethic of scarcity and the lure of constantly seeking more, readers can rediscover greater simplicity that leads to more freedom, contentment, and an ethic of enough.

Recognizing unbridled consumerism as a pernicious challenge, this book explores the use of money as both a spiritual issue and a powerful tool to help people put God first in their daily lives. Readers are invited to move further away from providing smorgasbord religious programs, and toward caring for one another and for the larger community as stewards of the Good News. Vital, passionate generosity can become the key to "soul making," as part of a sparkling, lifelong, whole-life adventure.

# Doing, Doing, Doing

Let's face it: there's so much *doing* in life that it takes deliberate intention to keep from being frenetic most of the time. When did you last feel frenetic—wildly excited or active, frenzied, and consequently distracted?[2] For millions of people, the frantic lifestyle includes what job ads call "a fast-paced work environment." Translation: Don't assume you'll have a minute's peace. Be prepared to multitask constantly and shift gears quickly. In a *Fortune* study[3] of career coaches, recruiters, and other job experts, one typical response was, "This means that the employer wants high productivity at all costs, and you'll be fielding a steady flow of emergencies."

Productivity is a key word in Western culture, where the do-it-yourself mentality runs deep, constant achievement is a virtue, and accomplishment is most often equated with success. Despite the reality of collaboration in many work settings, Westerners especially are encouraged to think individualistically, to "pull ourselves up by our own bootstraps." Employees are evaluated solely on their latest efforts, and they fear being edged out to the sidelines if their productivity slows.

Benedictine monk David Steindl-Rast notes that without realizing it, we can get trapped in a perspective in which only the useful counts.[4] In such a utilitarian world, we may lose our enjoyment of life—in music, in mountain climbing, or even a kiss.

"Much of Western culture is based on work and rewards," says Carl Hoffman, Presbyterian pastor:

> If we are not careful, our identities can be forged in this alchemy. We become what we do, and we are what we earn. Before we know it, our titles, diplomas, portfolios, roles, responsibilities, salaries, homes, and possessions begin to define us. We've worked hard to earn them, but they end up owning us.[5]

The philosopher Martin Heidegger believes that many of us have become so lost in "average everydayness" that we barely comprehend our more deeply authentic possibilities.[6] Whether or not we agree with his assessment, several recent studies tell us that unlimited use of technology can misdirect our attention, taking us away from being present to the people around us.

Technology itself is not the problem. In fact, a number of tech companies have had great success balancing work with play, some including profit-sharing and flexible work schedules.[7] Many Internet-related companies encourage employees to integrate different aspects of their lives by providing onsite child care and parental leave. The issue is how well we, the end users of their products, limit technology for our own purposes.

Constant work can box us into prearranged categories in the name of productivity, progress, and speed.[8] When people focus more on their electronic devices than they do on the people around them, they can become less attentive at work, slower to react defensively in their cars, and less attentive to relationships. They can still be "at work" electronically on an airplane or on vacation, and consequently miss out on being present to their family or friends. Their employers or supervisors also may assume they are available any time of the day or night, and so invade their personal time at home with incessant electronic demands.

We can choose another route for living. We can engage regularly in prayer, meditation, or worship. With consistent practices, we can learn to focus more on *being* than on constantly *doing*. In those moments, we realize that death is real, and each moment of life is precious. As we acknowledge our mortality, we may discover a greater freedom to explore our true possibilities and seek the opportunities that otherwise lie hidden in our lives.[9] This attitude opens us up further to "being–in–the–world," where we recognize the value of our involvement with others and are able to interact more meaningfully with our environment.

Clearly, just because we are busy does not mean we are living an inauthentic life. We can choose to live fully whether at a slow or fast pace. But at whatever speed we choose, how do we keep attentive to our relationship with God, which is the center of life's purpose? With the right priorities we are like a work of clay properly put at the center of a pottery wheel. But when we allow a zillion activities or mental and emotional distractions, we slip off-center on the wheel. Then the inevitable happens—the centrifugal force of our busy lives can unbalance us or even push us over the edge.

With more than thirty-six years as a pastor and church leader, I know some of these centrifugal forces firsthand. A combination of addressing regular ministry crises and my personal choices threatened to destroy personal boundaries and create a 24/7 work schedule. In my desire to "do it all," I often confused God's call as a Christian with an always-at-work mentality. The relationships and interactions were good in themselves but were not meant to take the place of God. Whatever our occupation, it takes effort to shift one's spiritual focus from compulsive doing to the quality of being present to God, to ourselves, and to others in a balanced way.

In the book *Death of a Hero, Birth of the Soul*, John Robinson identifies an emerging social movement of choosing "the consciousness of being over the compulsivity of doing." He draws on his experiences as a psychologist and psychotherapist when he says:

Being means knowing subjective experience in a perceptually pure and feeling way. It occurs, for example, when you simply feel into what you are, into your capacity for love. From this kind of awareness streams the natural rhythms of activity and rest, openness and closedness, work and celebration, introversion and extroversion. Compulsive doing, like the machine it emulates, violates this natural energy.[10]

While feelings are important, they may not be enough in themselves to inform our being. We need to reflect on our situations and choices, as well. In fact, John Wesley, founder of the Methodist movement, says that the process of good decision-making involves not only personal experience (including feelings) and reason, but also tradition, and how we understand the core messages of the Bible. He believes each of us relies on our unique mixture of these four factors—Scripture, tradition, reason and experience—as we gradually become the persons we were meant to be.[11]

As I write this, I am reflecting on my own past years of compulsive doing in pastoral and extension ministry, as I worked with individual congregations and across my denomination. But trying to make one's mark in the world is not limited to ministers or to Christians. People in a wide variety of careers feel the drive to be a success, and to make substantial accomplishments. They can become potentially disappointed when they look in vain for that new, magic program or daily spiritual practice that will cure all their ills.

As human beings, we may want to get off what seems like an enervating treadmill. At whatever age or stage of our lives, we might yearn to regain that sparkling sense of God's call to the persons we are and who, by God's grace, we can grow to become.

# Fragmented Living

Ever since the end of the Industrial Age, nations around the globe have moved more and more into a "knowledge economy,"[12] where economic systems have provided not only products and services, but also a globalized economy of knowledge resources such as the analysis and management of information. Some analysts of this new economy predict that it will "extend radically, creating a pattern in which even ideas will be recognized and identified as a commodity."[13] The explosion of computer technology has turned our time into a Digital Age. This technological leap, together with our expectations of increased productivity, can impact our sense of authentic living and our participation in a grateful community.

While not all people have access to personal computers, the invention of smartphones and public places with Wi-Fi access have transformed communications, even affecting entire social movements. Now millions of individuals around the world can transfer information freely and have instant access to knowledge that previously would have been difficult or impossible to find.[14] Ever since the implementation of the World Wide Web in the early 1990s, the Internet has become the ultimate platform for accelerating the flow of information.

This exponential burst of technology has acted as a two-edged sword. On the positive side, it has given us personal access to new worlds of expertise and phenomenal stores of information. Computers have made multiple subjects radically more accessible to us at advanced levels, so those who seek the information can range across limitless categories. But it has also intensified the need for professional compartmentalization in order to provide latest up-to-the-minute research in each specific micro-field.

Now with the ease, speed and scope of the Internet, users can demand more. At the same time, many of us continue to put on a pedestal the "go-getter" entrepreneurial spirit. This achievement orientation has produced amazing lives and achievements. But the flip side can be a professional self-image that depends upon ever-new discovery and a sense of value based on our latest assignment. As the saying goes, "you're only as good as your last project."

This pressure to profit from harnessing knowledge is the coin of our economy. Connections can dissolve into an extension of self-interest, leading to transactional relationships. If we view every relationship as a transaction, we remove the opportunity for mutual giving and receiving, and the delight of simply being with one another. Interactions are reduced to "you scratch my back, I'll scratch yours." While self-interest is always part of human experience, our care for other people increases as we mature, and go beyond purely personal advancement to seek the well-being of our community. With friends, neighbors, family members, and religious companions, both persons can change for the better when we share our life journeys with each other in gratitude, wonder, and deepening trust.

In addition to compartmentalizing ourselves professionally, we may unconsciously compartmentalize our different social identities. Someone could act like one personality in one role, and then have a totally different persona when he or she is engaged in a different task.[15] For example, a person might act compassionately in church on Sunday, but then be a cutthroat employer or employee the rest of the week, or a dictator in his or her own family.

But there is another level to compartmentalization, as well. It can also mean setting aside potentially conflicting aspects of a person's life into self-contained capsules. By putting different aspects of our lives into these "silos," we do not have to struggle directly with conflicting values or roles. For example, a doctor may recommend healthy living but personally overeat or smoke. An advocate for the environment or for justice might own personal stock in companies that pollute the air or produce weapons.

Many people need to devote most of their time and energy in one direction for a while, as parents do to raise their young children, or as one partner may work multiple jobs to support a spouse who is finishing school. But if excessive devotion becomes a lifelong habit, the successful businesswoman may feel insubstantial with her friends and family. The excellent school teacher or office worker may forget how to be fully himself with his wife or children.

Whenever we compartmentalize our lives, we can confuse what we do with who we are so completely that we lose touch with important aspects of ourselves.

Ministers can fall into compartmentalization in their roles, as well. "I can't imagine who I will be without the preacher's task to do, a congregation to listen to me and the satisfaction I get from the weekly attention," confesses L. Roger Owens, Associate Professor of Leadership and Ministry at Pittsburgh Theological Seminary.[16] Then he immediately admits that most spiritual directors today, as well as the biblical prophet Jeremiah, would call this idolatry: putting something that is not God in God's place, as the center of one's life.

I remember a time when I could not imagine being anything other than a pastor of a church. It's not that I thought I was indispensable or all that skilled at it, but rather that it seemed to be so intertwined with who I was as a person that I couldn't be me without it. I usually brought work along even on my vacations; otherwise I didn't feel useful.

Looking back, I realize I verged on addictive language about serving the church. "It's in my blood," I would say; "I can't imagine my life without it." Such statements, of course, were idolatry, putting something else—in this case, my pastoral role—in the place of God. Only God is the One we cannot truly do without.

We are all multifaceted human beings—much like jewels, reflecting differently when seen from another angle or in a different light. Living this way is lovely. But what is not lovely is "changing who you are; manipulating yourself in order to fit some kind of mold of what is or is not appropriate,"[17] if we do so for the sake of inauthentic appearances in contrast to who we really are.

So what would it feel like to dissolve many of these self-imposed compartments, and to move toward total alignment of purpose? As one writer said,

> When everything is completely integrated, when your heart, mind, and body are acting as one vehicle, your life starts to become something very beautiful. Your expression is natural, unique, and right. Your creativity flows. Your heart is opened.... Your existence becomes one of expressing and expanding the awesomeness of what already is.[18]

How do we live full lives in this world of technological accessibility, where both external demands and internal stresses can make it hard to reflect upon, let alone give full flow to all of who we are? Although many of us seek to live with a sense of balance, it has become easier to fall into fragmented living. We may over-attach to our public image, roles, or tasks, and thereby lose some important, long-buried aspects of who we truly are.

# "Doing" Church

With busier lives, the issues of productivity and compartmentalization tend to intensify. If you are active in a congregation or serve as a church leader, you may have found that church planning can fall into a lot of repetitive *doing*. Unless we intentionally streamline the process, every initiative requires multiple meetings. Searching for new ideas can become an endless stream of trying one program after another, looking for "the magic bullet" that will connect best with the congregation.

So how can we encourage people not to just *do* tasks, but to *be* in community with one another? How can we grow like a tree does, from the inside out, as Ephesians 3:16–19 so beautifully describes? Whether we are planning to lead others or are taking a serious look at how we live our own lives, how can we focus more on *being* the persons God intends us to be and continuing to mature as generous souls?

One cultural obstacle within the Western church can be an over-emphasis on achievement. Accomplishment is laudable. It requires not only skill but also a strong will, repeated practice, and unrelenting perseverance. Individual achievement requires boldness and ingenuity that makes a person stand out in the crowd. Yet many of us tend to see as larger than life individuals who demonstrate great courage, exercise special effort, or show superior ability.

Both Jesus and the Early Church in the New Testament reflect far more of a *team* ministry and *group* discipleship than a Lone Ranger style of service. While Jesus called most of his disciples one by one, he gathered them together as a group of people to train them and to minister alongside them. When they looked to him to feed more than five thousand listeners by the Sea of Galilee, he said, "You give them something to eat"—and then multiplied the gifts they brought forward (Mark 6:30–44 and parallels).

In the fledgling Church, Paul set up a network of house churches for worship and as a base for their outreach and mission. Here the early Christians also heard Paul's "epistles:" round-robin letters carried by personal messengers from one congregation to the next, to circulate among all the weekly gatherings in a given region (Romans 1:7; 1 Corinthians 1:2; and Ephesians 1:1. Note Colossians 4:5–17 and Philippians 4:2–3.)[19]

Here again, the issue of productivity arises. Trying to be fruitful in one's life can be motivating. Without goals to accomplish, we lose the sense of who we are and where we are going. The same is true for a congregation. Being a vital congregation requires teamwork in order to be active, involved, and effective. But it also requires sustainability. "Sustainability" is the ongoing strength of who you are together as a community, for mission and ministry.[20]

In a six-year study of more than seven hundred North American congregations, consultant Dan Dick identified how vital churches can strengthen both growth and sustainability. The measures of sustainability involve accountability for spiritual development, communal identity, and practicing specific "means of grace." They also include hours per week spent in spiritual formation and service, versus hours spent in meetings and planning; alignment of activities with values and vision; and decision-making processes, especially when dealing with conflict and contention. Two critical focus areas he names relate to sustainability, as well. They are: thinking holistically about the congregation and balancing the church's inward and outward focus.[21]

While church programs and events are useful in themselves, they can easily dissolve into an inward obsession. The outcome can be a church like the proverbial grease factory, where all the grease produced is used to lubricate the factory's machines.

Along with productivity, our society's extreme consumer behavior tends to affect our beliefs about church, in three ways.

- First, that members of the church staff are meant to do the ministry, while the congregation "buys" their services with their financial giving.

- Second, that the money we give allows us to dictate the church's ministry direction.
- Third, that "our" money is meant to raise our congregation's standard of living, not our standard of giving.

Such behavior also results in what Rt. Rev. Rowan Williams, former Archbishop of Canterbury, calls "programmatic secularism." In this mindset, we imagine each parishioner as "a lone figure facing a range of options, any of which may be adopted but none of which has any public validity."[22] In other words, we can come to expect church leaders at all levels to offer a smorgasbord of ministry program choices. Individual members of congregations pick and choose what they prefer—without their selection making any real difference to the church and society as a whole. Such an orientation leads to "selling" church programs, as if church members are primarily consumers or passive recipients.

This program orientation is complicated by the mobility of modern society. With more outsourcing, mergers, and plant relocations, more people than ever must travel to find or keep meaningful, financially adequate work, often out of necessity in an unpredictably shifting economy. So working-age church members are not as fiscally stable as they were thirty or more years ago. This leaves church leaders looking for how to attract and keep a gradually shifting group. Whether as leaders or participants, we can end up focusing unconsciously on one-shot programs and workshops, instead of working at the difficult but important task of creating a long-term plan for maturing, lifelong disciples.

Beneath these specific consumerist characteristics lies a set of distinctive attitudes. Considering many Protestants today, Sarah Wilson says, Evangelicals and Pentecostals, in their penchant for dividing and subdividing, mirror the capitalist market in providing a product for every taste. Mainline Protestants follow a franchise model, with each congregation expected to be the outpost of a central headquarters.[23]

Both models reproduce the interconnected individualism of the Internet, she asserts. Being able to migrate from one Christian community to the next reflects an economy and society based on individual preferences.

As the Church, while we often talk about how God owns everything, our heart still goes wherever we put God's money, usually thinking that it is our own. It's no wonder that Harvard professor Michael Sandel likens consumerism to "consumption," the old English word for leukemia.[24] Just as leukemia wastes one's physical body, consumerism is a "wasting disease" on our souls as part of the body of Christ. Whenever we connect money and possessions with power and control, we end up worshiping money, and challenging God's sovereignty.

So what is our hidden attraction to all this activity? We can swim with the tide of thinking church programs are our goal instead of a means to spiritual transformation. We can settle for bragging rights about what "our church" has done, while holding onto the limitless consumer ethos of our society. In this way we avoid digging deeper into our essential self, setting aside our preoccupations and the demands of the moment, to risk an encounter with the Living God.

## Being an Authentic Self

It is so easy to get lured into a kind of subtle inauthenticity. "Ironically, despite [our] emphasis on individual freedom," says professor William Avery,

> think of the ways our society does try to define us—by how much education and how prestigious a job we hold, by how much money we make, by where we live and what we wear. We are most often defined by what we do or have rather than whose we are. This secular and false self is fabricated by social compulsion...[25]

For most of us, this false self is not a deliberate attempt to deceive others, or even ourselves. Taking the lead from definitions of the term "false" in the dictionary,[26] a false self can develop because it is not solid or essential or is based on mistaken ideas. Depth psychologist David Benner says we may build our identity on an illusion—for example, believing that who we are depends only upon the amount and kinds of things we possess, or solely upon what we do and achieve, not on the persons we are from the inside out.[27] In that case, "the core of the false self is the belief that my value depends on what I have, what I can do and what others think of me."[28]

By contrast, we can aspire to a quality of life that is authentic. "Authentic" can mean according to fact or actuality (as in an *authentic* story); genuine, not counterfeit (such as *genuine* maple syrup); or sincere (as in true piety). It also may stress real existence or actual identity (as in *veritable* offspring).[29] When we apply these nuances to how we live, "authentic living" speaks of a kind of wholeness or integrity, where our outer appearances and behavior match the inner person, regardless of our situation. There is trustworthiness about the person we see. What they do flows out of who they really are.

When the different parts of our lives fit with one another, we move toward a sense of wholeness, or "integrity." In the process, we release some superficial preoccupations and become more in touch with our soul, or essential self. Greater receptivity allows us to widen our relationship with God. "Integrity means to live with congruence," says pastoral counselor Ronald Greer:[30] "connecting my life, its purpose and direction, with the God of its creation." When people live in basic alignment with "the essence of God's image placed within them[,]...it points to a self-identity grounded in humility and compassion."[31]

So here are some big questions: Beneath all the church programs and our preoccupation with doing, how can we focus on being, as generous stewards of God's grace? How can we develop and encourage generous souls, as we grow more into the image of God? We begin by starting from a place of authenticity: Christian stewardship and generosity.

# Stewardship

"I'm amazed at how easily jobs, people, things and even ideas weasel their way into taking a God's-job role in our lives," says Roger Owens.[32] He notes that prophetic Bible texts "help us to see those things we are holding onto in our lives, grasping at them because we believe they will give us identity, security and worth." By contrast, we can choose to receive our lives and our relationship with God as sheer *gifts*. With the help of friends with whom we can talk about our spiritual life, we are able to "discover the grace to loosen our grip so that we might learn to receive."[33]

Loosening our grip and learning to receive arise out of a basic stance of joyful, faithful stewardship. Great stewardship involves how we conserve, use and share all the resources of our lives. We might summarize this process as "managing all of life with Christ at the center."[34] As one denomination puts it, "stewardship is the free and joyous activity of the child of God and God's family, the Church, in managing all of life and life's resources for God's purposes."[35]

This fullness of living is "Spirited stewardship," in that it grows out of our receptivity to the Holy Spirit, active in and around us. Spirited stewardship is "a living process of growth in our personal and corporate relationship with God."[36] Spirit-oriented stewardship can change our various activities from a mere repetition of efforts into a fluid, dynamic, spiritual journey.

Becoming stewards who are receptive to the Spirit engages our attitude as well as our activities. So what are the primary characteristics of such Christian stewardship? Daniel Conway[37] names four: gratitude, responsibility, generosity, and the willingness to give back with increase. He says, "Stewardship is a lifestyle that reflects who we are and what we believe."[38]

Joyful stewardship reflects God, the most generous Giver of all. God's giving results in the life of all creation, and in the gift of the Holy Spirit among us. God's giving results in Jesus' life, death, and Resurrection on our behalf. Referring to James 1:17, one pastor says:

What matters in a gift is its source—all good gifts come from God. Such is the power of Christian stewardship: All good gifts come from above. By our giving in return, we show both the goodness and generosity of God, and come to know God's Spirit alive in us.[39]

After conducting a wide-ranging study of church members about money anxiety, one seminary professor said, "From a Christian perspective, security comes from healthy relationships—with family, community, and ultimately with God." She continued:

In order for people to change the way they think about and use money, the focus needs to shift from money as the measure of wealth and security to the only true security there is: placing your life in God's hands and learning to build healthy relationships in this life—healthy families, healthy communities, and a healthier world.[40]

By focusing on such relationships, we can begin to deal with even our most personal issues, including financial security.

With these aspects in mind, here is my core definition of stewardship: Stewardship is whatever we do with the Good News of God's love through the way that we live,[41] in every dimension of our lives—our relationships and use of time; nourishment of our bodies; application of our abilities; use of money and possessions; focus for our priorities, passions and values; and the ways we care for the Earth and all creatures.[42]

# Generosity

So if stewardship can be all that, why do we need a word like *generosity*?

First, we need another word because "stewardship" *can* be all that, but most of the time people have reduced its richness to simply "raising money for the church." In each generation, many pastors and church leaders have used the term as a theological cover-up for that dreaded annual commercial break in the congregation's program. Instead of seeing stewardship as living in the heart of the gospel itself, they have taken a paying-for-programs approach in order to underwrite what they have seen as the congregation's "real" mission.

"Stewardship has become a dirty word," states one church leader.

November brings with it the lurking threat of sermons on giving. At best, people treat it like a trip to the dentist: they sigh and try to imagine they are somewhere else. At worst, they go missing. Why does stewardship feel like a root canal instead of an invitation to deeper faith and worship? And how might we change that?[43]

In other words, the full depth of holistic, Spirit-led living withers down to a truncated stewardship. When that happens, it becomes a piecemeal borrowing of secular fundraising techniques in order to get church participants (read: customers) to pay more to support and expand the congregation's services. Such a consumer approach tends to hide the true meaning of authentic, Spirit-led stewardship. And if people are treated as the congregation's current or potential customers, it's no surprise that they become suspicious of selling techniques.

A second reason to use the word "generosity" is to emphasize some crucial facets of stewardship that are too-easily forgotten. For example, generosity is a passion for giving that is based in gratitude, not obligation, because it arises out of our awareness of "the riches of Christ,"[44] Jesus' "generous act" or "grace" (the same word in the New Testament language of Greek). In other words, what Jesus Christ did and continues to do for us in his life, death, and risen life present among us now, is an act of generosity that embodies God's grace.

In 2 Corinthians 8:9 Paul writes, "You know the generous act [Greek: grace] of our Lord Jesus Christ, that though he was rich, yet for your sakes he became poor, so that by his poverty you might become rich." Here Christ's riches are not measured in money or possessions, but in godliness, compassion, forgiveness, and self-giving. Jesus let go of his divine status and power in order to become human in our midst—and even one of the poorest and most vulnerable among us—so we could experience God's holiness, love, and generous self-giving in human terms.

Philippians 2:5–11 includes verses from the earliest Christian hymn we have. It describes this same self-giving another way:

> Let the same mind be in you that was in Christ Jesus, who, though he was in the form of God, did not regard equality with God as something to be exploited, but emptied himself, taking the form of a slave, being born in human likeness. And being found in human form, he humbled himself and became obedient to the point of death—even death on a cross.
>
> Therefore God also highly exalted him and gave him the name that is above every name, so that at the name of Jesus every knee should bend in heaven and on earth and under the earth, and every tongue should confess that Jesus Christ is Lord, to the glory of God the Father.

This means that the real value of our giving is not relative to what we have to give, or to what other people give. Instead, it arises out of God's relationship with us, as our response to God's graciousness, God's fundamental act of overwhelming generosity toward us. As a result, we seek to show "Jesus-like generosity embraced as a core spiritual value of our discipleship."[45]

Another key aspect of generosity is that it is not only an attitude but also part of one's character and a consequent habitual activity. In fact, the Science of Generosity research center at the University of Notre Dame describes *generosity* as "the virtue of giving good things to others freely and abundantly."[46] By this they mean that it is:

- A learned character trait that involves both attitude and action (both an inclination to give liberally and also an actual practice);

- A basic personal, moral orientation to life which not only expresses the moral good, but also rejects many vices, such as selfishness, greed, and fear;
- A way to give things that are good for others, including time, attention, and emotional availability, to enhance other people's wellbeing; and
- What is good for the giver in the long run and is good for the person who is helped. So "like all of the virtues, [it is] in people's genuine enlightened self-interest to learn and practice."[47]

While scientists describe generosity this way, other leaders address a distinctively Christian form of generosity. For example, Bishop Robert Schnase says, "*Generosity* describes the Christian's unselfish willingness to give in order to make a positive difference for the purposes of Christ."[48] When he adds the term "extravagant" to "generosity," he describes people who show "extraordinary sharing, willing sacrifice, and joyous giving out of love for God and neighbor."[49] Whenever they gather as vital congregations, they:

- Focus on the abundance of God's grace;
- Emphasize the Christian's need to give, based on who they are and what God has done for them;
- Talk explicitly about handling money as part of the Christian's walk of faith;
- Have a high sense of mission; and
- Desire keenly to please God by making a positive difference in the world.

The basis for such personal and congregational generosity is in "our extravagantly generous God, the Giver of every good gift, the source of life and love!"[50]

So bottom line, what does Christian "generosity" mean? Generosity is our passion for giving of ourselves and of what God has entrusted to us, out of gratitude for God's relationship of extravagant giving to us. It is a learned attitude and habitual action that seeks the other's welfare, not only to do good, but also to do no harm. It extends our care to others in a way that vitalizes both giver and receiver.

This is the definition of *generosity* which we will use as a basis for *Growing Generous Souls*.

I have had the joy of seeing both faithful stewardship and extravagant generosity in a variety of unique congregations. Whether we use the word stewardship or generosity, we can experience the reality of the gospel. We can also strengthen a culture of generous-hearted attitudes, actions, and relationships. Every time we reflect God's love in a facet of our lives, we are growing our grateful passion for giving to others, which gives back to us in turn.

# Turning Around

It was a stupid thing to do. But I was convinced it was right at the time. As a college student, I had taken earnestness to a new level. I went to all the classes and study groups, read the recommended texts as well as what was required, and nearly wore myself out doing everything a student could possibly do to be at the top of the class. I knew that I had been "too busy" to have proper time with God and felt the acute absence of what had been my primary relationship and friendship in life.

Wrapped up in my own universe, I was sure that I had been so busy from my side of the relationship that God "hadn't been able to get through." So in an exuberant combination of narcissism and naiveté, I resolved to go up a mountain somewhere to be "available," so God could get through to me.

In that first year of college, I had no means of transportation, so I asked my friend's boyfriend if he would drive me up to the mountains somewhere about an hour away and drop me off by the deserted two-lane highway, so I could spend the night with God. The boyfriend already thought I was crazy, so he did as I asked.

So there I was at the foot of an unknown mountain near twilight, with my sleeping bag, flashlight and a jar of peanut butter to get me through. God and I had been on more than speaking terms for years, so I didn't think I'd need anything else.

I began to climb the rocky slope, lightened by the prospect of spending some quality time with God. As I climbed higher and darkness descended, I found a place I could curl up against a downed tree to wait for God.

Almost immediately I heard an elegant silence. Like Elijah in his cave, I felt God's question, "What are you doing here, Betsy?" Only then did it dawn on me that there might be wild animals up here (any one of which might love peanut butter), that no one knew where I was, and that this was a dumb thing to be doing. But I was more embarrassed than afraid.

I clearly felt God's presence—and deliberate silence. Who was I to expect God to speak on my personal schedule? Yes, I was right that I had terribly fogged up my side of the window in our relationship, but that hadn't reduced God's ability to penetrate all my compulsive activities. I laughed at myself and knew God was chuckling along with me. God would speak when God chose to speak, whether I thought I was "too busy" or not. In my crazy busyness, I had forgotten which one of us was the Creator, and which one the creature.

I nestled into the log the best I could and looked up at the sparkling stars above. Recalling Psalm 8:4, "What are human beings that you are mindful of mortals, that you care for them?" I felt the irony of how tiny and vulnerable we human beings truly are.

It was a long night with little sleep, but not the longest night I have ever spent. In God's silence, I was reminded that this was the Living God who loves us despite ourselves and our tiny tempests. The next morning I scrambled back down the slope, praying that my friend's boyfriend would return for me. I felt heartily chastened, humored, protected—and loved by God all the way down to my toes.

As discussed earlier in this chapter, habitual compulsive doing can lead us in superficial, self-defeating directions, where we may believe that our survival and achievement come solely by our own efforts.

When we go down that road, we can overly focus on productivity, become fragmented and compartmentalized, and lose touch with our authentic selves.

So what can we do to reclaim the basis of who we are before God, with one another, and within ourselves? We can *turn around* and go the other way, toward true stewardship and generosity.

But it's that turning-around part that is the hardest.

The verb "to turn around" in the Hebrew Scriptures is *shuv*. It is an incendiary concept, whether it is going back home from whence we came or turning to charge forward. The Old Testament uses *shuv* to describe armies on the move, doing an about-face to retreat, or turning to charge into the enemy (Exodus 14:2; 2 Samuel 22:38; 1 Kings 22:34). This same verb is used to invite individuals to change their way of living, turning their lives around to face God (Deuteronomy 30:10; 1 Samuel 12:20f.; 1 Kings 8:33; 2 Kings 17:13).[51]

For example, the Bible challenges us to turn away from a lifestyle of indifference, injustice, and greed, and to turn toward following God's commandments. We are enjoined to listen to God's prophets about caring for widows, orphans, and people in poor circumstances. Whether speaking of an individual's total life change, or a national policy reversal, *shuv* initiates a qualitative change.

In Isaiah 30:15, the prophet Isaiah calls out to followers and curious onlookers alike. He says, "In returning and rest you will be saved; in quietness and in trust shall be your strength." The verb here for "return" is *shuv*.

What's more, the Hebrew word for "rest" is not a simple invitation to get comfortable or collapse in exhaustion. Rather, it has to do with physical and mental rest, led by a quiet mind or attitude[52] that turns toward God. It does not yield to uncertainty, anxiety, or fear, and trusts God's wisdom, justice, and power.[53] Because such confidence in God is a hard-won, intentional choice, it can persist even in the midst of external distractions, conflict, or chaos.

In the time of the first thirty-nine chapters of the Book of Isaiah, the twelve tribes called Israel found themselves squeezed between two world powers: to the south, the great empire of Egypt, and far to the east, the regional superpower of Assyria. Through the prophets, God had told them to be still and let God carry the whole burden of their defense.[54] But their political uncertainty got the better of them. Should they align themselves with Egypt against the greater threat of Assyria, and risk being assimilated by the Egyptians? Or should they invite Assyria's military within their borders to keep Egypt out, and risk Assyria's taking them over? In the middle of such uncertainty, Israel's leaders were afraid to do nothing and entirely trust God. Instead, they chose a military alliance with Egypt—and the great armies of Assyria swept over them all, to their utter defeat.

In this case, returning was not a political strategy; it was a matter of faith. Sometimes trust in God means doing a total about-face in our thinking and actions: relying upon God's work, albeit unknown to us, instead of on our own plans for survival. The result is that we can "rest" in God, regardless of our external circumstances.

Local churches can also make an intentional decision to "rest" in the sense of quieting their minds and seeking God's will for their next steps. For example, church leaders at McKendree United Methodist Church in Nashville, Tennessee, have done exactly that. Every day, they pray at 10:02 a.m. and 10:02 p.m., using Jesus' words from Luke 10:2—"The harvest is plentiful, but the laborers are few; therefore ask the Lord of the harvest to send out laborers into his harvest."

Stephen Handy, pastor of McKendree since 2008, says that prayer is the launching point for church vitality, which includes several important factors. "Pray for revival," he says:

> Wait expectedly for God's next move, create a culture of pastoral and congregational excellence, build a discipling system, equip the laity to be bold and courageous disciples of Christ, and then unleash them for ministry. Then set up a system to continuously invest in improvements.[55]

These days, the survival plans of many congregations and even denominations amount to only doing more of what we have been doing in the past. But the informal definition of insanity is doing the same thing over and over, expecting to get different results. So more than a few churches are leaving behind business-as-usual and attempting a total turn-around. For example, hundreds of congregations have used discipleship plans based on Eric Geiger and Tom Rainer's book, *Simple Church*; Jim Collins' *Good to Great and the Social Sectors*; Dan Dick's *Vital Signs*; or Robert Schnase's *Five Practices of Fruitful Congregations*.

Scores of families are turning around their habits, thanks to the work of Nathan Dungan, national stewardship consultant and founder of Share Save Spend. Dungan focuses on children by helping individual families shift effectively from a mode centered on spending to one that balances spending with saving and sharing.[56] Using a variety of Dungan's own resources, especially along with his book *Money Sanity Solutions: Linking Money + Meaning*, he guides them through a multifaceted model for families to develop and maintain healthy money habits. The process begins in young childhood and builds over time, as families make their daily financial decisions together.

Carefully thinking through the implications of our faith can prompt us to develop a different lifestyle. For example, when Shawn and Casey Englund-Helmeke prepared for their wedding, they wanted to reflect their commitment to simplicity. So they chose to use the odds-and-ends housewares they already had, and request donations to three charities instead of receiving wedding gifts.

Beyond that, they affirmed their intention in their married life to "bike, walk, or bus instead of drive, read a book instead of watching TV, cook together instead of [eating] out, and engage in any number of other 'slow' living practices."[57] Their purpose was "to have a richer experience of life, to tread more lightly on our Mother Earth, and to live out their faith by generally attempting to counter our culture of haste and thoughtless consumption."[58]

Turning around from obsessive doing toward qualitative being is an unfolding, lifelong process. As we risk trying some habits that may be new to us, we develop a deeper trust in God with a quieter attitude and mind. Strengthening our sense of identity in God's image, we can try out (or come back to) some practices such as meditation, prayer, simplicity, and service. These habits can help us focus on *being*—leaning upon God in the process.

A CORE DILEMMA faced by church leaders and people of faith is how to reduce the sense of fragmented living and compulsive *doing* in church involvement and daily life and focus more on *being* generous stewards of God's grace. The unending tasks of church, home, and work, on the one hand, and the desire to live meaningfully for God, on the other, create an ongoing push and pull in our lives. But a more holistic understanding of "stewardship" and "generosity" enables us, with God's help, to change our thoughts and actions to live a more authentic life.

## Questions for Reflection

1. To what extent do I feel frantic or fragmented? How can I focus more on authentic being?
2. In what ways am I generous with my time, abilities, money and relationships? Where do I share reluctantly or without joy?
3. How can stewardship and generosity help me make better choices? Where do I want greater balance and wholeness in my life?
4. Where do I need to make a total turn-around in order to face God more fully? Where do we need to do this as a congregation, or as a people?

## Endnotes

1. See Richard Rohr, *Falling Upward: A Spirituality for the Two Halves of Life* (San Francisco: Jossey-Bass, 2011).
2. *www.thefreedictionary.com.*
3. Cited by Brad Tuttle, reporter for *Time* magazine, in "Decoding Job Ads: Why to Avoid a 'Fast-Paced Work Environment,'" February 29, 2012, *http://business.time.com.*

4. Brother David Steindl-Rast, *Gratefulness, the Heart of Prayer: An Approach to Life in Fullness* (New York/Mahwah, NJ: Paulist Press, 1984), p. 218.
5. Carl S. Hoffman, "The Identity and Mission of God's People," *Upper Room Disciplines 2014*, (Nashville: Upper Room Books, 2013), p. 32.
6. Stephen Erickson, "Heidegger on the Meaning of Meaning," *Philosophy as the Art of Living, Course Guidebook* (Chantilly, VA: The Teaching Company, 2006), p. 82.
7. A job search site analyzed more than 72 million reviews to assess which companies are the best at encouraging work-life balance; *https://www.cnbc.com/2018/05/01/the-15-best-companies-for-work-life-balance-in-2018.html*. See also: *https://www.glassdoor.com/blog/tech-companies-work-life-balance*.
8. Stephen Erickson, "Heidegger on Technology's Threat," *Philosophy as the Art of Living*, CDs (Chantilly, VA: The Teaching Company, 2006).
9. ———, "Heidegger on the Meaning of Meaning," *Philosophy as the Art of Living*, CDs (Chantilly, VA: The Teaching Company, 2006).
10. John C. Robinson, *Death of a Hero, Birth of the Soul: Answering the Call of Midlife*, (Tulsa, OK, Council Oak Books, 1995, 1997) p. 317.
11. "Building on the Anglican theological tradition, Wesley added a fourth emphasis, experience. The resulting four components or 'sides' of the quadrilateral are (1) Scripture, (2) tradition, (3) reason, and (4) experience. For United Methodists, *Scripture* is considered the primary source and standard for Christian doctrine. *Tradition* is experience and the witness of development and growth of the faith through the past centuries and in many nations and cultures. *Experience* is the individual's understanding and appropriating of the faith in the light of his or her own life. Through *reason* the individual Christian brings to bear on the Christian faith discerning and cogent thought. These four elements taken together bring the individual Christian to a mature and fulfilling understanding of the Christian faith and the required response of worship and service." (*A Dictionary for United Methodists*, by Alan K. Waltz, cited under "The Wesleyan Quadrilateral" at *http://archives.umc.org/interior.asp?mid=258&GID=312&GMOD=VWD*.
12. This phrase was popularized by the famous management guru Peter Drucker in his book *The Age of Discontinuity*, cited in *www.wikipedia.com* under "knowledge economy." Drucker attributes the phrase to economist Fritz Machlup.
13. *www.wikipedia.com* under "knowledge economy."
14. *www.princeton.edu* under "Information Age."
15. See R. J. Crisp, *The Psychology of Social and Cultural Diversity*, pp. 16 and 39.
16. L. Roger Owens, in "Reflections on the lectionary: Sunday, September 1, Jeremiah 2:4–13," in *Christian Century* August 21, 2013.
17. "Jonathan," in response to a webinar at *www.paidtoexist.com*.
18. *Ibid.*
19. With the exception of Philemon, every one of the letters written by Paul or in his name was written to an entire congregation, not to an individual household. In Revelation 2 and 3, the message is written to the seven key house churches

throughout the region of Asia Minor, now the country of Turkey. Since most early Christians could not read, the epistles were read aloud during worship, and later exchanged with other congregations. In this way, over the first two centuries A.D., every house church heard all of the major epistles that were circulating in the greater Mediterranean world.

20. Dan R. Dick, *Vital Signs: A Pathway to Congregational Wholeness (Nashville: Discipleship Resources, 2007)*, pp. 9, 12f.

21. *Ibid.*, pp. 116f.

22. Samuel Wells' review of Rowan Williams' book, *Faith in the Public Square*, in *Christian Century*, May 28, 2014.

23. Sarah Hinlicky Wilson, "Lament for a Divided Church, *Christianity Today*, March 2014, p. 38.

24. Michael Fitzgerald, "Everyone's Got a Price," in *Newsweek*, April 23 and 30, 2012. In this review of Sandel's book, *What Money Can't Buy*, Fitzgerald says Sandel "argues that the spread of market philosophy has created what he calls 'a consumerist idea of freedom,' in which we think our highest freedom is what we consume. Our obsession with consumption limits our freedom to engage in a full civic life."

25. William O. Avery, "A Well-Formed Stewardship Leader Holds a Holistic Perspective," in *How Much is Enough? A Deeper Look at Stewardship in an Age of Abundance,* edited by Catherine Malotky (Columbia, SC, Region 9 of the Evangelical Lutheran Church of America/Lutheran Theological Southern Seminary Council on Stewardship Education), p. 16. Here he cites Henri J. M. Nouwen in *The Way of the Heart*, p. 22.

26. *Webster's Ninth New Collegiate Dictionary.* (Springfield, MA: Merriam-Webster, Inc., 1989).

27. David G. Benner, *The Gift of Being Yourself: The Sacred Call to Self-Discovery* (Downers Grove, IL: InterVarsity Press, 2004), p. 81.

28. *Ibid.* Here Benner cites Basil Pennington, *True Self/False Self*, p. 31.

29. *Webster's Ninth New Collegiate Dictionary* (Springfield, MA: Merriam-Webster, Inc., 1989).

30. Ronald J. Greer, *If You Know Who You Are, You'll Know What to Do: Living With Integrity* (Nashville: Abingdon Press, 2009), p. 39.

31. *Ibid*, p. 44.

32. L. Roger Owens, *op cit.*

33. *Ibid.*

34. Luther Seminary, Minneapolis, MN, publicity piece #LL1041–13b for Rethinking Stewardship event on July 28–30, 2014.

35. Stewardlife, the Lutheran Church. Missouri Synod, 8/11/2008, *www.luthersem. edu/stewardship.*

36. Betsy Schwarzentraub, *Afire With God: Becoming Spirited Stewards* (Nashville: Discipleship Resources, 2001, 2007), p. 27. See this book for more on the roots of true stewardship, as well as ways to grow it in the year-round life of the church.

37. Daniel Conway, *What Do I Own and What Owns Me? A Spirituality of Stewardship* (New London, CT: Twenty-Third Publications, 2005), p. 30.

38. *Ibid.*

39. Rev. David Lee Dobler, cited in *Radical Generosity*, at *www.umfnw.org.*

40. Carol Johnston, "Essay: Thinking Theologically About Wealth, Including Money," *www.resourcingchristianity,org,* cited in *Unleashing the Generosity of Our People* by Ken Sloane, General Board of Discipleship Ministries, The United Methodist Church.

41. One way of summarizing the gospel, or Good News, is in Romans 8:37–39: "No, in all these things we are more than conquerors through [the One] who loved us. For I am convinced that neither death, nor life, nor angels, nor rulers, nor things present, nor things to come, nor powers, nor height, nor depth, nor anything else in all creation, will be able to separate us from the love of God in Christ Jesus our Lord." Colossians 1:27 summarizes this Good News of Jesus Christ as "Christ in you, the hope of glory."

42. Cf. Betsy Schwarzentraub, *op cit.* p. 27.

43. Laura Heikes, "Mature Disciples Supporting New Givers," in *Leading Ideas*, August 31, 2011, e-newsletter of the Lewis Center for Church Leadership; *churchleadership.com/resources/Leading_ideas.asp.*

44. Bishop James Thomas used this phrase in "The Culture of Generosity" for the Yellowstone Annual Conference, at *www.yacumc.org.*

45. Michael Reeves, "A Strategic Plan for Generosity," written for University Church, San Antonio, Texas.

46. Science of Generosity, University of Notre Dame, at *http://generosityresearch.nd.edu/more-about-the-initiative/what-is-generosity.*

47. *Ibid.*

48. Robert Schnase, *Cultivating Fruitfulness: Five Weeks of Prayer and Practice for Congregations* (Nashville: Abingdon, 2008), p. 79.

49. *Ibid.*

50. ———, *Five Practices of Fruitful Congregations* (Nashville: Abingdon, 2007), pp. 108–109.

51. The late John Herbert Otwell, professor of Old Testament at the Pacific School of Religion, used "turning around" as the core metaphor for sin and repentance. Long before the Hebrew Scriptures described specific behaviors as individual "sins," he said, Early Israel developed the understanding of "sin" as turning away from God. Therefore the act of turning around was turning oneself back toward God's face. This action could apply to an individual, a group (such as religious leaders), or an entire people.

Old Testament scholar Gerhard Von Rad notes that all three of the classical prophets, Jeremiah, Isaiah and Hosea, have this same basic theology of returning to God as part of their proclamation of God's saving purpose. The latest prophet of the three, Jeremiah, emphasizes the human side in God's saving work. Jeremiah's appeals to return increasingly assert that it is God's decision to save us. Cf. Gerhard Von Rad, *Old Testament Theology, Volume I* (New York: Evanston, Harper & Row, 1962), pp. 216f.

52. Francis Brown, ed., *Hebrew and English Lexicon of the Old Testament* (Oxford: Clarendon Press, 1974), p. 629.
53. R. B. Y. Scott, "The Book of Isaiah Chapters 1–39," in *The Interpreter's Bible, Volume V* (New York, Nashville: Abingdon Press, 1956), p. 333.
54. Gerhard Von Rad, *op cit.,* p. 160.
55. "United Methodist church vitality increases in U.S.," by Heather Hahn, United Methodist news Service, at *www.umc.org/news-and-media.*
56. See *www.sharesavespend.com.*
57. Casey Englund-Helmeke, "Navigating the Jungle of Wedding Gifts: Why Donations are Just as Good," at *http://compassfaithandfinances.wordpress. com/2014/06/06. Compass* is a digital resource for young adults provided by the Ecumenical Stewardship Center, *www.stewardshipresources.org.*
58. *Ibid.*

# Being and Praise

MOST OF US want to let go of compulsive doing in one or more aspects of our lives, finding strength through quietness and trust in God. At the same time, how we see our responsibilities to others can make it difficult to admit to these longings. We may be stuck in overdrive when it comes to a sense of duty, preoccupation with work or family, the habit of people-pleasing, the striving for perfection, or some other dimension. How can we swim against the current of "the mighty river of urgency"[1] and anxiety that seems to sweep so many of us along?

It's easy to fall into a get-ahead, don't-fall-behind approach to life. But in the process, we can lose what Stephen Covey, the *Seven Habits of Highly Effective People* guru, calls "True North"—our essential connection with independent reality, from which we get our bearings and plan our life direction.[2] There is a reason we are called human *beings* and not human *doings*—by our intrinsic nature we find value in being alive. We can affirm that life has an "inside as well as an outside,"[3] that life offers spiritual depth as well as the roles of everyday living, and that our real worth is not found solely in how much we have, how others see us, or how much we do. While our daily activities and multiple roles are important to us and to others, many of us seek a healthier balance between these immediate activities and more time to reflect on bigger issues, such as who we are and our connection with God.

One way to turn ourselves around is by celebrating the intricate interdependence of living things on this earth, and our place among them. John Buchanan, editor of *Christian Century* magazine, finds that the changing seasons and different times of the Christian Year evoke "an awareness and celebration of the ways God comes into the world; the steady rhythms of nature with occasions of surprising beauty, the life force, the mystery of human birth, the simple fact of our being in the world."[4]

It is almost impossible to notice this network of relationships with our natural environment, if we do not allow time in our days for stopping and noticing. It is like whitespace that gives beauty to artwork and rests our reading eyes on the page, says author Bonnie Gray.[5] We need "spiritual whitespace" to give our souls repose, "a place to find balance and beauty."[6] A reviewer of her book, *Finding Spiritual Whitespace*, explains:

Spiritual whitespace makes room in our hearts for a deeper, more intimate relationship with God, room in our lives for rest, room in our souls for rejuvenation. To me spiritual whitespace would be comparable to just 'being,' being in the moment of peace, quiet, and reflection. We need times like these to help us face our problems and daily tasks with a renewed sense of well-being.[7]

When we set aside time to simply be part of creation and with God, we are not shutting ourselves off from the world, but rather becoming more deeply aware of it. For many people, the practices of yoga, Tai Chi, Qi Gong, or silent meditation of one kind or another result in a greater sense of aliveness and attention to one's own breath, body, and surrounding world. Likewise, various practices of meditation can clarify our ability to hear and respond positively to God's voice.[8]

Focusing on being does not mean denying the betrayals, suffering or injustice that we may have endured. Rather, it challenges us to value God's presence and love even—especially—in the midst of hardships. Jesus' stories prompt us to recognize the value of God's presence, love, and grace. As a natural result, we want to pursue and nurture these gifts, letting them change the focus of our being, and so make a difference in the quality of our lives.[9]

When we focus on being, we are not just "doing nothing." American Quaker educator Thomas Kelly describes it this way:

> I have in mind something deeper than the simplification of our external programs, our absurdly crowded calendars of appointments through which so many pantingly and frantically grasp. This amazing simplification comes when we "center down," when life is lived with singleness of eye, from a holy Center where the breath and stillness of Eternity are heavy upon us and we are wholly yielded to Him.[10]

Sometimes *being* insists its way into our lives. When a two-hundred-plus-pound, six-by-eight-foot glass partition fell on pastor Donna Fado Ivery,[11] it shattered parts of her brain. *Doing* became virtually impossible. "Thinking, writing, remembering, reading, grabbing, speaking, and walking were now strenuous activities," she says.

> In the first few months, a big day would be taking a shower or sitting in a recliner on our driveway to watch my four-year-old roller skate. Full-time care was found quickly for my baby, and my pastor husband became primary caregiver.[12]

In the years-long process of healing, Fado Ivery discovered that the common question about wellness, "How are you doing?" gradually transformed into what she calls the Sabbath question: "How are you *being*?" Living with this question drew her to focus, moment by moment, on the riches of God's creative grace. It oriented her to the movement of life within and around her and connected her more intimately to the Creator and all other creatures. She encouraged her own creativity to surge to the surface, and she has blessed countless other people through workshops and retreats, helping those dealing with suffering, including chronic pain.

Whether we are pushed by external events into doing less or drawn by choice into setting aside more time for qualitative being, something invites us to make decisions that come out of our inner core. We strengthen this shift when we think deeply about who we are and how we can reflect greater wholeness. We can also intentionally practice being in God's presence—by searching the Scriptures, as well as engaging in prayer, meditation, and contemplation. The more that we live out of our relationship with God, the more we can praise God with the whole of who we are, and nurture who we are meant to be.

# Who We Are

Being who we are is not as easy as it sounds. It is tempting to look outside ourselves to find what will make us whole.[13] We may adapt to family assumptions or a public role, or we might search for someone else to "complete" us emotionally. In and of themselves, these adaptations are not a sign of inauthenticity. But when we do these things for the wrong reasons, under duress, or with unreasonable expectations, we can lose touch with who we are deep inside.

In Romans 7:15, Paul admits that even when he *wants* to do the right thing, he ends up doing the opposite. Certainly he did plenty of that along the way, including supporting the execution of the first Christian martyr, and helping the Roman military arrest Christians to put them to death. Even after he became a Christian, no doubt he also regretted at least a few of the things he said to the fledgling house churches while trying to lay out ground rules for their Christian faith and behavior. His words and example kept them from assimilating the gods and lifestyle of their surrounding cultures. In addition, he must have felt some frustration while trying to keep them on course in their early years. (What pastor doesn't regret a few things said along the way?) But Paul is not remembered for these things. He is known for establishing the Christian movement across cultures and opening it up to Gentiles (non-Jews) around the globe, as well as for being the first Christian theologian.

Ultimately, God calls us to lead lives that only we can define, guided by the Holy Spirit. To do so, we may have to strip away our assumptions. But as our old patterns peel off, what do we try to put in their place?

Ronald Greer, minister and pastoral counselor, identifies seven values (attitudes or actions) that can develop into what he calls "virtues:" attributes that shape the fundamental character of who we are. These aspects can point our lives toward a sense of wholeness that is more authentically who God calls us to become:

- Compassion—Seeing opportunities to care for others and choosing to reach out and respond.
- Truth—Speaking honestly out of love (Ephesians 4:15), and not wavering on our "Yes" and "No" decisions (James 5:12).
- Character—Incorporating into our behavior a particular value often enough that it becomes a permanent part of ourselves (Romans 5:4–5).
- Courage—Reaching beyond ourselves in dangerous circumstances, despite our fear. This trait includes the willingness to keep going through difficulty or uncertainty, without being deflected from our course.
- Relation—Recognizing our relationships as a gift of God's grace, inviting us to connect with others in both good times and bad (Matthew 18:20).
- Fidelity—Choosing to remain loyal to vows, agreements, principles, and values; trustworthy in actions.
- Respect—Relating to others with dignity and consideration, acceptance, and understanding.[14]

These values are not absolutes. They are qualities we seek to develop and express repeatedly until they become habitual practices, like the path through a dense forest, guiding our thoughts and endeavors.

Granted, none of us has attained all of these qualities in full measure and no one practices them consistently. But God created us to be our authentic best, and it is our *desire* for God that is the deepest essence of who we are.[15] What God wants all human beings to know, says priest and author Henri Nouwen, is that, whatever we think or do, we think first about our human identity as God's beloved son or daughter (Luke 3:22).[16]

One of the biggest challenges in being who we are is that of "congruence." In general language outside the field of psychology, people speak of congruence as the state of agreement among different aspects of a person's life.[17] It takes personal maturity and intentionality to bring our actions more in line with what we claim we value and believe. But this task intensifies when we seek to be good parents. On the one hand, we try to model by our behavior what is important to us in life, hoping the children will follow good patterns. On the other hand, we attempt to teach our children to think for themselves, not merely imitating someone, or responding to coercion.

Thomas Merton, Trappist monk and author, says we are called to live out what we think and know, "making our knowledge part of ourselves," and by so doing seek to live as a unified body and soul.[18] Spiritual life is not only mental life, nor is it solely our emotions. It also includes our imagination, and more. "If [a person] is to live," Merton says, "he must be all alive, body, soul, mind, heart, and spirit."[19]

A sense of vitality does not protect us from pain or loss, but it can help us live more at ease with our sorrows as well as our joys. When we become aware of the larger picture of our lives thus far, as well as the lives of the people of faith who have gone before us (Hebrews 11), we can live with a more resilient spirit to weather times of anger, betrayal, or devastation. We can sense more congruence between God's assurances and our personal experiences of God's presence, so we are at least a bit more able to trust God as we move into unknown circumstances or a frightening future. Like marathon runners, we can each run our own race if we hold onto three key elements: sustained, disciplined focus on our goal; a community of support; and prayerful reminders of God's grace.[20]

"I believe we can do better by being less," says pastor Peter Traben Haas. "We can take a break from all our striving, sit down in the silence, and simply be with God."[21] The congregation he serves has committed itself to becoming a more contemplative congregation. Instead of starting their church meetings with normal business items, they begin in the chapel with "centering prayer," which focuses on consenting to God's presence. After developing that procedure as a regular habit, they branched out to other prayerful practices, including an early meditative service each Sunday, an eight-week study of centering prayer, a three-day prayer retreat, and a weekly Vespers service for children and adults that includes moments for silent prayer.

Whether in the church or in our personal lives, it takes time to shift from frenetic doing into acting out of meaningful being. It is a process of progressively opening to the presence of the Holy Spirit, trusting God to have a better plan than our do-it-ourselves attempts. Having to say goodbye to the way life used to be takes energy and trust, even when we long for new patterns of living, new routines, and new relationships. The apostle Paul experienced loss of the old life, despite his solid vision of where God was leading him. In 1 Corinthians 13:11, he writes about having to put an end to childlike ways in order to come into an adult faith.

In such transition times—letting go of our endings and getting ready for new beginnings—healing by the Spirit can take place through consciously seeking God's presence. "I've learned that there is healing in presence, healing that I don't make happen, but [it] heals all the same," says pastor Mary Elyn Bahlert, as she reflects on her life and ministry. She continues,

> I've learned that there is a mysterious wonder in every moment of life. I've learned to be grateful, just for now. I've learned to discern who and what gives me life energy, and who and what take me away from being fully present to the moment. Over time, I've become more accepting of myself and others.[22]

Robert Benson no doubt would agree. He is a lay church member who follows the Rule of St. Benedict and speaks and writes about spiritual formation. In his book *Living Prayer*, he says:

> I need time to listen, to examine, and to confess, time to take off some of the hats I wear. I need time to listen for the Voice, if for no other reason than so I will recognize it more clearly in the ways it speaks into the noise and bustle of the life I lead. The silence that I seek must be nurtured until it lives in me....[23]

Just as a fruit tree can produce, of itself, only its kind of fruit, what we say and do is inextricably linked to who we are. In Luke 6:43–49, Jesus points out this connection, and goes on to say that just as a healthy tree bears good fruit by nature, so a good person produces good "out of the abundance of the heart" (Luke 6:45). Eugene Peterson's Bible paraphrase, *The Message*, puts it this way: "The health of the apple tells the health of the tree. You must begin with your own...lives...."[24]

What do we mean when we refer to a person's character or essential being? One dictionary describes a person's character as "the attributes or features that make up and distinguish the individual."[25] So we might say our personal character includes the values and beliefs we want to pass on to our children or impress upon the world. Our character could also include trust in God, and basic beliefs, the causes that merit our personal involvement and financial support, the role modeling we try to do with others, or what is meaningful to us that prompts us to care and to give.

When it comes to generosity, science shows how these core components are linked to generous giving. For example, some studies demonstrate that a person's beliefs can affect his or her volunteer involvement in the community. In instance, volunteers in nonprofit organizations in Virginia,[26] the participants' belief in the "efficacy" of their volunteer work—meaning the positive impact of their efforts— was a stronger motivation than all other factors, including competing commitments, lifestyle change, personal growth, or influence by their social networks. Being aware of their potential to positively influence others made a powerful difference in the volunteers' lives.

Another aspect of character comes through in what researchers call "warm-glow giving," when people find pleasure in the act of giving itself. Researcher James Andreoni, who first coined the phrase, posits that there is no such thing as pure altruism (giving solely for the sake of others), since the act of giving has a positive side effect of good feelings in the giver.[27]

One study, done in 2007, tracked neural activity in the brain. It showed that even when giving to charity was mandatory, it elicited neural activity linked to the giver's sense of reward. But when the donors made gift transfers voluntarily, the neural activity showed they felt an even greater sense of pleasure.[28]

Research at The Lake Institute on Faith & Giving at Indiana University[29] show a strong correlation between the religious giving of parents and that of their adult children. Parents can increase their children's generosity in three ways. First, they can model helping behavior, such as serving food to the hungry or collecting supplies for people in need, in their children's presence. Second, they can point out to their children how their assistance benefits other people. Third, they can respond to a child's helping behavior by making positive comments about the child's helpful *character* rather than his or her child's helpful *act* (italics mine).[30] For example, they might say, "Honey, you were very generous in helping that younger child get a place in line."

While parents have a huge impact, community ministries also can help children and youth develop a generous character and emerge as lifelong "philanthropists:" those who love to help others through their giving. In Texas, a group of Austin-area benefactors, educators, and business professionals established A Legacy of Giving as an innovative education and service program under the nonprofit Austin Community Foundation. The program works with thirty-six public and private elementary schools, middle schools, and high schools[31] to incorporate philanthropy into the standard school curricula. Targeting community needs, they sponsor time-and-talent projects the students can lead, so the young people see the impact on their neighborhoods and make generous giving an integral part of their lives.

"When children become engaged in their community," says Linda Brucker, Executive Director, "they feel more invested, and over time continue to give."[32]

So how do the leaders of A Legacy of Giving do this? They provide monthly events throughout the school year, including academic assemblies on philanthropy, poverty, and building a community. They sponsor advocacy days on health and nutrition issues and on families in need, along with reflection activities with presentations from the teachers. They carry out a Drive for Coats and Cans; a Day of Service, involving student ambassadors from every school; and an invitation-only Youth Philanthropy Summit for middle school and high school Legacy students.

From 2007 to 2014, the children's annual drives for coats and canned food have contributed 42,709 coats and 258,842 pounds of food to the communities of central Texas. At the yearly Youth Philanthropy Summit, local philanthropic leaders inspire students to respect diversity among the students and follow their own interest in improving their community.

The practice of giving to help other people can help us better discover who we really are and were created to be, by deliberately selecting some specific friendships over others, and helping a less virtuous friend develop his or her generosity and humanity. In this way, our closest relationships can encourage God-directed living that arises out of *being*, instead of compulsive *doing*.

Most people have heard of "six degrees of separation," the theory that everyone is approximately six relationships away from any other person on earth.[33] But the theory of "three degrees of influence" is less well known. Posited by social scientists Nicholas Christakis and James Fowler, it says that whatever we say or do tends to have an impact on our friends (one degree), on our friends' friends (two degrees), and on those friends' friends (three degrees).[34] So the attitudes and behaviors we show in our relationships can spread, whether for good or for ill, across a surprising number of lives. These days, when we add in the exponential effect of social media, the potential impact on relationships can be immense.

Amazing things happen when we focus on building relationships, even in a one-time encounter. Sometimes God gives us something specific to say that touches the heart of an acquaintance or a stranger. Other times, God gives us "ears to hear" a deeper message within a person's comment that helps us deal constructively with our life situation. Such a message can be long-remembered and have a huge impact, whether the speaker was aware of it or not.

Relationship-building can take place in our communities, as well.

Within recent months, my family has seen three examples of the positive ripple effect when people intentionally build relationships. In one instance, just two weeks after new neighbors arrived on our street, they experienced a traumatic death in their immediate family. Because of the warm welcome we and other neighbors had already given them, they were able to rely on practical assistance and reassurance during their time of disorientation and loss. Having such immediate support helped them begin to cope with their tragedy.

In a second situation, church friends helped estranged parents work through their grief and frustration to apply necessary "tough love" with their adult daughter, challenging her to make a substantial life change.

In a third circumstance, leaders and shopkeepers in an isolated, rural community came together to sponsor a joint Halloween for the area children. They invited all the small-town residents to join in, thus turning a holiday of potential danger into one of safety and fun.

While many enduring friendships can be extremely rewarding, maintaining them for the long term can be challenging. Friendships don't always soar; sometimes they stall, says Paul Wadell, professor of religious studies at St. Norbert College in Wisconsin.[35] He states that longtime friendships "can be sustained only by a generosity of heart and spirit that enables the friends to work through the struggles and setbacks that mark any real relationship in order to recover its original grace." This is true of our relationships with family members, as well. For most of us, the emotional stakes in family relationships are higher, and the consequences are lifelong.

Some congregations are great places to deepen powerful, positive community. Many local churches describe themselves as a loving, welcoming family. But if those churches want to have a positive impact on their communities, the impressions of the newcomer and outsider count greatly. As with biological and adopted families, each congregation is unique. But some are more effective when it comes to encouraging growing relationships with one another, and hopefully with God.

One example is Worship Without Walls (WWW) at Providence United Methodist Church in Mount Juliet, Tennessee. "A church isn't a building. It's a collection of people. We know that firsthand," they say.[36] "We've met in a city park, a local hotel, a movie theater, an elementary school, and now a middle school. So, for us, church is definitely not about location; it's about people."

The "without walls" aspect refers primarily to their attention to people's stories, and how they can connect with one another. This is especially important since WWW has grown so rapidly. Their vision is "to see those who feel disconnected from God and the church find hope, healing, and wholeness in Jesus Christ." They invite each newcomer to join a group of fifteen to twenty people of all ages, called an "Offer Group." These group gatherings take place at least twice a month for food and sharing, Bible study, discussion, and prayer. Often, they form lasting friendships. "Almost immediately, we got plunged into an Offer Group that, over time, has become our small group family," says Valerie Craig in a personal post.

> Their friendships bring me great joy and their love for Christ and their desire to grow in Him constantly challenges me to do the same. God, in His never-ending faithfulness, brought my family to a church where we could continue to build relationships on earth while growing in our relationship with Him.[37]

The church does not target any particular age group, but interlaces its communications with social media, including Facebook pages, Instagram photos, a prominent column of tweets, and even up-to-five-star reviews. "Welcoming, worshipful, community-oriented" says one person. "Pastor Jacob, the band, the people, the attitude, the community spirit, and the outpouring of love is amazing!" says another.[38]

The other prominent aspect of Providence's ministry is their direct outreach and mission. They provide multiple hands-on opportunities throughout the year. One example is a "Clean Out Your Closet" event that provides clothes for people in their community, a non-profit campground, a transition house for women recently released from prison, a rural life ministry in the Cumberland mountains, a homeless shelter, and an orphanage in Honduras.

Every May, WWW holds its largest outreach event of the year, involving hundreds of participants. On that day they begin worship in the middle school as usual, and then fan out across three different counties to serve their community. In 2014 they accomplished more than seventy projects on that day, including:

- Landscaping at a city Police Department and repairs in twelve seniors' homes;
- Serving lunch to firefighters and at a facility for women in crisis;
- Fixing-up ten local schools and accomplishing a major facelift at a youth community center;
- Gleaning sweet potatoes and apples for local distribution and filling disaster-relief buckets;
- Worshiping at a transitional housing center and sewing clothes to raise funds for school construction in Haiti.[39]

So the theory of three degrees of influence reminds us of the power of being in relationship with one another, both individually and in our work, church, and neighborhood communities. Vital relationship-oriented ministries can help us do more through our personal connections than we could possibly imagine on our own.

But here is something even more stunning: Jesus brought all of us down to *two* degrees of separation between ourselves and God, through Jesus![40] "I am the vine, you are the branches. Those who abide in me and I in them bear much fruit, because apart from me you can do nothing," Jesus says. "This is my commandment, that you love one another as I have loved you." (John 15:5, 12) The fact of only two degrees between ourselves and Christ (as vine and branches) affirms that every one of us (church-goer or not) is a child of God, lovingly created in God's image. Given this close connection between God and us, it's not surprising that we are meant to reflect God's generosity and character.

# Identity

If we base who we are on *being* instead of only based on our *doing*, then what is our identity?

From a secular, social viewpoint, identity is multifaceted. One model[41] lays out four concentric circles surrounding a person's unique personality: the primary dimension, such as age, race and ethnicity; aspects of home and geographic location; various work relationships; and cultural, political, social and world events. Such models can be helpful in clarifying our multiple roles but tend to focus on external relationships.

A second way of describing our identity is to name essential attributes of an engaged, growing Christian as a follower of Jesus Christ. For example, one congregation[42] selected and described five traits: purpose, ethics, community life, worship, and peacefulness. These are helpful, but ideal attributes may not get us closer to our core identity.

A third view of identity is to name aspects of our spiritual well-being, as in The Wholeness Wheel.[43] This wheel identifies six sectors: emotional, physical, financial, vocational, intellectual, and interpersonal. Of greatest interest to us in this view is its depiction of the wheel's hub as "in baptism—a new creation in Christ."

Maybe our core identity is more like the hub of the wheel. But baptism is not inclusive enough. What if the core is that we are all children of God, made in God's image, whether baptized or not?

Jesus leads us in this direction when the Pharisees and others demand to know whether or not he endorses paying taxes to the emperor (Matthew 22:15–22). They think that if he says "No," they can arrest him, and if he says "Yes," he will lose popular support. But Jesus asks to look at a coin, and then asks whose image is on it. It is Caesar's, the head of the Roman government. Jesus says, "Give therefore to the emperor the things that are the emperor's, and to God the things that are God's." His meaning: *you* are made in the image of God; give yourself fully to God![44]

Clergy and church leaders have to deal with all kinds of challenges and conflicts along the way. So do people of faith who participate in meaningful ministries. Inevitably that means periodically dealing with failure. In the face of such an experience, one minister says,

> When my heart whispers these [challenging] questions, I remind myself of the truth of the gospel: my identity and worth—as a pastor and as a person—is not wrapped around what I do or how large my congregation is. It's not tied to how much clout or influence others think I possess. It is only based on one thing. I am a cherished child of the King."[45]

What we do is not entirely divorced from the people we are; our actions reflect our character. But our actions do not express all of our authentic selves, and only God can see all that lies hidden within us. No matter what we have done or not done with our lives so far, here is the Good News: we are still—and always—children of God. God continually offers us a new beginning, to value ourselves and others as God's priceless sons and daughters.

This fundamental news sometimes eludes us in the complications of daily living, with its climb-higher aspirations and inherent competition. Clay Oglesbee, a District Superintendent in Minnesota, reinforces this lesson. "We forget that the goal of life's development and calling is not sizable bank accounts, shelves of trophies or prestige in the eyes of our colleagues," he says.

> The goal of life, according to Paul, is to gain a specific spiritual character and a specific spiritual destiny by becoming Christlike. Romans 8:29 offers a similar word: we are to be 'conformed to the likeness' of Christ. . . .[46]

Once again, we return to our being created in the image of God, called to live in a way that reflects that likeness.

"Do you not know that you are God's temple and that God's Spirit dwells in you?" Paul asks the Christians in Corinth. (1 Corinthians 3:16) To the Athenian crowds, Paul introduces "the God who made the world and everything in it,... in [whom] we live and move and have our being. . . ." (Acts 17:24, 28) Psychologist David Benner puts it another way: finding our truly authentic self in Christ is different from the conventions of popular psychology. The foundation of our identity or being is "in Christ," (2 Corinthians 5:17) grounded in God. This places God's love as the basis for our identity,[47] giving both movement and direction to our lives.

John Wertz, Jr. is a local church pastor in Virginia. "Being a child of God is not a short-term, highly intensive activity that we can [intentionally] undertake for less than an hour before continuing on with the rest of the day," he says. "Each activity we undertake...is an example of how we use our gifts to live as God's people in the world."[48] Sparked by this insight, for a specific season he invited the entire congregation to pray intentionally for people "to make a stronger connection between their identity as a child of God and their daily activities," to see themselves as God's hearts, hands, and voices in the world.

So how might the church figure into this picture? "Given the market-driven and consumer-based realities of our world, the church too often comes off, or is perceived, as some sort of spiritual version of a community recreation center, simply offering up programs and experiences to meet people's needs," says author Rick Barger. "That the church has a story to tell—a true story!—that makes (extraordinary) claims about God and God's relationship with the world and all of humankind is obfuscated in the midst of this confusion."[49] The story we have to tell and to demonstrate is *good* news, news of God's love for us and our capacity for loving God and others in return.

One church that stands out for helping people claim their true identity is Church of the Resurrection (COR) based in Leasburg, outside Kansas City, Kansas.

COR is impressive in its clarity of purpose: "to build a Christian community where non-religious and nominally religious people are becoming deeply committed Christians." [50] Church members state their purpose not only on their website, *cor.org*, but also in two-foot high letters on the wall of their central lobby. Every COR program and event builds toward this goal. They are the largest United Methodist Church in the United States, with four physical campuses and one online congregation. But despite their size, they keep personal relationships and small-group life in the center of their ministry. Half of their ordained ministers focus fulltime on congregational care, visiting families, and strengthening relationships, without having to oversee the administrative, programmatic, and organizational matters that sole or senior pastors need to do.

As part of its purpose, COR defines "deeply committed Christians" as people who are on a journey of "knowing, loving, and serving God."

- Knowing God—"Becoming theologically informed: growing in insight and understanding as continual students of our faith."
- Loving God—"Being spiritually transformed: opening ourselves to being changed from the inside out through the work of the Holy Spirit."
- Serving God—"Making a difference: living out our faith daily in the world through our words and actions."[51]

This journey is one of discipleship. *Discipleship* means the process of following Jesus, learning more about his life and ministry, and drawing closer to him in our daily lives, as we seek to live in a more Christ-like way. Small-group life is the heart of COR's discipleship offerings, beginning with a six-week course called "Journey 101," and also providing a wide array of weekly classes for children, teenagers, and adults.

# Integrity

*Integrity* is closely connected to identity, since it means aligning our actions with our deeply-held values. Many of us tend to think of integrity as standing our moral ground, holding fast to right behavior (however we define that) against the winds that might blow us off our feet. While integrity has an important moral component, there is more to it than that.

"Integrity is the state of wholeness, of completeness, of being not divided, of being sound," says pastor Mike Harrell. "It's a process that's often two steps forward, one step back, as we continue to grow in our maturity."[52]

Sometimes integrity requires us to change course from what we used to think was our best way of doing things, in order to adapt to a new situation. Simply adding one new commitment or priority often does not work, especially when we try to do the old way *and* the new way at the same time. "If we don't let something go," says Harrell, "we're stuck with one foot forward, one foot back.... We need to move through the endings in our lives" to fully embrace the new beginnings.[53]

For example, a parent who is disappointed about how her now-adult child turned out may need to let go of trying to correct his behavior before she can move into an adult-to-adult relationship with him. Likewise, at a certain point, a child who has tried to measure up to his parents has to let go of those efforts in order to see them as peers and be able to go forward in his life. So while our identity as sons and daughters of God does not change as we live life, our understanding of who we are continues to evolve.

So again, what is integrity? Integrity means to live with congruence: keeping the same inner foundational principles, core beliefs and behavior, whether we are working at our jobs, presenting something formally in public, or relaxing with friends and family. Ronald Greer explains:

> *Personal* integrity is when we are authentically the persons we were created to be. It means living a life of wholeness and congruence. *Moral* integrity is when we do what is right simply because we know it is the right thing to do.[54]

Understood another way, integrity can be described as a new coherence in life, says Franciscan friar Richard Rohr. In his amazing book, *Falling Upward*,[55] he describes how human life develops in two essential stages. In "the first half of life," we build a sense of self and security, establish relationships, and find our place in community. This stage relates to self and survival and gives us the "container" for the contents of our lives.[56] It provides a sense of "home," telling us what we can assume about our place in the world around us.

What Rohr calls "the second half of life" can begin at any time after we experience a significant loss, failure, or suffering. In this second stage, we can choose to delve deeper to discover our inner blueprint. This truer self points to who we are from God's perspective.[57] Our true self, or soul, says Rohr, is the "pearl of great value" (Matthew 13:45–46), the inner abiding place of God's Spirit within us.

Rohr emphasizes the impact suffering can have on us, breaking open a new stance toward life. But some people may find that another sort of significant life event can have a similar effect. A period of multiple major changes such as moving across country, finding a new family, or suddenly retiring, might give us the impetus to redefine ourselves.

Whatever the form of such reorienting life events, they can draw us toward integrity as a "second simplicity," when we reflect on and learn from our experiences. Rohr says this experience "feels like a return to simplicity after having learned from all the complexity." Our lives become more unified, inclusive of paradoxes, as we look for all that we share in common with others.[58] Our actions become less compulsive because they arise out of a deeper understanding of ourselves, and of what we are called to do in the world. Once we act in such a way, we try to let go of excessive worry over possible negative consequences.[59] Integrity is congruence with the core person God has designed us to be, as we seek to freely experience the fuller life available to us when we live out who we truly are.[60]

# Being With God

For many of us, "we are starved for quiet, to hear the sound of sheer silence that is the presence of God himself," says seminary professor Ruth Haley Barton.[61] This special silence is not just the absence of noise. We want to clear away the distractions caused by the details of our lives, so we can focus on what is meaningful and lasting. Positive quietude is a stillness that we can nurture within us, "a solitude that is transcendent."[62]

But leaping directly from a full schedule of frantic running into total silence can be daunting, if not terrifying. Most of us need to experience the silence a bit at a time, to encounter and lovingly dismiss our inner voices, and start to discern the voice of God. It requires time to take off some of the hats we wear, to examine our lives, to confess shortcomings, see The Big Picture, and listen deeply. Only after some outer layers have stripped away, even briefly, can we begin to recognize God's presence or hear God's voice.

Being with God is not just a solitary venture. God also works in partnership with us. "What does it mean for God to work both in us and with us?" asks theologian Miroslav Volf. "God enters the very core of our selves [sic.], the place from which we direct our will. . . . It is I who wants, thinks, and does, and at the same time it is Christ who acts in and through me." In this way "God partners with us to reveal the wonder of grace to the world."[63] Volf says, "When loving truly, the self moves outside of itself to dwell with God and neighbor, and only then is it truly at home."[64]

The Reign of God "is a depth dimension of our lives together," says theologian Marjorie Hewitt Suchoki:

> It is an attunement to the call of God in the midst of ordinariness, an awareness of the roots of peace in the love of God. God's [Reign] is a future that pervades our present, changing the quality of our lives in conformity to the great love of God.[65]

In such a partnership, we are no more spectators of God's work than were the disciples, who "were no more spectators of Jesus than Jesus was a spectator of God—they are *in* on the action of God, God acting *in* them, God living *in* them.[66]

# Singing God's Praise

The Bible's Book of Psalms is a collection of sung prayers, mostly for use in group worship, and mostly ending in praise. As such, the psalms are poetic works of art. Psalm 119 is the most skillfully constructed "acrostic" psalm, as well as the longest. A simple acrostic poem in English has a structure of twenty-six lines, each new line of text beginning with the next letter of the alphabet, progressing from A to Z. But Psalm 119 is far more complex. It contains twenty-two strophes (paragraphs of verses) following the twenty-two letter Hebrew alphabet in order, with every line of each strophe beginning with the same consecutive letter. Its subject is "the word of God and the law of God as the decisive factor in every sphere of life,"[67] leading the psalmist to express praise.

This psalm is "a massive intellectual achievement."[68] Like a fugue in classical music which confines itself to the same notes in varying order, it reiterates the subject from different angles, while maintaining its precise framework.

The great twentieth-century theologian C. S. Lewis compares Psalm 119 to intricate embroidery, a result of the writer's disciplined craftsmanship.[69] Its precise literary structure reveals the poet's view that the "moral beauty" in God's Law is revealed in its intricate pattern. The psalm itself becomes a poem of praise to God for all the ways God reveals God's Self to us through God's Law.

In contrast to modern, Western views of "law" as external rules, God's Law (*Torah*) in Hebrew literally means God's "teaching." Here in Psalm 119, "the [T]orah is not a dead letter (2 Corinthians 3:2–6), but an active agent which gives life," says Bible scholar Walter Brueggemann. "That is, [Torah] is not just a set of rules, but it is a mode of God's life-giving presence."[70] The poet "thinks of the law in broad terms as being the truth from God; it is [God's] rule of life and [the psalmist's] ground of hope."[71] So Psalm 119 reveals that the structure of God's Law does not stifle our freedom, but rather brings us life, hope and delight.

Verses 15 and 16 of the psalm express the core of such joyful living. "I will meditate on your precepts, and fix my eyes on your ways. I will delight in your statutes; I will not forget your Word." The term for "ways" refers to one's mode of living or character. So here they become a synonym for the richness of all God can reveal through the Torah. When the psalmist says, "I will not forget your Word," he or she refers to God's "word" (*dabar* in Hebrew), which cannot simply be said, but must also be received. It is the word that spoke creation into being in Genesis 1 and has communicated to God's people ever since.

So the comprehensiveness and intricacy of Psalm 119 reveals a reliable, balanced, holistic approach to living. We experience this wholeness when we look to God to identify who we are as God's beloved children, and how we are to live in alignment with God's Word.

No one can see God directly, but we catch more than a glimpse of God's being or character through faithful people like the Jewish prophets, and particularly through Jesus Christ himself (John 1:18). Our awareness of God's being prompts us to be attentive to our own quality of being. We praise God by simply doing what we were created to do—dwelling in relationship with God—as do the wind, the mountain, and the rest of God's creatures.[72] God has breathed us into being in order to praise God. (Genesis 2:7; John 20:19–22)[73] We have a distinctive role in God's creation as stewards of the earth and of all God's creatures. (Genesis 1:26–27; 2:15; Psalm 8; and Psalm 24:1.)

WHATEVER OUR SITUATION, we can work on letting go of an excessive "get ahead, don't fall behind" mentality, to focus more on qualitative *being*—on nurturing our loved-and-loving relationship with God. As we look within, we can rediscover a certain congruity of our lives: our deeper identity and integrity as children of God, made in God's image. As we learn to give more attention to God's presence and Word, we can praise God out of a deepening recognition that we are anchored in God's life-giving framework for joyful living.

But how do we focus on being as part of our daily framework for living? How can we actually *practice* being present to God?

# Questions for Reflection

1. What and whom do I look up to in my life to tell me who I am? To what degree am I comfortable allowing them to help shape my definition of who I am?
2. What is the biggest challenge to me personally, as I try to get off the merry-go-round of endless doing?
3. Reflecting on the significance of the coin in Matthew 22:15–22, as I look at my life so far, where do I see the stamp of God's image upon the person I am?
4. Eric Law says a relationship-driven ministry emphasizes listening to one another's stories. What are my congregation's strengths and weaknesses in this area? What could I and/or my faith community do to value and improve relationships?

# Endnotes

1. Suzanne Guthrie, "A day with no agenda," *Christian Century,* September 17, 2014, p. 13.

2. Stephen Covey, *First Things First: To Live, to Love, to Learn, to Leave a Legacy,* pp.51, 215; and Dr. Stephen Covey, "The Moral Compass," October 9, 2011, at *http://betweentheradials.blogspot.com/2011/10/dr-stephen-covey-7-habits-of-highly.html.*

3. Novelist and memoirist Jeanette Winterson, quoted by Carol Zaleski in "Poetry and dogma," *Christian Century,* December 25, 2013.

4. John M. Buchanan, "Beauty and thanksgiving," *Christian Century,* November 27, 2013.

5. Bonnie Gray, *Finding Spiritual Whitespace: Awakening Your Soul to Rest* (Grand Rapids: Revell, 2014).

6. ———, at *faithbarista.com/finding-spiritual-whitespace*

7. Reviewer from Revell, Bethany House blog, in "A Simple Life, Really?" at *asimplelifereally.blogspot.com/2014/05/review-finding-spiritual-whitespace.html.*

8. This is Richard Foster's definition of Christian meditation, in his *Celebration of Discipline: The Path to Spiritual Growth* (New York: HarperCollins, 1978, 1988, 1998), p. 17.

9. See Peter Velander in his devotion "Love Prevails," in the *Upper Room Disciplines 2014* (Nashville: Upper Room Books, 2013), p. 249.

10. Thomas R. Kelly, *Holy Obedience* (Quaker pamphlet) from 1939 William Penn Lecture at Haverford College, Arch Street Meeting House, Philadelphia; at *quaker.org/pamphlets/wpl1939a.html.*

11 Donna Fado Ivery, "The Sabbath Question," *WellSprings: A Journal for United Methodist Clergywomen,* Fall, 2001(Nashville: Section of Elders and Local Pastors, Division of Ordained Ministry, General Board of Higher Education and Ministry of the United Methodist Church, 2001), pp. 55–58.

12. *Ibid,* p. 55.

13. Ronald J. Greer, *op cit.,* p. 28.

14. *Ibid,* pp. 73f, 81–107. Greer names these attributes; I paraphrased their summary definitions.

15. Ruth Haley Barton, Professor of Spiritual Transformation at Northern Seminary, in *Sacred Rhythms: Arranging Our Lives for Spiritual Transformation,* at *goodreads.com/author/quotes/47409.Ruth_Haley_Barton.*

16. Henri J. M. Nouwen, *The Spirituality of Fund-Raising* (Nashville: Upper Room Ministries and the Henri Nouwen Society, 2004), p. 34.

17. *wikipedia.com* for "congruence."

18. Thomas Merton, *Thoughts in Solitude* (New York: Farrar, Strauss, Giroux, 1956, 1958), p. 15.

19. *Ibid*, p. 16.

20. Rev. Arthur Gafke, reflecting on the annual Badwater Ultramarathon in Death Valley, California, in his "Choice and Focus" devotions, *Upper Room Disciplines 2013* (Nashville: Upper Room Books, 2012), p. 269.

21. Peter Traben Haas, senior pastor of Westminster Presbyterian Church in Waterloo, Iowa, in "Contemplative congregation," *Christian Century*, March 5, 2014, p. 25.

22. Rev. Mary Elyn Bahlert, "The Gift of Presence: God's Grace," in *Voices and Silences* (Richmond, CA: Donna Fado-Ivery, 2013), May 2013.

23. Robert Benson, *Living Prayer*, cited at *spiritualityandpractice.com*.

24. Eugene H. Peterson, *The Message: The Bible in Contemporary Language* (Colorado Springs: NavPress, 2002), p. 1418.

25. A Merriam Webster, Inc., *Webster's Ninth New Collegiate Dictionary* (Springfield, MA: Merriam-Webster Inc., 1989), p. 227.

26. Teresa A. Martinez and Steve L. McMullin, "Factors Affecting Decisions to Volunteer in Nongovernmental Organizations," at *eab.sagepub.com/content/36/1/112*.

27. See James Andreoni, "Impure Altruism and Donations to Public Goods: A Theory of Warm-Glow Giving," in *The Economic Journal*, Volume 100, No. 401 (June 1990), pp. 464–477; at *jstor.org/discover/10.2307/2234133?uid=3739920&uid=2&uid=4&uid=3739256&sid=21104375122431*. See also James Andreoni, "Giving With Impure Altruism: Applications to Charity and Ricardian Equivalence," in *The Quarterly Journal of Economics*, 1995; at *jstor.org/discover/10.2307/1833247?uid=3739920&uid=2&uid=4&uid=3739256&sid=21104375122431*.

28. William T. Harbaugh, Ulrich Mayr, and Daniel R. Burghart, in *Science* 15, June 2007: Vol. 316 no. 5831, pp. 1622–1625; at *sciencemag.org/content/316/5831/1622.short*.

29. The Lake Institute on Faith & Giving resides at the Center on Philanthropy at Indiana University. See *philanthropy.iupui.edu/research/copps/panelstudy.aspx*. Related to it are The Women's Philanthropy Institute, which studies how and why gender matters in philanthropy; and The Fund-Raising School, which incorporates the latest research while teaching fundraising professionals. The Lake Institute partners with several foundations to do its research. Its Philanthropy Panel Study is the largest longitudinal study of charitable giving among American households, now covering more than 8,400 families.

30. Mark O. Wilhelm, Eleanor Brown, Patrick M. Rooney and Richard Steinberg, *The Intergenerational Transmission of Generosity* February 2008, J Public Econ. 2008 Oct 1; 92(10–11): 2146—2156; doi: *10.1016/j.jpubeco.2008.04.004*, pp. 1, 5.

31. This number of schools is for the 2014–2015 school year. See *http://alegacyofgiving.org*.
32. *alegacyofgiving.org*.
33. See Frigyes Karinthy's 1929 short story, "Chains," popularized in John Guare's play, *Six Degrees of Separation*; cited in Eric H. F. Law, *Holy Currencies: Six Blessings for Sustainable Missional Ministries* (St. Louis, MO: Chalice Press, 2013), p. 18.
34. See Nicholas A. Christakis and James H. Fowler, *Connected*, pp. 26–30, cited in Eric H. F. Law, *ibid.*, p. 18.
35. Paul J. Wadell, "Shared Lives: The challenges of friendship," *Christian Century*, September 20, 2011, p. 13.
36. *http://provumc.net/worship-without-walls*.
37. Valerie Craig's "My Providence Story," at *ibid.*
38. *facebook.com/provumc?sk=reviews*, through *provumc.net/worship-without-walls*.
39. Oct. 29, 2014 email from Becky Yates, Director of Outreach, Providence Church, Mount Juliet, Tennessee.
40. Eric H. F. Law, *op cit.*, p. 20.
41. Adapted from Lee Gardenswertz and Anita Rowe, *Diverse Teams at Work* (Alexandria, VA: Society for Human Resource Management, 2003, 2008); used in *Readiness 360* training, California-Nevada Annual Conference, 2014.
42. Foothills United Methodist Church in Rescue, California, May, 2010.
43. Inter-Lutheran Coordinating Committee on Ministerial Health and Wellness of the Evangelical Lutheran Church of America and the Lutheran Church-Missouri Synod; used in Catherine Malotky, ed., *op cit.*
44. For a devotion based on this passage and metaphor, see Heidi Haverkamp, "Public Faith," *Upper Room Disciplines 2014* (Nashville: Upper Room Books, 2013), p. 347.
45. J. R. Briggs, "Transforming Failure: How God used a painful season of ministry to change my life," *Leadership Journal*, Spring 2014, p. 24.
46. Clay Oglesbee, District Superintendent for the River Valley District of the Minnesota Annual Conference of the United Methodist Church, "Reflections on the lectionary" for Oct. 2, 2011, in *Christian Century*, September 20, 2011.
47. David C. Benner, *op cit.*, pp. 13, 49, and 95f.
48. John Wertz, Jr., pastor at St. Michael Lutheran Church in Blacksburg, Virginia, "The Identity Which Shapes Our Lives," Luther Seminary Center for Stewardship Leaders e-newsletter, July 14, 2014.
49. Rick Barger, *A New and Right Spirit* (Herndon, VA: Alban Institute, 2005), p. 2.
50. See *cor.org*. The congregation first met in a mortuary, so they chose the name "Church of the Resurrection" to declare their Christian faith.
51. *cor.org*.
52. Rev. Mike Harrell, "Integrity Part I," Oct. 5, 2014, Foothills United Methodist Church, Rescue, CA.

53. ——, "Integrity Requires Change," Oct. 19, 2014, Foothills United Methodist Church, Rescue, CA.
54. Ronald J. Greer, *op cit.*, p. 9.
55. Richard Rohr, O.F.M., *Falling Upward: A Spirituality for the Two Halves of Life* (San Francisco: Jossey-Bass, 2011).
56. *Ibid.*, p. xiii.
57. *Ibid.*, pp. xi, 86.
58. *Ibid.*, pp. 114, 120.
59. *Ibid.*, pp. 105, 123.
60. *Ibid.*, p. 71.
61. Ruth Haley Barton, from *Invitation to Solitude and Silence: Experiencing God's Transforming Presence,* cited at *goodreads.com/author/quotes/47409. Ruth_Haley_Barton.*
62. Robert Benson, from his book *Living Prayer,* at *spiritualityandpractice.com.*
63. Miroslav Volf, *Free of Charge: Giving and Forgiving in a Culture Stripped of Grace* (Grand Rapids: Zondervan, 2005), p. 51.
64. *Ibid.*, p. 52.
65. Marjorie Hewitt Suchoki, "Remembrance and Anticipation," *Upper Room Disciplines 2012* (Nashville: Upper Room Books, 2011), p. 341.
66. Eugene H. Peterson in his introduction to the Book of Acts, *op cit.*, p. 1492.
67. Artur Weiser, *The Psalms: A Commentary*, trans. by Herbert Harwell (Philadelphia: The Westminster Press, 1962), p. 740.
68. Walter Brueggemann, *The Message of the Psalms* (Minneapolis: Augsburg Publishing House, 1984), p. 39.
69. C. S. Lewis, *Reflections on the Psalms* (NY: Harcourt, Brace & World, 1958), p. 58.
70. Walter Brueggemann, *op cit.*, p. 40.
71. William R. Taylor and W. Stewart McCullough in George Arthur Buttrick, ed., *The Interpreter's Bible Vol. IV: The Book of Psalms, The Book of Proverbs* (NY/Nashville: Abingdon Press, 1955), p. 623.
72. See Enuma Okoro, "The Word Brings Joy and Growth," *Upper Room Disciplines 2012* (Nashville: Upper Room Books, 2011), p. 375. Psalm 148 also expresses this thought.
73. Susan A. Blain, "The Word Is Very Near You," *Upper Room Disciplines 2013* (Nashville: Upper Room Books, 2012), p. 63.

# Practicing Presence

I T IS ONE thing to say we want to reorient our living from constant doing to being with God, but how can we develop the practice of living in the present moment with the One Who is present with us? And once we have experienced the difference, how can we encourage others in our families and congregations to risk making this change?

## Spiritual Disciplines

As we learn to be attentive to God's presence and word, we can choose to develop certain regular habits, what Christians traditionally call "spiritual disciplines." These are "disciplines" not in the sense of punishment, but rather as actions that provide a pattern or framework for our daily lives. The root word for "discipline" is "disciple," meaning "follower." So Christian spiritual disciplines are patterns of behavior that can help us grow as followers of Jesus Christ.

Different denominations have varying lists of them, but all include reading the Bible, prayer, meditation, and contemplation. Searching the Scriptures involves Bible study and devotional reading. Prayer is communicating with God, meditation is structured reflection on God, and contemplation is a gaze of love toward God. While these practices overlap to some degree, they are presented here as moving from more structured to more free-form experiences of choosing to be attentive to God.

"The spiritual disciplines are an inward and spiritual reality," says Quaker Richard Foster in his devotional classic *Celebration of Discipline*,[1] "and the inner attitude of the heart is far more crucial than the mechanics [forms of praying or prayer positions] for coming into the reality of the spiritual life." The fact of our praying, for example, does not bring God closer to us or have to be done in one specific way. Instead, prayer puts us in an emotional and spiritual place where we can be open to the God who has been trying to get through to us all along.

Spiritual disciplines are activities and attitudes that open us to God's transforming love and to the changes that only God can bring about in our lives.[2] They cultivate in us what the great Christian mystic Meister Eckhart calls a "gentle receptiveness to divine breathings."[3] All of us can have inner conflicts at times, to which we might respond with either a positive or negative attitude. The purpose of these spiritual practices is to help us avoid or replace old, destructive habits of thought with new, life-giving thinking and behavior that point us toward God, freeing us to center on Christ and draw closer to God's heart.[4]

# Searching the Scriptures

One of these disciplines is to search the Scriptures, through two distinctive avenues of Bible study and devotional reading. Whereas Bible study stresses interpretation, asking, "What does this Scripture mean?" devotional reading of the Bible emphasizes application, asking, "What does this Scripture mean *to me*?"[5]

When we do *Bible study*, we carefully direct our attention to a specific passage, going through a process that gives us an objective framework for understanding.[6] Author Richard Foster says that when we study such a text, we naturally flow through four steps:

- Repetition regularly channels the mind in a helpful direction, such as rehearsing God's good deeds toward us, thereby ingraining the habit of gratitude.
- Concentration focuses our attention on something we have decided is significant in our lives, such as the giftedness of each day, or opportunities to share with others.
- Comprehension comes when we consciously realize a truth that lies within the words, leading us to new insight and discernment by which to interpret the text.
- Reflection allows us to define the importance of what we are studying, which gives us wisdom, not just knowledge,[7] relating to our own lives the new understanding of what we have read.

John Wesley, founder of the Methodist movement, established a clear pattern for Bible study. First, he said we need to get away from the distractions of work and other busy places and give our undivided attention to the passage. Second, as we study the Bible, we come to trust that God the Holy Spirit is present, helping us understand its meaning. Third, we read with a particular spiritual goal in mind, for example to understand "the way to salvation" (one of Wesley's favorite phrases). Fourth, wherever there is something obscure or troublesome in the story, we can pray for guidance, compare this passage to other scriptures, and consult experienced Christians and other Christian commentators.[8]

The primary challenge in Bible study, says one author, is:

to learn to differentiate between that which is human, time-bound, culturally restricted, and that which is divine, eternal, and universal. In order to be able to do this responsibly, we must learn all that we can about every aspect of the biblical setting.[9]

Another resource says, "Better than asserting that the Bible *is* God's Word, is to understand that the Bible *contains* God's Word."[10]

Old Testament seminary professor John Herbert Otwell makes an even clearer distinction. "The Word of God is the divine response to our study of the Bible," he says. "[It] is my expectation as a Christian that God will continue to respond to my study of Scripture with what becomes to me the Word of God."[11]

In order to discover this Word, we begin by trying to discern the original setting and audience, through any of the commonly accepted types of biblical criticism:

- Literary criticism—Analyze the vocabulary, syntax, and style in order to identify the author, find the text's possible date, and clarify its meaning.
- Historical criticism—Identify the historical events surrounding the passage by applying evidence from archeology and scientific analysis.
- Form criticism—Mark common oral expressions surrounding the life situation when this story was customarily used. For example, it may be an everyday recitation, a family holy day ritual, an installation of a tribal chief, high priest or king, or litany for worship when all the people gather together.
- Patternism—Reconstruct the patterns of belief and action by which the people of that time responded to their environment.
- History-of-traditions criticism—Discern how people handed down the traditions related to people, places and institutions associated with this account.
- Redaction criticism—Study the editor ("redactor") who polished and put the pieces of text into their final form.
- Rhetorical criticism—Identify internal mechanisms that make this passage a particular literary form, such as a poem.[12]

These approaches allow us to study the Bible from different human angles, giving us various linguistic methods for understanding how God speaks to us through our interaction with the Scriptures.

The great majority of Christians see the Bible as neither a reference book on science or various other secular topics, nor a recipe book of how to make a certain thing happen.[13] The Bible "is the primary written witness to the love of God we know in Jesus Christ."[14]

It uses metaphors, parables, and other figures of speech to point to a deeper truth which God chooses to reveal to us. As John Wesley affirms, the Bible is one of the "means of grace" given to us, a way for God to reach out to us in love.[15]

By contrast, Bible literalists do not believe there are symbols, metaphors, or allegories within it, but that all references are to be taken at face value. The one exception is their belief that the "Lamb of God" is not an actual lamb but stands for Jesus Christ. They seek to make the Bible the authority in every aspect of living, including modern science, and see no contradictions between different Bible texts. With this view of "biblical inerrancy," if they perceive any appearance of discrepancy between one verse and another, they understand it as the fault of the writer of one of the verses in wrongly hearing God's specific words.

Often there are two ways to read sentences written in Greek, since the written language does not use many pronouns. As a result, a serious Bible student can read 2 Timothy 3:16 two alternative ways. One way is: "All Scripture is inspired by God and is useful for teaching, for reproof, for correction, and for training in righteousness." The second way is: "All Scripture *that* is inspired by God is useful for teaching, for reproof, for correction, and for training in righteousness." (Italics mine.) Annotated Bibles have a footnote that gives this alternative reading.

Those who take the Bible literally accept the first translation, concluding that every verse of the Bible is "inspired," meaning "God-breathed," transmitted directly from God to the human writer. Because of this perspective, literalists reject all types of biblical criticism. They place an emphasis on teaching specific theological beliefs and support their doctrines with verses chosen from throughout the Bible without reference to their context. Literalists stress "life lessons" over narrative in the Scriptures. They do not try to "interpret" the Bible but seek to move directly from reading a text to personal application.

By contrast, the majority of Christians understand 2 Timothy 3:16 the second way: stating that some scripture texts are inspired, but not all (such as Herod's slaughter of innocent children in Matthew 2:16–18). Therefore they see some types of biblical criticism as essential to be able to distinguish between what is inspired and what is not.

This discussion of the role of the Bible leads us to the second way we can search the Scriptures: *devotional reading.*

Christians across the generations have known that "reading is a fundamental spiritual practice and that books are tools that can serve our Christian discipleship."[16] This is especially true when we read the Bible to gain devotional insight: that is, looking for a message that speaks to our particular life circumstances at the moment.

Many Bible readers consider the Ten Commandments (Exodus 20:1–17) and Jesus' Greatest Commandment to love God and others as oneself (Matthew 22:37–40) as absolute standards to strive for in our living. At the same time, neither these passages nor any other part of the Bible give magic recipes for how to live perfect, stress-free lives. Thus the Bible is not an automatic recipe book. But when we read a passage each day with an open mind and spirit, we give our souls the opportunity to hear a message from God. God can break in at any time, of course, but it is much easier for us when we invite God to speak, or to show God's presence. A lot of people never hear an actual voice. Instead, their devotional time may give them a sense of peace or purpose, a challenge, or a thought of which they were not previously aware.

Devotional Bible reading involves slowly, softly engaging the Scriptures, sparking our imagination, and letting awe dawn upon us. We reflect on the mystery of how a loving Creator God speaks to us in the various times and places of our lives. "The depth of God's Word invites us to journey in faith and wonder, savoring as we go," says author Kirk Byron Jones. "Daily listening is the...only way to stay in tune with what God was up to back then and, even more importantly, with what God is up to right now."[17]

Many decades ago, I heard a preacher refer to "the amazing coincidence" of the Bible. No matter what our personal life circumstances at the time of reading Scripture, he said, God gives it a meaning for us, if we think it through and reflect on it with prayer. I have never forgotten that pastor's remark, because it still rings true for me now. The Bible is not a magic answer book, but it is amazing how it can speak to our lives when we reflect on the text in the light of the concerns and circumstances of our lives. Often it points us, not to self-contained answers, but to deeper, truer questions that challenge and stretch us.

Some people do devotional reading in a structured way. For example, they may go through sequential chapters in a Book of the Bible, as part of a read-through-the-Bible program over one or more years, or according to topics in a devotional book such as Rueben Job and Norman Shawchuck's *A Guide to Prayer for Ministers and Other Servants*.[18] Some people follow the Bible texts of the *Three-Year Common Lectionary* (a three-year church outline of Bible readings) with short devotional paragraphs, as in each year's *Upper Room Disciplines*. Others simply range through the Bible daily to see what catches their eye. We can develop a positive habit when we do this at the same time each day, such as the first thing in the morning, or the last thing at night.

Devotional reading can be part of a Christian's framework for living. Its purpose is to open us to a personal experience of God's presence. For example, we might memorize a Scripture text, so it stays in our thoughts throughout the day. Or we may read a short section of the Bible, then ask ourselves, "What does this phrase mean? What might God be telling me about God? About myself? About others?"[19]

One ancient way of devotional reading that has spread throughout different denominations is known as *Lectio Divina* (Latin for "divine reading"). We read a passage of Scripture slowly four times, trusting that we will hear a helpful word from God in the process.

- First reading—Read the story slowly and deliberately to get the plain meaning of the words.
- Second reading—Listen for a word or a phrase that speaks to you and reflect further on its meaning.
- Third reading—Write out your response to the key message you have heard, or the image you have seen.

- Fourth reading—Prayerfully reflect upon God and the selected phrase, seeking to fully be with God.

Surprising discoveries can come from searching the Scriptures, whether in the form of Bible study or devotional reading.

Reading and studying the Scriptures regularly can help us clarify our attitudes and shift into being in the world as a loved child of God. In those crystalline moments when we glimpse this deeper reality, we can affirm God's love for us and for all beings and express our love in return. By searching the Scriptures, we can begin to learn the specific meanings of Bible passages and explore God's Living Word for us.

My husband of more than thirty years is my soulmate, the greatest gift of my life. He and I are early risers, both by inclination and due to country living. A favorite part of our day is when we sit in front of the wood stove before dawn and read the Bible together. He reads one version aloud, while I silently read a different translation. One of us reads aloud the devotional paragraphs and prayer in our lectionary-based book of devotions.

Then comes the neatest part: we share with each other the meanings and impact of that Bible text, given our personal experiences and the Bible study we have done. As we watch the dawn come up over the crest of the mountain, blooming from peach to crimson against the silhouetted pines, we fall into silence together, simply seeking to be together with God. It is a beautiful, thought-provoking gift of God's grace, and a challenging way to begin the day.

# Prayer

Prayer is communicating with God, whether privately or with others in worship. It requires setting aside a time and place to reorient ourselves, giving God our undivided attention. But for most of us, that is not immediately easy, says author Richard Peace. Prayer is all about getting through the barriers that keep us from God, he states, reducing distractions so we can focus our thoughts on God. These barriers can be the noise of our body (This chair is uncomfortable); of our need (I'm feeling tired. Why can't I get this project done?); of relationships (How long is he going to stay mad at me?); or of problem and pain (How can I pay all my bills? I wish I felt better).[20] But in the end, Peace says, thankfully *God* is the One who prays *through* us, who prays for us on our behalf. Romans 8:26 says, "we do not know how to pray as we ought, but that very Spirit intercedes for us with sighs too deep for words."

Foster says, "All who have walked with God have viewed prayer as the main business of their lives," citing the Bible's David and such "giants of the faith" as Martin Luther, John Wesley, and George Fox.[21] But hearing such a statement can sound daunting to many of us. Prayer is not something ever truly "mastered," but instead is a learning process of seeking to better listen to and engage God with a loving heart.

Prayer is not something we merely say *to* God or do in *front* of God, but is rather an opening to dialogue *with* God. It can take many forms. One approach describes these forms as A-C-T-S.

- Adoration—Expressing our love for God;
- Confession—Admitting our actions and attitudes of estrangement;
- Thanksgiving—Thanking God for all God has given to us; and
- Supplication—Praying for ourselves and for others.

The most common prayer among Christians is the Lord's Prayer (Matthew 6:9–13 and parallels), which Jesus uses as a pattern or template to teach his disciples how to pray. "Jesus teaches us that prayer is fundamentally a loving listening to God as [God] continually communicates [God's] love to us at each moment," says one author. For Jesus it was "a permanent, ever-increasing state of being turned inwardly toward the Father at every moment in loving trust and self-surrender."[22]

More than anything, prayer is an inner attitude, where we deliberately attend to God. Brother David Steindl-Rast calls this

attentiveness "prayerfulness." It is that combination of concentration (centering our hearts) and "wonderment" (seeing things in
their most profound meaning), which results in "gratefulness." In
such times, we try to make our whole life a prayer to God, reflecting a prayerful understanding of God's call with thanks, praise
and blessing.[23] With this sense of prayerfulness in mind, we can
grasp the idea of "pray[ing] without ceasing" (1 Thessalonians
5:17), including keeping "our heart open for the meaning of life,"
says Steindl-Rast. These "moments in which we drink deeply from
the source of meaning"[24] can be times of prayer, meditation, and
contemplation.

Prayerfulness therefore involves living in the present, using all
our senses to glimpse God dwelling in the persons and events of our
daily lives.[25] It is a journey inward, down to the center of our being.
It prompts our awareness of the inner unity of all that exists—our
communion with all other human beings, with nature and all creatures, and all that God has made.[26]

One example of prayer is called the Prayer of Examen. It was first
developed by St. Ignatius, the founder of the Jesuits (Society of Jesus),
and is a way of assessing one's life before God on a regular basis. We
prepare ourselves by recollecting what has happened in our lives in
the previous twenty-four hours,[27] then making a list of our activities
over that time period, to prompt our reflection. Next, our prayer follows five steps:

1. *Gratitude* for encounters with people, events, experiences, and
   activities.
2. *Awareness of God* for when we particularly noticed that God's
   ever-present reality was especially real and apparent.
3. *Confession* of when we have been less than faithful to God or
   have failed to live up to our calling.
4. *Asking ourselves what we learned* from this experience—about
   this way of praying, about ourselves, and about God's call.
5. Finally, *closing* with a spontaneous prayer.[28]

While it is one thing to talk *about* God, it is another thing entirely to encounter the Living God. We pray as God's children through God's Son, and the Holy Spirit helps us in our prayer. But at the same time, prayer is a risk, requiring us to examine our lives in a way that may make us uncomfortable, leading us to let go of little self-deceptions and self-benefiting delusions. We stand in truthfulness before God, trusting God in our vulnerability. At the same time, in this moment of raw openness before the Creator, we know ourselves as loved. God reassures us: "Do not fear, for I have redeemed you; I have called you by name; you are mine." (Isaiah 43:1) "I will not forget you. See, I have inscribed you on the palms of my hands." (Isaiah 49:15–16)[29]

Jane Vennard, writer on spiritual practices, says, "Prayer is all about our relationship with a God who loves us. God calls all of us, just as we are, into relationship and offers us the possibility of intimacy."[30]

Such prayer leads us into what Jewish theologian Martin Buber calls an "I-Thou" relationship. ("Thou" is the intimate term for "you" in English, like *du* in German or *tu* in French.) "The primary word *I-Thou* can only be spoken with the whole being," says Buber. *Thou* creates a mutual, life-giving relationship, where the Spirit is in the relationship between us."[31] This relationship can turn every connection with others into prayer. In other words, in every encounter with a particular person ("you"), we get a glimpse of the eternal "you"—God.[32] This understanding fits with Matthew 25:31–46, where Jesus says that how we treat people who seem "the least" among us is how we are treating Jesus Christ himself.

In a life of prayer, "our wills and God's grace act together," says Evelyn Underhill, Christian mystic. "Prayer covers all ways in which our will and love reaches out to one Reality and Love in adoration, longing, penitence, confidence, and joy."[33]

One congregation that places a primacy on prayer is CrossRoads United Methodist Church in Phoenix. Like many local churches, they have an active prayer chain, in which prayer requests are shared regularly among the congregation electronically or by telephone.

But they also hold Morning Prayer every Monday, Wednesday, and Friday from 8:00 to 8:30 a.m. Anyone can drop in for prayer time in the sanctuary, to start their day focused on God's love.[34] "Worship is like breathing," they say:

> People worship God in different ways, but when we strip away [each individual form of prayer,] we are just falling forward before God (falling into God instead of away from [God] with our heart, mind, body and soul. We are humbling ourselves before our Creator and remembering who we are and who God is, as we become comfortable in our natural position [as God's creatures.][35]

Through prayer we seek to dialogue with God, in a process that can take many forms, but expresses our attention to God, and wonder and gratitude in response. Prayerfulness is a way of living in the now, in self-assessment, truthfulness, and vulnerability. It is the expression of our relationship with the Holy One who chooses to love us, as a sheer gift. Prayer helps us be with God as we live fully in the world.

# Meditation

Christian meditation is structured reflection on what God reveals about who God is, as we focus on specific thoughts, such as a Bible passage, in the context of God's love. Richard Foster says, "Christian meditation is the ability to hear God's voice and obey [God's] word," in order to "enter into the living presence of God for ourselves."[36]

He says it can take at least three forms:

- *Meditation upon Scripture*—Internalizing the passage; entering into the story to hear its message.
- *Recollection or Centering down*—Becoming still, entering into silence, and allowing our fragmented minds to become

centered. It involves turning over our concerns to God, and then opening up to receive what God wishes to show us.

- *Meditation upon God's creation*—Acknowledging that the heavens declare God's handiwork (Psalm 19:1), as we notice the trees, flowers, and all the humble acts of earth's creatures.[37]

To some extent, prayer, meditation, and contemplation overlap. In a process that quickly goes deeper than words can express, there is a commonality of experiencing God as the Holy One, and a palpable sense of God's love and of the unity of all God has created.

In Psalm 95, the psalmist invites us to worship God and listen for God's voice." Robert Benson understands this invitation to include two dimensions:

> We are to listen for the way God speaks to us through the breeze and through the rain, through the voice of a friend and the laughter of a child, through the thousand other ways God speaks into our lives.
>
> But we are to learn to listen for and to recognize the voice of God within us, as well.[38]

We can hear God's voice within us when we are "swept up in the symphony of the 'now,'"[39] with a larger and deeper awareness of God's presence in the world. It is a melting of distinctions between the "I" and all other living things.

What often comes as a surprise to even lifelong meditators is that God, "is not a What, not an object, but a living Subject,"[40] the Subject of our lives. The Living God can never be boxed in by theologies or words, by religious rituals or spiritual practices, or by human minds. So the result of meditation always awaits God's revealing, never to be taken for granted.

Brother Steindl-Rast acknowledges his own experience of this phenomenon:

> There are moments when, altogether gratuitously, we get an inkling of the ground of our being. We realize that we are both at

home there and on the way there. Some are bold enough to call this starting point and goal of our heart's journey "God." Nothing else deserves this name. We can call the two poles of this experience God's immanence (closer to me than I am to myself) and God's transcendence (beyond the beyond).[41]

In the process of meditation, we may discover another amazing thing: God and we act together. Richard Rohr calls it "co-breathing" with God, where our soul or true self, and God breathe back and forth, in and out, giving and receiving.[42] There is both intimacy and synergy in our relationship with each other, as we offer silence and space in our lives to receive from and give back to God.

"This deeper voice of God sounds a lot like the voices of risk, trust, surrender, soul, 'common sense,' destiny and love, of your deepest self," says Richard Rohr. "The true faith journey only begins at this point; up to now was only preparation." In some ways, it is like coming home, he states, but now home has a whole new meaning: "it *transcends but includes* one's initial experience of home."[43] (Emphasis in original)

Such an intimate interaction with God takes us outside our perception of time. Instead, we are in the eternal present with God. "Christ is not just present at the starting line and at the finish," says one devotional writer, referring to Revelation 22:13. "Christ actually is the source and the consummation of our life.... It is God who brought us to birth and God in whom our life will find its completion."[44] This description aligns with Acts 17:28, where Paul says God is the One "in [whom] we live and move and have our being."

Those who wish to enter into meditation through verbal prayer may choose to use a Breath Prayer, where they repeat two phrases over and over, timing them to their intake and outflow of breath. The best known of these is called the Jesus Prayer—(Inhale:) "Lord Jesus Christ," / (Exhale:) "have mercy."[45] Or we may use any other words or phrases, such as: "I receive your Spirit," / "I let go of fear." Or we might use Psalm 46:10, "Be still, and know" / "that I am God."

Likewise, people who want to enter into meditation using their senses may imagine a favorite geographical spot, a biblical setting, or a place of rest in which Christ comes to them or they encounter God. Meditation is not so much a matter of technique, but of simply seeking to see what God wishes to show us.

# Contemplation

Contemplation has been called "a gaze of faith" or "silent love."[46] Whereas meditation often begins with a consciously-directed sequence of thought, contemplation is effortless intuition, "an open waiting before God, resting quietly in God's love."[47] It is "a communion in something greater than the world, as great as Being itself, in order that in its deep peace we may find God."[48] Such an experience takes us beyond the markers of time, into an eternal present. Thomas Merton says, "we know, by fresh discovery, the deep reality that is our existence here and now, and in the depths of that reality we receive from [God] light, truth, wisdom and peace."[49]

Contrary to stereotypes, contemplation is not an esoteric practice done by other-worldly people. It is available to us all and points us to the fullness of life for which our human hearts long. Steindl-Rast says contemplation occurs whenever we realize the *gift* of all there is, and respond with thanks, blessing, and praise.[50]

Thomas Merton understands contemplation as a process for unmasking the illusion of our separateness from the rest of creation. The world is not a reality outside of us, he says. It is a mystery of which we are a part and to which we have access.[51] Often during contemplation the line is erased between the universe within us and the physical universe that surrounds our world.

While contemplation draws us inward, ultimately it directs us outward, in compassion toward others. "The gaze of God receives us exactly as we are, without judgment or distortion, subtraction or addition," says Rohr. "Such *perfect receiving* is what transforms us.... All we can do is receive and return the loving gaze of God every day." He continues, "Soon we...can pass on the same accepting gaze to all others who need it."[52]

When we care about others, our concern naturally flows into care *for* them and advocacy on their behalf. So contemplation prompts us "to bend deeply into God and to enter the stillness that activates God's deep inner movement in us so that we can be God's action."[53] David Steindl-Rast calls this stance "contemplation in action," where what we do with and for others is the way that we become a channel for love to flow to them.[54]

I grew up with parents who assumed that a person's faith influences his or her public life. Having raised four children while my dad provided the family income, my mom was officially a homemaker until she began teaching in a public school at age fifty, But unofficially all those years she was a community activist, and I became her willing tag-along.

There were plenty of things to learn in the 1960s, my high school years. Mom partnered with a male volunteer to pose as a white couple asking to rent apartments, along with a pair of black volunteers posing as a married couple to test fair housing laws in our state. I joined her, our pastor and a few other leaders of our congregation, to staff a Community House for mutual empowerment in a nearby low-income, black neighborhood, including doing office work for its job-search arm. One Easter Sunday we gathered with local residents before sunrise to march along the residential streets banging pots and pans and celebrating with "Christ is risen! He is risen indeed!"

When Black Power came to the fore, we handed over the keys and the leadership to the local community leaders, and to focus better on race issues in our own community.

Even as a teenager, I was clear that working for justice was much less a matter of political partisanship than an application of my Christian faith. During college years the linkage grew even stronger, in those days of civil rights, Cesar Chavez, inner-city unrest, and U.S. involvement in Vietnam. The base community in college for my nonviolent involvement was not a political party, but a campus ministry.

So while contemplation takes us on an inward journey, it also prompts us to make an outward journey of care-in-action toward other individuals and toward the social systems in which they live.

IT TAKES COURAGE, patience, and practice to be present to God in our daily living. We can design some "spiritual whitespace" into our days, seeking to simply *be* with God, by studying the Scriptures or doing devotional Bible reading, praying, meditating, or contemplating. These "spiritual disciplines" are habits that can more positively redirect our attitudes and build receptivity to God.

Engaging in biblical criticism and reading devotionally, such as through *Lectio Divina*, can help us recognize God's Living Word in the Bible. To express and address our relationship with God, we can pray in a variety of ways, from A-C-T-S or the Prayer of Examen, to spontaneous prayers with others or alone. Likewise, in meditation we can focus on God's creation or on Scripture or do silent centering within ourselves. Contemplation is "a gaze of faith" or "silent love," as we wait in openness before God. These and other practices encourage us to be attentive to the One who made us and loves us completely.

# Questions for Reflection

1. What are my current practices of consciously being present to God? Have I ever felt God's personal presence with me? What was the situation at the time?
2. How can I use Bible study and devotional reading to nourish my time of being with God?
3. What is the most natural way I usually pray? Is there a particular time of day, place, or way of praying that encourages me to spend more time with God?
4. What might prompt me to meditate or contemplate? How might I leave a space in "my" time to be more conscious of God's presence?

# Endnotes

1. Richard J. Foster, *op cit.,* p. 3
2. See the review of Ruth Haley Barton's book *Sacred Rhythms: Arranging Our Lives for Spiritual Transformation* (Downer's Grove, IL: InterVarsity Press, 2006) at *amazon.com.*
3. Meister Eckhart, *Meister Eckhart,* trans. C. de B. Evans, Vol. 1 (London: John M. Watkins, 1956), p. 50; cited by Richard Foster in *op cit.,* p. 57.
4. Richard J. Foster, *op cit.,* pp. 62, 110–111.
5. *Ibid.,* p. 69.
6. *Ibid.,* pp. 63ff.
7. *Ibid.,* pp. 65ff.
8. Gale C. Felton, ed. *How United Methodists Study Scripture* (Nashville: Abingdon Press, 1999), pp. 45f, 63f.
9. *Ibid.,* p. 103.
10. *Ibid.,* p. 98.
11. Dr. John Herbert Otwell, Professor of Old Testament at Pacific School of Religion, in the Pacific School of Religion's *Occasional Paper Number 10,* October, 1977.
12. Types of biblical criticism described by John Herbert Otwell, "Introduction to the Old Testament" first semester course, Pacific School of Religion, fall, 1973.
13. Gale C. Felton, ed., *op cit.,* p. 100.
14. Dick Murray, *Teaching the Bible to Adults and Youth* (Nashville: Abingdon Press, 1987, 1993), p. 167.
15. *Ibid.,* pp. 92f.
16. Byron Borger, co-owner of Hearts and Minds, an independent Christian bookstore in Dallastown, PA, cited in "One store, many churches," *Christian Century,* October 15, 2014, p. 11.
17. Kirk Byron Jones, "Wondering, Imagining, and Listening: The Hidden Bounty of Daily Bible Reading," *Circuit Rider,* May/June/July 2014.
18. Reuben Job and Norman Shawchuck, *A Guide to Prayer for Ministers and Other Servants* (Nashville: Upper Room Books, 1997).
19. For more suggestions see James Bryan Smith, *A Spiritual Formation Workbook: Small Group Resources for Nurturing Christian Growth* (San Francisco: HarperSanFrancisco Renovare, 1991, 1993), p. 52.
20. Richard Peace, *Meditative Prayer: Entering God's Presence* (Colorado Springs: NavPress, 1998), pp. 12f.
21. Richard Foster, *op cit.,* pp. 34ff.
22. George Mahoney, *In Jesus We Trust* pp. 36f., cited in Reuben P. Job, *When You Pray: Daily Practices for Prayerful Living* (Nashville: Abingdon Press, 2009), pp. 198f.

23. Brother David Steindl-Rast, *Gratefulness*, pp. 77f.

24. *Ibid.*, p. 211.

25. For stories that demonstrate this, see Sister Bridget Haase, O.S.U., *Generous Faith: Stories to Inspire Abundant Living* (Brewster, MA: Paraclete Press, 2009), pp. 11–46.

26. Maria Boulding, O.S.B., "Prayer: The Real Relationship," in John Mogabgab, ed., *Weavings* September-October 1990 (Nashville: The Upper Room, 1990), p. 39.

27. Richard Peace, *op cit.*, p. 55.

28. *Ibid.*, pp. 55–57.

29. Maria Boulding, O.S.B., *op cit.*, pp. 40–42.

30. Jane E. Vennard, *A Praying Congregation* ((Herndon, IL: Alban Institute, 2005), *p. 42*, cited in Rueben P. Job, *op cit.*, p. 122.

31. Martin Buber, *I and Thou, Second Edition* (New York: Charles Scribner's Sons, 1958), pp. 3, 39.

32. Phillip Cary, "Encountering the Biblical Other. Buber and Levinas," Lecture 28, *Philosophy and Religion in the West* CD (Chantilly, VA: The Teaching Company, 1999) and Martin Buber, *op cit.*, p. 75.

33. Evelyn Underhill, "Breathing the Air of Eternity," *Weavings* (Nashville: The Upper Room, 2002), May–June 2002, p. 8.

34. *crossroadsphx.com.*

35. F. Antonisamy, *An Introduction to Christian Spirituality*, pp. 76f., cited at *wikipedia.org* re prayer.

36. Richard Foster, *op cit.*, pp. 17, 24.

37. *Ibid.*, pp. 29–31.

38. Robert Benson, *The Echo Within: Finding Your True Calling*, cited at *robertbensonwriter.com.*

39. Sister Bridget Haase, O.S.U., *op cit.*, pp. 5, 8.

40. Walter Brueggemann, "Spirited remnant," *Christian Century*, January 9, 2013, p. 37.

41. Brother David Steindl-Rast, *op cit.*, pp. 196f.

42. Richard Rohr, *op cit.*, pp. 92f.

43. *Ibid.*, pp. 48. 87f.

44. Nicola Vidamour, "Worshiping Together," *Upper Room Disciplines 2013* (Nashville: Upper Room Books, 2012), p. 161.

45. Richard Peace, *op cit.*, p. 19. See also Harvey Seifert, *Explorations in Meditation and Contemplation* (Nashville: The Upper Room, 1981), pp. 67f.

46. *Catechism of the Catholic Church, 2724,* cited in *wikipedia.org* about prayer.

47. Harvey Seifert, *op cit.*, pp. 64f.

48. Thomas Merton, *op cit.*, p. 81.

49. *Ibid.*, p. 98.

50. Brother David Steindl-Rast, *op cit.*, pp. 77–82.

51. Thomas Merton, *Contemplation in a World of Action*: Second Edition, Restored and Corrected (Notre Dame, IN: University of Notre Dame Press, 2017).

52. Richard Rohr, *op cit.,* pp. 159f.
53. Doreen Kostynuik, "What God Requires," *Upper Room Disciplines 2011* (Nashville: Upper Room Books, 2010), p. 42.
54. Brother David Steindl-Rast in "The Spirit of Gratitude" presentation, *The Greater Good Gratitude Summit*, June 7, 2014, Richmond, CA.

# What Is a Soul?

A S I WAS growing up and through my college years, the word "soul" seemed to be used merely as a religious synonym for "person." After college, when I went to seminary, I heard that belief in "immortality of the soul" was different from belief in "resurrection of the body." I was excited about the true meaning of the Hebrew word usually translated as soul in the Bible. Since the only college philosophy course was an introductory class, all I knew about Plato was his Allegory of the Cave, where he described two different worlds: that of appearances (this world), and that of spiritual absolutes. I was sure it did not fit well with the Bible's view of the Incarnation: God coming to us in human flesh, in Jesus Christ. So I was eager to learn more about "What is a soul?"

What is a soul, anyway? The word *soul* is not exactly in the Bible. Also original Greek understandings of the word are burdened by dualism, thanks to Plato and some other Greek philosophers who followed him. But because of the term's long history and many facets, *soul* is still the best word to encompass the mystery of who we are as individual human beings, particularly in relationship to God.

So here is my working description of a soul, which we can compare with the insights of significant thinkers along the way. Our soul is our true self, the essence of who we are, seeking to grow more and more into the image of God.

# The Soul and the Bible

When I say that the word *soul* is "not exactly" in the Bible, I mean that there is no actual term for *soul* in the Hebrew Scriptures (what Christians call the Old Testament).

Jews in early Bible times knew that if you were not breathing you were no longer alive. If there is no breath, there is no life. So the word they used for life was *nefesh*, which literally means "throat." When their Scriptures were written, English translators often wrote the word "soul" for *nefesh*, depending upon the context. For example, Deuteronomy 6:5 says, "You shall love the LORD your God with all your heart, and with all your *soul*, and with all your might." This is the beginning of the *Shema*, the most important commandment in Jewish Law. It is also part of what Jesus called the greatest commandment.[1] We are to love God with all our being. The Hebrew word for *soul* here is *nefesh*. In this text it could also be translated as "one's being" or as "one's life."

Further, early Judaism makes no direct references to life beyond death.[2] It does not embrace the Greek idea of a person's soul that lives beyond this life. Even today, faithful Jews do not necessarily believe in individual life after death. The full Hebrew understanding of oneself is as body, mind and soul together as a person living in this lifetime.

Other Old Testament examples of *nefesh*—soul—reinforce this sense of the whole person.

- "You shall put these words of Mine in your heart and *soul*, and you shall bind them as a sign on your hand, and fix them as an emblem on your forehead. Teach them to your children, talking about them when you are at home and when you are away, when you lie down and when you rise." (Deuteronomy 11:18–19)[3]
- "Bless the LORD, O my *soul*. O LORD my God, You are very great! You are clothed with honor and majesty" (Psalm 104:1)

- "My *soul* waits for the Lord more than those who watch for the morning, more than those who watch for the morning." (Psalm 130:6)
- "Let me hear of Your steadfast love in the morning, for in You I put my trust. Teach me the way I should go, for to You I lift up my *soul*." (Psalm 143:8)

When we come to the New Testament, the writers use *psyche*, the Greek term for *soul*, borrowing it from the Greek culture immediately surrounding them at that time. These writers include the apostle Paul, author of most of the New Testament letters and in whose name several other New Testament letters were written. While Paul refers to higher and lower natures, a concept familiar to his Greek audience, he speaks of the *psyche* without embracing Plato's ideas of eternal Forms or of immortality of the soul.

Paul contrasts the higher and lower ways of living as living according to the "flesh" (*sarks*) versus living led by the "Spirit" (*pneuma*; cf. Romans 7:5, 8:12; Galatians 5:16, 19ff). In Romans 7:5 he links the way people live with where they focus their minds. While the older Greek term for "flesh" referred to one's actual body, by Paul's time its major meaning is creatureliness in contrast to God, and earthly character versus godliness. Paul uses the term to summarize the whole of a human being's physical existence and "the earthly sphere," which is limited and provisional, in contrast to "the heavenly sphere."[4]

The word *psyche* is a multi-layered word in the New Testament. It always links to the life of an individual, in contrast to life in a generic sense. In the four New Testament Gospels (Matthew, Mark, Luke and John) and also in the Book of Acts, *psyche* often connotes one's natural physical life, as in Mark 10:45, where a person may "risk" or "give" (the same term in Greek) one's *psyche* as a "ransom for many." In several instances in the Book of John, the use of *psyche* points to "the individual life which is possible after death."[5] Likewise in Acts and the Gospels, physical life and the life of faith cannot be separated, since the call to faith is a call to the true life which God originally intended.[6]

Jesus' well-known statement about saving and losing one's life (as in Mark 8:35) appears in four different forms in the Gospels. In each one of these instances, the word *psyche* refers to True Life in contrast to a purely physical existence. In Mary's song of the Magnificat (Luke 1:46), *psyche* is linked with *pneuma* (Greek for "Spirit" or "wind," similar to *ruach,* its Hebrew counterpart). Throughout the New Testament where the two terms are linked together, the work of a person's psyche is "ultimately the gift and work of God."[7]

Christians started using this linked concept of the soul from their beginning, as the early Christian house churches spread across the Roman Empire. While some Christians have been Platonic (as discussed in the following paragraphs), many have not. Church leaders and writers have used the term *soul* ever since, but without specifying a common definition.

# Plato

This divergence from Plato (born in 428 BC) is important, because the full Platonic concept of a soul has some major drawbacks for people these many centuries later.

One obstacle is the idea of eternal "Forms." In Plato's famous Allegory of the Cave, he says that everything in this life is merely a reflection of the Real, the ideal Form. Life is as if we are all chained inside a cave, facing the cave's inner wall. The cave wall only barely reflects the real, eternal life outside the cave, which basks in the direct sunlight of eternity.[8]

Through this allegory, Plato says that all of the physical objects in our mortal lives are merely a reflection of what they truly are in their ideal Form, in eternity. For example, a chair, a book, or any other object is part of the world of appearances, whereas their true being lies beneath, behind or above the objects we so imperfectly see in this life.[9] For Plato, these eternal Forms are both the soul's origin and its destination."[10] The soul *sees* Forms *before* it becomes embodied, before time, and before its fateful "Fall."[11] So "everything thus depends on the existence of the Forms and the soul's ability to see them."[12]

Plato's theory points to a central concept of Platonism called "intelligibility." It is the idea of profound kinship between the soul and eternal Forms, giving the soul its nature and possibilities. This connection empowers the soul to "recollect," recalling knowledge that it knew before time began, in eternity. Because of such a deep relationship with the Forms, the soul is able to look at itself and its relationship to the divine. Plato describes this self-regard as self-examination, discerning whether the soul is well-ordered within itself.[13]

In the *Phaedo*, Plato argues directly for the immortality of the soul, which holds that the soul is "akin to what is pure and everlasting, immortal and always the same."[14] Because of this special kinship, the soul is able to "see" eternal things. So when a person dies, Plato asserts, the soul separates itself from the body and from this perishable world that has imprisoned it. This understanding is the origin of the idea of "immortality of the soul," in contrast to the "resurrection of the body" in the Christian Bible.[15]

Many contemporary Christians have blurred this distinction between "immortality of the soul" and "resurrection of the body," but the two phrases lead to a crucial contrast. Immortality of the soul implies that a person is divided into parts, where some parts are more valuable than others. It also infers that the body is inferior: a mere husk that envelops the "spiritual" kernel of the soul. In addition, immortality of the soul assigns a lower worth to our physical existence and to the earth on which we live, since it imagines they will all pass away as being insubstantial in the end.

By contrast, "resurrection of the body" treats the human being as a whole person, fully valued and redeemed by God. It does not imply any hierarchy within creation. God as described in the Bible is involved, passionate, and participating in this world which God has created.[16] God abides in and among us and invites us to abide in God (John 15:4–8). The Greek word for "abide" means to remain, stay, dwell, rest, or endure. Even more, a distinctive characteristic of the biblical God is that God travels with us, literally in Hebrew "pitching his tent" alongside us wherever we go (John 1:14; Matthew 28:5–10, 19–20).[17]

The problem with Plato's dualistic view of appearances versus Forms is that it presents this life and this world as superficial and inauthentic in contrast to eternal life. At its core, it denies the Incarnation, since God loved the world so much—*this* world, *this* life—that God became incarnate (literally, "en-fleshed") among us. (See John 3:16.)[18] The Bible also says that human beings are created in God's image (Genesis 1:26–28) and are God's temple (1 Corinthians 3:16–17). We are meant to abide or remain in God and let God abide or remain in us (John 15:1–11; 17:1–11). It also affirms that the earth and all of its creatures belong to God, their Creator (Psalms 24:1–2; 104).

Plato's dualism also implies that we are divided selves where each person's soul exists before this particular life and is the only part of us that remains alive after our death. Ironically it is the part that is least expressive of our individual personalities or personal faith.

But despite these obstacles, Plato still contributes greatly to the concept of the soul. He affirms that each human being has an essential self that is deeply related to the divine. Because of this profound kinship, the soul is able to perceive life from an eternal perspective. This also means the soul is capable of looking at its own relationship to life and to the world.

## Aristotle and Plotinus

Aristotle (born in 384 BCE), describes the soul as the essence of a living thing; its nature or principle of life and growth:[19] "The soul is the entire vital principle of any organism," he says, "the sum of its powers and processes."[20] He criticizes Plato's theory of unchanging Forms, preferring instead to categorize living things of this world, where they change and grow according to their own nature.[21] For Aristotle, all movement is a process of change from potential to actual. For example, a child who grows into an adult human being becomes, by stages, the full human being that he or she truly is.

Also in contrast to Plato, Aristotle sees the soul as linked to the body by giving the body form, shape and purpose, and believes the soul also dies with the body.[22] At the same time, Aristotle says the human soul includes the intellect, which seeks to know nothing less than identity with God.[23] He asserts that rationality is what makes human beings distinct from all other creatures and involves desiring and making life choices.[24] We are meant to develop and use this ability to move toward "virtue," meaning excellence of living as a human being.[25]

As we reflect on Aristotle today, we can gain some important linkages. He sees the source of the soul in our human nature, in our being. At the same time, he believes the soul finds its identity in God. He also emphasizes that the soul inherently contains potential for growth and movement, as it develops from who we are now to the people we may become. Further, he says that the soul's movement aims toward a better quality of being.

PLOTINUS (born in 204 AD) has been called the founder of Neoplatonism, since he believes that the truth of being exists beneath the physical appearances we see all around us. It is a deep inner unity underneath the "many-ness" of the entire world we see in this life.[26] A person can access this inner unity only by finding the deep unity within his or her own soul.[27] Plotinus is the first philosopher to interpret Plato's "intelligible place" as an inner world located within one's soul.[28]

He mixes some intriguing quasi-scientific concepts with his philosophy in at least two ways. First, he pictures the soul as:

> a sphere revolving around the source of all light at the center of the universe and turning inward to see it. Our particular souls are each points of light on the revolving sphere, capable of looking outward upon the darkness or turning into the inside to behold the realm of light.[29]

Second, he ascribes to a hierarchy of being by believing that there are four levels of life. The top level, or "first principle," is the One, or the Good, which stands above all the intelligible world. The second level is the divine Mind. The third level is the soul, which is non-spatial, incorporeal, and immovable. It is both immortal and divine. And the fourth level is the material cosmos, including space and time, birth and death, bodies and motion.[30]

Today we could certainly argue with this "nesting doll" picture of the realm of light, and with the concept of the soul's immortality. But we might still appreciate how Plotinus connects the soul with light, a prominent metaphor for God in the Christian faith. He also notes that the soul can choose at any moment to focus either on the deep unity of life, or on its own state of being and relationship to the universal divine.

HAVING LOOKED at these early philosophers, we might find it easier to choose a different term than "soul," without the Greek-culture baggage of divided self, eternal Forms, and so on. But a substitute word would lose meaning and richness for many people today. When we say the word *soul*, it expresses the core of who people are, what contributes to their sense of wholeness, and what is meaningful and lasting about them as persons. It implies something of value in who we are, beneath all momentary roles and relationships. It also implies inherent movement from potential to actual, as we strive to become more and more the persons we were meant to be. At the same time, *soul* expresses our origin and deep kinship with the divine, and our ability to know and (in our creaturely way) reflect God.

As we explore the different interpretations of the soul by Plato, Aristotle, and Plotinus, we find that they differ from one another on some significant aspects of the soul. But at the same time, they reinforce the sense of the soul as one's true self, the essence of who we are, seeking to grow more and more into the image of God.

# Augustine

Some major Christian thinkers can offer further insights for our concept of the soul. Augustine of Hippo (born in 354 AD), is a Christian Platonist who has had an immense influence on subsequent generations. He states that the soul does not change in space but is changeable in time—therefore it is mortal.[31] The mutability of the soul—in this case, its frequent choice to focus on itself instead of on God—becomes the basis for his primary distinction between God and the human soul.

In contrast to the early Platonists, Augustine says that God is not only within the soul but also beyond it, as well.[32] This viewpoint fits with the core Christian belief that God is both "immanent" and "transcendent," meaning present both within us and also supremely beyond us. Augustine makes a clear distinction between God as the Creator and the soul as creature, asserting that there is a sharp "difference between the mind's eye and the divine light it sees."[33]

God guides one's soul to make what Augustine calls an "inward turn" so the soul can look at itself and assess its own cognitive powers. This inner process moves through four stages of intellectual inquiry. First, the soul examines how its mind receives the input of the senses, and second, how it correlates and unifies data from those senses. In the third stage, it reflects on how it discerns the truth. Then in the final stage, the soul examines how accurate its vision is, perceiving God as "That Which Is" (Note similarities with the personal name of God in Exodus 3:14).[34]

One of the greatest contributions Augustine makes in his understanding of the soul is his concept of "first in, then up." Having established that the soul is not divine but stands beneath God, Augustine says one's soul must not only turn inward but also look upward to see God, who reigns above us. In that interval between turning in and looking up, Augustine conceives of a new place:

an inner space proper to the soul, different from the intelligible world in the Mind of God. The soul becomes, as it were, its own dimension—a whole realm of being waiting to be entered and explored.[35]

From Augustine's writings, contemporary readers can gain at least three important thoughts about the soul. First, he confirms our affirmation that the soul is mortal and is not God. Second, the soul is able to move through an inner reflective process by stages, from initial assessment of our senses all the way to contemplation of the Holy One, the Living God. Third, Augustine's idea of "first in, then up" asserts the soul's free choice to focus on God or on itself, and declares the reality of an inner space, a realm of being, which is the soul or which the soul inhabits.

# Other Christian Thinkers

Several centuries later, the words of Thomas Aquinas (born in 1225) came to express the height of Scholasticism, the movement of medieval thought which sought to synthesize philosophy and theology in the service of the church.[36] Beginning in European medieval universities about 1100 AD, Scholasticism focused on articulating and defending the church's beliefs in an increasingly pluralistic context. It recovered Greek philosophy, particularly that of Aristotle,[37] in its method of debate and dialectical reasoning of thesis, antithesis, synthesis.

Aquinas says the soul includes but is not limited to the intellect. In this aspect, his teaching comes closer to the Christian Neoplatonism of Augustine than to that of Aristotle.[38] He states that while the soul is immortal and communicates with the body, it is not a complete substance without the body.[39] Both the soul and the body are supernatural gifts. Yet while the soul can exist without the body, it needs God to reunite them both and to infuse it with knowledge.

For Aquinas, humanity's purpose is to enjoy the vision of God.[40] Our reason alone is not enough for us to know God; both knowledge and faith are necessary. For us to grow in our knowledge of God,

God communicates with us through revelation, while we seek God through our reason.[41]

BONAVENTURE, born Giovanni di Fidanza in 1221, was a Franciscan theologian who took his scholasticism in a different direction from that of Thomas Aquinas. Named a Doctor of the Church at the same time as Aquinas, Bonaventure steered the then-flagging Franciscan Order on a moderate, intellectual course. He also made significant contributions to a union of the Greek and Latin churches.[42] But he is best known as one who sought to completely integrate faith and reason.

According to Bonaventure, one's spiritual quest begins with faith and develops through rational understanding: an accepted Scholastic approach to faith. But he goes on to say that this journey also influences one's affections and ultimately leads to a mystical experience of God.[43] Strongly influenced by Augustine, Bonaventure was a Neoplatonist. He affirmed ideal Forms as pre-existing in the divine Mind and envisions God as both Perfect Being and Perfect Goodness.

In *The Soul's Journey into God*, Bonaventure asserts that:

> there are two ways we know God: the book of nature, and the book of Scriptures. Through these two paths and then by looking inward into ourselves at our image created by God, we encounter God's presence at the heart of our very being. . . .[44]

Reflecting on Acts 17:28 which says, "In [God] we live and move and have our being," Bonaventure says that the oneness of creation is a direct, immanent expression of God, who transcends all human perceptions of existence.[45] "In this passing over" of the soul, Bonaventure says, "if [the soul] is to be perfect, all intellectual activities must be left behind and the height of our affection must be totally transferred and transformed into God."[46] Amazingly, such statements about the soul by Bonaventure were not considered panentheistic (meaning the belief that God resides within all things) and therefore not considered heresy by the Church.

But times change quickly, and doctrinal standards were stricter by the time the medieval mystic Meister Eckhart (born in 1260) became widely known. Earlier, the words of Plotinus had spoken of the soul's "union with" God. Church officials somehow interpreted this language as retaining the distinctiveness between creature and Creator. But Meister Eckhart describes the soul's union with God during contemplation as like a homecoming where the depth of the soul is identical with the depth of God.[47] Eckhart explains it this way: "In discovering its own depths, [the soul] discovers the depths of God that were always within it."[48] The church doctrinal leaders of his time—the Inquisition—held a very strict line between God as Creator and human beings as God's creatures. They understood Meister Eckhart's statements as erasing that line by implying that the soul itself is both eternal and divine. So they accused him of heresy. Meister Eckhart appealed his case to Rome, but he died before the Pope could rule on his appeal.

IN THE EARLY 1800s, the Danish philosopher Soren Kierkegaard (born in 1813) dared to ponder further about the soul. He stated that a "self" is not the same as a "person." While body and brain constitute a person, the self is an entire set of relations between that person and the world.[49] For Kierkegaard, the self is the total of these relations. We might imagine it like a set of rubber bands that expand and contract in all directions, radiating like the old model of electrons around the nucleus of an atom. Each rubber band connects the person with another human being or creature in this world. The individual even has a relationship with him- or herself, which today we might call self-awareness. And the most important level of relationship—that most essential rubber band that also is always in flux—is the person's relationship with God.

Kierkegaard focuses intensely on the individual, who can choose either to live for one's self or to live for God. He says that the self includes the will, which puts together all of one's aspects into a coherent whole. This includes one's ability or inability to make choices. In order to approach God, one must possess introspective faith, for which there is no organizational program or philosophical system. Kierkegaard asserts that people need religion on a personal level, but not on a societal level. He says that "institutions like the church claim to provide answers to people's troubles but in reality are simply providing excuses to avoid self-examination."[51]

When we have the courage to engage in self-examination, he says, we come into confrontation with God. Then we glimpse the chasm between our human anxiety on the one side and God's remoteness on the other.[51] Our anxiety comes from the "dizzying awareness of our freedom to define ourselves by our choices."[52] God's remoteness arises out of God's judgment of sin, which ultimately empowers the work of God's grace in our lives.[53]

For Kierkegaard, truth is "an objective uncertainty…held fast in passionate inwardness." Faith is not a Platonic search for the infinite and universal, but rather a deep resignation to our mortality, seeking infinite happiness in Kierkegaard's conception of the finite human Jesus.[54] Faith is the process of "not only finding God, but also 'becoming a self before God,' which is to become an existing self in the highest sense."[55]

In Kierkegaard's *Either/Or*, he describes three stages in which a person may decide to meaningfully engage life.[56] As we'll explore further in Chapter Five, most people live at a surface stage, shifting restlessly from one activity to another. Then in the second stage, they may seek to become more fully their true selves underneath multiple tasks and roles. At the same time, they acknowledge their ultimate failure at being able to find their true selves on their own.

When people come to realize the impossibility of discovering who they really are by their own efforts, they may choose to take a "leap of faith," seeking a direct relationship with God. At this point a person has fully exhausted his or her reason in the effort of self-discovery, and so is able to encounter "the God with Whom we can finally find our true selves, [or souls, which are] utterly transcendent of history and culture."[57] This leap is into "the absurd" because a person's actions at this point cannot be rationally explained or justified in any way.[58]

Reviewing this section, we can glean from the diverse insights of Thomas Aquinas, Meister Eckhart, and Soren Kierkegaard, several deeper dimensions of the soul. Despite Thomas Aquinas' belief that the soul is immortal, he stresses its need for the body, and our reliance upon God's gifts of both body and soul. He reminds us that we need both knowledge and faith to begin to know God. Bonaventure and Meister Eckhart emphasize the kinship between God and the soul, expressing in another way that we are made in the image of God (Genesis 1:26–28).

From Soren Kierkegaard we receive a major caution against presuming upon our relationship with God, or upon our ability to draw closer to God by our own reasoning or efforts. He challenges us with a definition of "self," or soul, that is a living web of relationships. He also emphasizes the abyss between our sinfulness ("missing the mark")[59] and God's transcendent holiness. He sees faith as a process, and our growth in the ethical stage as becoming more fully the true selves God intends us to be.

# The True Self

Two insights from psychology, one ancient and one modern, offer important nuances to our concept of the soul. The ancient insight comes from Augustine, who affirms God in three Persons: Creator, Christ and Holy Spirit. They are distinct from one another as different faces of the one God. When we look within ourselves, he says, we can see this same kind of interactive connection. He perceives our human "reflection of the Trinity in the inner self as created in God's image: the memory, understanding, and will."[60]

Our memory contains not only pure principles of mathematics and "affectations of the mind" such as joy, sorrow, desire and fear, says Augustine, but also memory itself, which is the collection of remembrances stored up within us. God chooses to dwell in our memory but also lives beyond it, since God is beyond us all.[61] Understanding is an inner word we speak from the heart when our knowledge joins the vision which God reveals to us.[62] Our will is what prompts us to choose to hold something in our memory or to let it go, and to look either toward or away from something we might understand. All three aspects are necessary—memory, understanding, and will—in order to fully express any one of these dimensions.

In Augustine's book *On Free Choice of Will*, he states that human beings do not merely play out parts given to us by past history, or by the laws of nature. To some extent, we are free to write our own scripts. "In that way we can truly be said to be in the image of God, Who created all things distinct from himself by a free and unconditioned act of will."[63] So by looking at the essence of our own souls, we can gain an understanding, albeit obscure, of the triune God.[64]

AN IMPORTANT modern insight comes to us from Carl Jung (born in 1875), Swiss psychiatrist and psychotherapist. He proposed and developed psychological types we use today, such as extrovert and introvert, created the concept of archetypes, and emphasized the importance of interpreting dreams. But his most striking contribution is his exploration of "the collective unconscious: the part of our unconscious that contains memories and ideas inherited from our ancestors."[65]

For Jung, "the Self [is] that center of the whole psyche, conscious and unconscious, that rules over the psyche and quietly (often secretly) regulates the whole system."[66] He sees the Self as the God-image within us, the part of our psyche which knows about God.[67]

So what is the collective unconscious? Jung says it is like an unceasing stream or an ocean of images that drift in and out of our dreams.[68] It contains instincts and patterns of life and behavior that lie hidden beneath our consciousness, reason and will. At the same time, these unseen instincts influence our waking life; they have an even greater effect on our major decisions than does our reason. This collective unconscious manifests itself "mainly in the form of contrary feelings, fantasies, emotions, impulses and dreams."[69]

The collective unconscious is essentially made up of "archetypes," Jung says.[70] These archetypes are definite forms in the psyche which are always present everywhere. When a person brings any of them up into his or her consciousness by means of dream analysis, active imagination, or free association, it is assimilated into the whole personality.[71] This process of assimilation is what Jung calls "individuation." When it occurs, we can recognize our *persona* (social mask) and delve beneath it to discover our purpose and to fulfill our potential.

Jung sees the human psyche as religious by nature. He says our unconscious is our "only accessible source of religious experience."[72] For most people, he states, the psyche is still an unexplored country of which we have only indirect knowledge.[73] Although our conscious self-knowledge is very limited, our ego takes it for granted that we know ourselves, and "mass-mindedness"[74] keeps us from digging deeper. For Jung, religion is one's dependence on and submission to the irrational facts of spiritual experience. As such, he says religion is a counter-balance to mass-mindedness, since it is there that an individual can develop his or her own "spiritual and moral autonomy."[75] Jung says that by exploring our own souls, we discover instincts and imagery that can be powerful potentialities in the persons we become.[76]

So the psychological viewpoints of Augustine and Jung can offer some intriguing dimensions to our concept of the soul. According to Augustine, as our memory, understanding and will remain distinct but act as one, we can glimpse in our inner selves a finite reflection of the interaction in God's own triune being. Even as God's creatures, our souls possess freedom of choice which reflects our Sovereign Creator.

Likewise, Carl Jung reminds us that our souls are not limited to what lies on the surface of our consciousness. We also tap into a collective unconscious, which can be a vehicle of individuation, moving us toward personal integration and natural awareness of God.

Writers today are more likely to describe the soul as a person's "true self."[77] Tragically, often we settle for a false self: masks we adopt early in life in order to avoid feeling vulnerable, which become an ongoing part of our public persona and are mistaken for our true self.

Our true self, on the other hand, is "as unique as a snowflake," says David Benner:

It is an originality that has existed since God first loved us into existence. Our true self-in-Christ is the only self that will support authenticity.... [It is] who, in reality, you are and who you are becoming.[78]

This true self is not a foreign entity which descends upon us. Rather, it is the combination of our gifts, temperament, passions and vocation, as we seek to live in truthful dependence upon God.[79] Like the combination of *psyche* and *pneuma* ("soul/life" and "Spirit/breath"), even as we seek to grow spiritually, we realize more and more that the true self we are becoming in God is less of an achievement, and more a gift from God. God has given us the gift of being capable of realizing our true selves, but it is up to us to choose to embark upon this process of realization, and to continue the conscious journey.

Paradoxically, we do not find our true self by seeking it, but rather by seeking God. The great twentieth-century mystic Thomas Merton (born in 1915) notes that "if we find our true self, we find God, and if we find God, we find our most authentic self."[80] The self is not God, but the honest, solid ground where God and self can meet. This finding and meeting involves a lifetime journey, and this journey brings us to realize three basic things about ourselves in relation to God: first, that we are deeply loved; second, that we are deeply sinful; and third, that we are in the process of being redeemed and restored[81]—a process in which we can choose to fully participate.

Across mystical traditions, says psychologist John Robinson,[82] there is an understanding that the true self is really an experience of the divine, and that even this spiritual self eventually has to give way in order to reveal the living mystery. So the true self is that unique experience of God we are able to be, after the false self has died. It is born out of our capacity to directly experience union with the divine.[83]

Fr. Richard Rohr, contemporary theologian, puts it this way:

I believe that God gives us our soul, our deepest identity, our True Self, our unique blueprint, at our own "immaculate conception." Our unique little bit of heaven is installed by the Manufacturer within the product, at the beginning! We are given a span of years to discover it, to choose it, and to live our own destiny to the full."[84]

Rohr says this blueprint is who we objectively are from the beginning, in the mind and heart of God. It is our substantial self and absolute identity.[85] When we surrender the trappings of our false self, we suffer the stripping away of much that we thought we needed to be. This painful process of uncovering turns out to be the very journey which allows us to find "the pearl of great price" (Matthew 13:45–46) hidden inside us. This is the inner abiding place of the Spirit, the place where we long for God. "The end is already planted in us at the beginning," says Rohr, "and it gnaws away at us until we get there freely and consciously."[86]

# Image of God

At the beginning of this chapter, we established a working definition of the word *soul*. We said, "a person's soul is our true self, the essence of who we are, seeking to grow more and more into the image of God." In this chapter so far, we have traced the soul through basic concepts in the Bible's Old and New Testaments and touched on philosophers Plato, Aristotle and Plotinus; Christian Neo-Platonist Augustine; and other Christian thinkers Aquinas, Eckhart, and Kierkegaard. We also explored aspects of the soul as our true self, including ideas from Jung, Merton, Robinson, and Rohr.

So how do these various understandings of the human soul relate to the Bible's claim that we are made in the image of God?

The core Bible passage for this phrase is Genesis 1:26, where God says:

Let us make humankind in our image, according to our likeness; and let them have dominion over the fish of the sea, and over the birds of the air, and over the cattle, and over all the wild animals of the earth, and over every creeping thing that creeps upon the earth.

The phrases for "image of God" in the Old and New Testaments have close meanings, since they rely on our connection with God, and our being given a divine task. In other words, what God calls us to do naturally rises out of who we are in God's sight. As one Bible scholar puts it, what finally stands behind all that the Old Testament says about human beings is the assertion that we are really alive only when we choose to fulfill what we truly are.[87]

Walter Brueggemann, Old Testament scholar, notes that Genesis 1:26 comes from the sixth century B.C. and addresses the able-bodied Jews who had been marched into exile in far-off Babylon after the destruction of their homeland. As such, this text refutes contrary claims of the Babylonians by asserting that Israel's God is not bound to the territory of the defeated. The people have not left their God behind, and the God of Israel is the Lord of all life everywhere.[88]

This passage makes a fundamental claim about God's sovereignty over all creatures, by proclaiming a new world empowered by God's Word. It says all creation is bound together in a relationship with God, "grounded in a mystery of faithful commitment" where "all of life is characterized by graciousness" as the recipient of God's grace.[89]

Methodist founder, John Wesley describes three dimensions of how God has created people in God's image. One aspect deals with our relationships and refers to God's call for us to care for the Earth and all its creatures. The second dimension (what Wesley calls the "moral image") includes the qualities and behaviors of "righteousness and true holiness" (Ephesians 4:24). The third dimension refers to our nature as spiritual beings.[90]

In Genesis 1:26, God says, "Let us make humankind according to our image and likeness." The Hebrew word for "humankind" is *adam*, which God creates out of *adamah* (feminine form, meaning "soil" or "earth").[91] So a more precise term for *adam* would be "earthling"—a potent reminder that people are organically connected to the Earth, and responsible for its care.

Taken in the larger context of Genesis 1:26–31, God refers to *adam* in both the plural and singular. This reflects how we are both human beings who stand together in solidarity before God, and also individuals who freely choose between living within or outside of the faith community to which God has called us.[92]

Old Testament scholars state that God made a divine resolution ("Let us make") only for the creation of human beings. Gerhard Von Rad says this shows that "God participates more intimately and intensively in this than in the earlier works of creation." He highlights the triple use of the rare verb, *bara* ("to create") in verse 27 alone.[93] This verb is different from humans "making" things and highlights the full creativity that only God can accomplish.

But for many readers, the surprise of this statement is God's use of the word "us." Since the hallmark of Jewish faith is that "God is one," clearly this does not refer to multiple gods. Walter Bowie suggests that the plural is used to declare majesty, a practice that is well-attested in the Hebrew Scriptures.[94] In this sense, it is similar to the royal "we" in the English language, referring to a monarch as an individual, and also as the embodiment of the realm.

Another interpretation of "us" imagines that Israel's God is surrounded by a council of heavenly beings over whom God rules. Old Testament scholar Gerhard Von Rad says this idea of a divine council is itself quite common in the Old Testament (as in 1 Kings 22:19f, Job chapter 1, and Isaiah chapter 6). Whether we call them cherubim, seraphim (which means "burning ones"), or the more popular term "angels," this idea of a divine council is not unique in Ancient Near Eastern religions. In the Bible, by having this angelic council, God is present and immediate, but also keeps us from seeing the mystery of God too directly.[95]

So what is God's "image," in which human beings are made? There is a stunning contrast here. On the one hand, God judges against any kind of idols, and solemnly declares that people make no graven images (Exodus 20:4–6). On the other hand, human beings are to be in "the image of God," disclosing our Creator in essential ways. We are to live in the "likeness" ("appearance, similarity, or analogy") of God, who governs by gracious giving of God's Self, caring for other creatures in order to bring their promise to fruition.[96]

Some Bible commentators emphasize different godly characteristics as being the crucial elements of living in God's image. For example, Adam Hamilton says we are in the image of God—reflecting God's character—when we love, reason, create, show compassion, give, sacrifice, and forgive.[97] But two Hebrew Bible scholars say we are in God's image as whole persons. Gerhard Von Rad states we reflect God in the way we are called into existence, in the totality of our being, and in our function of caring for the non-human world.[98] And Claus Westermann says the image of God we find in Genesis 1:26–31 "is concerned neither with the corporeal nor with the spiritual qualities of people; it is concerned only with the person as a whole."[99]

So if we are created in God's image, what is the problem? Clearly, we do not live in such purity, and often we are better at destroying rather than caring for the world and other creatures. David Benner says the crux of the issue is that we try to be like God *without* God.[100] But solely by our own efforts, the most we can ever do is make ourselves into competing gods, as we try to elevate ourselves to the level of our Sovereign Creator.

Yet there is Good News! When we admit our estrangement from God, our isolation or alienation, we can trust in God's mercy, asking to receive God's forgiveness and grace. The Bible speaks of this experience as letting go of the "old self" and allowing God to clothe us with a "new self, created in the likeness of God" (Ephesians 4:22–24).

But there is a purpose to being in the image of God: to "have dominion over" all the animals of the earth.

Despite generations of misuse and self-justification, the concept of "dominion" is the opposite of "domination." Instead of abusing and exploiting, God calls us to care for, feed, and tend all non-human beings on this planet. "The human creature attests to the Godness of God," says Brueggemann, "by exercising *freedom with* and *authority over* all the other creatures entrusted to its care."[101] This is basic stewardship—caring for others on God's behalf. It is the kind of rule that a shepherd gives, sometimes at great cost to himself or herself, to secure the flock against thieves, predators, or any other threat to their well-being.

This is not coercion / power-over, but empowerment / power-with. It is the way God exercises power: by inviting, evoking, and permitting. Modeled by Jesus Christ, we see that the one who rules is the one who serves (Matthew 23:11; Mark 10:42–45; Luke 22:26–27; John 13:12–15). Thus, we "rule" or "have dominion" by serving other creatures and creation itself.

This exploration of the image of God brings us back to our original definition of the soul as "our true self, the essence of who we are, seeking to grow more and more into the image of God." From the Old Testament we can affirm the intimate link between a person's soul and his or her "true self," including body, mind, and intention. The New Testament addresses the deep connection between our soul and our whole lives as creatures under God. It connotes our interwoven physical life and life of faith, linking our every breath with the Spirit, or Breath, of God.

ALTHOUGH MOST CHRISTIANS today do not adhere to Plato's belief in the immortality of the soul and dualism (division of human beings into body versus spirit), Plato has had a tremendous influence on our understanding that the soul is our essential self, related deeply to the divine. From Plato we get the concept of "intelligibility," or focus on the vision of God; and also the soul's ability to look at its own relationship to life and to the cosmos.

Aristotle contributes our sense of movement, connecting more deeply to the soul, as we seek to identify more closely with God, often by means of our moral choices and "virtues," or habits. In this way, who we are flows naturally into the decisions we make, developing from potential into the actual. Such concepts fit closely with this book's definition of the soul as "seeking to grow more and more into the image of God."

Plotinus adds the sense of the soul's inner life. He relates the soul to the "light" of God, which he calls "the first principle." He also points out that the soul can choose at any moment to focus either on the unity of life or on itself. This idea of choice is a precursor to the Christian concepts of free will and sin.

The great Christian philosopher Augustine affirms that the soul is mortal and can learn and grow. He states that God can work within us yet be far beyond us—what Christians call "both immanent and transcendent." Augustine also contributes the idea of "first in, then up:" the concept that the soul can look within to its own realm of being, to assess the accuracy of its vision of God, and then look "up" to glimpse the Living God, who reigns over us all.

Thomas Aquinas highlights the importance of reason, but says reason alone is not enough for us to know God—our faith is also essential, even as God reaches out to us through revelation. The mystic Meister Eckhart emphasizes the depth of union between the soul and God that is possible at any given time. Soren Kierkegaard expands our sense of the soul as the true self: a living web of relationships between the person and God, and between ourselves and every other creature. He stresses the impossibility of our approaching God on our own terms, which presses us to acknowledge the fact of death and the work of God's grace in our lives. He also emphasizes the aspect of becoming or growing, when he discusses three stages of life that are possible for us. If we choose to grow, we can move from restless activity and boredom, to intentional choices, to a "leap of faith."

Key psychological ideas by Augustine and Jung strengthen the concept of the soul as one's true self. Augustine states we reflect the Trinity, since who we are includes the three dimensions of memory, understanding, and will. Carl Jung helps us recognize our "collective unconscious," so that by exploring our own soul, we can discover powerful keys to the persons we can become. Jung employs the term *Self* to denote the center of who we are, the God-image within us, the part of our soul/self/*psyche* which knows God.

David Benner, Thomas Merton, John Robinson, and Richard Rohr reinforce these understandings of finding our true self in the experience of God, as part of a lifelong journey of discovery.

After exploring various meanings, I am personally convinced that the soul is one's true self, the essence of who we are, built around the core of our desire to be in loving relationship with God. Both authentic and unique to each one of us, the soul combines our gifts, temperament, and calling, as we live intentionally dependent upon God.

Further, the soul is not a division of oneself, as if separated from a person's mind or body, but rather the full expression of who we are or can be as whole persons, growing as we live and mature. The soul is capable of developing the qualities or characteristics of godly living. This is what the Bible calls being "in the image of God," our every breath connected to the Holy Spirit, the Breath of God.

# Questions for Reflection

1. Do my experiences and understanding fit in any way with the Bible's use of *soul* as a person's life or breath, and as the whole person linked with the Holy Spirit?
2. As I consider the viewpoints of Plato, Augustine, and the other philosophers named here, what aspects of the soul ring truest for me?
3. What do I believe about resurrection of the body versus immortality of the soul? Does that distinction make any difference to me?
4. Do any of Augustine's or Jung's psychological understandings resonate with my personal experience?

# Endnotes

1. Jesus linked this verse with Leviticus 19:18, "You shall love your neighbor as yourself." See Matthew 22:34–40 and parallels in Mark 12:28–34 and Luke 10:25–28. All three of these Gospels add the phrase "and with all your mind." This reinforces the idea that the Old Testament word for "soul" means an undivided, whole person.

2. The *Theological Dictionary of the New Testament, Volume IX* (p. 630) says, "The use of spirit for the dead lies outside the Old Testament field, cf. Luke 24:39. Even in death man remains a *nefesh*, i.e., either flesh which is given life by the *Ruach* or lifeless breath." (Note: *Nefesh* and *Ruach* are transliterated here from Hebrew and Greek.) The word *Ruach* means "Spirit, wind, or breath" (see footnote 4).

3. Here the Hebrew words are plural: "hearts" and "souls."

4. Cf. Gerhard Friedrich, ed., *Theological Dictionary of the New Testament, Vol. VII*, pp. 117f., 125f. The Greek word for "Spirit" means "wind" or "breath," and therefore also "soul" and "spirit" (*ibid., Vol. VI*, pp. 335f.). The Spirit is "the power of God which brings a [person] to faith in the cross and resurrection of Jesus" (*ibid.*, p. 432). In Galatians 3:2 and 5, Spirit is "the power which shapes the whole existence of the believer as one who lives by the event of salvation" (*ibid.*, p. 428).

5. ———. *Theological Dictionary of the New Testament, Vol. IX*, p. 638.

6. *Ibid.*, p. 639. When *psyche* is used in the story of the rich fool, for example (Luke 12:20), "the mere movement of the heart or drawing of breath is not enough," says Friedrich (p. 638). "Life has content here as the full life which God intended at creation." It can only properly be called life if it is "lived in God's service and praise."

7. *Ibid.*, p. 641.

8. Phillip Cary, "Plato. Metaphysics," *Great Minds of the Western Intellectual Tradition, 3rd Edition, Course Guidebook* (Chantilly, VA: The Teaching Company, 2000), p. 23.

9. *Ibid.*, p. 20.

10. Phillip Cary, *Augustine's Invention of the Inner Self: The Legacy of a Christian Platonist* (New York: Oxford University Press, 2000), p. 17.

11. Since this melding of Greek concepts with Christian terminology, many Christians have referred to Adam and Eve's expulsion from the Garden of Eden in Gen. 3 as "the Fall." However, there is no reference to a Fall in the Bible.

12. Phillip Cary, *op cit.*

13. *Ibid.*, p. 18.

14. *Ibid.*, p. 12.

15. In contrast to Tertullian and other Christians who railed against all classical philosophers, Justin Martyr (born 100 AD) was a Christian philosopher who risked showing positive connections between Christianity and non-Christian philosophers. Nevertheless, Justin also pointed out that "Christian hope is not

based on the immortality of the soul, but rather on the resurrection of the body." (Justo L. Gonzalez, *The Story of Christianity, Volume 1: The Early Church to the Dawn of the Reformation* (San Francisco: HarperSanFrancisco, 1984), p. 55.) See also Phillip Cary in Lecture 32 of *Philosophy and Religion in the West, Course Guidebook* (Chantilly, VA: The Teaching Company, 1999), p. 161.

16. Theologian Douglas Meeks says "the philosophical ontologies of the West" believe in a distant, unchanging god based on Greek metaphysics. He contrasts this distant concept with the God of Israel, who redeems by dwelling with those who are most vulnerable in this life (i.e., the poor and the homeless). Cf. *The Economy of Grace and the Market Logic*, pp. 10–11; at *councilofchurches.ca/ documents . . . economy/DouglasMeeks.pdf*.

17. Old Testament scholar Albrecht Alt says that this is the most distinctive characteristic of Israel's God. The gods of all other Ancient Near Eastern peoples were tied to their local shrines within the geography where they lived. So when people were captured and taken somewhere else, for example, their god was left behind. This was the Jews' key learning during the Exile: that God traveled with them and is sovereign over all people, no matter where they live. Cf. Albrecht Alt, *Der Gott der Väter: Ein Beitrag zur Vorgeschichte der israelitischen Religion*, Stuttgart: Kohlhammer, 1929, (Beiträge zur Wissenschaft vom Alten und Neuen Testament; 48 = Folge 3, H. 12). Translation of the title: "The God of the Fathers: a Contribution to the Prehistory of Israelite Religion."

18. Justo L. Gonzalez names Platonism as a danger to a Christian view of the Incarnation, the importance of this earth and of temporal realities, and seeing Jesus as a historical figure. (Cf. *ibid*, p. 319) On platonic dualism's denial of the Incarnation, see William Barclay, *The Letter to the Romans*, The Daily Study Bible (Philadelphia: Westminster Press, 1958), p. 168.

19. Jeremy Adams, "Aristotle. Metaphysics," *Great Minds of the Western Intellectual Tradition, 3rd Edition, Course Guidebook* (Chantilly, VA: The Teaching Company, 2000), p. 35.

20. Will Durant, *The Story of Philosophy* (NY: Simon & Schuster, 1961), p. 58.

21. Jeremy Adams, *ibid.*, p. 33.

22. ———, "Aristotle. Metaphysics," *Great Minds of the Western intellectual Tradition, 3rd Edition*, CD.

23. Aristotle, *On the Soul* 3:8, 431b20–432a2, cited by Phillip Cary, *ibid.*, p. 20.

24. Father Joseph Koterski, S.J., "What Is the Purpose of Life?" *The Ethics of Aristotle*, CD (Chantilly, VA: The Teaching Company, 2001).

25. ———, "The Philosopher of Common Sense," *The Ethics of Aristotle, Course Guidebook*, p. 5.

26. Phillip Cary, "Plotinus and Neo-Platonism," *Great Minds of the Western Intellectual Tradition, 3rd Edition, Course Guidebook* (Chantilly, VA: The Teaching Company, 2001), p. 87.

27. *Ibid.*

28. *Ibid.*, p. 11.
29. *Ibid.*, p. 5.
30. Plotinus agrees with Aristotle in this view of the soul (*ibid.*, pp. 25, 27, 188). Like Plato, Plotinus imagines the soul as divided, but he is unique in how he understands the divisions. He sees the lower part of the soul as that which is particular to the individual and as governing the body it inhabits (*ibid.*, p. 27). The higher part of the human soul is always contemplating and is "by nature immutable and therefore unfallen" (*ibid.*, p. 157).
31. Phillip Cary, *Augustine's Invention of the Inner Self*, p. 116.
32. *Ibid.*, pp. 38–39.
33. *Ibid.*, p. 39.
34. *Ibid.*, p. 65. Plato refers to the soul's "intellectual vision," and equates the intellect with the soul. But subsequent philosophers do not necessarily limit the soul to the intellect.
    In Exodus 3:14, God gives God's personal name as YHWH. In a seminal paper, *Yahweh and the God of the Patriarchs*, biblical scholar and linguist Frank Cross says this name is a verb phrase using the verb "to be" or "to become." Hebrew has no tenses, and this verb is unfinished, ongoing action. So a closer translation of the personal name is "He who causes all that is alive or becoming." Since Jews do not pronounce this sacred name aloud out of respect, they put in vowels for a different word and interpret it as "I Am Who I Am."
35. *Ibid.*, p. 39.
36. Martin E. Marty, *A Short History of Christianity*, Second Edition (Philadelphia: Fortress Press, 1987), p. 137.
37. Wikipedia, "Soul."
38. Jeremy Adams, "Aquinas and Christian Aristotelianism," *Great Minds of the Western Intellectual Tradition, 3rd Edition, Course Guidebook*, p. 94.
39. *Summa Contra Gentiles* II, 68, cited by SparkNotes editors, Thomas Aquinas (c. 122–1274), "Summa Theologica: The Nature and Limits of Human Knowledge" SparkNotes LLC. 2005. *sparknotes.com/philosophy/aquinas*.
    "The soul knows bodies through the intellect by a knowledge that is immaterial, universal and necessary, although only God can understand all things. The cognitive soul has the potential to form principles of understanding and principles of sensation. Individual objects of our knowledge are not derived from Platonic forms but rather from the mind of God." (*ibid.* accessed March 2, 2014).
40. Martin E. Marty, *op cit.*, p. 179.
41. Roland Bainton, *The Medieval Church* (Philippines: Anvil Publishing, 1952), p. 60. Emphasizing the role of reason, Aquinas says that the existence of God is a revealed truth, but reason can prove what faith accepts. As a result, he offers "five ways" or arguments for God's existence. (Cf. Justo L. Gonzalez, *ibid.*, p. 318.) In the Scholastic process, "the mind is summoned to something higher

than our reason here and now can reach" (so Thomas Aquinas in Roland Bainton, *ibid.*, p. 144).

42. Wikipedia at *http://en.wikipedia.org/wiki/Bonaventure.*

43. Noone, Tim and Houser, R. E., "Saint Bonaventure," *The Stanford Encyclopedia of Philosophy* (Winter 2010 Edition), Edward N. Zalta (ed.), cited in Wikipedia, *http://en.wikipedia.org/wiki/Bonaventure.*

44. Amazon.com reviewer Greg on November 17, 2006, at *amazon.com/ Bonaventure-Journey-Francis-Classics-Spirituality/product-reviews.*

45. Tom Corbett, amazon.com reviewer, on August 5, 2012, at *ibid.*

46. Bonaventure, *The Soul's Journey into God*, p. 113, cited by Steven H. Propp, amazon.com reviewer, on May 31, 2012.

47. Phillip Cary, "Mysticism and Meister Eckhart," *Great Minds of the Western Intellectual Tradition, 3rd Edition, Course Guidebook*, pp. 101ff.

48. Phillip Cary, *Augustine's Invention of the Inner Self*, p. 104. Meister Eckhart's doctrine is essentially Neoplatonic, since its goal is contemplation of the Divine, the God who is beyond all human concepts. Eckhart says that "before the foundation of the world, the ideas of all things that would exist were in the mind of God...." (Justo L. Gonzalez, *ibid.*, pp. 356f).

49. Comments on *Sickness Unto Death*. SparkNotes Editors. "SparkNote on Søren Kierkegaard (1813–1855)." SparkNotes LLC. 2005. *sparknotes.com/philosophy/ kierkegaard* (accessed March 3, 2014).

50. Analysis on *Either/Or* from Wikipedia, "Either-Or."

51. Martin E. Marty, *op cit.*, p. 256.

52. Commentary on preliminary Expectoration Part 1 in *Fear and Trembling*. SparkNotes Editors. "SparkNote on Søren Kierkegaard (1813–1855)." SparkNotes LLC. 2005. *sparknotes.com/philosophy/kierkegaard* accessed March 3, 2014.

53. John Von Rohr, *Profile of Protestantism* (Encino, CA: Dickenson Publishing Company, 1969), p. 105.

54. Phillip Cary, "Kierkegaard and the Leap of Faith," in *Great Minds of the Western Intellectual Tradition, 3rd Edition, Course Guidebook*, p. 249.

55. *Ibid.*, p. 250. "For Kierkegaard, faith doesn't just save you from the wrath of God; it is the way you become a self. coming to be related to yourself in the right way by being related to God in the right way." (Phillip Cary, *Philosophy and Religion in the West, Parts 1–3, Course Guidebook*, p. 128).

56. Stephen A. Erickson, "Kierkegaard's Passion," *Philosophy as a Guide to Living*, CD (Chantilly, VA: The Teaching Company, 2006).

57. *Ibid.*

58. Terms from *Fear and Trembling*. SparkNotes Editors. "SparkNote on Søren Kierkegaard (1813–1855)." SparkNotes LLC. 2005. *sparknotes.com/philosophy/ kierkegaard* (accessed March 3, 2014).

In *Fear and Trembling*, Kierkegaard takes Abraham's willingness to obey God by sacrificing his son Isaac as a primary example of a leap of faith. Human sacrifice is the ultimate abomination in Old Testament Judaism. Thankfully, at the last moment God provides a ram, caught in a thicket next to the altar. When we view Abraham's actions on the ethical level, we are horrified that he almost murders his only beloved son. Yet Kierkegaard lifts up the paradox that Abraham is praised as the father of faith, presumably because of his trust in God.

59. This is the literal meaning of *hamartia*, the primary Greek word for "sin" used in the New Testament.
60. Augustine of Hippo, *On The Trinity*, cited by Jaroslav Pelikan in *The Growth of Medieval Theology, 600–1300* (Chicago/London: The University of Chicago Press, 1978), p. 281.
61. Roger E. Olson and Christopher Alan Hall, *The Trinity* (Grand Rapids, MI: Wm. B. Eerdmans Publishing Company, 2002), p. 135.
62. Eleonore Stump and Norman Kretzmann, ed., *The Cambridge Companion to Augustine* (Cambridge: Cambridge University Press, 2001), p. 157.
63. Thomas Williams, ed. *Augustine, On Free Choice of the Will* (Indianapolis: Hackette Publishing Company, 1993), p. xiii.
64. Eleonore Stump and Norman Kretzmann, ed., *op cit.*
65. Wikipedia, "Carl Jung."
66. Ann Belford Ulanov, *The Female Ancestors of Christ* (A C. G. Jung Foundation Book), p. 4.
67. *Ibid.*, p. 11.
68. C. G. Jung, *Modern Man in Search of a Soul* (NY: Houghton Mifflin Harcourt Publishing Company, 1933), p. 186.
69. ———, *The Undiscovered Self*, trans. R.F.C. Hall (New York: Penguin Group, New American Library, 1957, 1958) p. 83.
70. *Collected Works of C. G. Jung, Vol. 9*, p. 42, cited in Wikipedia, "Carl Jung" related to *The Archetypes and the Collective Unconscious* (1934).
71. Wikipedia, "Carl Jung."
72. C. G. Jung, *The Undiscovered Self* (Boston: Little, Brown, 1958), p. 89.
73. ———, *Modern Man in Search of a Soul*, p. 75.
74. ———, *The Undiscovered Self*, pp. 17ff. When Jung writes about mass-mindedness, it is clear that he is referring to the Nazi state as a primary example, although he does not use the name. He writes searingly about those who manipulate the sovereign State by choreographing group thinking.
75. *Ibid.*, p. 23.
76. ———, *The Undiscovered Self*, p. 107.
77. For example, Phillip Cary calls the soul "the true self" in his surveys of philosophy from the time of Plato onward. See his chapter on "Plato.

Psychology" in *Great Minds of the Western Intellectual Tradition, 3rd Edition, Course Guidebook*, p. 29.

78. David G. Benner, *op cit.,* p. 15. Benner is a psychologist and Emeritus Distinguished Professor of Psychology and Spirituality at Richmond Graduate University in Atlanta, Georgia.

79. *Ibid.,* p. 103.

80. Thomas Merton, *New Seeds of Contemplation*, p. 36, cited in David G. Benner, *ibid*, p. 15.

81. David G. Benner, *op cit.*, p. 72.

82. John C. Robinson, *op cit.*, p. 269.

83. *Ibid.,* p. 270. Robinson says that our true self carries the gifts we were given to bring into the world, by being our truest selves. He describes the soul as our experiences of the divine.

84. Richard Rohr OFM, *Falling Upward*, p. ix.

85. *Ibid.,* p. 86.

86. *Ibid.,* p. 91.

87. Edmond Jacob in *Theological Dictionary of the New Testament*, edited by Gerhard Friedrich, p. 631. The two phrases for "image of God" use the terms we have considered in this chapter: *nefesh* in Hebrew, and *psyche* in Greek.

88. Walter Brueggemann, *Genesis*, Interpretation series (Atlanta: John Knox Press, 1982), p. 25.

89. *Ibid.,* p. 27.

90. John Wesley's sermons, "The New Birth," and "The End of Christ's Coming," *Wesley's Works, Third Edition, Vol. 6* (Grand Rapids, MI: Baker Book House, 1978), pp. 66 and 269f. Wesley's sermons also refer to our being made in God's political image, having dominion over the earth; see Austen Hartke, "God's unclassified world," *Christian Century* April 25, 2018, p. 29.

91. See Genesis 2:7, the second creation story, where God forms *adam* out of the soil or mud (*adamah*) and then breathes life into him.

92. Walter Brueggemann, *op cit.*, p. 34.

93. Gerhard Von Rad, *Genesis: A Commentary* , Old Testament Library (Philadelphia: Westminster Press, 1972), p. 57. For example, multiple Bible scholars say using the words three times in "Holy, holy, holy" indicates the superlative: that God is the supreme epitome of holiness.

94. Walter Bowie, Exposition, in "The Book of Genesis," in *The Interpreter's Bible, Vol. 1*, edited by George Arthur Buttrick (Nashville/NY: Abingdon Press, 1952), p. 59.

95. *Ibid.,* p. 58. This act of concealing God's direct presence fits with events elsewhere in the Old Testament, where angels stand in for God, and people entertain God unawares. A major name for God is "Emmanuel," which means "God Is With Us." God is personal advocate for the least likely, the poor, and the

marginalized. Jesus continues and embodies this theme of the Living God who is present and yet often concealed in our midst.

96. *Ibid.*, p. 33. An early Christian hymn, in Philippians 2:5–11, summarizes this Christ's giving of himself and God's response by saying, "Let the same mind be in you that was in Christ Jesus."
97. Adam Hamilton, *Forgiveness: Finding Peace Through Letting Go* (Nashville: Abingdon Press, 2012), p. 130.
98. Von Rad, *op cit.*, p. 60.
99. Austen Hartke, *op cit.*
100. David G. Benner, *op cit.*, p. 79.
101. Walter Brueggemann, *op cit.*, p. 32.

# Growing as Becoming

A S WE SAW in the last chapter, Aristotle observed that an essential part of all living beings is how they change and grow according to their nature. We recognize this in our own human experience: throughout our lifetime we cannot stay the same in our thinking, feeling and spiritual life, any more than we can retain the physical body of a baby or a young adult. How we relate to our parents now is different from when we were young children. How we understand poetry, respond to love, or deal with hurts and triumphs likewise changes. As circumstances sometimes force upon us, or as we further define the quality and direction of our lives, we discover the need for new maturity, and for greater depth and awareness of the world within as well as outside ourselves.

But how do we define *growth*, since each one of us has different life experiences and responds to them as unique human beings? The dictionary defines "to grow" as to come into existence from a source; to come to be by a gradual process, as a natural development; and to develop and reach maturity.[1] Applying this definition, we can say that our source is in God, who chooses to claim us as God's own. Spiritual growth is not something we can achieve by ourselves, but is empowered and matched by a gift of God's grace, as we intentionally practice becoming more attentive to God. Maturity is a relative term connected to where each of us has been in the past, not to an absolute, uniform endpoint in this life.

When we approach growing as *becoming*, we do not view these inner changes solely as an abstract notion of progress, as a series of greater social roles, or as improving stages of performance. To "become" means to grow in our being, to come into existence or change, to develop as a distinctive entity, or to mature into something or someone.[2] So our inner life is more a matter of who we are becoming than of what we do, each of us maturing in a distinctive way. Since our soul is our true self, the essence of who we are, we are seeking to grow—to become—more and more into the image of God.

"The life of Christian discipleship is a lifetime of becoming, a commitment to grow and change, develop and learn," says author Dan Dick. "To grow as Christian disciples we dedicate our lives to becoming who God wants us to be."[3]

But how might we *measure* growth and becoming? People have looked at growth in several different ways, including as a dimension of human development, or according to physical stages in our lives.

## Growth as Development

Some organizations look at faith development connected to how we mature in other aspects of human growth, such as our brain and physical abilities. For example, one general agency of The United Methodist Church[4] created a "Development Through the Life Span" chart to show general trends in twelve aspects of human development, in order to help Sunday school teachers gear their classes appropriately to participants of different ages. In the chart, they consider development in these areas: faith, physical, brain, mental and intellectual development; interpersonal relationships; values and ethics; sexuality; family relationships; needs of their age; gifts to share; vocation; and their expectations of the church.

These general statements are not meant to force people into one-size-fits-all categories, but rather to help church leaders benefit from developmental research and not assume that everyone grows in his or her faith the same way. In terms of "faith development," they characterize general trends of each age range with the following phrases:

- "Infants/toddlers to age 3—Beginning to trust. Comes to know self [as] separate from parents. Can say, 'No!' Senses love of parents and of those in Christian community.
- "Young children ages 4 through 7—Imitates religious behavior of adults. Begins to ask religious questions. Expresses wonder, joy, thanksgiving, and praise. Begins to use faith language.
- "Older children 8 through 12—Begins to identify with 'my' church. Learns stories of the faith. Understands God in concrete terms. Engages in acts of service and discipleship.
- "Early teens 13 and 14—Moving toward a more abstract concept of God. Asks deeper questions about God, faith, and the church. May see God as distant.
- "Middle teens 15 through 17—May see God as a personal companion. Beginning to have an owned faith. Influenced by faith of significant others.
- "Late teens 18 and 19—May begin to question faith in the process of developing an owned faith. Looks for the relevance of faith.
- "Young adults 20 through 34—May leave church and/ or return. Many seeking spiritual experience. Some want answers, others want to ask questions and search.
- "Midlife adults 35 through 64—Wants to understand the meaning of life and how faith relates to this. Taking responsibility for spiritual growth.
- "Older adults 65 and up—Wants arena to grow in faith and to accept life story. Need purpose and to feel life is worth living. May want to share life faith story with others."[5]

Some approaches have focused on specific aspects of generosity when it comes to raising children to be generous. For example, a section of *The Abingdon Guide to Funding Ministry, Volume 2*[6] says one way is to tell stories showing how children are good stewards by getting involved in mission and outreach, visiting a sick or lonely friend, or praying and exercising regularly.[7] Another way is to help children connect with others their age around the world through videos, letters, pictures, sharing prayers, or sending gifts, cards and electronic messages in both directions.[8]

Activities abound to teach children generosity. Delia Halverson's book *Let the Children Give*[9] provides age-level learning goals for comprehensive stewardship. It describes stewardship as part of every-Sunday classroom learning, as well as special projects, activities, and celebrations. Hands-on experiences speak louder than words, and young people learn the most from adults whose attitudes and behaviors offer positive models.

Some stewardship curricula give instructions for Sunday school teachers or Christian home-school parents to use with children at each specific age range. *Wrapped in God's Love: A Milestones Ministry Resource*,[10] written by the United Church of Canada, "plant[s] seeds of faith" and "grow[s] generous hearts" in infants to teenagers with a wide variety of creative activities for times of special recognition. Celebrated in Sunday school as the children grow, these "milestones" involve everything from a blanket on the baby's first Sunday in worship and saying thank you prayers, to nurturing self-acceptance, investing money and doing service projects. *Wrapped in God's Love* involves children and youth, their parents, caregivers and congregations. Age-appropriate themes for growing faith and encouraging generosity are listed below:

- Infancy—"Wrapped in God's Love"—"Celebrating God's Gift of Life"
- 2–4 years—"Welcomed by God's Family"—"Nurturing a Spirit of Gratitude"
- 8 years—"God is My Friend"—"Caring for God's Creation"
- 12 years—"Growing in Wisdom"—"Stewards of Self, Time and Talents"
- 16 years—"Growing in Freedom"—"Including God as I Make Choices"

- 18 years—"Moving Out Into the World"—"Partnering With God."

Another approach is to teach generosity by discussing stories already found in children's literature to "help children understand the value of sharing, giving to others and leading a life of generosity."[11] Virginia Knight's paper, *Teaching Children How to Live Generously*,[12] uses fourteen children's stories to show how living generously can make a difference, help children properly measure their giving, teach them cheerful giving, and motivate them to give to generations to come.

One program for teenagers is Sarah Arthur's six-session *Thinking Theologically About Money*.[13] Written in teen-friendly language, it emphasizes interaction with games and discussion. Using John Wesley's framework of Scripture, tradition, reason and experience, it addresses debt, tithing, banking, investing, and more. Role playing exercises explore shopping and brands, the pressure of our culture, and dealing with everyday money problems.

Various regional organizations have created their own curriculum to help children and youth learn about stewardship as they grow up. For example, "Generosity Across the Generations," designed by the Minnesota United Methodist Foundation and the Minnesota Annual Conference Christian Educators Fellowship, involves four-to eight-year-old children and their parents. Most of the congregations have used this curriculum in their Sunday school, others in Vacation Bible School. Four sets of lessons and activities based on these themes come in a packet ready for local church leaders.

1. "Our God is a Generous God!" (Genesis 1)
2. "We Can Be Generous, Too" (Luke 21:1–4)
3. "Our Giving Makes a Difference" (John 6:1–14)
4. "We Share Our Gratitude and Make Promises" (Luke 16:1–13)

The curriculum helps learners "discover not only how generosity touches each of our lives in our everyday ordinary places and spaces, but also how we may be vessels of generosity to others in very important ways."[14] It has a flexible, forty-five- to ninety-minute format of Bible stories, games, songs, and projects to show how God has been actively involved in the church's ministries, and how children and families can offer meaningful, important expressions of generosity in return.

One congregation providing hands-on stewardship opportunities for families is Maumee United Methodist Church in Maumee, Ohio.[15] Their leaders offer mission involvement for children and youth by hosting Lifetree Café, (a midweek coffeehouse ministry), and Chrysalis discipleship retreats for youth as well as Emmaus for adults. Three times a month they feed the poor, give away groceries, and offer contemporary worship in southern Toledo. Mission choices range from building local Habitat for Humanity houses, to Christian Appalachian Ministry in Southeastern Kentucky, and Heifer Project International. Attendance at their youth and children's events, small groups, and outreach programs sometimes exceeds the number of those in worship on weekends.

Helping children grow up with healthy money habits is a particular challenge in North American society, where children can be easy targets, especially for companies' sophisticated media-driven strategies. By as young as second grade, many children prefer the widely-marketed logos over lesser-known, equally usable items. Electronic "cookies" on computers and smart phones make them personalized consumer targets at a very young age.[16]

# Learning in Families

Family life can be a powerful context in which to learn about generosity and become more gracious stewards of our natural abilities, time, and possessions. Children, parents, and grandparents can intentionally teach and model good stewardship for one another.

Nathan Dungan helps youth and adults link their money decisions to their values.[17] In *Prodigal Sons and Material Girls: How Not to Be Your Child's ATM,*[18] he outlines disturbing facts about our pos-session-crazed society and materialistic distortions of the American Dream. Then he offers examples of how to use his "Share-Save-Spend" approach to money to reorient children and help their par-ents set a good example of financial management. His books and website, *sharesavespend.com,* give a framework for financial plan-ning in families, so they can make the distinction between needs and wants, and establish healthy financial boundaries.

Dungan's *Money Sanity Solutions: Linking Money + Meaning*[19] is an interactive guide for families to help them develop healthy money habits linked to their values. The book and DVD cover a variety of situations and provide discussion questions to spark family conver-sations. Offering more than budgeting basics, topics range from such subjects as consumer conscience and peer pressure, to vacations, paying with plastic, gratitude, and greed. Dungan has worked with clusters of churches to help them take their parish families through the comprehensive process.

Ron Hovland,[20] chair of the Stewardship Committee at Lutheran Church of the Good Shepherd in Minneapolis, says his congregation benefitted from both Dungan's speaking and his book *Money Sanity Solutions.* The church instituted a program of stewardship education over the six-week worship season of Epiphany (from January 6 until the beginning of Lent), with a common theme and text for all Sunday educational groups. In its first year they invited Dungan to speak at the first and the sixth weeks, and in the intervening weeks four chap-ters of *Money Sanity Solutions* became the catalyst for teaching and discussion in adult education, Sunday school for children and youth, and worship. In the second year they had him speak again, to high-light four different chapters of the book. Since the church also has a drama ministry, they wrote and performed skits to use with each of the themes. With eighty to ninety children and an average of forty adults in their Sunday school, their program affected hundreds of individuals and families.

Several resources give families options to use at home, to help chil-dren and youth practice generosity with their money, involvement, and possessions. In *Kids, Money & Values*[21] Estess and Barocas give parents games, role plays, and activities to help their children outgrow the "I want what I want when I want it" syndrome; learn to share, save and invest; make contributions; find youthful job opportunities; and become reasonable consumers. In *Giving Together: A Stewardship Guide for Families*,[22] Carol Wehrheim offers a five-session series or retreat format for several families to explore together how to set up family rules, let go of "too much stuff," and nurture generosity in the family and beyond. David Briggs' *Raising Financially Freed-Up Kids*[23] provides activities for parents to work with their children about allowances, making financial decisions, learning to budget, handling money and possessions, and planning for college costs.

The church in which I grew up used Sunday school materials that presented the same major themes every three years, using different Bible stories, life examples and discussions to match our growing development. If a congregation today were to add a fourth year with the theme of "Generous God, Generous Lives"[24] at every age level, we would grow a new generation of consciously generous Christians!

Whether or not such teaching takes place in church, the resources above enable parents, grandparents, or other adults to use any of the activities, celebrations, or "milestones," as a fun time together with children while teaching generosity in the process. A holistic approach such as *Money Sanity Solutions* is ideal, but even individual events can stick in a child's mind and make a difference.

Such generosity happened in my own life. I will never forget Miss Brewer, my seventh-grade English teacher, for giving up her own lunch hour twice to encourage and critique my extracurricular writing efforts. As a socially awkward preteen, I was amazed that she thought enough of me to sacrifice her own time to honor my efforts and show me how to improve them. The ripples of that one act of generosity and respect left a lifelong, positive wake.

It goes without saying that whatever resources parents may use to teach faith and generosity to their children, the parents' own behavior is the greatest influence on their children. This was confirmed in 2014 by the National Longitudinal Study of Adolescent Health of teens age thirteen to seventeen and their parents.[25] "Mothers and fathers who practice what they preach and preach what they practice are far and away the biggest influence related to adolescents keeping the faith into their twenties," says this landmark study of youth and religion.

By contrast, these findings showed just one percent of teens age fifteen to seventeen raised by parents who gave little importance to religion were highly religious in their mid- to late twenties. By contrast, eighty-two percent of children raised by parents who regularly talked about their faith gave great importance to their religious beliefs, and, later as young adults, were active in and beyond their congregations.[26]

Regardless of religious involvement, how do parents transmit generosity? Multiple studies done through The Lake Institute on Faith and Giving[27] have shown that children ages one through seventeen are more likely to help others when the parents do the following things (with each additional parental activity increasing the child's altruism).

- Positive modeling of generous / helping behavior.
- Verbal encouragement through "other-oriented induction" (noting the emotional state of the person needing help and describing how he or she will benefit from assistance).
- Reinforcement after the child's helpful behavior by attributing the child's caring action to his or her helpful mood or inclination.
- Providing opportunities where the child might be able to show caring.
- Helping the child identify his or her own experiences of receiving care from others, beginning with the parents' "warmth, sensitivity and responsiveness."

Other longitudinal studies have found that parents can affect their adult child's giving, when the adult child observes one or both parents volunteering, or someone in the family helping other people.[28]

My own parents talked about their faith with me. More importantly, they lived it in their family priorities, sometimes paying a price socially for their ethnic inclusiveness and support for civil rights. One of the original dozen couples who founded their local church, they gave generously to its ministries throughout their lives. They lived within their means so they could make periodic major gifts to help the next generation. My mother devoted most of her adult life to raise her four children. Then at age fifty she began teaching in an inner-city high school, empowering and affirming many low-income students for almost a decade. A scholarship she established at that school is part of her legacy. Dad refused work promotions in order to stay where Mom could express her gift for teaching. After he retired, he donated massive amounts of time in leadership of their denomination. They did not have to talk about generosity; I could see it in their lives.

# Stages of Faith

Another perspective on growth is to view our lifespan in progressive stages. Life stages are not automatic steps we must take, but rather increased spiritual capacities we may choose to actualize as we are able to develop mentally, physically, and in every other way.

Christian philosopher Soren Kierkegaard (born in 1813) focused on the individual's inward relation to God, identifying three basic "stages on life's way" to becoming a true self on the road of faith.[29] He said in "the aesthetic stage," a person attempts to escape boredom, anxiety and despair by pursuing immediate pleasures. Through faith in God—including "intense personal commitment and a dedication to unending self-analysis"[30]—one may attain a second level, called "the ethical stage." While in this stage, the person considers the effect of his or her actions on others, and values promoting social welfare over achieving personal gain. Yet this diverts one from self-exploration, he explained, since it requires an individual to follow a set of socially-accepted norms.

With another agonizing choice, the person may reach a split-level "religious stage," where he or she resigns to existence, "becoming a self before God."[31] Kierkegaard thought almost no one lives at this level, since one's relationship with God is exclusively personal, and he believed the large-scale religion (Christendom orientation) of the church actually interferes with one's personal spiritual quest.

A century later, American psychologist Lawrence Kohlberg (born in 1927) developed a model with six stages of moral development grouped into three levels,[32] expanding on that of Jean Piaget.[33] Kohlberg depicts Level One as where a person does the right thing to avoid punishment or to get rewarded (What's in it for me?). At Level Two, one does the right thing to uphold the community's rules and expectations, seeking to please others (How can I be a good boy or girl? What is the law-and-order response?). At Level Three, someone does the right thing out of appreciation for the values and principles behind it (How would this action express the social contract? What universal ethical principles are involved here?). By taking these steps, one moves toward "moral integrity," where what a person does when no one else is watching is congruent with what he or she believes.[34]

Most intriguing is the work of James Fowler, United Methodist clergy and developmental psychologist at Candler School of Theology. In his book *Stages of Faith*[35] he proposes six possible faith stages across one's life span, roughly paraphrased in the following ways:[36]

1. Intuitive-projective faith—Most typical of children from two to seven. Fantasy-filled, imitative phase, where one is strongly influenced by the visible faith of primary adults. Gives rise to the imagination, where the child begins to develop long-lasting impressions.
2. Mythic-literal faith—Usually children seven to twelve years old. Literally interprets moral rules, symbols, and attitudes. Forms and re-tells powerful stories, also using drama and myth. Emphasizes reciprocity and fairness, which may become a merit-based worldview.

3. <u>Synthetic-conventional faith</u>—This stage often arises in ado-
lescence but may become a permanent place for adults. Seeks
to synthesize all the spheres beyond the family that compete
for attention: school or work, peers, street society, media, and
perhaps religion. Pulls together a sense of self or identity and
looks to significant others to confirm it. Conforms to traditional religious authority. Tends to compose images of God as
extensions of interpersonal relationships.

4. <u>Individuative-reflective faith</u>—For many people, one does
not reach this stage until the mid-twenties to late thirties.
Re-examines one's faith in light of his or her experiences,
self-awareness, and reflection. Takes responsibility for one's
own commitments, lifestyle, beliefs, and attitudes. Faces
unavoidable tensions. Looks for a new identity beyond a com-
posite of roles. Shows concern about authenticity, and boundaries between oneself and others. Begins to take a new look at
key life stories and apply them to larger contexts.

5. <u>Conjunctive faith</u>—This stage is unusual before age forty.
Reclaims and reworks one's past. Integrates Stage Four's self-cer-
tainty with the earlier power of symbols. Realizes one's finitude
and so attaches less importance to oneself. Acknowledges the
unconscious and looks for one's "deeper self." Is alive to paradox and apparent contradictions. Knows defeat and the reality
of irrevocable commitments. No longer feels confined by the
identity of one's own community.

6. <u>Universalizing faith</u>—Fowler believes it is very rare for people
to get to this stage. Loves life and holds it loosely. Experiences
one's environment as including all human community. Shifts
the center of his or her experience from the self to participation in a power that transcends structures, unifies, and transforms the world. "Transcends the need for a system of beliefs
and becomes unified with a sort of universalizing spirit."[37]

Fowler's work on faith stages was seminal, as colleagues produced
an explosion of applications to various life aspects. For example, some

applied them to stages of cognition (Aurobindo); values (Graves); self-identity (Cook-Greuter); worldviews (Gebser); and even orders of consciousness (Kegan).[38]

In 1999 Gary Leak, Anne Loucks, and Patricia Bowlin, faculty at Creighton University, created The Faith Development Scale (FDS). The FDS is a quantified, "brief, global measure of religious maturity derived explicitly from Fowler's (1981) influential theory of faith development."[39] This eight-item scale creates a brief index of maturing faith development. Later, two four-year longitudinal studies[40] by the FDS creators sought to further validate the scale through its association with religious and personality characteristics, as well as through its methodology.[41]

Critics have made some significant points against various theories of "stages of faith." One objection is that stages might imply that spiritual growth is automatic or is the same journey for all people. Another concern sees stages as too closely tied to biological or mental development, not to a person's unique, intentional relationship with God. Several critics say the "higher" stages reflect the personal biases of the theorists. For example, some complain that Kohlberg's levels unduly emphasize justice over caring, while others say that Fowler's sixth stage reflects his own liberal Christian Protestant outlook.

Many have voiced concerns about a quantifiable scale that might be used as a measure for an individual's faith experience. Some critics point out the need for further content validity. Leak and colleagues admit the need for "a rigorous examination" of its scientific method beyond the two models they used to test it.

Nevertheless, viewing a person's faith development in stages may help many people avoid the assumption that one's spiritual life is a simple byproduct of biology. Stages also remind us of human beings' increasing spiritual capacities as we grow emotionally and reflect on our life experiences. This perspective reminds us of Aristotle's earlier point that actualizing our potential—in this case, in our relationship with the God who loves us—involves making a *choice*, unlike the non-intentional nature of physical maturation.

Any conception of life stages implies growth toward a higher level or goal, even though our goals may alter as we grow. Thomas Merton focuses on the endpoint itself. "Your life is shaped by the end you live for," he says. "You are made in the image of what you desire."[42]

David Benner, Professor of Psychology and Spirituality at Richmond Graduate University in Atlanta, describes this end as our vocation: "a call to serve God and our fellow humans in the distinctive way that fits the shape of our being" and that is "both best for us and best for the world."[43] Even as Jesus' understanding of God's call continued to develop throughout his life, says Benner, we also are called to keep developing our truest self in Christ, striving to align our being with absolute authenticity.[44]

Reviewing these "stage" approaches to spiritual growth, I find them helpful—as long as they are not conceived in an automatic, lock-step or one-size-fits-all way. Another caution is that they not be used to make judgments about who is more "spiritually mature" than others. Generally, the various theories of stages seem to reflect a similar process of movement from affiliating with significant adults, to developing an individual identity, to embracing a spiritually inclusive sense of being.

As with almost all interesting subjects, most of these stage theories are controversial in different circles—for example, Benner's idea that even Jesus changed and grew in his understanding of his identity and calling. (The four Gospels themselves give different viewpoints on this topic, although all agree that Jesus did not launch his ministry until he was grown.) However, if Benner's change-by-stages view of Jesus is true, it would give us powerful common ground with Jesus in his being "fully human," not just "fully divine."[45] If so, even Jesus needed to consciously pursue his own spiritual growth from one stage to another.

# Giving and Growth

"Generosity and stewardship are part of the spiritual formation of every growing follower of Christ."[46] But how do we grow in investing our energy, time, and funds, to follow God's call? And how can we invite others to join us in this journey of becoming more generous persons? How can giving—time, involvement, money, anything— help us grow in our relationship with God?

No matter what our life circumstances, when we realize how gracious and generous God has been to us, we naturally live more thankfully toward God, and more generously toward others. People whose lives have been spared in a natural disaster, or those who have lived through a traumatic circumstance, often band together to help others facing similar adversity.

I have seen this firsthand, living in a wooded area where fires have ripped through the canyons. Neighbors we did not know have come forward to offer a place for people to evacuate, or for their pets and livestock to have food, shelter, and safety.

But it doesn't take a crisis to impel many people to come forward. There are plenty of instances of everyday generosity toward others.

People do not have to believe in God to recognize the miracle and giftedness of our lives. Much of human "prosocial" (helping) behavior comes from knowing that we are, first of all, not givers but *receivers*—receivers of the wonders of this incredible natural world, and of the gift of human life and community. Lamentably, some children have been raised in want, in abusive or other inhumane situations. But most of the rest of us find it is a natural instinct to want to help others in return, if it is within our power to do so.

For Christians, the realization of being receivers first is exponentially stronger. As 1 John 4:19 says, "We love because God first loved us." John 3:16, a beloved text for millions of people, begins, "For God so *loved* the world that [God] *gave* [God's] only Son, . . ." (Italics mine) Even before getting to the gift of Jesus Christ himself, we are left with the stunning fact of God's love for us all, and of God's giving to us as the natural expression of that love.

"Our giving is a reflexive response to the grace of God in our lives," says author Randy Alcorn, who takes his cue from 2 Corinthians 8:1–6:

> As thunder follows lightning, giving follows grace. When God's grace touches you, you can't help but respond with generous giving. And as the Macedonians knew, giving is simply the overflow of joy."[47]

Being thankful naturally leads to being generous, seeking to give something back to God, no matter how small it may seem.

Growth in our giving involves not only values and decisions, but also a pattern of actions that we develop over time. Aristotle called these habitual actions "virtues:" skills we have intentionally developed over the years that have become "second nature."[48] These habitual actions are like a musician's or athlete's muscle memory. While we consciously seek to improve quality or consistency, the fact of our past behavior strengthens our ability each time we practice it. Aristotle sees virtues as implying excellence in a particular function, whether they are "virtues of mind" (speculative and practical wisdom) or "virtues of character" (including the cardinal virtues of justice, courage, temperance and prudence).[49] Using Aristotle's categories, generosity is a virtue of character—a pattern of giving based upon the value we give to God's grace, and our consequent decision to respond in kind to God by giving to others.

Because generous stewardship not only engages the mind, but also one's entire character, it is something to be practiced as well as learned. In *Beyond Money*, church consultant Dan Dick says that if *discipleship* is learning about following Jesus Christ, then *stewardship* is practicing our discipleship.[50] He describes growth in stewardship as a process where we begin by learning a lot and practicing a little of the more generous behavior. But as we continue to grow, we put more time and effort into practice, so "our learning becomes living."

The more we grow spiritually, the more we move from a childhood awareness of dependence, through to an illusory sense of independence at youth and young adulthood, and finally to midlife recognition of our interdependence with others every step of our journey.

Another way of understanding growth in giving comes from United Church of Christ minister and author William Green. He posits that people are "hard-wired for generosity," and for those who believe in God, describes a three-stage progression of spiritual growth in giving. First is *reciprocal generosity,* where we think, "I pat your back; you pat mine," imagining that God gives to us, so we give back to God.

Next comes *open generosity,* where we give simply for its own sake, without focusing particularly on either the recipient or God, who is the Source. Finally, there is *doxological generosity,* giving in order to praise God by all the ways that we give and live.[51]

Many stewardship leaders say that moving from a transactional model to a transformational one is the essential shift that needs to take place within us.

A transactional model is voiced as "I do something for you; you do something for me." It may come in many forms, from trying to make "bargain prayers" with God ("I'll worship You if You'll bless or protect me or my loved ones") to selling the church's services ("My financial support allows my congregation to serve my personal needs"). Our familiarity with marketing and sales techniques lies underneath such transactions, so the individual giver will meet the financial needs of the organization.

By contrast, a transformational model deals primarily with the giver's relationship to God, rather than to the church. "The same Lord is Lord of all and is generous to all who call on him" (Romans 10:12b). "For you know the generous act of our Lord Jesus Christ, that though he was rich, yet for your sakes he became poor, so that by his poverty you might become rich" (2 Corinthians 8:9). God's freely-given love for us, epitomized in Jesus Christ, prompts us to give love (*caritas,* or "love-in-action," caring for someone) to those around us. Transformation gradually takes place within the giver, as he or she seeks to refocus from being rich in material goods to being "rich toward God" (Luke 12:15–21). The ideal outcome is that the "giver becomes conformed to the image of Christ and becomes generous, like Christ."[52]

# Building Muscle Memory for Giving

Todd Harper, Executive Vice President of Generous Giving, presents a progression of how people can evolve in their reasons for giving, practice giving, and choose where to give.[53]

For example, *emerging givers* may give primarily because of relationships, in response to something that personally impacted them, and to pass on assets solely to their children and family. *Maturing givers* understand that everything belongs to God, see themselves as God's stewards, and have a growing desire to give as part of God's plan. They begin to understand giving as an investment in others beyond their immediate family. *Generous givers* view their giving as an outward expression of their spiritual commitment, see their possessions as a sacred trust, and seek spiritual guidance from others to aid their giving in all aspects of life.

Harper notes that giving begins with scheduled gifts and a "here and now" mentality. As we grow through our giving, we shift into creating some short-term giving strategies, and want to give increasingly more than a fixed ten percent, then do more systematic planning for giving generously out of both our income and property.

At every stage, he notes there are things to read and do, and offers some helpful questions for reflection. For example:

- How much is enough?
- What is an appropriate lifestyle?
- What are the dangers and opportunities of wealth from a spiritual perspective?
- What are the benefits of simplicity?
- How do I steward all that God has entrusted to me?

What begins as a journey often grows into a calling, as we seek to pursue God's will in every aspect of our lives, and to facilitate generosity and transformation in other people's lives.

The Lake Institute on Faith and Giving is connected with the Center on Philanthropy at Indiana University, and includes The Women's Philanthropy Institute and The Fund Raising School. This network offers a scientific environment for people to reflect on the role of money and charitable giving. It provides outstanding research, education, and training in the relationship between faith and giving within various religious traditions.[54]

Lake Institute studies have noted an increasing number of givers who see themselves as *investors* in the organization's cause, not merely as financial donors.[55] For example, most Millennial givers (born from 1981 to 1997) want to know where their money goes to improve people's lives. Since 1997, nonprofit organizations have been in a period of "intense accountability" to their contributors. Generation Xers (those born between 1964 and 1981), as well as the younger Millennials, want to see both informational feedback and measurable growth as a result of their giving.[56]

In addition, a 2006 study showed that a very high proportion of high net-worth givers (those with $200,000 or more income, or $1,000,000 or more in assets) also volunteered personal time to their charities. Sixty-one percent of them served on the Board of Directors for a nonprofit organization, and slightly more volunteered to help the charities raise funds.[57]

Another trend is that of "Giving Circles," where a small group of individuals gather together, often through the Internet, to decide as a group specifically where to give their personal charitable money. The number of Giving Circles has grown exponentially across the United States. One study shows that those who participate in Giving Circles "say they give more, give more strategically, and are more knowledgeable about nonprofit organizations and problems in their local communities"[58] than they would have been, had they researched charities on their own.

Dr. Michael Reeves, a leading stewardship coach, notes that when giving funds to God's work through the church, people tend to grow their commitment in three stages: first through annual, then major, and finally planned giving.[59]

The first stage is *annual giving,* as well as special offerings and projects when they arise. Local church leaders encourage this form of giving by developing and communicating a congregational budget, having sound financial policies in place, and providing stewardship education for all ages.[60]

After becoming accustomed to annual giving, many givers naturally consider periodic *major giving,* whether it is to buy land, build new or renovate old facilities, reduce debts, establish an endowment, or embark on a new mission. Often making a major gift takes rearranging family financial priorities in order to do this "second-mile giving."[61]

Most often, after one has adjusted to giving annually and periodically with major gifts, the third stage is *planned giving.* This occurs when the person chooses to include a particular church or other charity in his or her will, or through another uniquely-matched financial vehicle to make ministry available for future generations. While we do not know the particular form that presenting the gospel will take for our children's children, for example, we want them to hear the Good News and have their lives changed by it.

In the book *Contagious Generosity,*[62] Chris Willard and Jim Sheppard share a wealth of ideas from church leaders who are growing a culture of generosity in their congregations. Here are six practical things they say church leaders can focus on: 63

- Build trust—Look for multiple ways to communicate with people, creating an atmosphere of trust. Connect regularly in face-to-face interactions. In worship, highlight opportunities for generous habits: for example, with inspiring stories of a business owner who does home improvement work at no charge for seniors in the community, or a family that adopts a child from another country, all in response to God's grace.

- Cast and recast vision—Work to develop your ministry's vision. Constantly remind one another of it in various ways, so participants can absorb it and claim it for themselves.
- Shape culture—Encourage transformation through teaching, actions, and expectations. Invite people to change their hearts, minds, and habits toward generosity, giving freely to others in an authentic way.
- Demonstrate impact—Tell givers how their generosity has changed people's lives. Generous acts free givers from their attachment to things, and demonstrate God's love to the receivers, thus nurturing the souls of both donors and recipients.
- Enhance relationships –Encourage people to build relationships across a broad spectrum of members and participants and invite them to get involved with one another. Set aside time in your schedule to connect personally with those who support the church's vision.
- Highlight good stewardship of the money given to your congregation. Let people know about key decisions to use funds efficiently in your ministries.

The spirit and practice of generosity are "always an outward sign of an inward commitment," say the authors:

> Becoming a generous community…doesn't happen overnight. It is necessary to cultivate the culture, communicate core values, challenge people with clear opportunities, and imbed the vision for generosity in every area of life and ministry."[64]

One excellent way to encourage congregations to develop generosity on multiple fronts is through a challenge grant. The Wisconsin United Methodist Foundation has created a yearly Stewardship Challenge Grant, which rewards local churches for up to three years on a point system for their stewardship work in several ministry areas. Each grant is based on simultaneous work in four aspects of the congregation's life together:

1. Leadership for Stewardship,
2. Praise and Thanksgiving,
3. Creating a Culture for Giving, and
4. Education about Stewardship Principles and Concepts.

In this section we have seen that generous giving involves not only becoming aware of how we are first receivers, but also following a pattern of actions which give us "muscle memory" for giving. As we mature in our giving, we move from giving solely on impulse, to giving according to a plan, and on to giving to future generations. Our view widens when we try to use all our assets as part of God's design. Such growth prompts us to ask important questions about our lifestyle, and how to use all that we have. As church leaders, we can encourage this process of growth in giving, even as we seek to grow and model it in our personal lives.

I've been amazed by the simple beauty of transformational giving, whether in the church family or the wider community. In one town, three members of a tiny congregation helped an eleven-year-old child and her working single parent by taking her to day-long dialysis two days a week, every week—for years.

In another place, a caring neighbor made an anonymous financial gift so four young students could receive their very first music lessons, which their families never could have afforded on their own.

In yet another community, members of a local service club led their neighbors in raising funds to purchase an Allergy-Alert Dog named Peppermint Patty for a three-year-old girl with life-threatening nut allergies.

God's design for us takes shape with such spontaneity and beauty when people allow themselves to grow and be creative in their giving, following the flow of opportunities as they unfold.

WHEN WE IMAGINE spiritual growth less in terms of accumulated activities and more as a process of *becoming*, we discover a variety of ways to picture it as part of our natural human development, as learning within the family, or according to faith stages. Reminding ourselves and one another that we are first and foremost receivers of God's grace, we can build habits that give us a "muscle memory" for giving. But giving is not an end in itself: it is just one dimension of a generous personal life and congregational culture. We can build and strengthen such a culture whenever we empower trust among one another, cast and recast our vision as a community, highlight good stewardship of all we have received, enhance relationships, and demonstrate generosity's impact by sharing stories of transformed lives.

## Questions for Reflection

1.  Which view of spiritual growth makes most sense to me? Whichever model I use, where do I imagine myself in the process?
2.  Have I ever seen or experienced transformational giving? How was or is that different from merely transactional giving, perhaps in quality, presence, or purpose?
3.  Where in my life am I working together with God to become more fully the way God has seen me all along?

## Endnotes

1. *thefreedictionary.com.*
2. *Ibid.*
3. Dan R. Dick, Director of Connectional Ministries, Wisconsin Annual Conference, "Who Am I?" *Upper Room Disciplines 2011* (Nashville: Upper Room Books, 2010), p. 218.
4. General Board of Discipleship Ministries of The United Methodist Church. The Board says, "Children are born with an innate sense of wonder and faith that is real and authentic. As teachers and leaders our role is to provide a foundation

of experiences on which children build a life of learning and growth toward a mature and vital faith." (*gbod.org/leadership-resources/children*).

5. © 2008 General Board of Discipleship, now Discipleship Ministries. Used by permission.

6. Donald W. Joiner and Norma Wimberly, ed., *The Abingdon Guide to Funding Ministry, Volume 2* (Nashville: Abingdon Press, 1996).

7. Norma Wimberly, "Inviting Children to Be Stewards," in *ibid*, pp. 140f.

8. Jan Cox, "Guiding Young Stewards," in *ibid*, p. 145.

9. Delia Halverson, *Let the Children Give: Time, Talents, Love, and Money* (Nashville: Discipleship Resources, 2007).

10. United Church of Canada, *Wrapped in God's Love: A Milestones Ministry Resource. Planting Seeds of Faith, Growing Generous Hearts,* United Church Resource Distribution, 2005, at *ucrdstore.ca/wrapped-in-gods-love.* The updated digital resource is available through the Ecumenical Stewardship Center at *stewardshipresources.org/resources/item/257.*

11. Virginia Knight, *Teaching Children How to Live Generously,* at *tpf.org/files/uploads/philanthropy_curriculum.pdf.* Knight is Director of Education for Presbyterian Children's Homes and Services. The paper was sponsored by The Texas Presbyterian Foundation.

12. *Ibid.*

13. Sarah Arthur, *Thinking Theologically About Money* (Abingdon Press, 2004).

14. *mnumf.org* "Generosity Across the Generations" introduction.

15. 2015 United Methodist Program Calendar. See *maumeeumc.net.*

16. In 2009, Nathan Dungan reported that in Japan, Hello Kitty smart phones for children (with GPS trackers) were designed to make special sale offers to them for fast-food items at the nearby McDonald's on their way home from school. He said Japan had no laws against such behavior. Presentation given to the North American Conference on Christian Philanthropy.

17. See *sharesavespend.com* for more about Dungan's ministry.

18. Nathan Dungan, *Prodigal Sons and Material Girls: How Not to Be Your Child's ATM* (Solution Tree, 2003).

19. Nathan Dungan, *Money Sanity Solutions: Linking Money + Meaning (Share Save Spend, 2010).*

20. Phone interview, March 13, 2015.

21. Patricia Schiff Estess and Irving Barocas, *Kids, Money & Values: Creative Ways to Teach Your Kids About Money* (Betterway Books, 1994).

22. Carol A. Wehrheim, *Giving Together: A Stewardship Guide for Families,* (Westminster John Knox Press, 2004).

23. David Briggs, *Raising Financially Freed-Up Kids: Teaching Responsibility at Every Age* (Good Sense LLC, 2010).

24. Possible common key stewardship teaching across all Christian denominations, recommended by Mark L. Vincent in "The Whys & Hows of Money Leadership" workshop, 2003, at Los Altos United Methodist Church, CA.

25. Reported in "Parents are top influence in teens remaining active in religion as young adults," *Christian Century* December 24, 2014, pp. 17–18.

26. *Ibid.*

27. Richard Steinberg and Mark Wilhelm, Department of Economics, IUPUI (Indiana University. Purdue University Indianapolis) and the Center on Philanthropy at Indiana University, *Giving: The Next Generation. Parental Effects on Donations*, pp. 3–4 at *philanthropy.iupui.edu/lake.*

28. *Ibid, pp. 5–6.*

29. Phillip Cary, "Kierkegaard and the Leap of Faith," Lecture 57, *Great Minds of the Western Intellectual Tradition, 3rd Edition,* p. 249.

30. *sparknotes.com/philosophy/kierkegaard/themes.html.*

31. *Ibid,* p. 250.

32. Ronald J. Greer, *op cit.,* pp. 75–76.

33. Jean Piaget (1896–1980) was a Swiss developmental psychologist and philosopher known for his theory of cognitive development and studies of the mental framework created when a child interacts with his or her physical and social environments. Piaget specialized in the stages before children develop abstract reasoning between ages eleven to sixteen. See *en.wikipedia.org.*

34. *Ibid,* p. 76.

35. James Fowler, *Stages of Faith: The Psychology of Human Development and the Quest for Meaning,* Harper & Row, 1981.

36. See Joann Wolski Conn, ed., *Women's Spirituality: Resources for Christian Development,* pp. 226–232; John C. Robinson, *op cit.,* p. 251; *wikipedia.com* re. James W. Fowler; *amazon.com* about *Stages of Faith; kenwilbur.com/blog/show/509.*

37. "Applying James Fowler's Stages of Faith Development to Evangelism," by rdlang05, at *pinterest.com/pin/40743571604617237,* pinned at *rdlang05. hubpages.com.*

38. *pinterest.com* stages of faith charts.

39. Gary K. Leak (Creighton University), "Factorial Validity of the Faith Development Scale," at *tandfonline.com/doi/abs/10.1080/1.*

40. ——— , Anne A. Loucks & Patricia Bowlin, "Development and Initial Validation of an Objective Measure of Faith Development," in *International Journal for the Psychology of Religion, Volume 9, Issue 2,* 1999, pp. 105–124; at *tandfonline. com/doi/abs/10.1207/s15327582ijpr0902_2;* and Gary K. Leak's article, "Validation of the Faith Development Scale Using Longitudinal and Cross-Sectional Designs," in *Social Behavior and Personality: an international journal, Volume 31, Number 6, 2003,* pp. 637–641(5) at *ingentaconnect.com/content/sbp/sbp/2003/00000031/00000006/art00011.*

41. ———, "Factorial Validity of the Faith Development Scale," pp. 123–131, at *tandfonline.com/doi/abs/10.1080/10508610701879399.*

42. Thomas Merton, *Thoughts in Solitude*, p. 49.

43. David G. Benner, *op cit.,* p. 97.

44. *Ibid*, pp. 100–105.

45. The Council of Chalcedon (451 AD) declared that Jesus Christ has two natures in one person or substance. This statement that Jesus is both "fully human" and "fully divine" became the foundational phrase for describing Christ for all Roman Catholics and Protestants and for many Orthodox churches, as well as for some others. See Jaroslav Pelikan, *The Emergence of the Catholic Tradition (100–600),* Volume One of his three-volume Christian history, pp. 263f. See also John McManners, ed., *The Oxford History of Christianity,* pp. 79 and 145f.

46. Chris Willard and Jim Sheppard, *Contagious Generosity: Creating a Culture of Giving in Your Church,* The Leadership Network Innovation Series; Zondervan, (Grand Rapids, MI: Zondervan, 2012), p. 102.

47. Randy Alcorn, *The Treasure Principle: Discovering the Secret of Joyful Giving,* pp. 30f.

48. Father Joseph Koterski, S. J., *The Ethics of Aristotle* (The Teaching Company), CDs, Lecture Three.

49. ———, *The Ethics of Aristotle Course Guidebook* (The Teaching Company), pp. 1, 3 and 5.

50. Dan R. Dick, *Beyond Money: Becoming Good and Faithful Stewards,* pp. 10–13.

51. So Janet A. Long, pastor of Washington Avenue Christian Church, Elyria, Ohio, in her review of *52 Ways to Ignite Your Congregation... Generous Giving,* by William Green; at *centerforfaithandgiving.org/Review.*

52. Wesley K. Willmer, "Creating a Revolution in Generosity," in *Revolution in Generosity: Transforming Stewards to Be Rich Toward God,* ed. by Wesley K. Willmer, p. 39.

53. Todd W. Harper, "Discipleship as a Tool to Transform Hearts Toward Generosity," in Wesley K. Willmer, ed., *op cit.,* pp.240f. *Revolution in Generosity: Transforming Stewards to Be Rich Toward God,* pp. 240f.

54. *philanthropy.iupui.edu/lake-about-us.*

55. Melissa Brown, "Engaging the Next Generation," speaking at the 2007 Annual Meeting of the National Association of United Methodist Foundations, in Indianapolis.

56. *Ibid.*

57. *philanthropy.iupui.edu/lake-about-us.*

58. *Ibid.* These Giving Circle findings are from a report released by the University of Nebraska at Omaha, the Forum of Regional Associations of Grantmakers, and The Center on Philanthropy at Indiana University. More about Women's Giving Circles, including multiple firsthand accounts, and how to organize the circle,

recruit and retain members, can be found in Women's Giving Circles (a .pdf file) at *iupui.edu.*

59. Michael Reeves, "Dimensions of Church Stewardship," a Faith & Money Resource, created November 1, 2004.

60. Stewardship education for all ages is a crucial dimension of any congregation's year-round Generosity Plan. Many teaching resources are available geared toward learners from early childhood through adulthood. See Chapter Twelve for how to establish and use a Generosity Plan in your local church.

61. In Jesus' day, Jews were required to carry a Roman soldier's pack for a mile, if commanded to do so. But Jesus told his followers to carry it a second mile (Matthew 5:41). The phrase, "go the second mile" comes out of this saying, meaning to go beyond what is merely expected. Many churches speak of "second mile giving" as giving that is above and beyond one's regular financial pledge to the church's ministries.

62. Chris Willard and Jim Sheppard, *op cit.*

63. *Ibid*, pp. 97f., also pp. 30, 34, 96, 100.

64. Chris Willard and Jim Sheppard, *op cit.*, pp. 39, 41.

# Seasons of the Soul

E MBRACING A NEW season in our lives often requires us to
let go of familiar and seemingly good procedures. For example, when we get married, change careers, or become parents,
we need to let much of our former lives drop away. Leaving the old
life can be required for our spiritual lives, as well.

## Planting and Nourishing the Seed

When thinking about spiritual growth, it's not surprising for people to use a farming metaphor: as the farmer plants, nurtures, and
prunes, so the seed grows, bears fruit, and regenerates. But while it
is a natural process for the seed, it is not a guaranteed one. As Jesus
says, "Unless a grain of wheat falls into the earth and dies, it remains
just a single grain; but if it dies, it bears much fruit." (John 12:24)
Someone needs to bury the seed in soil—that is, let the seed die to its
old self—so its husk can break open, and a new life can spring forth.
In human terms, this means being willing to identify and let go of
the "husk" that has protected our growth thus far, but now may have
become an impediment to the transformation that lies ahead.

Sometimes the metaphorical seed is buried before we know what
will grow in its place. For example, members of the 31st Street Baptist
Church in Richmond, Virginia, bought a vacant block of land behind

their church building, with plans to construct a family life center, but the funding for the project did not come through. So they formed a new vision: to plant a garden to teach community residents how to be self-sufficient, to grow food for their neighborhood soup kitchen, and to provide a nutrition program for 250 people each summer, when children have no access to school lunch programs.[1] The result was a new ministry in a different direction, personally benefitting the lives of hundreds of families living right around them.

People may find that the planted seed brings forth abundant fruit, but of a different kind than they expected. A local-church minister examines his midlife vocation and becomes a community advocate. A woman goes to seminary to become a counselor but graduates as a traveling evangelist instead. An empty-nest homemaker goes to college to indulge an interest but discovers her passion and gifts for full-time teaching instead. The loss of a longtime partner sends a spouse's world spinning, only to emerge in an entirely new career.

Joseph in the Old Testament is a dramatic example. He was sold into slavery to a passing caravan by his jealous, frustrated brothers. Thrown into a foreign prison, he eventually became the equivalent of Secretary of State or Prime Minister for the Pharaoh over all of Egypt. As Joseph finally told his brothers, "Even though you intended to do harm to me, God intended it for good" (Genesis 50:20), since Joseph's placement in the Egyptian government made it possible for the people called Israel to survive and multiply in northern Egypt, despite years of famine in their homeland.

A key part of spiritual growth lies not so much in our periods of great activity, but in the times we focus on *being*. As with a field that needs to lie fallow periodically to be nourished once again, many of life's major transitions allow for a prior time of reflection, if we choose to learn from it.[2] In such times we may feel that something of significance is no longer working well, and that we need to make a change. We want to open ourselves to discover where God wants us to go, to renew our minds and discern God's will, instead of simply conforming to our old assumptions and behaviors. (Romans 12:2.) "This is akin to letting your future, the next direction in your life, lie fallow for a time," says minister and counselor Ronald Greer. "If you feel stuck in the process, stop working so hard at it. *Many of life's most important decisions are not made; they are discovered.*"[3] (Emphasis in original)

# Flowing Water

Another way to picture spiritual growth is by using the metaphor of flowing water. In *Holy Currencies*, Eric Law, Episcopal priest and Executive Director of Kaleidoscope Institute, describes six "currencies:" resources or behaviors meant to be converted for the sake of personal and community wholeness. At the same time, they act like "currents" flowing into one another to create fluid, sustainable ministries.

As people share and exchange one currency for another in response to new circumstances, they become a constantly changing "cycle of blessings." They are:

- Time and Place—Offer a time and place (a "Grace Margin") for transformative events to occur, where all may speak about the truth of their lives and their relationship with God.
- Gracious Leadership—Help leaders develop skills, tools, models, and processes to create a gracious environment for meaningful, diverse relationships.
- Relationship—Strengthen existing connections within our church or organization and with people of different attitudes, aptitudes, and outlooks, especially in our neighborhood, beginning by listening to the poor and the marginalized.
- Truth—Discover a comprehensive, inclusive understanding of the truth from the different perspectives of people living in our community.
- Money—Affirm and use money as a temporary medium of exchange to improve people's lives—not as something to hoard for its own sake, thereby taking it out of exchange.

- Wellness—Mobilize time and place, leadership, and relationships to help individuals and communities achieve physical, spiritual, social, ecological, or financial wellness.[4]

When we use these currencies as cyclical resources in a healthy way, they flow like natural water currents, moving in and out of our lives, multiplying blessings and enriching the entire community.

Considering one of these currencies, some people joke that money is like water—hard to hold, and too easily falling through our fingers. But in *The Soul of Money*, Lynne Twist uses this same metaphor in a more serious sense. "Money is a current, a conduit for our intentions," she states. "Money carries the imprimatur of our soul."

When Twist was a fund raiser for The Hunger Project's commitment in Africa, she met a woman named Gertrude in New York's Harlem, who told her:

> Now I ain't got no checkbook and I ain't got no credit cards. To me, money is a lot like water. For some folks it rushes through their life like a raging river. Money comes through my life like a little trickle. But I want to pass it on in a way that does the most good for the most folks. I see that as my right and as my responsibility. It's also my joy. I have fifty dollars in my purse that I earned from doing a white woman's wash, and I want to give it to you.[5]

Gertrude's generous gift came with a sense of integrity and heart, carrying the energy of her commitment and contribution of spirit. She understood that her money was not really *her* money, but a currency meant to flow in and out, helping to nourish the entire human community. Learning from Gertrude that day, Twist concludes, "Our money carries energy and generates relationships and partnerships, where everyone feels able and valued."[6]

# Seasons of Our Lives

In our personal lives, we might view a lifespan of spiritual growth as seasons of a year, correlated to the spring of our childhood, summer of young adulthood, fall as full adult engagement, and winter as retirement and old age. Brian McLaren's book *Naked Spirituality* uses this pattern, identifying the major theme and three practices that can nurture our souls in each season.[7]

Springtime is the season of *Simplicity*, he says: a time of God-drenched enthusiasm. "In Simplicity, we reach out to God in happiness," he states. "We see the world as it should be."[8] Three helpful practices can cultivate our attentiveness to God: noticing God's presence, giving thanks, and experiencing "jubilant wonder" in response to God's abundance and creation.

Summer is a time of *Complexity*, when we become aware of pain, failure, and limitations. We look for forgiveness and seek positive change. Helpful practices at this point are self-examination and confession (including elements of sorrow, regret, and mercy); petition (looking for help, guidance, strength, and wisdom); and compassion that leads us to pray for others.

Autumn is a time of *Perplexity*, says McLaren, when we notice how we are braided together with others, and (I would add) assessment and thankfulness. It may also include a period of disillusionment, suffering, and ambivalence toward God, understanding that estrangement can be an organic part of spiritual life. Practices one might develop at this time could include a sense of desperate survival and lamentation.

In our spiritual winter, we experience *Harmony*, as we learn to separate the *reality* of God from our concepts and words *about* God. In this season, we might see God and other people more acutely, as well as ourselves as God's children. We can perceive the world as bathed in God's compassion, and develop the practices of beholding God, resting in contemplation, and deepening by joining with God and other people to transform people's lives.

These four spiritual seasons may occur at different times of a particular person's life, or even overlap in various respects, depending upon when he or she encounters significant life events. Wherever we are in our natural life rhythms, thinking in terms of seasons may prompt us to breathe more freely, and allow for fluidity in our lives. We can appreciate the times of lying fallow, as well as of fruitfulness. We can come to accept the flow of cyclical resources that enrich not only ourselves, but also our communities. As we embrace change unfolding within us, we find it is often not a sudden metamorphosis nor a lock-step progression, but a gradual becoming.

# Moving from False Self to True Self

Previously we discussed the difference between a person's "false self" and "true self." Most of us pick up some behaviors molded by our circumstances early in life to help us find our place in the world, to hide our vulnerability, or to highlight our worth to others. As we learn more about ourselves, we need the masks less and less to define us. But when we hold onto these masks thereafter as part of our public persona, we can create a sense of self that is not true to who we really are.

By contrast, our "true self" is our soul: the essence of who we are as we seek to experience God and grow more and more into the person God intends us to become.

Author David Benner says that the core of the *false* self is the belief that our value depends solely on what we have, what we do, and what other people think of us.[9] By nature, our false self requires constant bolstering, projecting an idealized self (what we want others to think we are) that is maintained only by conscious control. But the core of the *true* self is who we are in reality, and who we are becoming. God has placed our God-given, true selves within us, but it is up to us to choose to develop our fuller identity.

While growing toward our true self requires conscious work to pursue our call or vocation, it also depends on having the capacity for positive change. Both of these are gifts: our willingness to develop new habits, and our ability to change. When we are motivated to help others, we can discover joy and contentment in the process. But if our goal is merely to gain wealth or status, those victories do not answer our deeper human desires, leaving us wanting more.[10]

Ambition can strain people in all walks of life, but for ministers, it often takes the form of needing to be needed. For people in non-profit helping professions, this mask of "the one who can fix it" may be harder to face and overcome because of the pedestalization that many people give us—treating us as if we are were more saintly or closer to God than others. Especially for those who work in the service professions, it is liberating to nurture relationships where we can interact as peers more than authorities, admitting our struggles as well as our strengths.

For most people, the early stages of our lives are ego-driven, as we have to be, says Franciscan Richard Rohr. But his designation of the true self is who we objectively are from the beginning, in the mind and heart of God:

> It is your substantial self, your absolute identity, which can be neither gained nor lost by any technique, group affiliation, morality, or formula whatsoever. The surrendering of our false self, which we have usually taken for our absolute identity, yet is merely a relative identity, [is] hidden inside this lovely but passing shell.[11]

While God knows the true self from the beginning, we may spend much of our lives discovering it. Many of us start out following the roles and expectations of significant adults in our lives, but then begin to "feel our way" onto different paths. It can be a unique process of exploration as we navigate families, relationships, and careers throughout our lifetime.

Over many years of psychiatric practice, Carl Gustav Jung noted a common pattern. He identified "the morning" of our life when we develop as an individual and find our place in the world. For example, we may focus on being useful and efficient, or making a mark in our society. Moving further into the metaphorical day, we may shrewdly steer offspring into good jobs and suitable marriages.[12] Yet at some point, Jung says, we no longer need to exercise our conscious will, but in order "to understand the meaning of [our] individual life, [we] must learn to experience [our] own inner being."[13]

Transition times encourage us to examine and scrape away layers of the false self, and to re-discover and nurture who we are becoming on a truer, deeper level. At various periods in our lives, such as when our vocations have settled in or our children have left home, we are prompted to contemplate our journey thus far. These times can engender a new trust in oneself—a new center of equilibrium, which heightens the feeling for life, and maintains its flow.[14]

The pressure of midlife prompts this internal shift, says psychotherapist John Robinson. It is "the urgency of the unlived self to recover its own deep, powerful and independent voice."[15] At that point, the other-directed parts of one's personality collapse internally, and those hard-won early contests of life crack open like the husk of a seed, for a more authentic center of personality to burst forth. In the end, the self becomes merely "a practical reference point, rather than something to defend, protect, strengthen, or inflate."[16] This is the heartfelt path. No one else can dictate a person's new purpose or direction; finally it must be intuited and welcomed from within.

Whatever our stage of life, we are capable of reflecting on deeper meanings. In the inherently busier times of adult living—such as when we are moving out on our own, developing our careers, or raising children—it may require more conscious commitment to carve out regular times to study the Scriptures and, for example, pray, to learn more about who we are called to become. Such conscious habits can provide a rudder to faithfully steer us through the exciting, sometimes chaotic waters of daily living.

# Growing From the Inside Out

In *Five Practices of Fruitful Living*, United Methodist Bishop Robert Schnase describes spiritual growth as the result of a life-giving blend of five behaviors:[17]

- Radical Hospitality—Cultivating receptivity, opening ourselves to God's unconditional love.
- Passionate Worship—Loving God in return, allowing God to change our hearts, and seeing the world through God's eyes.
- Intentional Faith Development—Cooperating with the Spirit as we seek to follow Christ more closely.
- Risk-Taking Mission and Service—Discerning God's call to make a difference in other people's lives.
- Extravagant Generosity—Realizing that all that we have and are belongs to God.

These practices are intertwined, interactive, and interdependent, where each aspect strengthens each of the others. They do not come in a set order and can be surprisingly unpredictable. Schnase encourages a gentle sense of urgency about the direction in which these dimensions lead us, but also patience about the progress, since following Christ is a lifelong endeavor.[18]

In Ephesians 3:16–19, Paul talks about growth as similar to that of a tree, growing from the inside out.

I pray that, according to the riches of [God's] glory, [God] may grant that you may be strengthened in your inner being with power through [God's] Spirit, and that Christ may dwell in your hearts through faith, as you are being rooted and grounded in love. I pray that you may have the power to comprehend, with all the saints, what is the breadth and length and height and depth, and to know the love of Christ that surpasses knowledge, so that you may be filled with all the fullness of God.

According to this glorious prayer of blessing, the growth begins in our inner being, thanks to the "power" of the Holy Spirit (*dunamis*, from which we get the words "dynamic" and "dynamite"). While this is an internal force, the word for "you" is plural: Paul is addressing the Christians in Ephesus as they gather together. So this process is personal but not necessarily private: a spiritual dimension that is intensified by being shared. The recipients do not need to be an official congregation. Whenever two or more people meet in Christ's name, the Spirit is working among and through them. (Matthew 18:20) To use the tree metaphor, trees in a grove intertwine their roots, finding strength with one another as together they dig deep into the soil of the Spirit.

When Paul prays that "Christ may *dwell* in your hearts through faith," he uses the verb that means to live a long time, to settle in, to make that place one's home. So here Paul's prayer for the Ephesian Christians is that Christ will make his longtime home within their pattern of living, in the unspoken witness of their lives.

But there is even more to learn from this biblical metaphor. The paradox of "personal but shared" grows even stronger when Paul prays that the Ephesians "are being rooted and grounded in love."

For decades I believed the old adage that "the deeper the roots, the more the tree grows." Yes, tree growth is related to its roots. But recent botanical studies show that, except for a few tap root trees, growth comes from how interlaced the tree's roots are with the roots of other trees of its kind. The most dramatic example of this phenomenon is the Aspen tree. Because of the intertwining of roots, biologically an entire Aspen grove is counted as a single Aspen tree![19] So when we share our spiritual lives with one another, we intertwine our experiences and insights, nurturing not only ourselves, but also the entire faith community.

Thomas Moore, former friar turned psychotherapist,[20] seems to have this same tree metaphor in mind when he describes those who choose to "live from the soul."

Living from the soul, your actions are more in tune with the root of your experience and less influenced by passing social fads and your personal views. Your life has a primal quality, some of it going back beyond your birth to your ancestors and your far distant primitive source. As you age, you sink more into the earthiness of your identity and become less interested in the surface glitter of culture.[21]

So *living from the soul*, he says, means trying less to control aspects of your life, and living more in touch with your intuition and emotions. It means being less focused on the self, and more identified with others and with nature.

But Paul does not stop there. He goes on to pray that the Ephesians' growth will bring them to "have the power to comprehend, with all the saints, what is the breadth and length and height and depth, and to know" [a verb of firsthand intimate relationship] "the love of Christ that surpasses knowledge, so that [they] may be filled with all the fullness of God"—in other words, so that their lives can be filled with the presence of God, whose very character is generosity and love!

When we seek to grow from the inside out, we begin on the inside, in our relationship with God. Yet as we connect deeply with other people, we make room for Christ to dwell within us personally and among us in community with one another. The intertwined roots of faith encourage us to "live from the soul," reflecting God's love in many ways, including the five practices of fruitful living.

# Responding to God's Grace

From Paul's prayer in Ephesians 3:16–19, we know that the power working individually within us and exponentially within our faith community is not our power, but the power of God. It is God's grace at work among us whenever we allow God to work through us, and to work through others upon us. When we respond positively to God's grace, the fullness of God continues to grow in our lives.

"Sanctification" is the church word for how we live in response to God's grace. The dictionary defines it as "the state of *growing* in divine grace as a result of Christian commitment after baptism or conversion." (italics mine)[22] Its generic meaning is "the state of proper functioning," referring to someone or something that is set apart for its designer's use. "A human being is sanctified, therefore, when he or she lives according to God's design and purpose."[23] The New Testament Greek word often translated as sanctification means "holiness." Even though no creature shares the holiness of God's essential nature, God calls people to be holy as God is holy (See 1 Peter 1:15, "be holy yourselves in all your conduct;" and Leviticus 11:44, "be holy as I am holy.")

As we noted previously, God and we can act together when we engage in spiritual disciplines—patterns of behavior that point us toward God and help us order our lives. When we do this, "grace is engrafted on our nature and the whole [person] is sanctified by the presence and action of the Holy Spirit."[24]

In Colossians 3:3–14, Paul lists three specific ways we can respond to God's grace, in obedience, in spiritual strength, and by growing in knowledge of God's will. Together, these practices point to the Colossians' leading "lives worthy of the Lord." Paul says he has learned that the gospel has been bearing fruit among them from the day they heard it and truly comprehended the grace of God.

Our gratitude is not only our *response* to God's grace, but also the *reflection* of God's mercy.[25] So it arises both from our initiative and as a gift from God. "Every breath we draw is a gift of [God's] love," says Thomas Merton:

> Every moment of existence is a grace, for it brings with it immense graces from [God]. Gratitude therefore takes nothing for granted, is never unresponsive, [and] is constantly awakening to new wonder and to praise of the goodness of God. For the grateful [person] knows that God is good, not by hearsay but by experience. And that is what makes all the difference.[26]

WHEN WE THINK of spiritual growth as a process of becoming, we may picture it like planting and nourishing a seed, allowing currents of water to flow, shifting from a false self to our truer self, or moving from one season to another across our lifespan. But regardless of which way we imagine spiritual growth, we can grow from the inside out, responding to God's grace.

With this perspective of seasons of the soul, we can encourage ourselves and others to grow from being uninvolved, distant financial donors, to becoming personally invested in a particular project as part of God's work, mindful of the people affected by it and the ways it will improve their lives. We can shift from merely engaging in transactional giving, to participating in transformational relationships. We can help ourselves and others grow from the inside out as loved and grateful children of God, created to live more fully in God's image.

# Questions for Reflection

1. In what ways do the metaphors of nourishing seeds or letting currencies flow through us help me more deeply understand my spiritual journey thus far?
2. Have I ever seen or experienced transformational giving? How was or is that different from merely transactional giving, perhaps in quality, presence, or purpose?
3. At what times have I grown spiritually by listening to and sharing with others, benefitting from the "interlaced roots" of one another's experiences?
4. When have I let go of surface preoccupations to "live from the soul?" Are there other times where I would benefit from doing so?

# Endnotes

1. Debra Dubin, "Congregations tend soil and soul with gardens," *Christian Century*, June 12, 2013, p. 17.
2. Ronald J. Greer, *op cit.*, pp. 54f, 60.
3. *Ibid.*, p. 54.
4. Eric H. F. Law, *Holy Currencies*, pp. 3f.
5. Lynne Twist, *The Soul of Money: Reclaiming the Wealth of Our Inner Resources* (New York, London: W. W. Norton & Company, 2003) p. 97.
6. *Ibid.*, p. 103.
7. Brian D. McLaren, *Naked Spirituality: A Life With God in 12 Simple Words* (HarperOne, 2011).
8. Lauren F. Winner, book review of *Naked Spirituality* in *Christian Century*, December 13, 2011, pp. 44f.
9. M. Basil Pennington, *True Self / False Self*, p. 31, cited in David G. Benner, *op cit.*, p. 81.
10. Ronald J. Greer, *op cit.*, pp. 44, 83.
11. Richard Rohr, *Falling Upward*, p. 86.
12. C. G. Jung, *Modern Man in Search of a Soul*, pp. 109f.
13. *Ibid.*, p. 71.
14. *Ibid.*, pp. 71f.
15. John C. Robinson, *op cit.*, p. 103.
16. *Ibid.*, p. 272.
17. Robert Schnase, *Five Practices of Fruitful Living* (Nashville: Abingdon Press, 2010), p. 163.
18. *Ibid.*, p. 164.
19. Father Diarmuid O'Murchu, "Becoming More Adult In Our Faith," retreat, July 16, 2008, Mercy Center, Auburn, CA.
20. Thomas Moore has been a member of a religious order, a musician, a university professor, and a psychotherapist. Today he lectures widely on holistic medicine, spirituality, psychotherapy, and ecology.
21. Thomas Moore, *Dark Nights of the Soul: A Guide to Finding Your Way Through Life's Ordeals* (New York: Penguin Random House, 2004), p. 294.
22. *merriam-webster.com/dictionary/sanctification*.
23. *biblestudytools.com/dictionary/sanctification*.
24. Thomas Merton, *op cit.*, p. 37.
25. *Ibid.*, p. 109.
26. *Ibid.*, p. 33.

# Gratitude

G RATITUDE IS THE bedrock upon which generosity is built, the soil in which it grows. So what does it mean to be grateful? Out of which kinds of relationships does gratitude come? Is it just a feeling, or more? An attitude? A way of life?

In recent years, an entire body of "gratitude research" has emerged, as scientists have studied its effects on a person's health, emotions, relationships, and even longevity. Further, there are activities a person can engage in to become more aware of life's gifts and more grateful for them. Most of us instinctively respond to a gift by giving something in return or giving something to others, in a cycle that opens us up to a deeper realization of the gifts we've been given. Together this flow of gratitude and giving provides the basis for a rich, deeply-lived life. In this chapter, we'll explore these aspects, leading to a multifaceted understanding of Christian gratitude.

## The Gratitude Process

What do we mean by the term *gratitude*? Most of us gain a threefold sense of the concept from our everyday experiences. When grateful, we:

- Willingly acknowledge that we have received a gift from outside ourselves;

- Intellectually recognize the value of the gift; and
- Emotionally appreciate the giver's kindness or other positive intentions in giving the gift to us.[1] The gift may be a benefit or personal gain which is material, emotional, or spiritual, adding meaning or quality to our lives.

Gratitude is also inherently motivating, moving us to share the goodness we have received from others.[2] It gives us the opportunity to enjoy, learn, or act in a way that benefits other people. We show our gratitude not merely by saying "Thanks," but by doing something positive with what has been given to us.[3]

We can see three natural stages in the gratitude process.[4] First we *stop* for a moment from our usual round of doing, in order to pay particular attention. Second, we *look* with mindfulness or "loving awareness,"[5] to experience the gift itself, or to value the positive surprise of life in this specific moment. And third, we *do* something with the gift, or give something to someone else in response. Throughout this process, "gratitude is a felt sense of wonder, thankfulness, and appreciation for life."[6]

The biblical Moses gives us a dramatic example in his encounter with God at the burning bush (Exodus 3:1—4:20). He is tending sheep near Mount Horeb (also called Sinai), and sees a bush that is burning but not consumed by the flames. "I must turn aside and look at this great sight," he says. (*Stop*, first stage.) When he arrives at the bush, he realizes that the Living God is calling to him out of it, and he takes his shoes off in awareness that it is "holy ground." (*Look*, second stage.) Finally, he responds with awe and gratitude for this divine encounter by following God's command, leaving the wilderness and all that he has acquired. God tells him to return to Egypt, where he is wanted for murder, to confront Pharaoh on behalf of his people. (*Do*, third stage.)

We can see the internal dynamics of this three-step flow of gratitude in many of the Psalms, as well.[7] First, they recognize receiving a favor; second, they experience a powerful contrast of emotions (such as tears in the evening and cries of joy the next morning); and third, they jubilantly share their experience with others.

Such a response of gratitude is not only to the gift, but also to the goodness or positive intention of the giver. It is also a response that can deepen over time with multiple experiences. Psychologist Charles Shelton, a leader in the scientific study of gratitude, charts increasing levels of gratitude that are possible for us as we move from:

Thank You, to
Thankfulness, to
An Attitude of Gratitude, to
Gratitude as a Trait, to
A Disposition, and finally to
Gratitude as a Way of Life.[9]

At each of these levels, the person graduates from a slight focus on goodness to a commitment to pass on goodness to someone else, from minimal thought about the gift to a profound intent to give back in some way, and from few gestures of compassion to continual acts of kindness.

# A Joyful Response of Praise

All of this leads to a sense of joy in living! Brother David Steindl-Rast, one of the leaders in gratitude research, says that when you receive and enjoy something, "the heart fills up with gratefulness to overflowing, and then it overflows with joy."[10] Jack Kornfield, his Buddhist colleague in the gratitude movement, says, "The joy is allowing ourselves to shift from doing to the quality of loving awareness, gratitude, sacred presence—to the mystery of being here."[11]

In Old Testament times, *todah* was the praise offering made in the Jerusalem Temple. It involved burning a sacrificed animal and a loaf of bread on the altar. It was considered an act of praise through remembering God's saving deeds in the past: an action accompanied by song.[12] The word for "offering," *minha*, literally means "gift," so the sacrifice was meant to "give back" something to God.[13] In the Bible, the Hebrew word *todah* is variously translated into English as "praise," "thanksgiving" or "gratitude," depending upon its context.

In modern Hebrew, *todah* has come to mean "thank you." Today, Judaism teaches two themes related to gratitude: first, cultivating gratitude to God; and second, nurturing gratitude in human relationships.[14] Jewish prayers, teachings and related concepts such as the practice of giving thanks all reflect these two understandings.

This sense of "sacrifice of praise" carries over into the Christian practice of Holy Communion. The Greek word for this meal of bread and cup is *eucharistos*, or Eucharist. It means an "act of giving thanks."[15] *Charis*, the Greek word for "thanks," goes back to the sense of a person's "gracious address to another" and one person's turning to assist another.[16] As *charis* was used in relation to God, over time it developed into a description of God's "grace" or "graciousness," and found its true place within worship liturgy and praise of God.[17]

Paul uses *charis* as his central concept of grace: describing God's freely-given gift of Jesus' life and death for us. In Romans 5:20–21, he says that God's Law increases our awareness of sin so that God's grace multiplies even more—by God's "justifying us," or "turning us around" to be able to face God once again. In Paul's letters to the Christians in Rome and Corinth, he uses "grace" to express thanks to God, and to the Gentile congregations for supporting the Jerusalem church as it aided its region during a long famine.[18]

Truly giving back to God is impossible, since everything belongs to God already. So praise—giving, receiving, and giving back—is both a duty and a delight. The delight is the practice of gratitude itself, praising and thanking God. The duty is the flip side of gratitude: showing loving responsibility for all that God has entrusted to us. As Old Testament scholar Walter Brueggemann says, "Praise is the duty and delight, the ultimate vocation of the human community."[19]

One example of this two-pronged gratitude is the L.A.S.T. program: Learning And Serving Together. In the summer of 2013, more than two hundred youth from nineteen United Methodist churches participated in an eight-week, hands-on mission venture in Portland and Eugene, Oregon. The participants came from congregations in Montana, California, Idaho, Washington, and Oregon.

They engaged in activities that had an impact, including making 2,000 lunches a day for a free lunch program in a park in Eugene, organizing donations at a new food bank, and playing all day with at-risk children at a local community gathering place. Some groups working in Portland tore down walls of a 100-year-old church building to turn it into a community center. They also tended a new community garden. Other groups spent time at Dignity Village, a homeless community near the Portland airport. All of this was with loving responsibility. But it was also the delight, as each evening the group members at all the sites reflected on their experiences, and on how Jesus' life and ministry call us to go beyond our comfort zones, into our communities.[20]

Another example comes from Grace United Methodist Church in Three Springs, Pennsylvania. The largest congregation in a six-church parish, Grace has 90 members with 40 to 50 in worship on a Sunday. But their gratitude and ministries are larger than their numbers. Since 2006, they have hosted a 90-minute after-school program called Mondays with Jesus. Children ages five through twelve jump off the school bus for the program that includes a snack, a Bible lesson in three age-group classes, a craft or recreation, and closing with everyone singing together or seeing a video or puppet drama.

In the spring of 2013, the church began a health ministry program to educate members of the church and the community on health-related topics. Then they initiated an annual dinner to show their appreciation to the local volunteer firefighters and ambulance personnel and their spouses. Next, a small group of their young adults began Hot Grace, where they prepare and freeze casseroles and soups to give to community members in the midst of crisis. In the fall of 2013, they heard about the need for backpacks for some local elementary-school students and managed to buy and stuff six backpacks with school supplies for one child in each grade, kindergarten through fifth grade. Meantime, their contemporary Christian music praise team began traveling to other churches in the area, and to local extended-care residential facilities. They appropriately named the music effort Grace Unplugged.[21]

So what about the "delight" side of their service to others? "The teachers at Mondays With Jesus say the kids are more of a blessing than they are work for them," reports pastor Ken Grundon.[22] "We consider ourselves 'first responders in faith.' If there's a need in the community, we try to fill it. Our delight is the joy of serving Christ and meeting the needs of our sisters and brothers in the world today."

Thus far, we have seen that gratitude is a joyful process where we *stop* to pay attention, *look* at the gift or wonder of life, and *do* something to give to or share with others in response. But gratitude is also a relationship, where we receive, often accept our dependence upon something provided by someone else, and then desire to do something positive in return.

After receiving a heart transplant that saved her life, one woman put it this way:

> I have found that it is not enough for me to be thankful. I have a desire to do something in return. To do thanks. To give thanks. Give things. Give thoughts. Give love. So gratitude becomes the gift, creating a cycle of giving and receiving, the endless waterfall. Filling up and spilling over. To give from the fullness of my being.[23]

Her wish to give does not come from a sense of obligation. "Rather, it is a spontaneous charitableness," she says. "It is the simple passing on of the gift."[24]

Henri Nouwen, Catholic priest, psychologist, and devotional writer, says that gratitude flows out of our recognition that who we are and what we have are gifts for us to receive and share.[25] Generosity and gratitude are not two sides of some prescribed agreement. A grateful person is much freer and feels vastly different from a person who is in debt.[26] The person who has received a gift not only appreciates his or her pre-existing relationship with the giver, but also often is inspired by that kindness to enter into a relationship of helping others in some way in the future.

Pastor Don Lee grounds this relationship in God's relationship with us when he tells his congregation,

> In our own personal experiences of "resurrection," it is never our doing that brings the shift to new life, but only through God's gracious action toward us and all creation[, often seen by others' generosity toward us]. We are left with the privilege of response: gratitude. It is with gratitude that we are called to be alive. It is with gratitude that we can wake in the morning and lie down at night. It is with gratitude that we can give some part of ourselves to something bigger than ourselves. And like a circle or spiral of life, when thankfulness is our response to God's graciousness, then blessings abound and new life is multiplied over and over.[27]

In the process of this two-way relationship with God and other people, grateful persons help sustain a healthy community.[28]

Glenn Taibl, then Co-Director of Luther Seminary's Center for Stewardship Leaders, suggested that we replace the traditional "Three T's" of stewardship—Time, Talent and Treasure—with Thanksgiving, Trust, and Transformation.[29] Giving thanks invites us to look at the time God has given us as a precious gift, and to search for ways to use it wisely. God trusts us so much that God gives us all the abilities we need to create community, heal what is broken, and bring hope where there is indifference or despair. Transformation takes place when we allow God to change the way we look at everything we have received (our lives, our minds, our talents, everything) in order to live out our values. Because of the fundamental trust God has for us, says Brother David Steindl-Rast, in most situations we can "respond gratefully to every given situation, out of trust in the Giver."30

# A Grateful Perspective

So gratitude is both a threefold process and a mutual relationship between giver and receiver. But it is also a distinctive emotion—a feeling that depends upon attitude and thinking. The receiver is prompted not only by the giver's kind action, but also by the receiver's own understanding, reflection, and openness to accepting the giver's goodness in giving[31]—what Charles Shelton calls "grateful reasoning."[32]

Henri Nouwen affirms how gratitude involves a conscious choice, despite our feelings, as we focus our thoughts on "all that is worthy of praise." (Philippians 4:8–10)[33]

We cannot change most of the circumstances that happen to us, whether they are good or bad. But we can change the way we intentionally react to the situation.[34] Even as we may feel loss or injury, we can seek support from friends, pray for God's guidance and comfort, participate in exercise, look for a life lesson, or engage in some other positive activity. And the longer we think about the gifts we have received, the more sustained our gratitude becomes. After keeping a daily gratitude journal as part of a study, one person said, "It is so easy to get caught up in the process of daily living that I sometimes forget to stop and remember the reason why I get up every morning. Your study helped me to form a pattern to take time each day to remember the beautiful things in life."[35]

The more we involve ourselves in the gratitude process, relate gratefully to God and to other people, and think about the goodness of those who have given to us, the more we develop an ongoing attitude or worldview of gratitude. It begins to overcome its opposites: thoughtlessness, forgetfulness, superiority, selfishness, and a sense of entitlement.[36] Studies have confirmed that gratitude is like a muscle: it becomes stronger the more we use it, giving us a brighter outlook on life as a whole.[37]

In her book *Attitudes of Gratitude*, M. J. Ryan writes,

Gratitude is like a flashlight. It lights up what is already there. You don't necessarily have anything more or different, but suddenly you can actually see what is. And because you can see, you no longer take it for granted.[38]

With sustained awareness and intentionality, gratitude becomes "a generous acknowledgement of all that sustains us, about our blessings great and small."[39]

This worldview brings us to live fully in the present, but not to grasp it with white-knuckled fierceness. By contrast, psychologist David Benner says that people struggling with a false self can develop excessive attachments. One person might cling to her possessions, accomplishments, or space. Another may seize on his dreams, memories or friendships. These things are a "blessing when they are held in open hands of gratitude," but they become a curse when they are grasped tightly in fists of entitlement and viewed as solely "mine."[40]

Such attention to and enjoyment of the present gives us hope for the future, as well. In 1 Corinthians 1:4–7, Paul says, "I give thanks to my God always for you, because of the grace of God that has been given to you in Christ Jesus, for in every way you have been enriched in him. . . ." Note that in each present moment God *already* has given us all kinds of gifts out of God's grace, including "speech and knowledge of every kind . . . so that you are not lacking in any spiritual gift."

Later in the same letter, Paul tells us that among the gifts God has given us are: wisdom and knowledge, faith and healing, miracles and prophecy (1 Corinthians 12:8–11), as well as the "still more excellent way" of love itself (1 Corinthians 12:31; 13:1). Based upon our experience of God's generous gift-giving already in our lives, we can wait with patience for God to fulfill all God's promises to us, and to creation (Romans 8:25).[41]

Thus far we have seen that gratitude is a process, a relationship, an emotion-plus-thought, then becoming an attitude that can translate into a worldview. Likewise, as the various aspects of gratitude deepen, they become a way of living. "Being disposed to be grateful may now, if [someone] practices it, become what we call her 'character,'" says Margaret Visser.

> Gratitude arises from a specific circumstance—being given a gift or done a favour—but depends less upon that than on the receiver's whole life, her character, upbringing, maturity, experience, relationships with others, and also on her ideals, including her idea of the sort of person she is or would like to be.[42]

Charles Shelton notes that when gratitude becomes a way of life, its qualities are transformed into a commitment to give away goodness; a profound intent to give back; continual acts of kindness; a view of the world as filled with gifts; memory focused on the theme of "gifts given me;" radical openness to the world, and to others; a welcome sense of dependence upon other people; emotional experiences that lead to humility and hope; and the willingness to find meaning and strive for growth out of suffering.[43]

In other words, gratitude becomes more than a disposition or worldview, instead soaking into the nature of the person. Philosopher Soren Kierkegaard "suggested that, in thankfulness, a person's relationship to God and others gives birth to a self-awareness that constitutes his being."[44] This points to the value of how gratitude can shape our identity in a beneficial way.

As gratitude takes hold of our soul or essential self, it increasingly serves as a catalyst for how we perceive and act in the world. Gratitude becomes a "moral habit"—that is, a habitual pattern of right choices and actions based upon them.[45] Gratitude is a "right" choice not because we are obligated to respond a certain way, but because it seems natural and right to acknowledge a gift. Recipients can learn to notice gifts given to them, and to assess what the giver's motives may be in giving. They can also decide to recall events regularly and to "reframe" them to emphasize what they have gained rather than what they have lost. In this way, gratitude becomes "second nature."[46]

In the fundraising classic *The Seven Faces of Philanthropy*, authors Russ Prince and Karen File report on studies that identify several primary motivations for giving among major donors. In it, they say ten percent of those who make large gifts to nonprofit organizations can be called "repayers." These givers see themselves as doing good in return for having received a significant gift from the organization: often healing in a hospital or education from a school. Their own experiences shifted their perspective on life or on the purpose of giving. Having personally benefitted from the charity, they now choose to give back, to help others in a similar situation. This pivotal experience transforms them into different persons from who they were before they received the gift.[47]

Two other types of major donors give out of a sense of gratitude that has become part of their character. One type (21 percent of them) is what Prince and File call "devout." They see themselves as doing good, because it is God's will or because of the moral teachings of their religion. For them, giving is not a contractual exchange, but a way of giving something of themselves. The other grateful-character type is the "altruist" (nine percent of major donors). They give because it feels right, and their giving offers a greater sense of purpose. They tend to associate giving with spiritual development and social causes.[48]

Whatever one's reason for giving, the gratitude that has become part of a person's character tends to stand out over a lifetime. Such is the case with Milton and Catherine Hershey. Unable to have children of their own, they used part of the wealth from their chocolate business to found the Hershey Industrial School in 1909. That year, the school opened its doors to four young boys to attend classes there and to live in Milton Hershey's home. After Catherine Hershey died a few years later, Milton Hershey gave virtually his entire fortune to the school to provide for its future continuation. Today, Milton Hershey School is the country's "largest pre-kindergarten through grade 12 home and school for boys and girls from families of low income and social need."[49] It provides free education and housing, clothing, and meals for all the years of the students' residence there, as well as free medical, dental, religious, and other services.

# The Benefits of Gratitude

"Gratitude has the power to heal, to energize, and to change lives," said researcher Robert Emmons at the 2014 Greater Good Gratitude Summit.[50] "We're here to celebrate the science and the spirit of gratitude." These comments came from a university professor of psychology who oversees scientific studies that measure the physical, emotional, and relational effects of gratitude. Supported by three-year major funding from the John Templeton Foundation, he and other leading researchers oversee more than two dozen ongoing studies measuring evidence of gratitude's effects.

Most people in a Christian community have heard about gratitude within the context of our faith, as a primary response to God's love. So the surprising element for us in recent years has been to hear about *scientific studies* of gratitude in secular academic circles. Professors and scientists from various universities have been conducting the studies largely since the year 2000 in centers such as the Greater Good Science Center at the University of California, Davis and at institutions of higher education including Harvard Medical School, Cornell University, other universities across the United States, and the University of Stirling in England. Projects at other institutions are taking place, as well, including Massachusetts General Hospital.

In 2011, in collaboration with the University of California, Davis, the Greater Good Science Center launched a three-year project called Expanding the Science and Practice of Gratitude. Since then, they have sponsored twenty-nine original research projects, launched a digital Gratitude Journal called *Thnx4.org*; published dozens of articles and videos about new studies, and shared their research through talks, seminars, and major press coverage.

The overall effects of gratitude are that it is good for our bodies, our minds, and our relationships.[51] The types of research in progress cover an amazing range. For example, Robert Emmons and Michael McCullough conducted a study on persons with neuromuscular disease, where the gratitude-outlook group "exhibited heightened well-being across several, though not all, of the outcome measures."[52]

A University of British Columbia study of children showed how "kids get a happiness boost from sacrificing for others."[53] Twenty toddlers, all a month or two shy of their second birthday, were introduced to a monkey puppet who "likes treats." Through a series of activities, observers reported that the children:

> appeared happier when they gave away a treat than when they received a treat, and they displayed the greatest happiness when they gave away one of their own treats; this "costly giving" even made them happier than giving away a found treat at no cost to themselves.[54]

A third study asked college students to do five acts of kindness per week for six weeks. One group of students did all five acts of kindness in one day, a second group could spread out their acts of kindness over the week, and a third (control) group were given no instructions about kind actions. Those who did all five acts in one day saw the greatest change. "You start to see yourself as a generous person," says researcher Sonya Lyubomirsky, "as interconnected to others. It makes you interpret other people's behavior more charitably, and it relieves distress over other people's misfortune. . . ."[55]

Gratitude has positive side effects for the whole person. Gratitude allows us to celebrate the present by magnifying our positive emotions. It also blocks toxic, negative emotions such as envy, resentment, regret, and even depression. Grateful people are more resistant to stress, recovering emotionally more quickly from adversity. In addition, grateful people have a higher sense of self-worth. They feel that others have provided for their well-being, or that they have a network of past and present relationships that is helping them get to where they are right now.

In fact, author Charles Shelton describes nine possible positive effects of gratitude in a person's life:

- Maturity—Feeling more like an adult by taking greater responsibility for one's actions;
- Inspiration—Encouraged to become a better person in one's various roles;
- Insight—Recognizing the blessings in what one has; not taking it for granted anymore;
- Positive behaviors—Increasingly sensitive and generous toward others, responding with more care and greater understanding;
- Prompting other positive emotions—e.g., impelled to feel more hope or less worry or anger;
- Dependency—Sensing one can rely upon others, leading to an experience of interdependence;
- Greater awareness—Acknowledging goodness in the world, treasuring things more, or being touched by awe and wonder;
- More than enough—Having a sense of inner fulfillment and peace, which creates a sense of contentment, regardless of the amount of one's possessions;
- An open mind—Able to venture beyond personal biases and preconceived notions, to see the generosity of others or new ways of viewing one's world.[56]

One Greater Good Science Center study has been exploring gratitude's effects on health and longevity. Results so far show that gratitude contributes to better well-being, lowers anxiety and anger, creates more social connections with others, improves sleep quality, and lowers blood pressure both at rest and during activity. Biologically, gratitude produces oxytocin in the body: a neuropeptide associated with affiliation, cooperation, and trust.[57]

In addition to general physical benefits, increased gratitude produces stronger immune systems, more exercise, better care of his or her health, and fewer aches and pains.[58]

Four studies illustrate a direct biological connection.

Recent research on organ donations showed that "the more grati-tude a recipient of an organ feels, the faster that person's recovery."[59] When seventy-four participants were questioned about their feelings at receiving such a "gift of life," those who expressed their gratitude directly or indirectly in their journals felt physically better and func-tioned at a higher level than those who did not.

The second study, conducted in 1995, found that just five minutes focusing on gratitude can shift a person's nervous system toward a calm state.[60] That physiological state, called "resonance," is usually experienced during deep relaxation and sleep. It occurs when a per-son's heart, breathing, blood pressure, brain rhythm, and electrical potential of the skin are synchronized.

A third set of findings correlated a person's level of appreciation with rises in some of the body's immune antibodies, which can be a major defense against disease.[61]

The fourth study was conducted by Jeff Huffman, a professor and psychiatrist at Harvard Medical School. It measured the effects of gratitude on heart attack survivors. By testing people while they are in the hospital, two weeks later, three months and six months later, he noted that people who show gratitude (by both self-check and biomarkers) exercise more and eat healthier foods and have a better quality of life. Results showed that gratitude has positive biological effects, and protects against a sense of hopelessness, as well as car-diac events.[62]

Further research showed that since gratitude is a source of human strength and relational well-being, emotions and relationships go hand-in-hand.[63] Emotional benefits of gratitude include feeling more alert, alive, and awake, and having higher levels of positive emotions, more joy, pleasure, and optimism.[64] Benefits spill over into social relationships, as well. The grateful person acts more gener-ously, compassionately and helpfully toward others, is more outgo-ing and forgiving, and feels less lonely and isolated.[65]

The relationship between gratitude and joy is particularly strong. A 1998 Gallup survey of American teenagers and adults found that over half of the respondents who saw themselves as grateful felt extremely happy, and 95 percent of them felt at least somewhat happy. The report concluded, "Grateful people tend to be less materialistic and thus more easily satisfied with what life brings them."[66]

Greater Good project advisor Philip Watkins is a professor of psychology at Eastern Washington University. His research revealed how gratitude enhances well-being through cognitive processes, and increases one's desire to affiliate with others, even when there is a cost to oneself. It found that gratitude enhances our tendency to include more people in our lives, helps us each out to others, and reminds us of those who are helpful to our well-being, as well as bringing us closer in our existing relationships.[67]

The long-term benefits of gratitude can reverberate down the years, as the practice of gratitude becomes a discipline or pattern of living. "Our research has led us to conclude that experiencing gratitude leads to increased feelings of connectedness, improved relationships, and even altruism," says Robert Emmons. "We have also found that when people experience gratitude, they feel more loving, more forgiving, and closer to God."[68]

In one study of women in midlife, those who had received mentoring by older adults when they were young were much more likely twenty years later to be mentors themselves.[69] Over time, positive emotions such as gratitude broaden and increasingly influence how we think and act.[70]

We are not grateful *in order to* receive all these benefits. But it is amazing how the impulse to give, out of gratitude, ends up rewarding the giver just as much, if not more, than the recipient.

## Practicing a Grateful Attitude

The more aware we are of God's gifts, the more grateful we tend to be. Granted, there are no sure-fire exercises to guarantee our joy. But there are intentional activities that can help us savor the moment and notice the goodness in our lives.

So what are some ways that we can express our gratitude and practice it regularly? Reminiscent of Steindl-Rast's three-part gratitude process of stop, look, do, Charles Shelton's *Daily Gratitude Inventory*[71] offers a great four-part exercise we can practice:

*Pause* to breathe deeply, letting go of our surface preoccupations;

*Review* what has happened in the previous twenty-four hours: everyday experiences, significant people;

*Relish* the reasons for our gratitude, slowly repeating after each one a phrase such as "I am gifted;" and then

*Respond* by reflecting on how we could give back in gratitude for the gifts we have received today. I can note who I am (my life history, strengths, and situation), and what I feel moved to do.[72]

Another way of reviewing the day and expressing gratitude is by *stating the reasons we are grateful and rating the level of our commitment each day.*[73] On a scale of 1 to 5 (with 5 meaning most grateful), we list various reasons for our gratitude. For example, I may reflect on how being grateful helps me make a difference, allows me to recognize God's faithfulness, deepens my sense of meaning and purpose, enhances my well-being, or nurtures friendship. We can build our own list of reasons and then rank them, finally circling our top five priority reasons for being grateful.

An alternative activity is to *spot the reasons for our gratitude throughout the day.* Noting each gift as it happens, we can whisper, "Thank you."[74] This way we increase our awareness immediately and give ourselves an opportunity to respond.

Or we can write down our reasons in a *Gratitude Journal.* Use of a Gratitude Journal is a common practice in many of the scientific gratitude studies undertaken so far. Participants choose a regular time of day, such as the first thing each morning, or the last thing each night. While it may feel odd at first, listing what we feel grateful for and what joy the day has brought lifts a person's mood. We can recall moments of gratitude associated with events, personal attributes, or valued people in our life. The act of writing them down affirms a source of goodness in life and may help us reframe a difficult situation. Reading past days' entries gives a larger perspective and can get us in the habit of countering bad things in our day with reflections on the good.[75]

For example, Jo-Ann Tsang of Baylor University tested to see if daily Gratitude Journals might improve the physical and psychological well-being of Alzheimer's caregivers. For two weeks, half of the participants wrote down what they were thankful for each day, while the other half listed daily hardships they had experienced. Those who journaled about their blessings celebrated small victories, such as "Bill called me by my name," or he "remembered it was July, not January."[76] The caregivers who kept Gratitude Journals experienced reduced stress and lower depression levels and had an increase in their overall well-being.

But expressing our gratitude does not have to require words. For example, we may bring photos or magazine *pictures that reflect our gratitude* to a special "Expressions of Gratitude" bulletin board. Or we may post pictures from our Instagram page to the congregation's Instagram, Facebook, or website page. Other means of cultivating an attitude of gratitude include: finding ways to *connect with loved ones on a regular basis*; inviting people to join us more often in our regular activities; and creating a *whimsical photo album* of good memories to enjoy from time to time.[77]

Staying active is one important non-verbal way to encourage gratitude. One session of *physical exercise* can raise our mood for up to six months, whether we are gardening, exploring our neighborhood on foot, or socializing with a friend while taking a walk. Social support encourages healthy behaviors. One study showed that participants recruited with friends for a program of weight-loss and exercise had a 95 percent completion rate, versus 76 percent for those recruited alone. Sixty-six percent of them kept all their weight off for six months, versus 24 percent of those recruited by themselves.[78]

*Adults modeling grateful behavior* makes a difference, too. In one study of youth conducted by a Harvard psychologist, 80 percent of the participants said their parents were more concerned about their teenagers' achievements than whether or not the teens cared about other people.[79] So he developed a five-point process for parents to express daily thanks for people who contributed positively in their lives, in order to teach and model caring for their children. He also recommended parents include people of other communities and cultures in their circle of care.

One way to increase gratitude in the congregation is by *engaging a Gratitude Coach*. Wesley Leake, a business coach and spiritual leader in Brisbane, Australia, launched the Gratitude Coach movement by starting a Thirty-Day Gratitude Challenge, to help people live happier, more enriched lives.

In the United States after retiring from pastoral ministry, Kent Millard became a volunteer Gratitude Coach for churches of the Indiana Conference of the United Methodist Church. "I invite congregations not to start the conversation about giving with the needs of the congregation," Millard says. "I encourage them to start talking about the blessings God has already given each of us." He continues:

When people begin to count their blessings, they realize that God has blessed us abundantly. And if we feel any sense of gratitude for these blessings, we want to give to God in appreciation for all God has first given us.[80]

In Millard's book, *The Gratitude Path: Leading Your Church to Generosity*, he offers "a balanced practice of ministry" designed to be a process of faith formation to "transform your stewardship from a once a year event to a year round practical philosophy of generous giving."[81]

# The Basis for a Life of Gratitude

Gratitude became embedded in me from a very young age, through camping in the mountains. I have never lost the sense of wonder and thankfulness at seeing a crimson sunrise over a high meadow, the intricacy of a flower, or afternoon light sifting through the trees. I marvel at the generosity of our artist God, who lets human beings enjoy God's creation. Through many adult years, hiking has been a form of meditation and grateful prayer, filled with a sense of being with God.

For people of faith, gratitude always starts with God's generous giving. Benedictine Brother David Steindl-Rast uses the term *gratefulness*, which he defines as "that fullness of life for which all of us are thirsting," a kind of "heart-vision" where we see that "all is gratuitous," meaning freely given to us.[82] He understands gratefulness as comprising the ongoing actions of thanksgiving, blessing, and praise. Such a rhythm is our whole-hearted reply—meaning the response of the whole person—to God's presence and love.[83]

A cycle of thanksgiving, blessing, and praise can form the basis for a lifetime of gratitude, with at least three dimensions:

- First, openness to being thankful for the gifts that life brings;
- Second, awareness that many of these gifts come from beyond ourselves and beyond humanly-made circumstances; and
- Third, a desire to pass on our gifts to the world in which we live.

Whatever its form, a grateful response does not have to include traditional church involvement or being institutionally religious. Renowned sociologist Robert Wuthnow of Princeton University says that most people define "spirituality" as "their relationship to God."[84] He notes that a few people prefer to substitute the phrase "higher power" or "divine being," but they still see it as a "transcendent connection," looking beyond the limits of our mortal lives. Any of these terms for God fit with many mystic expressions such as those of Br. David Steindl-Rast and Buddhist monk Jack Kornfield, who spoke at a Greater Good Gratitude Summit. "Gratitude is a generous acknowledgement of all that sustains us, about our blessings great and small," said Kornfield. "As gratitude increases, it gives rise to joy."[85]

Steindl-Rast immediately agreed. "This is the nature of deep, authentic spirituality," he said. His book, *Gratefulness: The Heart of Prayer*, echoes this joyous true-self theme. In it he notes the many dimensions of expressing our gratitude by giving thanks: our *intellect* recognizes that all that exists is fundamentally a gift;[86] our *will* acknowledges the interdependence of the giver (God) and the human "thanks-giver;" and our *emotions* celebrate the joy of our belonging to each other.[87]

We are saved by God's generosity, states Miroslav Volf in his remarkable book, *Free of Charge*.[88] He asks, What does God, the Creator, Christ, and Holy Spirit, give to us? "The [Creator] gives existence and grounded trust," says Volf. "The [Redeemer] gives salvation and active love. The [Consummator] gives eternal life and living hope."[89]

Volf makes three crucial points about God as giver:

- God is the *first* giver, giving to us from what originally and exclusively belongs to God. (Romans 11:35) By contrast, as 1 John 4:19 tells us, we give love only because God first gave love to us.
- God is the *infinite* giver, since God exists without measure and can give without measure. God's vitality and resources are never depleted. (2 Corinthians 9:8.)
- God is the *utterly loving* giver. "God doesn't just love; God *is* love." (1 John 4:16.)[90]
- "[God] showers a world gone awry with the gifts of eternal life and deliverance from sin," says Volf.[91] "The true God gives so we can become joyful givers and not just self-absorbed receivers."[92] God intends for us to flourish and to help others flourish, just as God blessed Abraham and his descendants in order for them to bless the world (Genesis 12:1–3).[93]

God's unlimited giving prompts us to full gratitude and joyful thanksgiving! Paul invites us, "Rejoice always. Pray without ceasing. Give thanks in all circumstances; for this is the will of God in Christ Jesus for you. Do not quench the Spirit." (1 Thessalonians 5:16–19)

This passage reveals three key aspects of a genuine faith community: they pray individually and together, they are thankful, and their gatherings are marked by joy.[94] Paul's words here to the Thessalonian Christians link the prayer life of the congregation with a resulting atmosphere of joy. Temporary happiness can occur because of fortuitous outward circumstances, but a deeper, more enduring joy comes from within: from a healthy relationship with God, with one's self, and with others.

Prayer without ceasing does not have to involve words or a certain outward ritual. It can be an underlying awareness of God's presence as we participate in our daily activities. It is an "attitude of the heart," a continual communication with God.[95] In this way, prayerfulness turns our entire lives into prayer, as we focus on our purpose, and lean into the meaning God can give to our lives.[96] Grateful living is itself continuous prayer, whatever our circumstances. As we pray, we can learn to live increasingly "by every word that comes from the mouth of God." (Matthew 4:4)[97]

Prayer can help us glimpse events from God's perspective, even if for a moment, by giving us a deeper understanding of the Scripture's intent, and by allowing us to sense more clearly God's will for our lives. As we pray, we can pray with attentiveness, with a growing trust in God, and with persevering love.[98]

Thus, First Thessalonians 5:16–19 guides us toward a deeper understanding of Christian gratitude. Researcher Charles Shelton defines Christian gratitude as "gratefully experiencing the grace-filled presence of Jesus within us." He says God has already gifted us with the goodness we seek, and the more that we accept and experience it, the more we want to share other people's goodness with those around us.[99]

As we move from periodic thankfulness toward expressing an entire lifetime of Christian gratitude, our internal gaze is transformed from one cherished moment of delight to the conscious joy of knowing God continues to love us, as the One who has loved us from the very beginning. (1 John 4:10).[100] This incomparable Good News prompts us to see ongoing gratitude as "a freely rendered and loving response to grace."[101]

Thomas Merton, the great Christian mystic and activist, writes, "Our knowledge of God is perfected by gratitude: we are thankful and rejoice in the experience of the truth that [God] is love."[102] Because prayer always reminds us that we depend upon God for everything, gratitude is "the heart of the Christian life."[103] At the same time, our gratitude is our freely-given response to God, and also reflects God's mercy, revealing us as made in God's image.

As WE HAVE SEEN, generosity grows out of human gratitude for the gift of life itself, which in turn arises out of God's generous giving. Gratitude embraces not only our feelings, but also our thinking and our will. It can move from a specific thank you to a basic stance, on to an attitude and a trait, and finally to a disposition which becomes the way that we live. Our gratitude naturally flows as both an inward sense of joy and an outward act of giving to others, out of who we are, and what we have. As gratitude defines more and more of our self-understanding, it becomes a moral habit, where we see gifts as intrinsic to the world and to life events, and where giving becomes an essential part of our character. We can consciously practice being grateful and expressing it to God and to other people. In this way, we are able to transform into the grateful, praising persons whom God intended us to be all along.

# Questions for Reflection

1. Thinking back to the turning points in my life so far, to whom and to what am I grateful, for keeping me heading in the direction of wholeness?
2. Thinking of Shelton's levels of gratitude, how have I experienced gratitude primarily as general thankfulness, a disposition or a trait, an attitude, or a way of life? What practices help me remember God's grace in the past, and be grateful?

3. Describe a time when I gave thankfully in response to a sense of God's presence and love.

# Endnotes

1. Robert A. Emmons, *Thanks! How Practicing Gratitude Can Make You Happier*, p. 3. Emmons cites two studies (in 1985 and 2001) showing that gratitude includes recognizing: first, that the receiver has received a positive outcome, and second, that an external source provided it at a cost to himself or herself (R. A. Emmons and Michael McCullough, *The Psychology of Gratitude*, p. 9).
2. ———, *Thanks!* p. 4.
3. Brother David Steindl-Rast in *The Practice of Grateful Living* DVD.
4. *Ibid.*
5. Jack Kornfield in *ibid.*
6. Robert A. Emmons and Charles M. Shelton, "Gratitude and the Science of Positive Psychology," in *Handbook of Positive Psychology*, ed. C. R. Snyder and Shane J. Lopez (New York: Oxford University Press, 2002), 460; cited in Charles M. Shelton, *The Gratitude Factor: Enhancing Your Life through Grateful Living* (Mahwah, NJ: Hidden Spring, Paulist Press, 2010) p. 86.
7. Margaret Visser, *The Gift of Thanks: The Roots and Rituals of Gratitude* (Boston, New York: Houhhton Mifflin Harcourt, 2008) p. 165.
8. *Ibid.*, p. 382.
9. Charles M. Shelton, *op cit.*, p. 159.
10. Br. David Steindl-Rast in *The Practice of Grateful Living* (DVD).
11. Jack Kornfield in *ibid.*
12. Margaret Visser, *op cit.*, pp. 264f.
13. *Ibid*, p. 166.
14. R. A. Emmons and Michael McCullough, ed., *The Psychology of Gratitude*, (Oxford University Press, 2004), p. 12.
15. Zondervan Publishing House, *The Analytical Greek Lexicon (1975), p. 177.* See also Alfred Marshall, *The Interlinear Greek-English New Testament,*(Grand Rapids, MI: William B. Eerdmans Publishing Company, 1974) p. 812 re. 1 Thessalonians 5:17.
16. Friedrich, Gerhard, ed., *Theological Dictionary of the New Testament, Volume IX*, p. 377.
17. *Ibid.*, p. 379. Luke 1:30 uses the term for "to find grace," and Acts 7:46 uses it for "to give." Luke 2:40 uses the word to refer to God's "grace" resting on the child.
18. See Romans 6:17; 7:25; 1 Corinthians 15:57; and 2 Corinthians 8:16; 9:15.
19. Walter Brueggemann cited in John M. Buchanan, "Duty and Delight," *Christian Century* November 14, 2012.

20. "Learning and Serving Together (L.A.S.T.)," California-Nevada Conference *Instant Connection*, January 9, 2014.
21. Ken Grundon, "Putting feet to faith in the 'shadow of the steeple,'" Susquehanna *LINK*, Fall 2013.
22. August 27, 2014 phone interview of Rev. Kenneth B. Grundon, co-pastor of the Three Springs United Methodist Parish, Pennsylvania.
23. Elizabeth Bartlett, cited in Robert A. Emmons, *Thanks!* p.7.
24. *Ibid.*
25. Henri J. M. Nouwen, *The Spirituality of Fund-Raising*, p. 33.
26. Margaret Visser, *op cit.,* pp. 282f.
27. Rev. Don Lee, Sierra Pines United Methodist Church, Auburn, California, newsletter, April, 2007.
28. In *Living Into Community: Cultivating Practices That Sustain Us*, Christine D. Pohl names gratitude as one of four core practices that sustain a healthy community. She identifies the other three practices as promise-keeping, truthfulness, and hospitality.
29. Glenn Taibl, "Thanksgiving, Trust and Transformation: The Three T's of Stewardship," Luther Seminary's Center for Stewardship Leaders, March 11, 2014; *luthersem.edu/stewardship/newsletterarchives.*
30. Brother David Steindl-Rast, *Gratefulness,* p. 198.
31. Margaret Visser, *op cit.,* p. 2.
32. Charles Shelton, *op cit.,* pp. 53ff.
33. Henri Nouwen cited in Robert A. Emmons, *Thanks!* pp. 17f.
34. *Ibid.,* p. 24.
35. *Ibid.,* p. 47.
36. Margaret Visser, *op cit.,* p. 365.
37. *Wall Street Journal,* December 23, 2013, cited in *Christian Century,* January 22, 2014.
38. Cited in "Grateful Heart, Joyful Heart," from *Awakening Joy: 10 Steps to Happiness* by James Baraz and Shoshana Alexander; *gratefulness.org/readings.*
39. Jack Kornfield in "The Spirit of Gratitude" presentation, *The Greater Good Gratitude Summit,* June 7, 2014, Richmond, CA.
40. David G. Benner, *The Gift of Being Yourself,* p. 81.
41. See Christine Chakoian, pastor of First Presbyterian Church in Lake Forest, Illinois, "Reflections on the Lectionary, 1 Corinthians 1:3–9," in *Christian Century* November 15, 2011.
42. Margaret Visser, *op cit.,* p. 287.
43. *Charles* M. Shelton, *op cit.,* pp. 159–163.
44. P. S. Minear, "Thanksgiving as a synthesis of the temporal and eternal," in *A Kierkegaard Critique,* pp. 297–308, cited in R. A. Emmons and Michael McCullough, *The Psychology of Gratitude,* p. 13.
45. Charles Shelton, *op cit.,* pp. 153f; Margaret Visser, *op cit.,* pp. 292–4.

46. Margaret Visser, *op cit.*, p. 294.

47. Russ Prince and Karen File, *The Seven Faces of Philanthropy: A New Approach to Cultivating Major Donors* (San Francisco: Jossey-Bass Nonprofit and Public Management Series; November 30, 2001).

48. The seven different types of major givers are: Communitarian (26 percent); Devout (21 percent); Investor (15 percent); Socialite (11 percent); Repayer (10 percent); Altruist (9 percent); and Dynast (8 percent).

49. *Milton Hershey School* booklet.

50. June 7, 2014 Greater Good Gratitude Summit in Richmond, CA; sponsored by the Greater Good Science Center, an independent, donor-supported institute based at the University of California at Berkeley.

51. Robert Emmons, "Why Gratitude Is Good," at *http://greatergood.berkeley.edu/article/item/why_gratitude_is_good*.

52. —— and Michael McCullough, "The Blessings of Gratitude," abstract in the *Journal of Personality and Social Psychology, Vol. 84*, February 2003, pp. 377–389; from *http://psycnet.apa.org/journals/psp/84/2/377*.

53. Study by Lara Aknin and colleagues at the University of British Columbia, reported in "Being Kind Makes Kids Happy," by Delia Fuhrmann, August 1, 2012, at *http://greatergood.berkeley.edu/article/item/being_kind_makes_kids_happy*.

54. *Ibid.*

55. Sonja Lyubomirsky, "Happiness for a Lifetime," at *http://greatergood.berkeley.edu/article/item/happiness_for_a_lifetime?*

56. Charles M. Shelton, *op cit.*, pp. 98–106.

57. The Greater Good Science Center, *The Science of Gratitude: Proving the Power of Thanks*, p. 6; also presentation by Wendy Berry Mendes on panel, "The Gratitude Effect: Physical, Psychological and Social Benefits of Gratitude," at The Greater Good Gratitude Summit, June 7, 2014.

58. Robert Emmons, "Why Gratitude Is Good."

59. Stephen Post and Jill Neimark, *Why Good Things Happen to Good People* (New York: Broadway Books, Doubleday, 2007), p. 30.

60. Dr. Rollin McCraty, director of research for the Institute of HeartMath in Boulder Creek, California, cited in *ibid.*, p. 31.

61. Barbara Fullerton, "Generosity and Gratitude: Those who [practice] generosity and gratitude live longer," *Mandate*, November 2010.

62. The Greater Good Science Center, *The Science of Gratitude: Proving the Power of Thanks*, p. 5; also presentation by Jeff Huffman on panel, "The Gratitude Effect: Physical, Psychological and Social Benefits of Gratitude," at The Greater Good Gratitude Summit, June 7, 2014.

63. Robert A. Emmons and Cheryl A. Crumpler, University of California, Davis, in their abstract on "Gratitude as a Human Strength: Appraising the Evidence," at *guilfordjournals.com*.

64. Robert Emmons, "Why Gratitude Is Good."
65. *Ibid.*
66. Stephen Post and Jill Neimark, *op cit.*, pp. 40–31.
67. Greater Good Science Center, *The Science of Gratitude: Proving the Power of Thanks*, p. 11.
68. Robert Emmons, *Thanks!* p. 12.
69. Stephen Post and Jill Neimark, *op cit.*, p. 30.
70. Psychologist Barbara L. Frederickson, "Gratitude, Like Other Positive Emotions, Broadens and Builds," *The Psychology of Gratitude*, ed. Robert A. Emmons and Michael E. McCullough, p. 148.
71. Charles Shelton, *op cit.*, p. 53.
72. *Ibid.*, pp. 23–25.
73. *Ibid.*, p. 53.
74. Marilyn Brown Oden, "The Word and Our Words," *Upper Room Disciplines 2012* (Nashville: Upper Room Books, 2011), p. 23.
75. For reflections on a six-week experiment with this practice, see Catherine Price, "Stumbling toward Gratitude," at *http://greatergood.berkeley.edu/article*.
76. Robert Emmons, *Thanks!* p. 169.
77. Wayne Perry, "Seven Tips to Cultivate an Attitude of Gratitude," at *livescience. com*.
78. Sonja Lyubomirsky, "The How of Happiness: A Scientific Approach to Getting the Life You Want," at *amazon.com* re. *The How of Happiness;* Robert A Emmons, *Thanks! pp. 24, 200.*
79. *Washington Post* July 18, 2014, cited in *Christian Century* August 20, 2014.
80. Kent Millard, *The Gratitude Path: Leading Your Church to Generosity* (Nashville: Abingdon Press, 2015), cited in "The Gratitude Campaign," August 11, 2015, at *http://www.ministrymatters.com/leadl/entry/6228/the-gratitude-campaign*. A leadership team has turned this into an annual financial commitment campaign on the Conference website. Unfortunately, such a connection may reinforce public views that all references to "stewardship" are simply a lead-up to church requests for funds instead of its wider holistic understanding. A more powerful use of the Gratitude Sunday would be to hold it at a different time of year without reference to funding the church.
81. Rosanna Anderson's book review of *The Gratitude Path: Leading Your Church to Generosity*, at *www.umcdiscipleship.org/resources/book-review-the-gratitude-path-leading-your-church-to-generosity*.
82. Brother David Steindl-Rast, *Gratefulness, the Heart of Prayer*, pp. 88, 77.
83. *Ibid.*, pp. 82, 26.
84. *Religion and Ethics Newsweekly*, online companion to PBS.org television news, April 26, 2002, Episode No. 534.
85. Greater Good Gratitude Summit, June 7, 2014.
86. Brother David Steindl-Rast, *ibid.*, p. 201.

87. *Ibid.*, p. 216. These three aspects of the true self may remind us of Augustine's inner trinity: memory, understanding and will.
88. Miroslav Volf, *Free of Charge*, p. 20.
89. *Ibid.*, p. 74.
90. *Ibid.*, p. 62.
91. *Ibid.*, p. 64.
92. *Ibid.*, p. 28.
93. *Ibid.*, p. 60.
94. William Barclay, ed. *The Letters to the Philippians, Colossians, and Thessalonians*, The Daily Study Bible (Philadelphia: Westminster Press, Second Edition 1959), p. 240.
95. Brother David Steindl-Rast, *op cit.*, pp. 211, 41.
96. *Ibid.*, pp. 77f.
97. *Ibid.*, pp. 59, 11.
98. Francois Fenelon, "The Saints Converse With God" (sermon on 1 Thessalonians 5:17), in *20 Centuries of Great Preaching, Volume Two: Luther to Massillon, 1483. 1742*, by Clyde E. Fant, Jr. and William M. Pinson, Jr. (Waco, TX: Word Books, 1971), p. 381.
99. Charles Shelton, *The Gratitude Factor*, p. 158.
100. *Ibid.*, p. 163.
101. Margaret Visser, *op cit.*, p. 377.
102. Thomas Merton, *Thoughts in Solitude*, p. 31.
103. *Ibid.*, p. 105.

# Scarcity and the Lure of More

**M**OST OF US don't want to feel unsatisfied or lacking in any way. We don't think of ourselves as greedy or acquisitive. It's just that, at some important times, we want *more*—more time, more salary, more savings, more peace, more security, more rest, more achievement, more recognition, more *something* to feel more attractive, fulfilled, or loved.

A daily avalanche of advertising targets and threatens to engulf us. The average American family watches television at least seven hours a day, over 51 hours a week—complete with loads of commercials. "With only six percent of the world's population, America consumes 57 percent of the world's advertising," say marketing experts.[1] The average American receives 5,000 daily advertising impressions, designed to create and reinforce the false idea that spending money on an array of products necessarily leads to happiness and fulfillment.[2] Commercials constantly use images of wealth, fame, and sex appeal to sell everything from medications to jewelry to hamburgers, from cars to mortgages to online travel sites. They show up everywhere on virtually all media, from traditional print and television to all kinds of online platforms.

Many of us have houses full of stuff. We have garages that cars cannot fit into because the space is already full. We may even have storage lockers for what our houses and garages cannot hold. By contrast, many others ask themselves, "How can I deal with not having enough to make ends meet?" or "How can I live with wanting more than I can pay for?" When it comes to answering the question, "What is *enough* to live on?" a huge gap exists between rich and poor families, both worldwide and in our own communities.

Whether we think we have too much or not enough, Jesus tells us, "Do not worry about your life, what you will eat or what you will drink, or about your body, what you will wear. Is not life more than food, and the body more than clothing?" (Matthew 6:25) While we need to plan for the logistics of living, he warns us, "Take care! Be on guard against all kinds of greed; for one's life does not consist in the abundance of possessions." (Luke 12:15). Easy to say, hard to do.

# The Lure of More

Statistics may surprise us when we reflect on the cumulative results of our desire for more. Research published in 2012[3] showed that eighty percent of Americans feel stressed about the economy and their personal finances. Fifty-six percent are concerned about their job stability. Two-thirds of Americans are living paycheck to paycheck. Fifty percent worry they cannot meet their family's basic needs.[4] While the national economy has generally continued to improve since 2012, not all economic sectors, and certainly not all Americans, have shared proportionally in the recovery.

Meantime, Americans have the highest level of private consumer debt—and the lowest rate of savings—in the industrialized world.[5] American children ages eight through seventeen average slightly more than a dozen trips to the mall each month, spending an estimated $3,600 a year while there.[6] And for many adults, the bumper sticker slogan is all too true: "I owe, I owe, so off to work I go." Setting sights on a certain standard of living, many people get caught in the trap of spending first, then working to pay for it. As a result, a Harris Research poll shows that since 1973 our free time (for family, friends, and healthy personal balance) has fallen nearly forty percent.[7]

At the same time, three billion people around the world live on less than two dollars a day.[8]

"We have a love affair with 'more,' and we will never have enough," says theologian Walter Brueggemann.[9] Many Americans feel their rampant consuming is an entitlement, as long as they have the money to buy more and more things. Stewardship writers Tanya Barnett and Tom Wilson agree with Brueggemann's assessment. Referring to Psalm 62:8, which calls us to trust God as our refuge, they ask, "Have we been pouring our hearts into the bottomless pit called 'never enough' or into the abundant 'refuge' that is the Creator and Sustainer of all that exists?"[10]

Every society has an economy of one kind or another. An economy in its broadest sense describes structured relationships among individuals and institutions to allocate resources so people have what it takes to live.[11] Participation in the economy gives us access to important life-sustaining resources: a place where we are known, where we will be cared for, included, and given sustenance.[12] For example, in our market economy we exchange money for products and services, in what is called "commodity exchange."[13]

Exchanging goods and services can be a wonderful thing. But problems arise when we become what political economist Karl Polanyi[14] calls a "market society." Such a society exists, he says, when not only land, labor, and money are treated as commodities, but also all spheres of social goods—such as clean air and water, literacy, cultural opportunities, financial independence, and health care[15]—are produced and distributed as if they were commodities, as well.[16] Vanderbilt Divinity School professor Douglas Meeks states, "It is therefore possible for such a society not to be outraged when many of its children no longer have access to what it takes for them to live and live abundantly."[17]

While economists and politicians may discuss causes of this situation from various angles, those who try to follow Jesus are challenged to choose between lives of commodity or lives of covenant based upon grace.[18] Ethically-minded people can ask, "To what degree am

I helping people in need based upon my personal profit, instead of on God's call to care for one another?"

Even as we deal with daily concerns to provide for our families and communities, biblically-oriented people may recall "the everlasting covenant between God and every living creature of all flesh that is on the earth" (Genesis 9:16).

A "covenant" is a treaty, promise, or vow, in this case given to us by God. We find biblical covenants within Exodus, Joshua, and as the framework of the entire Book of Deuteronomy.[19] God has committed to be our God, and to claim us as part of God's people,[20] inviting us to reflect God's priorities in our everyday dealings. When Jesus names the greatest commandment, he challenges us to "love the Lord your God with all your heart, and with all your soul, and with all your mind, and with all your strength," and to "love your neighbor as yourself" (Mark 12:30–31). In stating this, Jesus summarizes God's ongoing covenant of relationship with us by saying, "Love one another just as I have loved you" (John 15:12).

On an individual level, if our heart constantly hungers for *more*, then we never feel fulfilled, and have thereby cut ourselves off from true gratitude and joy.[21] As we have seen in the previous chapter, gratitude naturally leads to giving to help one's neighbor, as it did with the "good Samaritan" in Luke 10: 29–37.

For many of us, letting go of obsessively seeking more begins by *unlearning* three false messages we have been taught (consciously and unconsciously) along the way:

- Your worth is in what you own;
- You are what you buy; and
- If some is good, more is better.

It takes a maturing sense of identity—an inherent sense of worth in who we are as children of God—to counteract all the messages of needing more all around us.

At the same time, our consumer-oriented misconceptions can lead us to realize three truths:

- If we believe more stuff will make us happy, it will never be enough;
- If we believe more stuff will make us important, it will never be enough; and
- If we believe more stuff will bring us security, it will never be enough.[22]

Catherine Malotky, philanthropic advisor to Luther Seminary in Minneapolis, reminds us that stewardship comes from a distinct perspective: the steward's calling is to manage his or her life on behalf of someone else, and for the sake of someone else. "Perhaps the church can help us learn to think of ourselves as stewards, choosing a [conservation-management] perspective rather than a consumption perspective," Malotky says.[23]

# The Rich Fool

Jesus tells a story in Luke 12:13–21 about a rich man who has such a big surplus of crops that he has no place to store his most recent harvest. So he says to himself,

I will do this: I will pull down my barns and build larger ones, and there I will store all my grain and my goods. And I will say to my soul, "Soul, you have ample goods laid up for many years; relax, eat, drink, and enjoy yourself."

Jesus continues:

But God said to him, "You fool! This very night your life is being demanded of you! And the things you have prepared, whose will they be?" So it is with those who store up for themselves but are not rich toward God.

In Bible commentaries, this story is commonly called "The Rich Fool."

The man in the story is *not* called a fool because he is rich. It is not bad to be wealthy, as long as we have been ethical in our dealings with others. The problem comes when, instead of being good stewards for others, those of us who already have enough are still obsessed by money and things and let our craving for more define who we are.

So what makes this man a "fool?" We can call him foolish because:

- He thought he owned his profits (his crops) and assets (his grain and goods), to do with entirely as he wished, for his own sole purposes, as part of "a life centered on attaining more, on making oneself rich and living off the excess;"[24]
- He thought he was in control of his health and life, unrelated to God's mercy and goodness;[25]
- He did not consider his relationship with other people (family or community), and particularly with those who were in need;
- He believed that he owned and directed his soul, and that material things would give peace, meaning, and joy to his soul; and
- He lived his life without reference to God, whether in prayer asking for guidance, or in giving thanks for what he had been given.

Whether we are drowning in debt or making substantial financial headway, says author Jeff Manion, if we equate our self-worth with our net worth, we are poor.[26]

Such "foolish" beliefs do not come out of nowhere. Our cultural and economic milieu does much to encourage rampant consumer behavior. Author Christine Roush[27] says the two most significant developments that have resulted in our becoming a consumer society were "the invention of the credit card and the decision to make products that become obsolete over time."

The credit card makes it possible for people to buy almost anything over an extended time. When credit cards were created, a record number of Americans took advantage of the new system. Whereas in 1929 only two percent of homes had mortgages, by 1962 only two percent of homes did not.[28] By 2006, Americans owed more money than they made.[29] In 2007, "years of cheap money, excessive spending and negative savings rates"[30] added to other factors, including encouraging buyers to assume mortgages that could not realistically be repaid, granting mortgages without a normal financial vetting process, and selling high-risk mortgages to financial institutions. Together, these created a "perfect storm:" a worldwide recession that impacted all areas of the economy, beginning in the United States when an 8 trillion-dollar housing bubble burst.[31] It officially lasted until June, 2009, but its impact is still being felt today. The housing drop led to cutbacks in consumer spending and business investment, as well as job loss[32]—a steep price paid by many for others' financial speculation, bank deregulation, and Wall Street greed.

Planned obsolescence ensures repeated sales. If the quality of a product is too good, people keep the item too long. So many manufacturers discovered they could benefit by lowering the product quality, increasing their advertisements to create attachment to a specific brand, and emphasizing how recent products are "new and improved."[33]

But sometimes even the physiological characteristics of our own brains can work against us. Scientific researchers are discovering that, as individuals, our brains may be more or less hardwired for spending or for saving, as well.[34] A part of the brain's prefrontal cortex makes us willing to defer gratification and save for the future. It can send "calm down" signals to the midbrain's "I want it now" circuits. Also a good short-term memory can help people imagine and plan for themselves in the future. Likewise, the hormone in the brain called oxytocin—which individuals have in differing amounts—makes some people less anxious and more patient, and therefore more willing, for example, to receive a larger amount of money later instead of a smaller amount now.

"The choice to spend rather than save reflects a very human—and some would say American—quirk: a preference for immediate gratification over future gains," says researcher Sharon Begley.[35] When we add this to our instant-access culture of Internet buying, overnight deliveries, and movies on demand, slowing down endless acquisition can seem like a lost cause.

But there is good news for our brains! "Being unable to delay gratification is not something we're stuck with for life," says psychologist Walter Mischel. "You develop willpower and patience through practice."[36] In other words, our brains can learn to look forward to future rewards, and not give in to impulse consumption. Even children can train their brains to recognize that forgoing pleasure now can bring a greater payoff later. Doing today's homework can bring better grades next month and saving a small allowance to buy a nice item later on will be more pleasurable than buying cheap junk each week.[37]

# Needs versus Wants

One essential lesson for learning how much is enough is the distinction between *needs* and *wants*. *Needs* are things or conditions we must have in order to live, such as water, food, and shelter. *Wants* are those potentially limitless things that are desirable, but not essential to our survival.

Many of us may be familiar with Abraham Maslow's motivational theory that says people aim to meet basic needs first, and then seek to meet successively lower-priority needs.[38] Popularly called Maslow's Hierarchy of Needs, it places physiological needs, such as air, warmth, and sleep, at the base of the pyramid, with less essential needs forming the pyramid's higher levels. But as the elemental needs are fulfilled, the difference between needs and wants can blur in our minds. Having first satisfied our physical needs, the theory says, people look for safety, next move up to a sense of belonging and love, and then try to satisfy their need for esteem, including achievement, responsibility, and reputation. Finally, Maslow identifies the need for "self-actualization," meaning personal growth and fulfillment.

But how we understand our need can vary hugely from person to person and depends upon our placement in the culture. A homeless person may consider his or her physical needs met long before a wealthy suburban resident does. "Although between 75–80% of us say [the United States] is too materialistic," says Christine Roush, "overall half the population in the richest country in the world says they cannot afford everything they need. And it is not just the poorer half."[39]

The cause of this insatiability may not only be a lack of money but can also be fostered by exposure to incessant advertising messages, and the tendency to see our expansive desires as basic needs. "We expect to have cable television, mobile phones, and the latest computer games," says Abingdon Press writer Ella Robinson. "As we turn these luxuries into essentials, we allow them to become what pastor Mike Slaughter calls 'shiny gods.'"[40]

Referring to how biblical Israel molded a golden calf to worship (Exodus 32), Slaughter identifies "shiny gods" as "whatever distracts us from experiencing the generosity of God."[41] These self-made gods may be good things in themselves but become detrimental when we use them to supplant the true God. For example, bank accounts, stocks, or bonds may ensure financial security, but they can also become a powerful obstacle to faith, if an adult refers to them constantly, equating them with self-worth. Electronic communications can provide invaluable knowledge and pleasurable entertainment, but if someone sees them as her entire world, they can become destructive idols.

"If you think about it, needing everything you can afford is a pretty silly way to define a need," says stewardship leader Lynn Miller.[42] "Needing everything your neighbor has is equally silly," he continues. "Likewise, needing what the media says you deserve is a bit of a stretch since the media doesn't have the faintest idea who you are."[43] In contrast, Miller chooses to define a "need" as whatever thing or service is essential for us to fulfill God's personal call to us. For example, if our call is to offer housing and meals to strangers, we will need a bit more money for housing and food. If our call is to transport people to their medical appointments, we may need a larger vehicle.[44]

Miller proposes we list by various categories where our money goes for a year, to determine what are essential expenses to meet our needs, versus other expenses about which we have more flexibility.[45] It takes a logical, tracking approach and honesty in assigning expenses to categories to accurately assess where the line is between our wants and needs.

This process is counter-cultural in a consumer society that defines "success" based on the quantity of possessions we have and teaches us that we can never get enough.[46] Ultimately, whatever our possessions, they cannot fulfill our deepest needs. So it is no surprise that three studies found that people who aim for more wealth above other factors in their lives (such as happiness and love) tend to have a lower sense of well-being.[47] The market trades on convincing us of an artificial sense of scarcity, so advertising becomes the market's evangelism, says Douglas Meeks.[48] Such constant advertising, notes Pope Francis, gives "absolute autonomy [to] the marketplace and financial speculation."[49]

Think about your own financial situation. When you compare your income with your needs, how does it come out? In 2 Corinthians 9:8, Paul says God will not only meet our needs, but will also give us enough to do good works for others.

# Scarcity Thinking

Much of what keeps us endlessly buying things and impedes our gift-giving is the scarcity mindset. "As a society we have been conditioned to believe that more is always better," say members of the Rock Recovery Ministry in California, "yet we can never obtain enough." They explain:

Drugs and alcohol, money, food, clothes, sex, hi-tech gadgets; the list of our wants is infinite and our temptation to get them is almost overpowering. The temptation of greed can consume the soul as we selfishly succumb to its fatal grip. Greed strips us of our spiritual supply [sense of positive connection in the world, compassion, and loving relationship with God], and we trade in our moral standards for mere moments of make-believe bliss.[50]

As recovering drug addicts, these Rock ministry participants have learned firsthand that whenever we begin with an attitude of scarcity, more never brings enough of whatever we crave.

But the scarcity myth goes even deeper than that. Scarcity is like a lens we look through even before thinking, says money expert Lynne Twist. It prompts us to think, "I don't have enough" time, or money, or food, or anything. Twist says:

It's the siren song of consumer culture, but it's not just about money. It dribbles over into every aspect of life.... It becomes '*I'm not enough*,' and it's the source of so much of our suffering.[51]

Such scarcity thinking makes us feel as if we are living in a deficit relationship with ourselves, as if we need more money and things to even be acceptable as persons.

The ethos of the U.S. consumer culture is an ethic of scarcity, says Elizabeth Hinson-Hasty of Bellarmine University. In classical economics, she says, an ethic of scarcity "assumes resources are limited, and human desire is unlimited."[52] In the church, she notes, this same ethic arises partly out of fear of decline in the number of people attending worship and congregational activities, when we fear we do not have enough "revenue" in money or in members.

Hinson-Hasty names several driving forces behind this cultural ethic of scarcity. The first is increased inequality in distribution of wealth over the past thirty or more years. The second is commercial exploitation of consumer appetites. For example, she says Americans spend on luxuries ninety times the amount of money needed to provide clean water for every person around the globe! The third factor is climate change, aggravated by our energy consumption. At less than five percent of the world's population, the United States annually consumes one-third of the world's resources, and one-fourth of its yearly production of fossil fuels. Implicit in these last two factors is the false assumption that unlimited growth is both possible and sustainable.[53]

When it comes to the Bible, it contains two contrasting viewpoints, says Old Testament scholar Norman Gottwald. While one assumption is that of scarcity, "the other is a consensus of abundance."[54] For example, both Mary's song of praise (Luke 1:47–55) and Jesus' first sermon (Luke 4:18f.) imply ultimate abundance when they speak of how the mighty are brought low and the lowly are lifted up, anticipating God's final rebalancing of inequality and scarcity in the human social order.

These competing perspectives of scarcity and abundance are still with us today. As a nonprofit fundraiser and global activist, for many years Lynne Twist has been engaged with people living in crushing conditions of want, and also with others who have wealth way beyond their needs:

> Yet, surprisingly in that world of over-abundance, too, the conversation is dominated by what they don't have and what they want to get. No matter who we are or what our circumstances, we swim in conversations about what there isn't enough of.[55]

This scarcity mindset prompts many of us to feel we do not have enough time, work, profit, power, or weekends. For those of us who have more than our basic needs, the mantra of *not enough* can become our default setting as consumers,[56] whether we are conscious of it or not.

Twist identifies three false "truths" that underlie such a toxic mindset:

1. The perception that "there's not enough" drives our efforts to overcome a feeling of lack and generates a fear of being left out or of losing out to others.

2. The idea that "more is better" motivates us to focus constantly on the next thing, whether it is a car or job or vacation or the latest electronic item, so we hardly experience the gifts of what we have now.
3. The conviction that "that's just the way it is" tells us that life is unfair, others have more than we have, and we live in a hopeless, unequal world with no way out.[57]

Altogether, the subliminally-reinforced stories many of us unwittingly believe foster continual discontentment. We keep trying to fill in the gap with things, as if they can assuage our deeper hunger.

By contrast, *contentment* has to do with where and how we look to compare our lot in life. If I stand somewhere at the middle of the social ladder and look *up*, says author Christine Roush, I may see my boss' car, or the house a television celebrity lives in, and consequently will never be happy with my more modest home and station wagon. But if I look *down* the ladder, I see billions of people! My residence is a safe haven and place of retreat compared to the low-income housing across the way, or single-room-occupancy apartments across town—much less the refugee camps, slums, or streets where the homeless live.[58]

We cannot open our hands to give freely when we're holding tight to what we have. One extreme example is hoarding, which has even become the subject of a television show. Another is the thousands of self-storage units—once nearly nonexistent—which have exploded all over the American landscape.

IT IS HARD TO LET GO of a scarcity mindset unless we stop to analyze our expectations, sort between true needs and mere wants, and test the validity of our fears of not having enough. But we can face and name our addiction to more and choose not to believe the false "truths" we may have subconsciously embraced.

The Bible can help us identify God's reversal of scarcity thinking. Apart from our need to be discontent with injustice and oppression, we can learn to be content with what we have been given, for example in possessions, special relationships, or quality time, to improve life for God's people and creatures. Once we take a step back to reflect on our assumption of scarcity, we can begin to recognize the true abundance God has given us. Being spiritual or religious does not keep us from falling prey to a scarcity mindset. Only when we admit the temptation to grasp at an unlimited *more* of everything in our lives, can we loosen our grip to see the fullness of what already surrounds us, and recognize so much of it as sheer gift.

# Questions for Reflection

1. In what aspects of my life do I experience the lure of *more*?
2. Where do I find a balance between my wants, and the needs of others around the world?
3. What inner attitudes and outward practices might help me live more simply and reduce material possessions? Which practice of simplicity would I like to strengthen?
4. What do I consider to be my "fixed expenses," and why? Considering my response, in what spending categories can I be more fluid?

# Endnotes

1. *Positioning: The Battle for Your Mind*, by Al Ries and Jack Trout (New York: McGraw-Hill, 2001), pp. 11–12.
2. Nathan Dungan, "Financial Freedom: A Journey to Transformation," in "Live Free," *Giving: Growing Joyful Stewards in Your Congregation* (2015), by the Ecumenical Stewardship Center.
3. Jim Forsyth, "Living Paycheck to Paycheck," *The Huffington Post*, September 20, 2012, *huffingtonpost.com/2012/09/20/living-paycheck-to-paycheck_n_1899685. html*, cited in *shiny gods: finding freedom from things that distract us Leader Guide*, by Ella Robinson, p. 7.
4. Adam Hamilton, *Enough: Discovering Joy Through Simplicity and Generosity*, (Nashville: Abingdon Press, 2009), p. 5.

5. Lynn A. Miller, *The Power of Enough: Finding Contentment by Putting Stuff In Its Place* (Nappanee, Indiana; Evangel press, 2003), p. 68.

6. "*USA Today* Snapshot," Gannett Company; *usatoday.com/snapshot/money/ snapindex.htm* cited in Christine Roush, *Swimming Upstream: Reflections on Consumerism and Culture* (Kohler, WI: Design Group International, 2009), p. 11.

7. Harris Research poll cited by Christine Roush in *op cit.*, p. 53.

8. Ronald J. Sider, *Rich Christians in an Age of Hunger: Moving from Affluence to Generosity*, cited in Christine Roush, *ibid.*

9. Walter Brueggemann, "The Liturgy of Abundance, the Myth of Scarcity," in *Money & Faith: The Search for Enough*, cited in *umfnw.org/radical generosity* by Tanya Barnett and Tom Wilson, Stewardship Emphasis staff, Pacific Northwest Conference of the United Methodist Church.

10. Tanya Barnett and Tom Wilson, United Methodist Foundation of the Northwest, *umfnw.org/radical generosity.*

11. M. Douglas Meeks, *God the Economist: The Doctrine of God and Political Economy*, pp. 29–45, cited in M. Douglas Meeks, *The Economy of Grace and the Market Logic; councilofchurches.ca/wp-content/uploads/2013/12/DouglasMeeks. pdf.*

12. *Ibid.*, pp. 3–4.

13. M. Douglas Meeks, "Discover Gold!" National Association of United Methodist Foundations annual meeting, Oct. 22–27, 2012. Thompson Reuters defines a commodity as "a raw material or primary agricultural product that can be bought and sold, such as copper or coffee;" *thompsonreuters.com.*

14. Author of *The Great Transformation* (Boston: Beacon Press; 1944) about the rise of the modern market economy in England.

15. *investopedia.com/terms/s/social_good.asp.*

16. M. Douglas Meeks, *The Economy of Grace and the Market Logic*, p. 4; *councilofchurches.ca/wp-content/uploads/2013/12/DouglasMeeks.pdf.*

17. *Ibid.*

18. M. Douglas Meeks, "Discover Gold!" presentation.

19. See Exodus 19:3–8; 20:1–17; 24:3–8; Joshua 24; and the Book of Deuteronomy, which is structured in the form of a covenant.

20 –See Exodus 6:7; Leviticus 26:12; Jeremiah 30:22; 2 Corinthians 6:16; and Revelation 21:3.

21. Brother David Steindl-Rast in *The Practice of Grateful Living* DVD.

22. Rev. Dr. Michael Dent's sermon, "It's Never Enough," September 9, 2012, Trinity United Methodist Church, Denver, Colorado. There is only one thing in this life that we can never get enough of, says Dent: "knowing the love of Jesus Christ."

23. Catherine Malotky, "Stewardship as Vocation," from Luther Seminary's Center for Stewardship Leaders, *communic@luthersem.edu*, May 20, 2014.

24. Tanya Barnett and Tom Wilson, *Radical Gratitude*, (Luke 12:13–21), Pentecost 10 of Year C; *umfnw.org*.
25. Daniel Conway, *op cit.*, p. 45.
26. Jeff Manion, *Satisfied: Discovering Contentment in a World of Consumption* (Grand Rapids: Zondervan, 2014).
27. Christine Roush, *op cit.*, p. 20.
28. Dave Ramsey, *Financial Peace*, p. 8, cited in *ibid*.
29. Jessica Bennett for *Newsweek* August 8, 2006, *msnbc.msn.com/id/14251360/site/ newsweek*; cited in Christine Roush, *ibid*.
30. *study.com/academy/lesson/what-was-the-great-recession-timeline-facts-causes-effects.html*.
31. *stateofworkingamerica.org/great-recession*. A real estate bubble of inflated prices precipitates houses that "go underwater," where the owners "[hold] negative equity (a mortgage debt higher than the current value of the property)." (*en. wikipedia.org/wiki/Great_Recession*)
32. *stateofworkingamerica.org/great-recession*. Effects of the recession were far greater than just in housing or just in the United States, but housing is used as one example.
33. Richard Tedlow, author of *New and Improved: The Story of Mass Marketing in America*, notes that the mass market became possible toward the end of the nineteenth century, mainly due to technological advances in manufacturing. These advances allowed for standardization of parts (which enabled the establishment of nationwide railroads, telegraph, and telephone networks), and then development of the assembly line in the early 1900s and mass production of consumer goods such as cars and refrigerators. In response, by the early decades of the twentieth century, business firms began segmenting the market. They targeted distinct groups according to demographic information and varying lifestyles, highlighting the "special value" of the product independent of production costs. This specialized approach has led to strong individual attachment to particular brands. *tandfonline.com/doi/ abs/10.1080/00076799100000148?journalCode=fbsh20*.
34. Sharon Begley with Jean Chatzky, "Stop! You Can't Afford It," *Newsweek*, November 7 and 14, 2011, pp. 50–54).
35. *Ibid*, p. 54.
36. *Ibid*.
37. *learning-theories.com/maslows-hierarchy-of-needs.html*
38. Christine Roush, *op cit.*, p. 45, citing Juliet Schor, *The Overspent American: Why We Want What We Don't Need*, pp. 113 and 6, respectively.
39. Ella Robinson, *shiny gods: finding freedom from things that distract us, Leader's Guide* (Nashville: Abingdon Press, 2013) p. 7.
40. *Ibid*, pp. 17–18.
41. Lynn A. Miller, *op cit.*, p. 56.

42. *Ibid.*

43. *Ibid.*, p. 58.

44. *Ibid.*, p. 57, gives us a list of possible needs to consider as we put together our own list of needs versus wants.

45. David Bell, Executive Director and President of the United Methodist Foundation of Michigan, "Consumerism and Faith: Conflicting Views of Money," at June, 2011 United Methodist Stewardship Gathering; adapted from *Behind the Stained Glass Windows: Money Dynamics in the Church*, by John and Sylvia Ronsvalle.

46. Susan Hawks, "Teaching Youth About Money Can Decrease Their Materialism And Increase Their Self-Esteem," September 2013, citing an article published online on July 16, 2013 in the peer-reviewed, scientific journal, *Motivation & Emotion*, DOI 10.1007/s11031-013-9371-4. That article is: "Changes in materialism, changes in psychological well-being: Evidence from three longitudinal studies and an intervention experiment," by Tim Kasser, Katherine L. Rosenblum, Arnold J. Sameroff, Edward L. Deci, Christopher P. Niemiec, Richard M. Ryan, Osp Arnadottir, Rod Bond, Helga Dittmar, Nathan Dungan, and Susan Hawks. The intervention experiment was Nathan Dungan's "Share Save Spend" approach, which helps youth and adults develop healthy money habits that link to their values.

47. David Meyers, Professor of Psychology at Hope College, notes that people coming from upper middle-class backgrounds are *less* likely to report that they are happy than people living at lower socio-economic levels (Christine Roush, *op cit.,* p. 5).

48. M. Douglas Meeks, "Discover Gold!" National Association of United Methodist Foundations annual meeting, Oct. 22–27, 2012, p. 6 of handouts.

49. Pope Francis, "The Joy of the Gospel," cited in *Christian Century* December 25, 2013, p. 7.

50. A ministry of the Rock Church, San Diego, California, offering outreach and residential support for people struggling with addiction. The Rock Recovery Ministry, "Temptation," in *Upper Room Disciplines 2013* (Nashville: Upper Room Books, 2012), p. 197.

51. Lynne Twist, author of *The Soul of Money*, interviewed by Oprah on OWN Television, Super Soul Sunday, April 23, 2017.

52. Elizabeth Hinson-Hasty, Associate Professor of Theology at Bellarmine University, in "Grace-Filled Economy: The Way Around the Ethic of Scarcity Toward the Ethic of Enough," Midwinter 2013 lectures at Austin Presbyterian Theological Seminary, February 4–6, 2013, podcast.

53. http://www.washingtonpost.com/blogs/fact-checker/wp/2015/04/30/does-the-united-states-really-have-five-percent-of-worlds-population-and-one-quarter-of-the-worlds-prisoners/

54. Catherine Malotky, ed., *op cit.*, p. 30. Here she refers to Norman Gottwald, *The Tribes of Yahweh: A Sociology of the Religion of Liberated Israel,* (Maryknoll, NY: Sheffield Academic Press, 1999).
55. Lynne Twist, *The Soul of Money,* p. 43.
56. *Ibid.,* p. 44.
57. *Ibid.,* pp. 49–55.
58. Christine Roush, *op cit.,* pp. 4f.

# An Ethic of Enough

O NCE WE ACKNOWLEDGE the false allure of constantly wanting more, we can begin to rest in a sense of contentment and open our eyes to the abundance that underlies and surrounds our lives. We can experience God's abundance in at least five ways: through the profusion of creation all around us, in God's advocacy on our behalf, through our daily access to the Holy Spirit, by using our resources for the good of those around us, and in living deeply in the present moment.

## An Abundant Partnership

*Creation*—This physical world reveals God as the source of incredible abundance! One of the most popular hymns of all time reminds us of all the works and worlds that God has made: the stars, light, and entire universe—the forests, birds, and brooks, the mountain majesty, and even the gift of God's own Son, Jesus Christ. All of this prompts millions of people to sing: "How great Thou art!"

The Bible includes songs that praise God for the vastness, intricacy, and interdependence of creation, as well—particularly in Psalms 8 and 104, and Job, chapters 38 through 41. For God, scarcity is absurd, says a contemporary author. "God is desperate to show us a generosity that makes a mockery of our smallness of mind and our conviction of the difficulty of getting things that we want and need."[1]

*God's advocacy*—God is the Creator of all that is above, around, beneath, and within us. But God is also the "Redeemer," a church word which could be understood as "hugely abundant, generous and *for* us."[2] The Hebrew word for "redeemer" used in the Old Testament is *go'el*. This term refers to a specific person in the tribe whose relationship to us is closer than any other family member (father, brother, sister, mother), who makes things right on our behalf as far as is possible in this life. In the early Old Testament times, when the Jews depended upon tribal relationships, every person had a *go'el*, or redeemer, who would right the balance of justice (*shalom*) by retrieving from the thief what he or she had stolen from his kin or killing his kin's murderer to redress the wrong. (In this sense the phrase "an eye for an eye" averted escalating tribal war.)

The Hebrew Scriptures speak of God as our personal *go'el*. By using this word, they are saying that the great, cosmic Creator God is closer to us than any human relationship, and the One who ultimately rights the wrongs done to us by others. This role covers not only our things but our person, as well. The New Testament builds upon this Old Testament understanding, when Jesus calls God *Abba*, or "Daddy" (Mark 14:36), and Paul invites *us* to call God *Abba* as well, declaring us as God's own children. (Romans 8:15f.) God is our protective "Father" and "Redeemer."

Both Testaments also refer to the abundance of God's mercy in forgiving us after our rebellions (Acts 10:43; Ephesians 1:7; Matthew 6:12). They also point to the power of God's promise of "a new heaven and a new earth" (Isaiah 65:17; 66:22; Revelation 21:1)—a whole new creation in which to live, once this existence ultimately passes away.

*The Holy Spirit*—But God's abundance is not only related to creation and to redemption. God offers us an ongoing partnership and abundant relationship. Thankfully we are not called to some kind of spiritual anorexia, as if starving our dreams were a virtue! Jesus says, "I came that they may have life, and have it abundantly" (John 10:10). As the original Hebrew wording of Zephaniah 3:17 tells us,

God rejoices over us whether we are in times of singing or—amazingly—in periods of God's silence. In those times of silence, we may feel anxious about not hearing God's voice. Of course, God speaks in an incredible array of ways, but for a variety of reasons, including our preoccupation and over-busy minds, we may have forgotten how to truly listen.

Our partnering relationship with God is described in different ways. Poet Samuel Longfellow uses the metaphor of our soul as the sacred page on which the Holy Spirit, God's unseen presence, can write.[3] This image captures the sense of holy relationship with each other. But we are not merely recipients; we can also be participants in something God has already placed within us. God's love confronts us in the stillness of meditation and prayer. One author describes this as "the most intense intimacy a human being can experience."[4]

*Our resources for others*—An abundant partnership with God can heighten our sense of overflowing blessing, despite the gap between us as creatures and God as our Creator. "And God is able to provide you with every blessing in abundance," Paul tells the Christians in Corinth. "So that by always having enough of everything, you may share abundantly in every good work." (2 Corinthians 9:8) Paul's phrase *so that* shows that the point is not for us to simply accumulate blessings of various kinds, but to use the blessings—of time, energy, relationships, and all the rest—in order to *share abundantly with others* in every effort in which we engage.

But Paul goes on. He says, "[The One] who supplies seed to the sower and bread for food will supply and multiply your seed for sowing and increase the harvest of your righteousness." (2 Corinthians 9:10) Here he claims that God both supplies the raw materials ("seed") and gives us the human ability to turn the harvested grain into "bread," multiplying the results, so we can feed ourselves and others. In Hebrew, the term for "bread" also means any kind of food. But in this passage Paul implies not only food, but any human effort, as well.

In addition, there is a double meaning here, because the term "righteousness" also might be "benevolence." So we can read Paul's statement as saying that God gives us the resources, energy, and ability to be "righteous," meaning rightly facing God and in right relationship with others, while being "benevolent:" doing acts of kindness and giving generous gifts.

This enriching partnership with God is not just a "me and Jesus" affair. "What abundance do we see in Jesus Christ?" asks Charles Lane of Luther Seminary in Minneapolis. "In him is an abundance of forgiveness, an abundance of hope, and an abundance of community."[5] Citing Colossians 1:21, Lane says that we human beings were once estranged from one another, as Jews versus Gentiles. Now both groups Paul dealt with can come together in Jesus, trusting that our differences from one another will not ultimately divide us from each other or from God. So Lane asserts, "This is the ground of true community."[6]

Some years ago, the United Methodist General Board of Discipleship Ministries launched what they called The Best Practices Romans 12 Project, to identify emerging trends among congregations that are "actively making disciples of Jesus Christ for the transformation of the world."[7] One of the trends they discovered was that most vital congregations are *"living out of a sense of abundance, with an expectancy of God's presence and guidance."*[8] [Emphasis in original.]

"Every week I hear about someone doing something outside of their comfort zone in the name of God...mission work, elder care, leadership roles, etc.," says a member of one small-but-mighty Romans 12 congregation.

> There is a strong unselfish generosity among the congregation when donations are requested for missions and individuals in need, whether community, national or world.... We are not "bumps on a log." Stuff happens in our church. We have a "can do" attitude and faith that with Christ we can accomplish anything.[8]

Sometimes an individual or a family catches this sense of abundance and acts on it, making a huge difference. Years ago a family in Waterloo, Ontario, Canada heard of the need for potatoes to feed the hungry—and raised 2,000 pounds on their own! This developed into "an annual February potato blitz, raising 300,000 pounds for distribution throughout the year," said a retired Mennonite pastor living in that town.[9] Prompted by that example, she added her own experience:

> Perhaps I can help set the stage for such miracles when I pay attention to my own cravings for more. I can pray with Isaiah, "Why do you spend your money for that which is not bread, and your labor for that which does not satisfy? Listen carefully to me and eat what is good." [Isaiah 55:1–3] For when my spirit is nourished, I catch a glimpse of God's economy of abundance.[10]

*This moment*—We have another important way to understand God's abundance, as well. It is the abundance of the moment, of living now! Stephen Mitchell, Bible scholar and translator, describes it this way:

> When Jesus talked about the kingdom of God, he was not prophesying about some easy, danger-free perfection that will someday appear. He was talking about a state of being, a way of living at ease among the joys and sorrows of our world. It is possible, he said, to be as simple and beautiful as the birds of the sky or the lilies of the field, who are always within the eternal *Now*. This state of being is not something alien or mystical. We don't need to earn it. It is already ours.[11]

Most of us lose this sense of the now as we grow up and become self-conscious, Mitchell says, but it always resides within us, waiting to be reclaimed. It's an approach to time regardless of our degree of wealth. Because young children have not yet developed a solid sense of past and future, he states, they "accept the infinite abundance of the present with all their hearts, in complete trust." When we choose to reclaim this childhood awareness, we are entering the kingdom of

God, says Mitchell, feeling that "we are being taken care of, always, at every moment."[12]

## The Problem With Abundance

But we can get into problems when we emphasize God's abundance without recognizing the vast chasm between the rich and the poor of this world. For many of us who consider ourselves middle class in the developed countries of the globe, "abundance" can come to mean "sharing out of our excess," without recognizing that although all the resources needed in the world may exist, they do not get equitably distributed to all people.

For example, while the United States makes up 5 percent of the world's population, it consumes between 25 and 40 percent of the world's natural resources.[13] While many middle-class Americans learn as children to be generous, their later consumer lifestyle lures them into overspending and overextending their financial obligations. As they continue to grow, they become locked in a pattern of private spending, feel they have less, and therefore less to give to help people in need.[14] The result of such a complex scarcity-based system has been "a substantial increase in poverty, [an increasing acceptance of it,] the deterioration of poor neighborhoods, and alarming levels of crime and drug use."[15]

Ministry of Money founder Don McClanen wrote, "The problem with money is not with God's supply but with [humanity's] distribution."[16] The lilies of the field and the birds of the air (Matthew 6:25–34) are nourished from the system to which they have committed themselves. In the same way, McClanen said, God has given human beings all we need to live, *if* we distribute our resources appropriately. When enough people consistently do God's will on earth, both poverty and riches will disappear.[17]

At least up through the 1980s, a powerful part of the American dream was the belief that the next generation could have a better life or accomplish more than their parents did. This attitude tends to create a personal expectation of "more and better." While it is not a bad thing to hope that our children will do better than us, this hope needs to be paired with awareness that the earth's resources and individual opportunities are not unlimited.

Yet for millions of Americans, reality is the "habit of more." Recalling the California Gold Rush, author Laurence Shames describes this attitude, born of mingled history and myth, that:

> There would always be another gold rush.... The next generation would always ferret out opportunities that would be still more lavish than any that had gone before.... Frontier, opportunity, more. This has been the American trinity from the very start.[18]

Out of this habit has arisen what economist Kenneth Boulding calls "cowboy economics,"[19] referring to the viewpoint of economists who believe that limitless expansion is not only possible but required for society's stability. Considering the real ecological limits of this planet, James Child, of Trinity Lutheran Seminary, calls such expansionist thinking "humanity's tragic defiance of its own finitude."[20]

Richard Foster agrees. "In a world of limited resources, our wealth is at the expense of the poor. To put it simply, if we have it, others cannot," he says. "Our lifestyle is not our private affair," he continues. "The [gospel] demands more of us: it is obligatory upon us to help one another hammer out the shape of Christian simplicity in the midst of modern affluence."[21]

God's abundance is real, but as author James Alison notes, "it can really be enjoyed only if we are celebrating the source of abundance and only if there are no victims of our abundance."[22] The fact is, there are two sides to *enough*. On one side, the majority of the world's people, God's children, need to *obtain* in order to have enough (clean water, sustaining food, protective shelter, or clothes to wear). On the other side, a privileged minority of God's children need to *refrain* in order to have *just* enough to right the balance.[23]

This uncomfortable reality prompts us to evaluate our lifestyle choices, both personally and as congregations and communities.

While agreeing on personal lifestyle choices can be a complicated process, it is possible to stand on common ground in a given congregation. For example, the Enough for Everyone program of the Presbyterian Church (USA)[24] includes four projects called the Presbyterian Coffee Project, Sweat-Free Ts, Investing in Hope, and Electric Stewardship. They address fair trade, sweatshops, debt and credit, and energy efficiency.

Other examples of evaluating our lifestyles take place when a person or family decides to live on less in order to give more for others. Like the couple who chose to move to a less expensive home and community in order to be able to give more generously, through their global Mennonite Mission Network, to people locked in poverty in other countries. Or like the man who came to understand "Communion" as "union with" poor people in Mexico whom he visited repeatedly on mission trips. The more time he spent with these people of faith, the more he distinguished his "needs" from his "wants," eventually giving up a car and being content with a bicycle for transportation, so he could pour more of his resources into that community.[25] In both of these situations, the givers embody the kind of sharing between Gentile and Jewish Christians described by Paul in Romans 15:27f. Some had material blessings to give, while others shared the spiritual blessings of their heritage and direct relationship with God.

In summary, we can experience God's abundance in many powerful ways: through God's creation; God's "redemption" as our Advocate and the One who ultimately rights the balance of justice for us; in our ongoing personal partnership with the Holy Spirit; and by consciously deciding to use resources for the good of ourselves and of others. We can also strive to experience God's abundance by living fully in the present moment whenever we can. The way we live may seem to be our own private affair, but affects others, near and far. When we claim God's abundance in any of these ways as individuals, families, or congregations, we brim with vitality, living out of a sense of abundance, accepting God's presence and guidance along the way.

# Contentment and an Ethic of Enough

The opposite of scarcity is not necessarily abundance. In human experience, a truer opposite of scarcity is contentment,[26] or "enough-ness." The best way to describe it in English is *an ethic of enough*—a sense of sufficiency that leads us to act responsibly toward others in gratitude for all that we've received.

In the New Testament the root term used for contentment or satisfaction is *arkeo,* "to be sufficient" or "to suffice, be enough for, or satisfy."[27] It is used in statements that people should be content with the goods allotted to them. For the New Testament, "this freedom from want is grounded in God. [God's] provision is sufficient."[28]

For example, we see this message in the following texts:

- 2 Corinthians 9:8—"And God is able to provide you with every blessing in abundance, so that by always having enough of everything, you may share abundantly in every good work."
- Philippians 4:11—"I have learned to be content with whatever I have. I know what it is to have little, and I know what it is to have plenty."
- Hebrews 13:5—"Keep your lives free from the love of money, and be content with what you have; for [God] has said 'I will never leave you or forsake you.'"

Being content is not the same as becoming secure and complacent, imagining ourselves as self-sufficient, needing neither God nor human community.[29] Note especially in the first passage: the purpose of such contentment is not self-sufficiency in an isolationist way. Whether we have a lot or a little, we are meant to have enough, *so that* we can do good works and benefit others. This greater purpose of contentment is reinforced in 1 Timothy 6:17–19, where those who are wealthy are warned not to trust in their riches, but to "do good, to be rich in works, generous, and ready to share...."

Author Christine Roush summarizes the concept this way: "Happiness and contentment seem to be a lot less about having what you want, than actually wanting [valuing] what you have."[30]

Pastor Adam Hamilton boils it down to four keys to contentment (with my distillation listed after each point):

- Remember that it could be worse.
  Recognize that no matter what we may not like about a thing, relationship, or circumstance, we can always find good aspects to focus on, if we choose to do so.
- Ask yourself, "How long will this make me happy?"
  When considering whether to make an impulse buy, reflect on your personal priorities, how much you want to pay for time-saving items, and then ask yourself this bulleted question.
- Develop a grateful heart.
  As Paul tells us in 1 Thessalonians 5:18, "Give thanks in all circumstances." When we begin with gratitude, we are more able to be content with what we have, and with who and where we are.
- Ask yourself, "Where does my soul find true satisfaction?"
  What gives our restless hearts a sense of contentment and feeling that we are at home? How can our relationship with God help deepen this feeling of contentment to deepen?[31]

Valuing what we already have can change a congregation, as well. Under the influence of society, members of too many churches, whether giant or small, have been internally focused consumers of the church's "goods and services," imagining their local church solely as a provider, and themselves as recipients. "We need to strike a healthy balance between internal health and external reach," says church consultant Matthew Thomas. "This means moving church members from customers to co-laborers by developing intentional strategies to train and launch people in missional living."[32]

Contentment does not come from a program. It is fundamentally internal, multifaceted, and evolving, so it prompts a person's soul to do ongoing work. Bishop Robert Schnase says contentment results from four formative factors.

- A deep, cultivated sense of gratitude.
  When we see graciousness in common experiences, everyday tasks, and ordinary friendships, we become more grateful for God's gift of life in all its dimensions. Making a daily list of at least five things we are grateful for can be a powerful way to increase our awareness. (See 2 Corinthians 12:9, "My grace is sufficient for you, for power is made perfect in weakness.")
- The practice of generosity.
  By intentionally choosing not to spend all we have on ourselves, we can open our hearts to others. Repeated acts of generosity nurture our relationships and can break even the most extreme obsession with one's possessions.
- The spiritual awareness that God has already provided us with all we need to flourish.
  With a sense of sufficiency, we are more able to distinguish the difference between needs and wants and are released more often from worry about lacking enough to survive.
- Persistent interior work and cooperation with the Holy Spirit.
  When we allow the Spirit to work within our thoughts and decisions, we align our regular activities more closely with our values. Our daily practices (including the spiritual disciplines) help us keep from merging our sense of identity and worth with what we own or want to have.[33]

Living fruitfully is not so much a question of having something to live *on*, but to live *for*, says Schnase. After people are able to meet their minimal financial requirements to support themselves, they look beyond mere physical survival. "Purpose, connection, love, service, friendship, family, generosity—these sustain contentedness."[34]

So what is *an ethic* of enough? Many of us may be familiar with the field of ethics: the branch of philosophy that deals with morality, concerned with distinguishing good from evil, and right from wrong.[35] But what about an *ethic*, in the singular form? The dictionary describes it as a set of moral principles, a guiding philosophy, or the consciousness of moral importance.[36] In other words, an *ethic of enough* is an attitude of material contentment ("enoughness") that allows us to act upon a sense of responsibility toward others.

For example, a person might develop a conservation ethic that prompts her to value caring for the earth and its creatures. Out of this set of principles, she might live more simply in order to use fewer natural resources. She may share her garden produce, rescue or advocate for endangered animals, or work with others on an environmental project. This ethic or sense of values and actions could increase her experience of contentment, drawing her into more expansive, generous living.

In this way we realize that this ethic or sense of responsibility involves both a decision and a process. For example, if I choose to consume fewer of the Earth's resources in specific ways, I take some responsibility to care for the Earth itself. In that same act, I also seek a closer relationship with people around the globe who live on far less. But one decision is not enough to create a lifestyle. It takes a pattern of similar decisions to establish a personal ethic.

Whatever ethic we embrace also requires us to mature, deepening in our understanding of interconnectedness. For example, Methodist founder John Wesley came to realize that a General Rule for Christian living is not only to *do good*, but also to *do no harm*. By "doing good" he meant positive acts of kindness and mercy, as far as is possible, toward all people. The more challenging General Rule was to "do no harm," avoiding evil of every kind, not only directly, but also by thinking of those who might be influenced incidentally by our actions.

For example, Wesley chose to "do good" by giving food and clothing to those in need, regularly visiting people who were sick and in prison, and employing other Christians. Likewise, he decided to "do no harm" by living and dressing simply to counter the distinctions between rich and poor; abstaining from alcohol in a society where that was a major addiction and an economic burden; and not charging interest, which produces both profit and debt.[37]

Another example is Paul's advice to the first-century Christians in Corinth about whether or not to eat meat that had been prepared in a public butcher shop, where the shop owner had cut off a piece of meat and symbolically offered it to an idol (1 Corinthians 8:4–13). Although Paul knew no rival gods truly existed, he did not eat publicly-sold meat, in case it would hurt the conscience of those Christians who thought idols might be real.

Both John Wesley's "do no harm" and Paul's advice to the Corinthians reveal an ethic of responsibility. Both challenge us to reflect on unintended consequences of our actions, lest our choices contribute to someone else's misfortune. Because society is complex, each person often draws his or her own conclusions as to what is the right action. As one pastor puts it, there is no single "good" option versus the rest. Instead, God is interested in *how* we make the choices we make,[38] as we try to embody God's priorities in Micah 6:8—"to do justice, and to love kindness, and to walk humbly with [our] God."

"Do good" and "do no harm" may sound simple, but they are not easy—especially in the face of two "diseases" that run rampant these days in so many developed countries.

The first is *affluenza*, a term first coined in a Public Broadcasting System television program. Comparing it to a virulent case of influenza, the producers defined affluenza as "the modern-day plague of materialism."[39] For example, the program stated that:

- The average American shops six hours a week but spends only forty minutes a week playing with his or her children.
- By the age of twenty, Americans have viewed one million commercials.[40]

Pastor Adam Hamilton[41] calls this phenomenon "the constant need for more and bigger and better stuff—as well as the effect that this need has on us. It is the desire to acquire, and most of us have been infected by this virus to some degree."

The second greed-borne disease is what Hamilton calls *credit-itis*.[42] In *Simple Rules for Money* Rev. James Harnish describes Hamilton's term as "the 'buy-now-pay-later' addiction to an unhealthy use of credit cards. Credit-itis has spread like an epidemic through our culture."[43] While credit cards may be used responsibly, millions of people find them too easy to use, resulting in their paying interest on interest, engaging in unhealthy spending, and affecting others by their bad financial decisions. But the temptation behind overuse of credit is not a new phenomenon. As Proverbs 1:19 says, "Such is the end of all who are greedy for gain; it takes away the life of its possessors."

What can we do to cleanse our personal and community consumer habits? Authors Rob Dietz and Dan O'Neill recommend the following steps as a way to begin.

- Turn marketing on its ear.

  Use successful marketing techniques to "sell" sound cultural values—such as well-being as our way of life—instead of more and more consumer goods. For example, Freecycle Network is a global, grassroots movement of people who give and receive things for their homes and towns, without cost, through the Internet. The movement focuses on reusing items and keeping goods out of landfills.[44]
- Harness the power of art.

  Participate in the creative, collaborative processes that produce art, thereby playing a direct role in bringing about a better world.
- Be the change.

  Reject unnecessary consumer items and set a positive example by living our values. Some ways to do this include participating in local initiatives and producing things   locally.
- Recruit influential individuals.

  Search out key figures in social networks to become potent agents of change toward a sustainable lifestyle. For example, talk with a local teacher or civic leader about publicly supporting the idea of a community garden.

- Juxtapose mindless consumerism with the nonmaterialistic good life.

  Establish living examples of dynamic communities that encourage a sustainable lifestyle, such as the Transition Town movement, which engages communities in home-grown, citizen-led education and action.[45]
- Eliminate planned obsolescence.

  Reduce your reliance on short-lived, disposable products, in favor of durable items that do not diminish the earth's finite resources.
- Limit advertising.

  Encourage the marketing community to regulate themselves. Seek ways to reduce or ban advertising aimed at children, as did a 1980 ban in Quebec, Canada.
- Cultivate non-consumerist institutions.

  Communities and governments can empower organizations, such as cooperatives and land trusts, which focus on managing assets and meeting needs, rather than on repeatedly selling unlimited products.[46]

Any one of these initiatives might help a family, neighborhood, or congregation consider how deeply consumerism has become embedded in our everyday life and take some local steps to encourage a more responsible approach.

The best way to counteract the lure of more and develop an ethic of enough is to start with what we have, not with what we lack. Jesus challenged his disciples to start there, when a crowd of more than five thousand people had been following them and had nothing to eat (John 6:1–13). "Where are we to buy bread for these people to eat?" he asked, to test them.

Philip replied, "Six months' wages would not buy enough bread for each of them to get a little."

Then Andrew noted, "There is a boy here who has five barley loaves and two fish. But what are they among so many people?"

Yet that was all Jesus needed. He had the disciples tell the people to sit down. Then he took the bread, gave thanks, and distributed it to all who were seated. He did the same with the fish. "When they were satisfied, he told his disciples, 'Gather up the fragments left over, so that nothing may be lost.'" And when they gathered up all the fragments of food, they had filled twelve baskets with the scraps of bread.

We can draw several lessons from what the disciples learned from Jesus' feeding that crowd:

- With God, nothing is wasted, nothing is lost. (The number "twelve" here in the twelve baskets indicates fullness and wholeness—as in the twelve tribes of Israel, the twelve disciples, and the twelve gates to the New Jerusalem.) This is part of God's economy of grace.
- We can begin by looking for our assets, not our needs, moving away from scarcity thinking to discovering abundance.
- No gift is too small for God to use! We cannot limit God's ability to provide or to multiply what we offer to others.
- God gives us what we need, sustaining us and thereby prompting us to nourish others around us. When we live out of a sense of God's abundance and our "enoughness," we can expect God to guide us through seemingly impossible situations. As Paul says in Romans 14:8, "whether we live or whether we die, we are the Lord's."

To summarize, when we pause to assess the lure of more and the trap of scarcity thinking, we can reflect on God's abundance, and how, by giving to others, we can make our world less divided between rich and poor. Personal experiences can invite us to a sense of contentment or "enoughness," where we seek to act responsibly toward those around us. Even in financially difficult situations, we can start with what we have, acknowledging that God's provision is sufficient, and valuing what we have been given. We can choose to claim an "ethic of enough"—a set of moral principles or guiding philosophy—that causes us to mature, seeking not only to "do good" but also to "do no harm." When we realize how *affluenza* and *credit-itis* distort our values, we can start cleaning up our consumer habits in specific, local ways, focusing on managing the assets we have, and meeting people's needs.

# Simplicity as Freedom

A Spanish proverb says that habits begin as cobwebs and end up as chains.[47] The saying is particularly true when it comes to our way of living, the routines we fall into, and all the things we buy and use to sustain ourselves. "If we do something a thousand times, it is hard *not* to repeat it," says theologian Martin Marty. "What we do so habitually often creates illusions of security and holds us captive."[48]

Richard Foster, author of the modern classic on Christian spiritual disciplines, describes *simplicity* this way:

> The central point for the Discipline [sic.] of simplicity is to seek the kingdom of God and the righteousness of his kingdom *first* and then everything necessary will come in its proper order.[49]

This paraphrase of Matthew 6:25–34 is the touchstone that prompts us to become quiet within and to allow God to reshuffle our priorities, eliminating the froth.[50] Foster asserts that the heart of Christian simplicity points us toward a way of living in which everything we have comes to us as a gift, is cared for by God, and is available to others when the time is right.[51]

One key concept in beginning to live more simply is what Mennonite theologian Lynn Miller calls "inherent usefulness." For example, he says, a car's inherent usefulness is its ability to get us from one place to another. The inherent usefulness of a house is its ability to give us a place to live.[52] When we peel off the added symbolic meanings of status, sexual appeal, and financial success, we are able to determine our needs versus wants, and make more sensible financial choices. We might decide to downsize our responsibilities (such as a smaller home, a different job, or less costly entertainment) to reduce our attachment to so many things, in order to focus better on doing justice, loving kindness, and walking humbly with God (Micah 6:8).

Every person's responses will be different, but Foster offers some practices, or "principles," to develop a stronger personal habit of simpler living. Here are four of them:

- Learn to enjoy things without owning them.
  Regularly go to the library instead of the bookstore.
- Develop the habit of giving things away.
  Some people give away clothes at the end of the summer and winter seasons. Others buy and donate clothing and housewares at thrift stores. Still others keep an empty chair at the dinner table and encourage family members to invite a friend or stranger to eat with them.
- Look at all "buy now, pay later" schemes with healthy skepticism.
  Resist impulse buying, including purchasing things on layaway. There is a reason the company always makes a profit.
- Develop a deeper appreciation for creation.
  Instead of paying for entertainment activities, go for a walk or a hike, take the family camping, or spend a day exploring a park or nature area. Make the activity fit for you, your family, and your situation.[53]

The examples above show many ways we can tweak our lifestyles in our current situations. But for one North Carolina couple, one step naturally led to another, then another. Susan Carlyle and her husband discovered that living more simply is not as much about living on less as it is living with "a different kind of plenty," when they decided to homestead and do sustainable living. "Simplicity is about putting God first and setting aside anything that gets in the way of a life centered in him," she writes. "Integrity means living a life where your outward actions match your inward self."[54] Little did she know that their ecological and economic exercise would become a whole new way of life.

They started by giving things away: three truckloads to the Salvation Army of extra things she said they did not need anyway. Then they went from two cars to one. They put up a clothesline, cooked more, planted a vegetable garden, and started baking their own bread. Then they decided to move to a place where they would have no electric or water bill and could grow their own food. They wrote up a budget, retired early, bought a plot of land, and built a small, passive solar home. Susan says,

> We've homesteaded here in the mountains for 15 years, living sustainably on far less than we used to. The biggest surprise is that our lives have become richer in all respects. Kim and I still work much of the time but it's work that is satisfying to the soul."[55]

While not every family would go as far in simple living, we all have the opportunity to reassess our goals and find our own balance of time, effort, and convenience.

The discipline of simplicity directly challenges over-burdened, affluent lifestyles. In contrast to an excessive way of life, simplicity offers us a sense of freedom—freedom within, freedom from anxiety, and freedom from being endlessly consumer-driven.

Freedom within comes when we see living more simply not as an achievement, but as a gift of God's grace. No matter what stage of life at which we find ourselves, we hunger to be near the One who gives us a focus for life.[56]

"We work but we know that it is not our work that gives us what we have," says Foster. Then he names three inner attitudes of simplicity.

- We receive what we have as a gift from God. "We live by grace even when it comes to 'daily bread.' We are dependent upon God for the simplest elements of life: air, water, sun."[57]
- It is common sense to care for what we have, and take reasonable precautions against potential criminals, such as

locking our doors. But if we thought our precautions alone guard our possessions and lives, we would be riddled with anxiety. As we simplify our possessions, we feel freer to trust God for these and all things.

- We are more willing to share our goods with others in appropriate ways, because we know God will care for us. While we hold onto our essential possessions, we can let go of other things we have, to help someone else who is in need.

Such attitudes toward what we own can tend to reduce the weight of complex mental agendas, such as obsessing over how to protect what we have, or how to get the newest version of an electronic device. A simpler perspective can also help pry us out of anxiety about possible economic downturns tomorrow. These kinds of internal turmoil and uneasiness can make us forget to whom we belong, and why we were created. "Until we relocate the heart and its quest in God, we can never find life to be simple," says Marty. "But at the crucial moment, grafted back into the heart of God, human hearts find true repose. . . ."[58]

The majority of middle-class North Americans and Europeans live most of the time above the level of day-to-day subsistence. But even families who are struggling to gain basic financial security know that worry does not help them find their next meal. To those who have relative material comfort, Jesus' challenge comes as a particular shock. He warns us not to worry about having enough food, clothing and other logistics for existence (Luke 12:22–31). "Can any of you by worrying add a single hour to your span of life?" he asks. "If then you are not able to do so small a thing as that, why do you worry about the rest?" (verse 25) Then he says, "Instead, strive for [God's] kingdom, and these things will be given to you as well." (verse 31)

The bottom line is to trust God, even as we do our best to plan against negative contingencies. Our trust is not that what happens to us will always be positive, but that God cares about us, and loves us in the little things as well as in the big ones. The key (and we're all still working on this) is to keep remembering the big picture: God is in charge, and God loves us. If we seek a secure relationship with God, it becomes easier to be less insecure about our circumstances, to live simply, and to be generous. With the apostle Paul we can say,

> Not that I am referring to being in need, for I have learned to be content with whatever I have. I know what it is to have little, and I know what it is to have plenty. In any and all circumstances I have learned the secret of being well-fed and of going hungry, of having plenty and of being in need. I can do all things through [the One] who strengthens me." (Philippians 4:11–13)

This is not to say that nothing bad will happen to us. On the contrary, many accounts in the Bible talk about pain and loss, and our own life experiences bear this out. But no matter what our situation in this life—or even in the next—we still belong to Jesus Christ. (Philippians 1:21) The regular practice of simplicity can help us find our quiet center, strip away excess baggage and non-essentials, and focus on our relationship with God. As Richard Foster says, simpler living can "allow God to reshuffle [our] priorities and eliminate unnecessary froth."[59]

Spending for pleasure is not always "froth," as long as it comes *after* sharing and saving and paying for necessities—in other words, as long as it is intentional, and in line with the priorities we embrace. Each family's assessment of that balance will be different. But we may realize that we're embarking on the wrong path whenever we let our indulgences become a substitute for a healthy relationship with God or with other people.

Whenever we are tempted to take such a path, renewed awareness of incessant advertising and the lure of *more* can help free us from trying to buy our way (directly or indirectly) to love and status. "My needs for comfort, ego, stroking, and prestige could be met elsewhere," says Lynn Miller. He continues:

Now that I think of it, no amount of "stuff" could give me the love and status I get from having one sinless man in history give his life for mine. Nothing I can buy can do that—only the free gift of salvation in and from Jesus Christ (Romans 5:15–17).[60]

When Miller puts it that way I think, What greater abundance or security could I ever have?

IN THIS CHAPTER we have pointed out a major dilemma: saturated with advertising and weighed down by consumer debt, many families battle mightily with the lure of more, confusing wants with needs, and struggling to let go of obsessive consumption. We specified three false truths about the scarcity mindset: that if some is good more is better, that you are what you buy, and that your worth is in what you own. After characterizing the disease of "affluenza," we drew contrasting life lessons from John 6:1–13 and 2 Corinthians 9:8.

On further reflection, we discovered four dimensions of God's abundance—in the luxuriance of creation, in God's advocacy for us, in our daily relationship with the Holy Spirit, and in using our efforts and abilities to provide resources to benefit the people around us. Delving into the Bible's term for "contentment," we noted individual, family, and church examples that display an ethic of enough. Finally, we examined a life of simplicity as an attitude of inner freedom based upon life as a gift from God. We also explored some consequent practices of simpler living, from learning to enjoy things without owning them, to valuing possessions for their inherent usefulness instead of as symbols of competition or success.

# Questions for Reflection

1. What is my personal understanding of "inherent usefulness" for each of the following: house, car, salary, food, clothes, cash savings, and retirement savings? How much is "enough" of each of these things for me?

2. How do I deal with the gulf between people who do not have enough to survive, and those who are burdened with too much? Where do I find a personal balance in my own way of life?
3. In what areas of my life do I struggle with being content? How can I begin to address those issues?
4. To what degree do I feel an internal freedom from incessant advertising and the lure of *more*?

# Endnotes

1. James Alison, author of *Broken Hearts and New Creations: Imitations of a Great Reversal*, in "Reflections on the Lectionary" for March 3, 2013, *Christian Century* February 20, 2013, p. 21.
2. *Ibid.*
3. Samuel Longfellow, hymn: *One Holy Church of God Appears*, in Rueben P. Job and Norman Shawchuck, editors, *A Guide to Prayer for Ministers and Other Servants*, p. 254.
4. James C. Fenhagen, from *Ministry and Solitude*, in Rueben P. Job and Norman Shawchuck, editors, *ibid*, pp. 252f.
5. Charles R. Lane, "A Well-formed Stewardship Leader Trusts God's Abundance," in *How Much is Enough? A Deeper Look at Stewardship in an Age of Abundance*, edited by Catherine Malotky, p. 2.
6. *Ibid.*
7. Deb Smith, General Board of Discipleship (now Discipleship Ministries), "Romans 12. Emerging Trends In Vital Congregations;" *http://www.umcdiscipleship.org/resources/romans-12*. The quoted phrase is the official mission of The United Methodist Church.
8. *Ibid.*
9. Sue Clemmer Steiner, "Reflections on the Lectionary" for August 3, 2014, in *Christian Century*, July 23, 2014, p. 21.
10. *Ibid.*
11. Stephen Mitchell, *The Gospel According to Jesus: A New Translation and Guide to His Essential Teachings for Believers and Unbelievers*, excerpted for "A Morning Prayer Service," Retired Clergy Association Spring Fling, 2014, California-Nevada Conference of The United Methodist Church.
12. *Ibid.*
13. Christine Roush, *op cit.*, p. 11.
14. James M. Childs Jr., *Greed: Economics and Ethics in Conflict*, pp. 109f.

15. *Affluenza*, a coproduction of KCTS/Seattle and Oregon public Broadcasting (Bullfrog Films, 1997), cited in *ibid*, p. 110.
16. Don McClanen, *Ministry of Money* newsletter, September, 1982, p. 2.
17. *Ibid.* Here McClanen is citing Clarence Jordan, scholar, author and civil rights activist, in his book *The Sermon on the Mount*, pp. 96 and 98.
18. Laurence Shames, *The Hunger for More: Searching for Values in an Age of Greed*, pp. 21f., cited in *Greed: Economics and Ethics in Conflict* (Minneapolis: Augsburg Press, 2000), by James M. Childs, Jr., pp. 8f.
19. James M. Childs Jr., *op cit.*, p. 10.
20. *Ibid.*, p. 11.
21. Richard J. Foster, *Freedom of Simplicity: Finding Harmony in a Complex World*, quoted on *goodreads.com/work/quotes/1869385-freedom-of-simplicity-finding-harmony-in-a-complex-world*.
22. James Alison, "Reflections on the Lectionary" for February 17, 2013, p. 23.
23. Melanie Hardison, "A Theology of Enough for Everyone," *Stewardship presbyterian.typepad.com/enough*, p. 14.
24. *Ibid.*, p. 15. To learn more, she cites three key resources: Enough for Everyone at *pcusa.org/enough*; Sabbath Economics Collaborative at *sabbatheconomics.org*; and the World Alliance of Reformed Churches at *warc.ch*.
25. Both of these examples are real people I have met, protected here by anonymity.
26. See "Subversion and hope," James C. Howell's book review on Walter Brueggemann's *Sabbath as Resistance: Saying No to the Culture of Now* (*Christian Century*, June 25, 2014, pp. 32f.). Howell notes that Brueggemann calls the Sabbath, the weekly day of rest, an alternative to our workaholic, consumer culture, and an antidote to the market ideology of endless acquisition. God "is about restfulness not restlessness," asserts Brueggemann (on p. 32). It counteracts the attitude of anxious commodity, best expressed in the Book of Amos: "When will the new moon be over so that we may sell grain, and the Sabbath, so that we may offer wheat for sale...?" (Amos 8:5)
27. Oxford Clarendon Press, *An Intermediate Greek-English Lexicon: Founded upon the Seventh Edition of Liddell and Scott's Greek-English Lexicon*, London: Oxford University Press, 1975, p. 117.
28. Gerhard Kittel, editor, *Theological Dictionary of the New Testament, Volume 1*, p. 465.
29. *Ibid.*
30. Roush, Christine, *op cit.*, pp. 4f.
31. Adam Hamilton, *op cit.*, pp. 59–65.
32. Matthew Thomas, blogging for Design Group International, at *designgroupinternation.com/blog*.
33. Robert Schnase, *Five Practices of Fruitful Living* (Nashville, Abingdon Press, 2010), pp. 128f.
34. *Ibid*, p. 129.

35. "ethics." *The American Heritage New Dictionary of Cultural Literacy, Third Edition.* Houghton Mifflin Company, 2005. 20 Aug. 2015. <Dictionary.com dictionary.reference.com/browse/ethics>.

36. "ethic." *Merriam-Webster Dictionary.* An Encyclopedia Britannica Company, 2015. 20 Aug. 2015. <merriam-webster.com/dictionary/ethic>.

37. Wesley named three "General Rules" for Methodists: do no harm, do good, and attend on all the ordinances of God. This third General Rule included public worship, Scripture study, the Lord's Supper, prayer, and fasting. See David Lowes Watson, *The Early Methodist Class Meeting* (Nashville: Discipleship Resources, 1995), p. 205.

38. Rev. Mike Harrell, May 10, 2015 sermon, Foothills United Methodist Church, Rescue, California.

39. *Affluenza* was a one-hour television special produced by John de Graaf and Vivia Boe, which explored the high social and environmental costs of materialism and overconsumption. It was a production of KCTS/Seattle and Oregon Public Broadcasting, made possible by a grant from The Pew Charitable Trusts. See *pbs.org/kcts/affluenza.*

40. *Ibid.*

41. Adam Hamilton, *Enough Stewardship Program Guide* (Nashville: Abingdon Press, 2009), p. 68.

42. ——, *Enough: Discovering Joy Through Simplicity and Generosity* (Nashville: Abingdon Press, 2009), pp. 16–20.

43. James A. Harnish, *Simple Rules for Money: John Wesley on Earning, Saving, and Giving* (Nashville: Abingdon Press, 2009), p. 29. Here he cites Hamilton's book *Enough*, pp. 15f.

44. *freecycle.org.*

45. In Dietz and O'Neill's book, *Enough Is Enough: Building a Sustainable Economy in a World of Finite Resources,* (San Francisco, Berrett-Koehler Publishers, Inc., 2013), p. 163, they cite Rob Hopkins' book, *The Transition Handbook: From Oil Dependency to Local Resilience* (White River Junction, Vt.: Chelsea Green Publishing, 2008). The Transition Town movement uses a multi-stakeholder planning process to increase local self-reliance and resilience; *transitionus.org/ transition-town-movement.*

46. Rob Dietz and Dan O'Neill, *op cit.*, pp. 162–164.

47. *i.imgur.com/ULRv15R.jpg*

48. Martin Marty and Micah Marty, *When True Simplicity Is Gained: Finding Spiritual Clarity in a Complex World* (Grand Rapids, MI and Cambridge, U.K.; William B. Eerdmans Publishing Company, 1998), p. 31.

49. Richard J. Foster, *Celebration of Discipline: The Path to Spiritual Growth,* 25th Anniversary Edition (San Francisco: HarperSanFrancisco / Harper Collins, 1998), p. 86.

50. ———, *Freedom of Simplicity: Finding Harmony in a Complex World*, cited at *goodreads.com/work/quotes/1869385-freedom-of-simplicity-finding-harmony-in-a-complex-world*.
51. *Ibid.*
52. Lynn A. Miller, *op cit.*, p. 46.
53. Richard J. Foster, *Celebration of Discipline*, pp. 90–95.
54. Susan Carlyle, "A Different Kind of Plenty," *Guideposts*, September 2012, pp. 78–81.
55. *Ibid*, p. 81.
56. Martin Marty, *op cit.,* p. 16.
57. Richard J. Foster, *Celebration of Discipline*, p. 88.
58. Martin Marty and Micah Marty, *op cit.*, p. 19.
59. Excerpt from *Freedom of Simplicity: Finding Harmony in a Complex World.* Richard J. Foster, "Freedom and Simplicity," at *spiritualtyandpractice.com/books/excerpts.php?id=19074*.
60. Lynn A. Miller, "Living on Enough," in *Money Mania: Mastering the Allure of Excess* by Mark L. Vincent (Goshen, IN: MMA, 2005, p. 97.

# 10

## Generosity and Money

WHETHER WE HAVE a little or a lot, money is a powerful force in our lives. For millions of people, it is the unspoken measure of worth in our society. We hear about money all around us in people's unconscious language. As the old song goes, "She's a million-dollar baby," the words implying that our assets equal our worth as persons. As God's children, I would say that we are "priceless," but that term brings up a credit card ad!

Surprisingly, at every level of income, many people believe a little more money is the answer to their financial needs or woes. At the same time, almost all of us know those who barely get to see their loved ones because of all the work hours they must put in to provide for their families. Money can be a powerful driver.

Yet unconsciously, a lot of us are taught that money is tainted. It's interesting how many people misquote 1Timothy 6:10, thinking that *money* "is the root of all evil." No, Timothy says it is the *love* of money that is the root of all evil. Here 1Timothy explains that evil gets its foothold if we love money more than anything else, including God.

We often have conflicting feelings about money. On the one hand, messages all around us say to strive for greater wealth and the possessions it brings. An extreme version of this view is the bumper sticker that says, "The one who dies with the most toys wins." On the other hand, people can fear that money itself is a bad thing, and be afraid to spend and leverage it, as if making money were a less-than-godly endeavor.

# The Big Taboo

Confusion about money is compounded in the church and other respectable places when we think we are not supposed to talk about it. It becomes the proverbial "elephant in the room." So while advertising and so much of our society revolves around money, thousands of spiritual or religious people are uncomfortable discussing it. By making it a taboo subject, we let money gain more tacit power, since we never get a chance to evaluate its proper role.

Our confusion can increase when our experiences teach us conflicting lessons about money. For example, they might tell us:

- "There's never enough money to go around."
- "Money is meant to be used for good."
- "The more money you have, the greater your worth as a person."
- "If you work hard, you'll always have enough money to live on."
- "To whom much is given, much is expected in return."
- "Church leaders only talk about money when they want people to give."
- "The purpose of work is just to make a paycheck."
- "The more money you have, the more power you have over others."
- "Money is meant to be shared."
- "If I earn money, it belongs to me alone."

As we mature, these lessons may or may not prove to be true for us. This is why it helps greatly to write a Money Autobiography at different points in our lives, to clarify our experiences and help us assess which lessons remain valid.

A *Money Autobiography* is a written reflection on the role money has played in our lives, including our attitudes and assumptions about money and possessions. Our early personal experiences with money may have left us feeling magical, worrisome, fun, or fearful about having enough. Given our adult experiences, we can reassess the childhood messages we received through our parents' attitudes about money and how they made family financial decisions. We can write three to five pages about our feelings and actions related to money as a helpful part of our spiritual journey.

Church consultant Dan Dick has provided an excellent set of reflective questions we can use in this process, pondering one question a day over a four-week period.[1] For example:

- What is your earliest memory of money?
- Did you feel rich, poor, or neither growing up? Did you worry about money when you were a child? A teenager?
- In what ways are you a spender? A saver? Generous? Stingy?
- In what ways are you a good or poor manager of money?
- How does your relationship with money affect your faith? How does your faith affect your relationship with money?

Another good source of Money Autobiography questions comes from Jan Dockter's *Money & Faith Study Circle Handbook*.[2] A church or ministry can also design a spiritual retreat for individuals to go through such a process together.[3]

Within the family, Nathan Dungan suggests several positive efforts that can jumpstart money conversations with children:4

1. Lead by Sharing—Sensitizing children to the needs of others teaches them the impact of generosity. Give them numerous opportunities to share their money and time, responding to the world's needs.
2. Set Savings Goals—Goal-setting can counter the demand for instant gratification. When children save for something they want, they develop patience and discipline.

3. Start Talking—Children learn healthy money habits and shared values through conversations and experiences with their parents and other responsible adults.

4. Walk the Walk—Adults' money habits and values can influence for decades how their children and grandchildren use money. Periodic re-evaluation of our practices can help us realign our behavior with our desired outcome.

When we embrace opportunities to talk about these issues as a family, we provide important building blocks for the next generation to establish a healthy view of money.

# How to Talk About Money in the Church

Allowing ourselves to refer to personal finances in church can bring a burst of new life to the whole congregation. I am not talking about asking for money, but rather discussing money as part of life in a non-anxious way. Money is a factor in all of our lives, not solely related to our giving. We deal with money whenever we earn, save, spend, manage, or share any of our material resources. And whether our income is high or low, we all have to live within financial limits.

How might we talk about money in a healthy way? To begin, we can affirm that we all use money as a resource and have to make choices about where our funds will go. From a Christian viewpoint, once we have gained the funds we need for a basic livelihood, the most important thing is not the amount of money we have, but what we do with it for God's purposes. (That is stewardship, after all.) In our daily life as a congregation, we can choose to become a safe place to discuss money and our personal values, where we can learn from one another's experiences as well as from the Scriptures, trusting the Holy Spirit to guide us.

One example is at North Point Community Church in Alpharetta, Georgia, where the church leadership makes the conversation about faith and money so natural that people don't get anxious when the topic comes up. Their pastor, Andy Stanley, says, "Generosity is something we want *for* you, not *from* you."[5]

Breaking the ground first helps grow greater comfort around references to money. For example, leaders might:

- Encourage and celebrate non-monetary giving, such as: sharing garden produce, sending words of encouragement to other church members, mailing get-well notes, and following up on people for whom prayers are given, committing time for personal involvement in the community, and giving in-kind goods to help others.
- Work with the church treasurer to treat giving as a way to pursue issues of pastoral or spiritual care. For example, when people suddenly give less, they may have lost their job, experienced a divorce, heard bad news about their health, or lost a sense of connection with their faith community. Any of these situations provides an important opportunity to support people and show they care.
- Help the congregation transfer leadership from one generation to another, particularly in the field of finances. Focus more on the common goal of making disciples of Jesus Christ than on preserving the methods of how things have been done in the past.
- Train the church's youth group to define its own goals and manage its own money.[6]
- Offer a "Money" class that helps people put their financial lives in better order. For example, they may choose programs from Freed-Up Financial Living,[7] a version of Financial Peace University,[8] or Crown Ministries.[9] Also, each year the pastor might hold a sermon series based on biblical texts. For years at Ginghamsburg United Methodist Church in Tipp City, Ohio, pastor Michael Slaughter offered a "Money" sermon series every January. Historically more people attended worship at Ginghamsburg during those weeks than at any other time of the year.

When it comes to congregational worship, the time when we give our money offerings and silently give our hearts to God can be a highlight of the service, arising out of worshipers' spiritual need to express love and devotion to God.[10] The offering time gives each person the opportunity to show gratitude to God for all that God has done for us. We give thanks to God, to whom everything belongs.[11] Sharing stories during this time can affirm God's goodness and help people celebrate changed lives and spiritual growth.

The purpose of this time in worship is not only to receive money to pay the church's expenses, but also to give people a chance to participate in God's work through a range of local and global ministries. In contrast to some televangelists and other preachers who unethically bilk money out of people for their personal profit, authentic churches tell people where the money goes, have audits and show accountability, and report back showing how people have been helped.

This has also been a time of giving back in the worship service, particularly during the 2008 recession. Some churches hosted "reverse offerings," allowing people in need to take from the offering plate. Still other congregations distributed funds periodically to members, encouraging them to find people to receive the money. Then they posted the stories about their giving on a website for the entire congregation to see.[12]

For example, in early 2009, when giving had slumped at Cross Timbers Community Church, Argyle, Texas, pastor Toby Slough knew the members had to be hurting from the recession. So he suggested to the Church Board that they give away much of the money held in the church's reserve fund. The following Sunday "they told the congregation that if anyone had a need, they were to take money from the plate instead of giving to it," or to "pass it on" to others in need.[13] For the two months after that Sunday, the three-campus megachurch gave extra money for the purpose, so they were able to give more than $500,000 to members and non-members who were struggling financially. That effort sparked more outreach to people in need, as the congregation gave designated gifts and distributed

$200,000 through four missions that fed and clothed people experiencing hard times.

Reverse offerings can give more than money, as well. For example, many congregations have cited Jesus' parable of the "talents" (Matthew 25:14–30) to take a small amount of money and make it grow for the community's benefit. One spectacular example is the Coats of Kindness program sponsored by All Saints Lutheran Church in Cottage Grove, Minnesota.[14] In 2009, All Saints member Eric Wenzel received such a dire cancer diagnosis that he decided to give away some of his coats. When All Saints offered a fifty-dollar pay-it-forward initiative, he and his family bought coats to give to people who had none. The manager of the coat store heard about the cause and dramatically reduced coat prices, and other shoppers in the checkout line spontaneously contributed money.

A year later, Coats of Kindness was organized as a nonprofit organization, and continued to collect and give away winter wear. Every year, Coats of Kindness continues to expand its reach, involving corporations and even an elementary school in Iowa.

Through worship, leadership, classes, and small groups, the church can help people become less anxious about money—not merely to encourage more church giving, but to help them establish a healthier relationship with money and feel more contentment in their lives.

# A Would-Be God

It is hard to experience fulfillment when, in many ways today, people's money-related attitudes and actions make it seem like a god.[15] For example, money:

- Outlives us. It was here before we were born and will be here in one form or another after we are gone.
- Can extend our circle of influence. Money lengthens our reach to make a difference in people's lives and circumstances.

- Is associated with mystery. Unexpected developments can happen on Wall Street, for example, or with our investments or pension funds. Such financial surprises can change our lives in dramatic ways.

Because money seems eternal, powerful, and mysterious, it seems to live in the realm of what human beings are tempted to worship. To many people, money's purchasing power mimics what God promises about the New Jerusalem, including health, dignity, peace, justice (Isaiah 65:17ff.), healing, and direct access to the Source of life (Revelation 21:1–22:5).

In even more ways, money can seem to act like a god:

- Money can be used for good or for ill. We can wield it as an extension of our own body, using it as a sword to attack others, like a shield for protection, or as a scalpel for healing. We can also do great things with money to improve people's conditions. But sometimes, even with good intentions, our money-related decisions harm other people anyway.
- In some ways, everything can become the subject of economic conversation. For example, we might look at God's ministries through the church and think that we are just "raising the budget" instead of transforming people's lives.
- Money can even seduce us into thinking *we* are God: that we are in control, all-powerful, and capable of exerting our presence everywhere.

So if money is not meant to be a god for us to worship, how are we to view it? Philip Jamieson, foundation director and theological teacher, says money is "a key aspect of faithful Christian discipleship."[16] Congregants' money management practices such as budgeting, investing, saving, and spending are inseparable from Christian discipleship.[17] In this way, money is a power that is neither good nor bad in itself. Depending upon our use of it, it can lead people away from God, or it can be a dynamic tool to uplift, support, and empower people as part of God's mission in the world.

# Getting Out of Debt

While constant "more-is-better" advertising and too-easy use of credit cards surround us, many of us have come to assume that debt is an inevitable part of the American way of life.

But several places in the Bible give us a different message. The person who borrows ends up morally and legally obligated to the lender (Proverbs 22:7). If we have any debts, we are to repay them as quickly as possible (Psalm 37:21; Proverbs 3:18). If we co-sign a loan, guaranteeing someone else's future payments, we could lose our home (Proverbs 22:26f). Paul tells us to pay everyone what we owe them, including taxes to the government, giving respect and honor to those who are worthy (Romans 13:7). Continual, excessive, or inappropriate debt also denies us the opportunity to learn the "self-control" (Galatians 5:22f) which is evidence of the Holy Spirit. Living in ongoing debt also reduces our respect for God's mysterious work beyond our efforts and our lifetime. Because accumulating debt presumes that it can be paid off easier later on, it robs us of learning how to master worry about meeting our future material needs (Luke 12:22–34).

Both Financial Peace University and Freed-Up Financial Living give specific instructions and worksheets for reducing our indebtedness, as part of their comprehensive materials for helping families get back on track with their finances. We can also use some technological aids. For example, a person may choose to enroll in the Acorns program at *www.acorns.com*. It automatically rounds up to the nearest dollar on our purchases and invests the difference, which we can use to reduce our debt.

Several structured programs can help us guard against further unwise debt. For example, one friend has arranged with her bank to take one dollar out of every credit card purchase she makes and put it into her savings account. Another friend uses the electronic Mint program at *www.mint.com* to help him manage his money, pay his bills, and track his credit score. In addition, four alternative Apps are available at the iTunes App Store: Debts Break Pro, Debt Free-Payoff, Debt Manager, and Payoff Debt. Each one of these costs less than five dollars to initiate.

Whether or not we use a structured program, Mike Sullivan, of Take Charge America,[18] outlines these basic steps for getting back in the black:

1. Define a specific goal—"Get out of debt" or "save more money" are too broad for goals. A realistic, attainable goal might be "save $100 from every paycheck," or "reduce credit card debt by $100 every month."
2. Make an ongoing automatic commitment—If people receive a paycheck, they might add a payroll deduction to go into their savings account, or to make a gift to their church or another charity. If they are building funds for retirement, they could increase their automatic contribution on their 401k.
3. Get creative with paying off debt—We can consider payment opportunities beyond our regular monthly payments, such as reevaluating student-loan repayment options, consolidating high-interest credit card debt into a fixed personal loan, or getting into a debt-management plan sponsored by a nonprofit agency.
4. Reevaluate monthly bills to see what can be eliminated or reduced—For example, we might cancel premium television cable services or some other indulgence, get new quotes for auto insurance, refinance the home mortgage to a lower rate, or decide if the gym membership is really worth it.
5. Track our progress—People are more likely to accomplish their goals if they set up specific, measurable timelines and accomplishments. Telling family members or close friends about our goals can help us be accountable and give us someone with

whom to celebrate the milestones or discuss and hopefully resolve difficulties along the way.

The above steps are suggestive only. But if we choose one of them, we could start a New Beginnings small group at our church or pick a partner for mutual encouragement. Our new behavior could make a big difference!

Using money in a healthy way requires an active, fluid balance as we deal with the ups and downs life can bring, readjusting spending priorities to suit changing needs and circumstances. Sometimes the best we can do is to be intentional about making wise financial decisions. The goal is to manage our money according to values we have carefully set, rather than have our money manage us.

# A Spiritual Issue

"Money is not a financial issue. It is a spiritual issue. Money is not about your bank account. It is about your heart for God and others," says Mennonite stewardship leader Steve Ganger.[19] When we work for pay, money is simply something for which we trade our life energy. At the same time, when we give money, it tends to increase our passion for the cause (Luke 12:32–34). So the ways we use money help shape our values and priorities. At the same time, when we have encountered God's grace in some way, generosity is our natural and appropriate response.[20]

Jesus talks a lot about money. One in every sixteen verses in the New Testament is about money and/or stewardship. In fact, "the Bible has more verses about a person's relationship to possessions and giving than about prayer, believing, and love combined."[21] The only topic Jesus discusses more than finances, giving, and stewardship is the Kingdom or Reign of God.[22]

How we steward, or manage, money is a key measure of our spirituality. Stewardship is not just how much we manage and give; it is what we do with whatever we have. Trying to manage money prompts each of us to ask ourselves, "What do I own, and what owns me?" In a book by that name, Daniel Conway says:

> The question *What do I own?* calls attention to all the spiritual and material gifts that we have received from a good and gracious God. The second question, *What owns me?* probes the state of our souls. Have we freely given over our life and our will to the Lord? Or are we still holding back—possessed in some way by our possessions, by the seductive influences of status, wealth, or the illusion of control?[23]

These questions encourage us to consider issues at the intersection of our faith and our resources. Reflecting on these concerns can help us cultivate a spirit of openness in community with others who are on a similar journey.

When we let Jesus challenge and guide us, we can "develop into disciples who, in gratitude, compassion and justice, are eager to align their money with the needs of God's created order."[24] Money is a tool to serve God. When we pause to think about money in this way, we can intentionally use it according to our faith for God's purposes, thereby benefitting our personal lives and our faith community. We are able to use money as a tool to serve God, as we can with every other gift God has entrusted to us, including our abilities and talents, time, possessions, and ministries.

In an integrated life, money does not exist for its own sake. Throughout the Scriptures it is linked with helping people in need. For example, in Deuteronomy 15:1–11, God commands the Israelites to care for less fortunate people in their tribes. In Proverbs 11:25, the author connects generosity with helping others, and in Proverbs 19:17 we read, "whoever is kind to the poor lends to the LORD." In Matthew 25:31–46, Jesus equates feeding the hungry, clothing the naked, and caring for the sick with putting God first.

Stories surround us today about how giving financial support can empower people to meet others' needs. For example, having "covenant relationships" with local congregations—including supportive prayer, financial gifts, and missionary visits—empowered The Soul Family Center in Missouri to change lives. "Occasionally those we assist ask why we're here, why we don't charge for what we do," said one deaconess serving at the center. "Their response is wide-eyed wonder at the idea that because of God's love, people they never will meet also love and choose to be a part of their lives."[25]

The Bible also inherently connects financial giving with right living.[26] Cheating or stealing from one another is a sin against God (Leviticus 6:1–7). God does not want offerings that are given just to show off, without our trying to live in a way that honors God (Amos 5:21–24; Micah 6:6–8; Luke 11:42).

Sondra Wheeler, Christian ethics professor at Wesley Theological Seminary, makes a dramatic case for interweaving giving and living: "You are already giving your life for something, pouring it out at some altar, spending it on something. Sell it dearly!" She continues:

Trade it for warmth for someone out on the street on a freezing night; trade it for all the milk a hungry child can drink; trade it for comfort for the dying in Haiti, or down the road in the local AIDS hospice. If not for them, then for yourself! For your own sake, share in God's joy....[27]

Bible scholar N. T. Wright seems to agree. He says, "The Kingdom that Jesus preached and lived was all about a glorious, uproarious, absurd generosity."[28] In response, our spiritual journey should guide our generosity (with money, care for others, and right living) more than the size of our financial assets.

For example, one ten-year-old girl heard her bishop urging children to help fight against malaria by providing treated mosquito nets. She started collecting bottles and cans and recycled them for money. She added the money she received for her birthday, Christmas, and other special events. In worship on Health Sunday, she announced she had raised more than $1,000, saying she wanted to give her sisters and brothers in Africa a chance to live.[29]

Generosity is not rooted in our bank balance, but in the habits of our hearts.[30] Consultant Nathan Dungan teaches future pastors at Luther Seminary, Minneapolis, six habits to increase awareness of money's influence and make financial decision-making more fruitful:

- Reflect on who and what shaped your early money habits;
- Learn to recognize your strongest money-related habits, and discover how they impact other aspects of your life;
- Discover new ways to communicate about money and values effectively and proactively;
- Develop a financial decision-making process that honors your values;
- Learn how to set realistic money goals that include saving and sharing; and
- Get simple, implementable ideas and tools, such as budget forms and online helps, to support healthy money habits.[31]

The money we have is not our money—it belongs to God. Yes, we earned it, but God gives us the capacity to want to earn and seeks to inspire us to work for the right reasons. Also other people help us earn it, from the employers who gave us our jobs, to our coworkers and the complex network of supply and demand that makes it possible. God gives us the ability to share, to save, and to spend. In sharing we can develop the virtues of generosity and gratitude. In saving we can grow patience and discipline. In spending we can learn the difference between basic needs and passing wants.[32]

As we saw previously in Eric Law's Cycle of Blessings, money is one of six currencies, along with time and place, gracious leadership, relationship, truth, and wellness. But there is another helpful metaphor, as well. When we receive, use, and pass on money in life-affirming ways, it brings well-being, similar to blood that must flow to all parts of the body in order to bring health.[33] But when we let our "holdings" hold us back from using money in other-oriented ways, money no longer carries positive energy and intent. Instead we are dominated by fear of losing it, defensiveness, and an unhealthy need to control.

Money by itself cannot do anything. As Jeavons and Basinger say, "You can have all the money in the world, but if you don't have people of faith to use it wisely... for the right things, God's work will not be done."[34]

Whatever we do with money, the key is to live in right relationship with it. The Bible's central message about money is not that we should be happy with just a small amount of it, says stewardship leader Sanford Coon:

> The recurring message is about trusting God to provide sufficiently for us, [which] allows us tremendous freedom from fear, uncertainty, and even regret. This understanding allows us to receive and manage dollars that come to us with a sense that they are bountiful evidence of God's sacred generosity.[35]

Such trust requires that we live not without fear, but in spite of our fears about money. We may fear that we will never have enough. We may fear that people value us only because of the things we can give to them. Or we may fear that we are loved only because of what we can do to help others.

Fear also can arise as a symptom of the class distinctions people make, giving some individuals less worth as persons compared to those who have more. Money has a community value, after all, which both the giver and the receiver share. In fact, money in any of its forms is worthless if it is not part of a system of exchange of goods and services.[36] Only through participating in that exchange system can one earn or accumulate wealth at all. And how we make and spend our money always affects others. This is especially true if we habitually say we *need* something we merely *want*. Such repeated buying decisions leave us less money available for generosity toward others, making it harder for those less fortunate to fulfill more basic needs.

Considering the effects on others flowing from how we acquire and use money affects others can lead us to acknowledge our affluence in relation to the world as a whole. "I am wealthy because I have access to adequate food, shelter, clothing, work, education, transportation, and health care," says Jean Blomquist. "Yet it is not always easy for me to recognize... usually because I compare my situation to those who have more than I do."[37]

Sometimes a way to get into a better money relationship is not to spend more resources, but to use those resources more creatively. For example, a businessperson who owns two hardware stores in a city may not need to sell one store in order to have money to be generous. He or she may provide jobs more creatively, house a neighborhood center as well as a business, explore new practices of employing the poor, consider equal salaries, or rotate managers.

LOOKING BACK at our use of money as a spiritual issue, we can see that how we steward it is a key measure of our spirituality. Money doesn't exist for its own sake but relies on its use in an economic system for its value. In the Bible, money is inherently connected to helping people in need. It is also linked to right living, awareness of its influence on our lives, spiritual commitment, daily habits of good money management, and fruitful monetary processes.

Even as we realize that we earn our money thanks to God-given gifts, we need to do our best to plan, share, save, and spend it more wisely. This process urges us to overcome the fears we have had about money into a more confident faith. We can acknowledge our affluence relative to those who have less rather than to those who have more and consider how our money habits influence others' lives. We are able to work on ways to use our resources creatively to benefit the wider community.

# Questions for Reflection

1. How have I experienced money's power in my life? Are there any ways in which I have treated or regarded it as a would-be god?

2. Has the atmosphere in our congregation allowed church members to talk about money in the church in a beneficial way? Would any of the five healthy ways listed in this chapter free us to deal with money as more faithful, positive stewards?
3. How could I get out of debt, or become more faithful in staying away from it? Which of the ideas here might help my church assist its members in their individual and family financial situations?
4. What are some ways I can use my resources creatively to benefit my wider community?

# Endnotes

1. Dan R. Dick, "A Money Autobiography," *www.gbod.org*, Aug. 6, 2003. These questions work well in small groups, too.
2. Jan Sullivan Dockter, *Money & Faith Study Circle Handbook*, March, 2002; published by Ministry of Money and available from *www.ministryofmoney.org*.
3. See Mark L. Vincent, *Speaking About Money: Reducing the Tension* (Scottdale, PA and Waterloo, Ontario: Herald Press, 2001), pp. 33–35 for preliminary questions and a proposed schedule for a Money Autobiography retreat.
4. Nathan Dungan, "Teaching Generosity in an Era of Austerity," *www.sharesavespend.com*, Nov. 23, 2011.
5. Chris Willard and Jim Sheppard, *Contagious Generosity*, p. 67.
6. For these first four points, see Mark L. Vincent, *op cit.*, pp. 89–100.
7. Freed-Up Financial Living provides stewardship resources and training for churches, organizations, and Christian leaders. Its core curriculum for families is *Freed-Up Financial Living: How to get there with biblical principles,* by Dick Towner and John Tofilon with Shannon Plate (Colorado Springs: Willow Creek Resources, NavPress, 2008).
8. Financial Peace University is founded by Dave Ramsey. It teaches "God's ways of handling money" in nine sessions, using video teaching, class discussions and interactive small group activities. Participants can take a version of the course in different individual or group formats.
9. Crown Ministries was founded by Larry Burkett. Its core course is the Crown Biblical Financial Study, for leaders, and for students, as well as a Life Group Manual, Practical Application Workbook, and more. For more information, go to *www.crown.org*.

10. Mark Allan Powell, *Giving to God: The Bible's Good News about Living a Generous Life* (William B. Eerdmans, Grand Rapids, 2006), p. 12.
11. Melvin Amerson, "Celebrating the Offering," National Association of United Methodist Foundations Annual Meeting, June 24, 2008.
12. Chris Willard and Jim Sheppard, *op cit.*, pp. 66f.
13. *Ibid*, pp. 65ff.
14. Charles (Chick) Lane, then Director of the Center for Stewardship Leaders at Luther Seminary, in "Coats of Kindness," *Stewardship for the 21st Century* e-newsletter, Jan. 15, 2013.
15. Mark Vincent, "The Whys and Hows of Money Leadership workshop" at Los Altos United Methodist Church, 2002.
16. Philip D. Jamieson, Executive Director of The Tennessee United Methodist Foundation and former Assistant Professor of Pastoral Theology at the University of Dubuque Theological Seminary, in *Ministry and Money: A Practical Guide for Pastors*, by Janet T. Jamieson and Philip D. Jamieson (Westminster John Knox Press, Louisville: 2009), p. 8.
17. Practicing money management as disciples is one of eight steps Richard Foster proposes for allowing Christ, not wealth, to be one's master, in *op cit.*, p. 192.
18. News release, "Take Charge America helps consumers establish realistic financial goals and identify steps to achieve goals," *Georgetown Gazette,* January 7, 2016. Take Charge America is a national nonprofit credit counseling and debt management agency.
19. Steve Ganger, Director of Stewardship Education, MMA, in Mark L. Vincent, *Money Mania*, p. 147.
20. Chris Willard and Jim Sheppard, *Contagious Generosity*, p. 37.
21. Michael Reeves and Jennifer Tyler, *Faith & Money: Understanding Annual Giving in Church* (Nashville: Discipleship Resources, 2003), p. 12.
22. —— in "Book Notes: *Faith and Money*" by Ronnie G. Collins, on *www.imagebearerblog.com*.
23. Daniel Conway, *What Do I Own, and What Owns Me?* p. 40.
24. Ministry of Money newsletter, 2002.
25. *Here I am, Lord! Devotional Guide for the Advance for Christ and His Church*, United Methodist Communications.
26. Herb Miller, *Full Disclosure: Everything the Bible Says About Financial Giving* (Nashville: Discipleship Resources, 2003), p. 47.
27. Sondra Wheeler, "A Celebration of Grace: The Economics of Fearlessness," *Giving: Growing Joyful Stewards in Your Congregation* magazine, Ecumenical Stewardship Center, 2002, p. 27.
28. N. T. Wright, *Luke for Everyone*, p. 73, cited at *www.generouschurch.com/15-generosity-quotes*.
29. "10-Year-Old Raises $1,000 for Imagine No Malaria," *Instant Connection*, California-Nevada Annual Conference, United Methodist Church, April

30, 2015. The congregation was Hayward First United Methodist Church in Hayward, CA.

30. Herb Miller, *op cit.*, p. 81.

31. Nathan Dungan's workshop, "Mind Your Money," described by Glenn Taibl and Gerry Rafferty in the Center for Stewardship Leaders e-newsletter, August 19, 2014.

32. Nathan Dungan, *www.sharesavespend.com.*

33. Lynne Twist, *op cit.,* p. 105.

34. Thomas H. Jeavons and Rebekah Burch Basinger, *Growing Givers' Hearts: Treating Fundraising as Ministry* (San Francisco: Jossey-Bass, 2000), p. 33.

35. Sanford Coon, "Sacred Money," in *The Cornerstone*, by the New Mexico Conference Methodist Foundation, March 2010.

36. Jean M. Blomquist, "My Money, My Self: Moving from Fear to Faith," *Weavings* "Singleness of Heart" issue, March/April 2003, p. 44.

37. *Ibid.*

# Putting God First

L IVING GENEROUSLY INCLUDES far more than how we give from our assets; it expresses who we are and seek to be: faithful, joyful disciples of Jesus Christ, authentically seeking to grow in God's grace.

For many people trying to move from fear to faith, the most difficult step can be to believe that who we are is not intrinsically tied to what we have or what we do. While we don't consciously set out to create a false personality built from our financial assets and public roles, it's common to hold the false belief that our net worth equals our self-worth. Sometimes we confuse the amount of our possessions with our core identity. As we become more aware of the pull of materialism around and within us, we can more readily realize to whom we belong.

## Moving Beyond Materialism

There is nothing like a natural disaster to put possessions in their place. Floods were always a possibility when I served as pastor for a church in the Sacramento river delta. Specific local residents checked the levees regularly for "boils:" places where the packed dirt might let river water seep through. In 1986 a great flood came, after excessive rains and a sudden release of water from overfull dams in the mountains. Within twenty minutes walls of water swept into homes, covering thousands of acres of low-lying farmlands.

Worship that Sunday was full to the brim, as evacuees and survivors gathered to pray and reclaim their lives together. I asked them, "What did you pack in your cars to be ready to evacuate?" The answers revealed a common theme. Beyond a few essential documents, they took what had greatest personal meaning: family photographs and symbolic treasures that reminded them of who they were and where they came from. They left everything else.

As one person said, "People come first. The rest are just things."

When we are caught up in materialism, we evaluate our life values or objectives solely according to how they relate to our material well-being.[1] In this section we will challenge all-too-ubiquitous materialism, by examining several strategies:

- Helping one another create a plan to get out of debt;
- Teaching children and youth how to handle money;
- Living more simply in a consumerist culture; and
- Establishing some essential financial planning practices.

Getting engulfed in spending, building wealth, or paying on endless debts leaves little room for generosity.[2] The pull of hyper-consumerism tends to limit our perspective by keeping us focused on our own investments, abilities, jobs, homes, insurance, pensions, education, leisure, and possessions. This restricted focus compromises our ability to balance personal or family finances with generous stewardship. In the church, we can fall just as fully into privatism, viewing our giving more as a fee-for-service responsibility than as an essential spiritual practice.

Even if we are paying personal debts and loans responsibly, we may ask ourselves some questions. For example, First Fruits teacher Lynn Miller wonders why Americans are so good at making payments on consumer loans, but so bad at making savings deposits. "We have the highest level of private consumer debt in the industrialized world and the lowest savings rate," he says. "That's baffling, since a loan payment is nothing more than a savings deposit going in the other direction!"[3] The answer is that procuring loans to buy things before we have the money and paying on debts afterwards has become the norm for so many of us. We've never learned what it feels like to save up for major purchases.

When we manage money better, we can avoid some of materialism's pitfalls. For example, the authors of *Kids, Money & Values* start with a parents' guide for children ages five through fourteen that lists the children's capacities for arithmetic skills, interest in money, sense of personal property, and view of honesty and truthfulness.[4] Next they provide a quiz to help the adults clarify what they want their children to value. Looking through these lenses, parents can review specific activities geared to children from preschoolers on, including everything from shopping with a parent to earning money, saving, receiving allowances, and more.

Allowances should come with a weekly "money conversation" that fits the child's age and situation.

For example, an adult named Billy attended a workshop from Nathan Dungan that taught him to set up a "Share Save Spend" allowance. Billy reported big changes after almost a year of the weekly allowance conversations. His younger son, Leif, noticed the number of homeless people on Minneapolis street corners, and decided to give his "share money" to a homeless shelter. Billy located a local nonprofit helping homeless youth and adults, called Street Works. Now Leif is its youngest donor. "Not only is Leif learning how to make wise money decisions," says Billy, "but he is also beginning to understand that his resources can make a difference in the world—even as an eight-year-old."[5]

When it comes to allowances, national radio talk-show host Ric Edelman adds a surprise. He says children should be doing four things with their money:

1. Giving some to charity;
2. Saving some for a long-term goal;

3. Spending some; and
4. Withholding some for taxes!

"Children need to be taught from a very early age that they don't get to keep everything they earn," he says.[6] He boldly recommends the parent withhold one-third of the child's allowance, birthday money, or babysitting earnings. Put that amount into their savings or an investment account, he advises. When the child is ready to buy a car or go to college, hand over the account.

A parent can give a positive lesson about taxation by explaining that some of the child's money could be his or her contribution to the local playground, community library, or other organization the child recognizes as benefitting the community. This alternative use of the child's "tax" money could emphasize how taxes are withheld in order to strengthen the common good.

For young children, interacting with money in a positive way can lead to positive habits. Church practices can help a family note milestones along the way, linking them with stages in growing a generous heart.[7] As soon as children are old enough, parents might want to use the online tool called FamZoo.[8] It is a virtual bank that allows family to move money between the parents' accounts and their children's savings. Allowances can be distributed to internal categories such as sharing, saving, and spending. The card activity is available to the parents. The adults can configure credits and debits for completing jobs or failing to do chores.

Our teen years constitute a prime time for learning an essential part of financial responsibility: how to earn money dependably and then allocate it in ways consistent with our values. When children enter the teenage years, they can build upon the concepts of Share, Save, Spend. Mark Vincent recommends dividing spending into two categories: "providing" and "consuming."[9] *Providing* is taking care of the basics, such as groceries, housing, required clothing, and reliable transportation. Depending upon family circumstances, young people may pay for some or none of these. *Consuming* pays for things and experiences we do not need but want, such as eating out, additional clothes, gift giving, and entertainment. When youth and adults learn the difference between these two kinds of spending, they can determine priorities with the money they acquire.

Vincent advises that families allocate percentages for each financial category. For example, if an adult plans to give 10 percent and save 15 percent, he or she may spend 65 percent on providing, and 10 percent on consuming.

Given the same categories, Vincent says a teen may decide to give 10 percent, provide 20 percent, and consume 10 percent. That would leave a full 60 percent to put into savings for future providing and consuming: 5 percent for short-term saving goals, such as an electronic device or a bicycle, and 55 percent for long-term savings, perhaps toward a car or a post-high school education.[10] With some parental help to set goal percentages, young people can develop positive habits in their use of income, thereby strengthening future positive behaviors.

One outstanding resource is *Wrapped in God's Love: A Milestones Ministry Resource*.[11] Designed by several Canadian denominations, it is their jointly developed educational plan to teach young people about money, within the larger context of growing a generous heart. The material shows how at age twelve, youth can intentionally explore what it means to be stewards of one's self, time, and talents. By the time they are sixteen, they can receive adult encouragement to pray for God's guidance when making financial choices. By age eighteen, they might discern how to partner with God as they consider future life directions.

A practical stewardship curriculum specifically for youth is *Money Matters for Youth: Integrating faith and finances*.[12] In seven sessions it introduces primary understandings peppered with interactive exercises, journaling, games, and video clips. The topics include exploring our personal assumptions about money, becoming God's trustees, how to budget, wise decision-making about debt, saving for the future, giving a tithe, and determining how much is "enough."

Teens and young adults can also learn the time value of money through the power of compound interest and its reverse, compound debt. Even when young people are not adding to their income, through the compounding process, their savings continue to increase. Unfortunately, unpaid debts also keep growing through compounding. As teenagers babysit, do yard work, or have other part-time jobs, they can add to a personal bank account and see their money grow. Parents, mentors, or youth group leaders can help them reflect on the cumulative impact, and prompt them to imagine how they might reinvest interest on money earned for God-centered goals. Adults can also help youth organize their daily lives around time and relationships, not simply focusing on making and spending money.

When youth give specific amounts of time for hands-on service, their volunteer time combats consumerism, as well. Often called "service projects" or "mission trips," these experiences can teach inspiring lessons in compassion, justice, and solidarity with the poor. While repairing homes, building schools, or doing other direct mission work, they see firsthand how little money and few things most people have in poorer regions.

Such lessons are desperately needed. Previously I noted children's spending, but as they grow into the teen years, Americans aged from twelve to nineteen:

- Spend a total of about $153 billion each year for personal consumption. Initially teen males buy things for an average of $55 a week, while teen females average $60 a week. By the time they are sixteen to seventeen years old, they have nearly doubled that amount.
- Those same teens average, 3.1 hours in shopping malls per week.
- At the same time, despite the spending habits of wealthier teenagers, one in five young people under the age of eighteen lives below the poverty line.[13]

A two-year project by The Search Institute[14] discovered several themes among youth related to giving and serving:

- Despite living in a consumer-oriented culture, thousands of American youth find hands-on service a powerful way to shape and practice their faith. Yet many congregations do not invite them to give some of their own money to the same mission purposes. This omission causes youth to miss out on the deep connection between mission service and financial giving.
- Most congregational leaders appear to be uncomfortable talking about money, especially with young people. In addition, many church leaders do not advocate for young people to share their money to benefit others.
- Youth need to be involved in designing and leading their service activities. Such experiences deepen their faith,[15] especially when it is accompanied by structured reflection.

In families and congregations, youth can strengthen their understanding of the connection between giving and serving, and thereby gain exciting personal life lessons. "The church needs to step up and reclaim its voice as a countercultural leader," says Nathan Dungan. "Millions of youth and adults are eager to live differently and to think more deeply about aligning their faith, money and values."[16]

One example of countercultural leadership took place in the Episcopal Diocese of Colorado when Nathan Dungan spoke at their 2006 annual meeting. With financial help from the diocesan foundation, they invited any congregation within its bounds to participate at the end of the conference in a training session based on Dungan's *Share Save Spend* curriculum. As a result, leaders in many churches received intergenerational workshops on money, values, and culture.[17]

Stewardship teaching makes a positive difference in the lives of youth. For example, the Council for Economic Education's 2011 Survey of the States revealed that only fourteen of the fifty U.S. states require high school students to take a course in personal finance.[18] But where courses in financial education were mandatory, the students were less likely to become compulsive buyers, to make late credit card payments, and to spend up to their credit card limits. They were also more likely to save, take reasonable financial risks, and pay off credit cards in full each month. In addition, studies show that teaching youth about money and its role in their lives can decrease their materialism and increase their personal self-esteem.[19]

When we recognize that we are affluent in relation to the world as a whole, we "differentiate between our self-identity and our consumer-identity."[20] In the process we come to recognize that our consumerist self-image, foisted upon us through multiple media, is a false sense of who we are.

At the same time, practical financial planning can help us nip materialism in the bud when we take these foundational steps:

- Create a budget and track our expenses;
- Make our First Fruits giving *first*, before we pay anything else;
- Simplify our lifestyle by living well within our means;
- Establish an emergency fund;
- Use credit wisely, pay off credit cards, and use cash or debit cards for purchases; and
- Practice long-term savings and responsible investing.[21]

These regular practices will help us relegate materialism to the edges of our thoughts and actions.

We have seen in this section that at every age we can learn and teach how to counter the materialistic myth that the good life requires an ever-growing amount of money and possessions. From preschool on, children can learn how to value and manage money. Adults can link money conversations to allowances, and children can use their money in a plan that has them first share, then save, then spend. The family's congregation can teach stewardship lessons with each milestone as the child grows. Parents also can utilize online tools such as FamZoo to help their kids do First Fruits Living.

Youth are able to distinguish "providing" from "consuming," and allocate percentages for each budget category. They can learn about compound interest and compound debt, *before* learning the hard way with actual credit cards. Their natural focus on helping others can assist them to connect hands-on service with financial giving, thereby strengthening positive adult habits. Recognizing how much we have and practicing basic financial planning encourage positive financial habits and help us mature in our relationship with God.

# Money and Giving

Donating money is certainly not the only form of giving, as we have seen. But sharing financially to improve other people's lives helps us grow as Jesus' disciples. People may choose to give for many reasons, several of which result in a grateful, joyous attitude on the part of the donor. In addition, churches can help people increase their financial giving and understand it as part of their response to God's grace. In this section we will touch on each of these dimensions.

Financial giving is indispensable to Christian discipleship in at least three ways:

1. By assigning part of our resources to God's priorities according to biblical teachings, our giving helps declare our personal love for God, Who identifies with the poor and the outcast (Matthew 25:35–40). Herb Miller, longtime stewardship consultant, notes that our money is a tangible extension of the life God gave us for God's purposes.
2. "Jesus told us that if [we] want to know what a person really loves, we should follow the trail of his [or her] money," says one blogger. He pointedly asks if we see our resources solely as ours to benefit from, or as opportunities to be generous to others.[23] Our giving shows we care about people in need, confirming our view of them as being those whom God loves. We give to make their lives better by increasing their safety and improving their living conditions, beginning with the basics of adequate shelter, clean water, and nourishing food.

3. The process of giving also helps us mature spiritually, when we express more fully our faith and values by correlating our actions with our beliefs.[24] As James 2:16 says, we do no good at all if we tell a hungry person to go in peace, stay warm, and have a nice meal, but do not give the person some food, a coat, or a blanket.

"Giving is not an option in our Christian living," says pastor Matt Smith.[25] "It's an essential in who we are, living into the fullness of God's grace." So authentic giving from the heart does not come with a burden of guilt or obligation, but rather with a feeling of lightness and freedom. At the same time, it brings a sense of deeper connection to God and to one another.

Members of Maplewood United Methodist Church in Maplewood, Missouri know that feeling. For the first time in at least twenty years, in 2007, they paid their entire expected share of denominational mission ministries. They had already considered using old-style approaches such as focusing on the needs of their congregation, hounding the participants to "pay up," dividing up church bills, or playing the loyalty card—all to no avail.

When the day came that they were no longer sure how to make payroll, "we realized it was time to reevaluate our approach to church finances," said Courtney Stotler, their Finance chair.[26] So they designated ten percent of all the missions offerings they had received to help people beyond their local church. Next, their pastor encouraged them to attend a stewardship workshop to ease any obsession about their financial deficit.

Their church newsletter began to adopt a more positive tone. "It was like a virus. It was a good virus that began to spread among members of the Finance Committee and the rest of the church," said Maplewood's Stewardship chair.[27] Then the Finance Committee members personally agreed to tithe or to gradually increase the percentage they gave to eventually reach ten percent. After a year of this new practice, the congregation deepened its commitment to fund ministry around the world and to reach out to their community.

Finance chair Stotler said:

This is about faith. It's not a gimmick. This is connected to your
personal life. Allowing God to play a role in your finances lets you
know that God is real. This has brought about real change in my
family's life, and I know it can bring about real change in the lives
of others.[28]

"Letting God play a role" in our financial lives involves personal
reflection and prayer, and also often requires help from a curriculum or a consultant. One dramatic example is a congregation called
"Northland, A Church Distributed," in Longwood, Florida. During
the recent economic meltdown, the church launched hundreds of
small groups of congregants to study Dave Ramsey's *Financial Peace
University* and learn the "much-needed basics of financial stewardship."[29] In that context, the church developed a comprehensive
Generosity Plan that included budget counseling, estate planning,
will seminars, and periodic sermon series dealing with financial
issues.

The act of giving also can lead to greater personal investment, as
we hear stories about the difference our giving makes.

Once when I joined the professional staff of a four-year regional
capital campaign, I felt I needed to make a financial commitment
to the ministry we would be leading. So I filled out a commitment
card with a reasonable, minimal amount. Then as I began to talk
with people who would receive the funds, my heart was moved by
the authenticity of the ministries, and how people's lives would be
transformed by the effort. So I filled out a second commitment card
promising a more substantial amount. I kept working with church
leaders, writing down and sharing the stories I heard, and encouraging people to participate.

After a time we began to see some results of the money already
raised—an exciting new congregation launched, a Christian campground upgraded—and I wrote and distributed those stories, too. So
I revised my financial pledge one more time: this time up to a more

generous level. I felt better about the purpose of the funds raised and about my involvement in the enterprise as a whole. Now I finally could see the greater vision for the entire effort.

Giving provides a natural antidote to obsessive consumerism. "The practice of generosity is God's gift to us," say leading generosity strategists Chris Willard and Jim Sheppard. "It helps us resist the snare of consumption and the idol of greed."[30] It also gives us a chance to learn about our global neighbors, and how we can support them as part of the international community.

For example, the open-source curriculum called *Lazarus at the Gate*, by 2011 had guided more than 400 people in more than thirty "Lazarus Circle" groups to give away a total of $200,000.[31] In eight sessions, which used the Bible story of poor Lazarus who sought help at a rich man's gate (Luke 16:19–31), evangelical and mainline Christians (plus college students of various faiths) have learned that investing a few dollars of their own goes a lot further in the developing world.[32] Founded by Christians in their twenties and thirties, *Lazarus at the Gate* mobilizes people to "alleviate poverty and promote stewardship through personal, community, and public policy change."[33] Sharing confidentially, participants talk about their money habits, discuss how poverty fuels social problems, and decide on a collective gift to fight poverty, such as microfinancing, encouraging sustainable agriculture, or rescuing women and children from oppressive situations.

So what prompts people to give to a specific charitable cause? A substantial study of more than 1,100 congregations from two dozen denominations, called the Spirituality and Giving Project,[34] revealed a broad range of motivations for giving to churches and other charitable organizations. In order of importance, the top six reasons for giving were:

1. Commitment to Christ—43.4%;
2. Desire to support the church's program—20.1%;
3. Belief that giving is a spiritual matter, and that generous giving benefits one's spiritual life—9.1%;

4. Identification with the people supported by the church's ministries—7.5%;
5. Discipline or habit developed over the years—6.6%;
6. Desire to make a difference in the world—3.5%.[35]

Most often, reasons for giving to charities have more or less weight for different age groups. The most commonly-used way of dividing North American generations is the following:

Great or G.I. Generation . . . . . Born before 1925
Silent Generation . . . . . . . . . . . 1926–1945
Baby Boomers . . . . . . . . . . . . . . 1946–1964
Generation X . . . . . . . . . . . . . . . 1965–1981
Millennials . . . . . . . . . . . . . . . . . 1982–1998[36]
Generation Z . . . . . . . . . . . . . . . Born since 1999

Age differences don't automatically determine giving patterns, but they often link to life experiences that help shape each generation, such as length of education, experience of worship, views of marriage and family, and amount of income.[37] For example, because formal education continues longer for most Generation X and Millennials, these two groups tend to move more often, delay marriage and children, and contend with higher levels of debt than their older counterparts.[38] Most Generation Z youth are fiscal conservatives, having experienced the 2002 and 2008 American recessions in their childhood. They are more likely to contribute personal involvement than money, and naturally think more like entrepreneurs than employees.[39]

Being younger, Generation X and Millennials face a comparatively long-time horizon for both personal and national security, as well as greater urgency in their desire for world change. So even more than other generations, they want to sense results from their giving, such as visible change, measurable growth, and audible feedback.[40]

Members of Generation Z are often called "the iGeneration," not just because of their lifelong facility with the Internet, iPod, iPad, and iPhone. They also tend to expect to "interact" with the people their giving affects, and, more than preceding generations, consider "international" causes as within their scope of giving.[41]

Such generational variations prompt people to respond differently when asked to contribute money to social service organizations. So it makes sense to appeal to each generation differently through communication channels most natural to them, and by articulating the reasons they value the most.

When people financially support the work of churches for any of the top six reasons listed above, their intrinsic attitude toward giving is both intentional and joyful. In 2 Corinthians 9:6–12, when Paul says God loves a "cheerful" giver, he uses the Greek word that means "hilarious!" This term confers a sense of giving with an attitude of joyful abandonment. Paul makes this statement in the context of saying people should give what they have planned in their hearts, not with hesitation or because of being pressured to give. The purpose of giving, Paul notes, is so givers will have everything they need and also that they "may share abundantly in every good work" (2 Corinthians 9:8). As a result, we are encouraged both to plan ahead for generous giving, and also to delight spontaneously in the moment of giving itself.

Why might people feel so joyful about giving in such circumstances? "Jesus set the example for giving passionately and generously to those in need," says *Ministry Matters* blogger Samantha Tidball.[42] While a lot of non-Christians may also be generous givers, she says to Christians, "When we give to others, it is a visible manifestation of God at work within us.... Giving has the power to transform the world by reflecting the love of Christ to everyone." This generous attitude presents a contrast to the more perfunctory "discretionary obligation" which the book *Passing the Plate*[43] says motivates typical American Christian giving.

When Calvary Chapel members in Fort Lauderdale, Florida celebrate generous giving, they challenge one another to change their attitudes. Pastor Bob Coy says this approach assists the congregation in four ways:

1. By celebrating the cause of Christ, they place their priorities with his kingdom rather than with their personal gain;
2. By celebrating integrity in finances, they keep themselves from abusing resources;
3. By celebrating generosity, the church comes together to see what giving does for the kingdom, enjoying the privilege of obedience together; and
4. By celebrating frugality, they set aside as many resources as they can for God's work, storing up their treasure for God rather than in personal gain.[44]

Such positive reinforcement helps us "provoke one another to love and good deeds" (Hebrews 10:24).

With care and intentionality, church leaders can help people grow in their financial giving and see their sharing as part of their response to God's grace. The same comprehensive Spirituality and Giving Project study mentioned earlier identified ten overall strategies (directly quoted below) as the most effective ways to increase congregational giving:

- "Connect individual giving directly to the spiritual life of every person.
- Begin practicing stewardship education as a twelve-month process which involves children, youth, and adults.
- Encourage tithing or proportionate giving.
- Let people make pledges and regular gifts to more than a single fund, encouraging designated giving.
- Provide the opportunity for people to give from both checking and savings.
- Promote special offerings effectively.
- Encourage the pastor to be actively involved in stewardship education and fund-raising.
- Send frequent financial statements to members and constituents who support the church.

- Emphasize the mission and vision of your church rather than the line item budget, and remember that people give to people and God, not to budgets.
- Help people plan future giving through their wills, living trusts, life insurance policies, and similar means."[45]

People of all ages are most affected by hearing stories of how their gifts changed others' lives. Such stories shared during worship can turn the offering time into an authentic celebration involving members of all ages.[46] During the offering and in a variety of other church settings, church leaders can connect the giving "to changed lives, to nurturing disciples, spreading the gospel and meeting the needs of the hungry, hopeless and helpless,"[47] thereby building an environment of celebration.

The same principle is true when people give for a distinct purpose, such as in response to disaster relief or other immediate public crisis. Hearing from someone who has been rescued from a life-and-death situation, such as seeing women and children pulled free from the rubble of an earthquake, brings joy to people around the world, prompting them to give even more.

"When we celebrate generosity, we gain a front-row seat to [God's] work in people's lives," note veteran pastors Chris Willard and Jim Sheppard.[48]

In this section about money and giving, we have noted how the fact of (not the amount of) financial giving is essential to Christian discipleship and have identified some resources that can help us intentionally let God influence our financial lives. Giving is a natural antidote to obsessive consumerism as well as greed, and the amount of time, effort, and money we give tends to increase as we become more committed to a specific cause.

# Ask, Thank, Tell

The best stewardship rhythm for a congregation's life in this regard is an ongoing pattern of "ask, thank, tell." In a book of that same name,[49] Charles Lane states that in many churches solid, biblical stewardship has been held hostage by a villain named "Paying the Bills." The way to free the hostage is to change our assumptions and shift our primary question from "What does the church need?" to "How is God calling me to respond to God's presence in my life?"

In the flow of a congregation's life, *ask* refers to two aspects. The first is conducting an exciting, well-planned annual financial commitment program. The second is providing multiple giving and serving opportunities throughout the year that build interest in new ministries, create new relationships beyond the congregation, and strengthen individuals' connections to the church and its Lord.[50]

Lane's term *thank* refers to creating a culture of giving thanks within the congregation in immediate and personal ways. These forms of giving thanks may include saying Thank You to volunteers, offering trips for church members to see ministries firsthand, acknowledging community recognitions, and having the pastor write personal thank-you notes in a variety of circumstances.

In the process, it is essential to *tell* the congregation's mission story: why it exists; what it does for participants, the community and the world; and what has been achieved thus far. Additional giving to local, national, and global ministries that focus on people, not organizations, can be better balanced with a monthly schedule of different mission projects. Such stories tell members what their gifts are doing, and why they make a vital difference.[51]

A major biblical theme is that we are given God's blessings in order to bless others. For example, God blessed Abraham and Sarah with the ability to have children in their very old age—*so that* they could become a great people who would bless all the nations of the world (Genesis 12:2). Whenever we give from the perspective that God has blessed us, we look to God as our source and security (Matthew

6:31–33), realizing that "every generous act of giving, with every perfect gift, is from above" (James 1:17). Giving helps us mature as Jesus' followers with an attitude of joyful abandon, encouraging one another to ask, thank, and tell stories of changed lives through the work of Jesus Christ among us all.

People can give for a variety of reasons, many of which lead to an attitude of celebration and joy. We are inspired when we hear real stories about people whose lives have been transformed thanks to our giving. A regular rhythm of "ask, thank, tell" in the congregation's life is a powerful way to encourage one another to celebrate the ways God works through generous people to help heal the world.

# From Tithing to First Fruits

The best way to practice generosity is First Fruits Living. It is a critical part of contentment, a down-to-earth way to put God first in our lives, and the bedrock upon which a person can build a life of joy and generosity.

Over the past centuries, most church leaders have called people to give a percentage of what they have earned, inviting believers to practice tithing (giving ten percent) as the starting point or norm for financially supporting God's work in their midst. The Bible's Old Testament is full of references to giving tithes on different seasonal occasions. For example, in Deuteronomy 26, God told the people to give the first of their crops, as well as tithes and offerings, in yearly cycles. Their giving was meant to be an act of worship and thanksgiving to God. In a later generation, King Hezekiah called the people to give ten percent of their crops and livestock to support the priests and Levites as they worked on the people's behalf (2 Chronicles 31:4–10).

Later yet, in Jesus' time, the tithe was a regular part of religious life. It was meant to be a means of putting God first in one's awareness and actions, not as an end in itself. In Matthew 24: 23–24, Jesus criticized the religious leaders who were scrupulous in giving exactly one tenth of all they had—even down to a tenth of each of their spices!—but who forgot the more important matters of God's Law: justice, peace, and faith. "It is these you ought to have practiced, without neglecting the others," Jesus said.

Unfortunately, in our day some people who have embraced tithing have become just as legalistic, turning the tithe into a formula or magic number, instead of using it as a guide to faithful living. Others have made tithing a requirement for participation and membership in a church. Still others have fallen into the attitude that they are "paying for services" from the church or its staff, as if giving were a business transaction.

Yet others lapse into preferential treatment of those who have more money or give more money to the church organization. The Book of James doesn't mince words about such favoritism. "For if a person with gold rings and in fine clothes comes into your assembly, and if a poor person in dirty clothes also comes in," says James, "And if you take notice of the one wearing the fine clothes and say, 'Have a seat here, please,' while to the one who is poor you say, 'Stand there,' or 'Sit at my feet,' have you not made distinctions among yourselves, and become judges with evil thoughts?" (James 2:2–4)

While tithing can remain a healthy standard for giving, First Fruits Living approaches sharing from the other end. Whereas tithing asks, "How much can I give, before I spend anything anywhere else?" First Fruits Living prompts us to ask, "How little can I live on in order to reflect God's generosity?" When we engage this second question, we focus not on the amount given, but on the process of making God's work a top priority. This is a far more challenging question, whatever the percentage we are able to give at a particular time.

Mark Vincent, pastor, organizational consultant and first fruits educator, offers several examples of first fruits giving, including a farmer setting aside for world relief the first produce grown on a part of his or her acreage; a musical group's gift of income from its first concert of the year; an individual's dedicating the first book read each year, or the first day of vacation to spiritual purposes; or a Christian's commitment of the first hour of the day for Bible study and prayer.[52]

Financial stewardship consultant Nathan Dungan communicates the same message of giving first with the phrase, "Share, save, spend."[53] Once we choose appropriate levels of giving, his phrase tells us the order of what we're meant to do: give first, then save, then spend. Through his website, *sharesavespend.com*, and his extensive teaching and speaking, he works with churches and denominations on how to teach and implement the practice—particularly within families and bringing up children. His book *Money Sanity Solutions* presents a multifaceted approach to help families reorient and get out of the maze of consumerism.[54]

One nationally-known pastor and author[55] describes First Fruits Living this way:

> We need to give the first part of our day in meditation to God. We need to give the first part of our week in worship of God. We need to give the first part of our income to God. We need to give the first part of our social life to fellowship with other Christians. Each of these four kinds of giving keeps our mental compass focused in God's direction. Remove any one of them, and spiritual growth slows.

Giving our first fruits is not only a financial commitment, but a way of being intentional about growing in our faith journeys, out of a holistic understanding of stewardship.

So what is First Fruits Living? It is not only giving to God the first and the best of what we've been given, but also managing all the rest according to God's generosity.[56] It is about both the percentage we are able to give and what we do on God's behalf with the 100 percent of who we are and what we have been given.

Here are more exciting examples of First Fruits Living:

- Each month before paying any bills, a family writes its first check to God's work through its congregation's ministries.
- A businesswoman offers a certain number of hours each month using her computer expertise at the local Grange, community clothes closet, or national advocacy organization.

- A young adult commits to volunteering specific days with Habitat for Humanity or at the local food giveaway program, before setting up the rest of his monthly schedule.
- A working man makes his monthly financial gift by Electronic Fund Transfer to a nonprofit halfway house or a community homeless shelter, so the amount gets to work immediately on the first of each month.
- A young couple decides to eat at home more often and get more books at the library than the bookstore, so they can be more generous in an online Giving Circle or supporting their denomination's global missionaries.
- A family makes a priority of spending an evening each month with a different family in their congregation, to get to know and encourage one another.

This is giving to God's work first and prioritizing our lives the best we can from what we know about God's generous grace as experienced in Jesus Christ.

If you feel you're less than perfect in this way of living, don't get discouraged! It takes a lifetime to grow more fully into it. But how refreshing it is! This is not merely a way of *giving* but of *living*, since it relates to all our resources and relationships, not just to the religious sector of our lives.

When we search the Bible, we find that people who give their first fruits also:

- Tell stories of God's faithful acts on the people's behalf;
- Offer themselves back to God in love through their worship and service to others;
- Host community feasts and support buildings as houses of worship and service; or
- Employ their community roles as ways to distribute goods to people in need.

In this way, First Fruits Living is dedicating one's entire life to passing on God's gifts to others.

While the Old Testament practice speaks of giving the first fruits of one's harvest to people in need, the New Testament builds on the idea, by exhorting us to give *ourselves* first to God. For example, in 2 Corinthians 8:1–7, Paul relates how the Christians in poor, rural Macedonia "gave themselves first to the Lord," then begged to be able to participate in the offering to sustain the Jerusalem Christians, who were helping their neighbors survive a three-year famine. Despite the Macedonians' own financially-limited circumstances, they gave beyond their means, in a "wealth of generosity."

When we seek to live generously with "all the rest" of life, we ourselves *become* God's first fruits, as the first of those who live in a freed-up, joyful way. One congregation sought to learn this concept together. Guided by the Barnabas Foundation,[57] the Third Christian Reformed Church in Zeeland, Michigan took this calling seriously. They formed a First Fruits Committee, studying together Robert Heerspink's book, *Firstfruits*.[58] "It was a powerful way for us to learn a common language," said Stewardship Chair Lyle Ahrenholtz,[59] "a way to talk about goals and mission, a way to quietly keep stewardship in front of people."

There is an air of risk and excitement when we seek to live this way. "Living as God's [first fruits] offering means living as entrepreneurs of the gospel," says *Firstfruits Living* author Lynn Miller. "It means putting our money and our time to use as signs of the kingdom of God," such as caring for creation, one another, and our Creator. "It is offering to God from the first of what we receive, before calculating the risk or counting the cost, before deciding if we can afford to be God's kind of steward."[60]

This is why First Fruits Living is so important. When we give a percentage of what we have for God's work first, we reorient our priorities—instead of spending first and then seeing what we have left over for others.

"Giving first to the Lord is a central goal for any Christian family," says Vincent. "[It] is the pivot point around which the rest of our financial management rotates." He notes that giving first to God is a "hymn of praise to the God who provides" everything, including life, meaning, relationships, and love.[61]

It is crucial for a church to do this with its budget, as well—to demonstrate both faith and financial health by giving first to its Shared Ministries funds—whatever percentage commitment its members have made as a congregation—*before* they save for deferred maintenance and spend for current programs and staff. Vincent's book *The Whys and Hows of Money Leadership*[62] demonstrates how a local church can do this, by comparing it to how a family sets up First Fruits Living with its own budget. After all, why should church leaders ask their members to do First Fruits Living if they're not first modeling it in the congregation?

IN THIS CHAPTER we have addressed generosity and money in four ways. First, we acknowledged the benefits of open congregational discussion about money and giving in our society. After identifying some of the conflicting lessons our experiences with money often teach us, we explored doing a personal Money Autobiography as a helpful way to clarify how money influences our lives. Several congregations counter the money-is-taboo tradition by talking purposefully about money in the church in ways that increase members' comfort level and skill in handling their family finances.

Second, we examined dealing with money as a spiritual issue. While many people attribute a godlike status to money, if rightly used, it can be a powerful tool for Christian stewardship. We also explored attitudes toward money and giving, including reasons people give generously, and cited examples of faith communities moving from a place of fear when it comes to monetary issues, toward a fuller trust in giving as a response to God's grace.

Third, we looked at the potentially debilitating impact of debt, basic steps for getting back in the black, and aspects of positive financial planning. Some excellent ministry programs were highlighted for teaching young people ways to move beyond materialism, and appropriate strategies to deal with money for all ages.

Fourth, we emphasized tithing and First Fruits Living as practical, foundational ways of putting God first in one's life.

# Questions for Reflection

1. Thinking about family income, how do my saving and spending percentages differ from those in this chapter's Adult Allocation pie chart? What adjustments am I willing to consider so my percentages better fit my financial goals?
2. How have I been teaching the children and youth in our family about managing money? Could any of this chapter's resources help that process? In our congregation, how could we be more intentional about teaching children and youth about money?
3. In what ways do my money habits harm or help others? Are there ways I can scale back my wants in order to benefit those who are needier than I, and to help sustain natural resources?
4. What might First Fruits Living look like in my life? How would my priorities change? What would stay the same? How well am I "managing all the rest" as a reflection of God's generosity?

# Endnotes

1. Merriam-Webster, Inc., "Materialism," *Webster's Ninth New Collegiate Dictionary* (Springfield, MA, 1989).
2. Clayton L. Smith, *Propel: Good Stewardship, Greater Generosity* (Nashville: Abingdon Press, 2015), p. v.
3. Lynn A. Miller, *The Power of Enough: Finding Contentment by Putting Stuff in Its Place* (Nappanee, Indiana: Herald Press, 2003), p. 68.
4. Patricia Schiff Estess and Irving Barocas, *Kids, Money & Values: Creative Ways to Teach Your Kids About Money* (Cincinnati: Betterway Books, 1994), pp. 4–9.
5. Nathan Dungan, "From Idea to Action," *sharesavespend.com.*
6. Ric Edelman, "Add Another Duty to Your Parenting List," August 2013, originally published on November 2012 in *Inside Personal Finance*, at *www.ricedelman.com.*

7. In *Money Mania*, p. 37, Mark Vincent lists how the congregation can connect with children and youth by stages. This is an adaptation of the Canadian resource, *Wrapped in God's Love* (see footnote 11 below).
8. Steve Oelschlager, Stewardship Program Coordinator for the Evangelical Lutheran Church in America, "Measuring Your Life. Websites and Smart Phone Apps That Help and Teach," *Giving: Growing joyful stewards in your congregation* magazine, "Live Simply" issue, 2016, p. 29.
9. Vincent, *Money Mania*, p. 48.
10. *Ibid.*, pp. 26–27, 48–49.
11. In *Wrapped in God's Love: Planting Seeds of Faith, Growing Generous Hearts*, The United Church of Canada provides a tangible symbol and brief curriculum for each age range through age eighteen. See Item TLKT1144 at *http://www.stewardshiptoolkit.ca/education*.
12. *Money Matters for Youth: Integrating faith and finances, Teacher's Guide and Student Pages*, created by the Everence organization for the Church of the Brethren, found at: *brethren.org/stewardship/documents/money-matters-for-youth.pdf*.
13. Notes from Peter Zollo's book, *Wise Up to Teens: Insights into Marketing and Advertising to Teenagers*, in Eugene Roehlkepartain, "Cultivate Generosity: The Antidote to Consumerism," in *Giving: Growing Joyful Stewards in Your Congregation* magazine, the "Remember" issue 2002, p. 15.
14. The Search Institute specializes in the healthy development of children and adolescents. In an exploratory project, they conducted a two-year initiative to interview innovative Jewish and Christian leaders of youth, national experts on youth trends, and focus groups with young people in congregations, about their experiences and perspectives on giving and serving.
15. Roehlkepartain, *op cit.*, pp. 13f. The article also offers eight ways a congregation can help youth shift into intentional lifelong habits of generosity (p. 18).
16. Nathan Dungan, "Talking and Teaching about Money: An Essential Stewardship Opportunity for Your Congregation," from The Episcopal Network for Stewardship's e-newsletter, *The Steward's Well*, at *tens.org/resources/free-resources/free-resources-blog/the-stewards-well*.
17. *Sharesavespend.com*, cited in Betsy Schwarzentraub, "Teaching Healthy Money Habits: Christ Church, Richmond, VA," March 16, 2011 for the General Board of Discipleship (now Discipleship Ministries) of the United Methodist Church; also at *generousstewards.com*.
18. Ric Edelman, *op cit.* The mission of the Council for Economic Education is to promote economic and personal-finance education for kindergarten through twelfth-grade in U.S. schools.
19. Nathan Dungan, "Teaching Youth about Money Can Decrease Their Materialism and Increase Their Esteem," *sharesavespend.com*, study on motivation and emotion in *Motivation and Emotion*, Vol. 37, No. 2: June, 2013. A report on the study is in *Scientific American*, July 2014, p. 19.

20. Jean M. Blomquist, "My Money, My Self: Moving from Fear to Faith," *Weavings: A Journal of the Christian Spiritual Life*, March–April 2003, issue on "Singleness of Heart," p. 42.
21. Adapted from Adam Hamilton, *Enough*, pp. 43, 105–108.
22. Herb Miller, *op cit.*, p. 29.
23. J.D. Greer, "Three Ways the Gospel Changes our Generosity" blogpost, Nov. 19, 2014, at *www.generouschurch.com/15-generosity-quotes?inf_contact_key=6034ae-c29491114f3a1f5da8a1f1d49ac05b91adf5d42d002eb69fe12ee08951.)*
24. Michael Reeves and Jennifer Tyler, *Faith & Money*, pp. 17f.
25. Rev. Matt Smith during worship at The Table at Central United Methodist Church, Sacramento, California, April 22, 2015.
26. "Connecting faith and giving leads to financial turnaround for church," January 17, 2008, at *www.fivepractices.org.*
27. *Ibid.*
28. *Ibid.*
29. Chris Willard and Jim Sheppard, *op cit.*, p. 57.
30. *Ibid*, p. 172.
31. G. Jeffrey MacDonald, Religious News Service, in "Christians shatter taboos on talking about money," *Christian Century*, July 12, 2011, p. 17.
32. *worldvision.org/resources.nsf/main/Lazarus_at_the_Gate-Economic_Discipleship.pdf/$FILE/Lazarus_at_the_Gate-Economic_Discipleship.pdf?open*
33. *Ibid.*
34. Holly Carcione, Steve Clapp, Kristen Leverton, and Angela Zimmerman, *The Desires of Your Heart: Financial Giving and the Spiritual Life* (1997, Fort Wayne, Indiana: Christian Community, Inc.), pp. 12–14.
35. *Ibid.*, p. 19. The study required people to list their top three reasons for giving. This is their response for their top reason. Tithing was frequently mentioned in their second- or third-listed reasons.
36. Researchers vary in the end date for Millennials, but most scientists studying the younger Generation Z begin it at 1999.
37. Melissa Brown, Associate Director of Research for the Center on Philanthropy at Indiana University, at the 2007 Annual Meeting of the National Association of United Methodist Foundations. See also the list of generational shaping experiences in my "Generational Stewardship Chart" at *http://generousstewards.com/wp-content/uploads/2017/07/Generational-Stewardship-Chart.pdf.* The chart reflects responses from hundreds of United Methodist Church members who attended fourteen "Spirited Stewardship" workshops in California and Nevada.
38. Melissa Brown, *op cit.*
39. Christopher Wolf, "Gen-Z Matters More Than Millennials," video at *www.goldmansachs.com.* See also Betsy Schwarzentraub, "Gen Z givers grow through generous involvement," 2017 issue of *Giving: Growing Joyful Stewards in Your Congregation* magazine.

40. Melissa Brown, *op cit.*
41. *www.wikipedia.org,* "Gen Z."
42. Samantha Tidball, "The power of giving," Feb. 2, 2016, at *www.ministrymatters. com/lead/entry/6650/the-power-of-giving*
43. Christian Smith and Michael Emerson, *Passing the Plate* (New York City: Oxford University Press, 2008).
44. Chris Willard and Jim Sheppard, *Contagious Generosity*, p. 154.
45. Holly Carcione *et al., op cit.*, p. 22. This excellent book contains one chapter on each of these ten strategies.
46. For ideas on how to make the offering more dynamic and meaningful, see two resources from the Ecumenical Stewardship Center: the "I Have Called You Friends" issue of *Giving: Growing Joyful Stewards in Your Congregation*, and *The Offering as Worship*, both at *www.stewardshipresources.org*. Also see two books by Melvin Amerson and James Amerson: *Celebrating the Offering* (Nashville: Discipleship Resources, 2008) and *Fruit for Celebrating the Offering* (CreateSpace Independent Publishing Platform, 2012).
47. Brad N. Hill, "Ways of giving," *Christian Century*, September 7, 2010, p. 29.
48. Chris Willard and Jim Sheppard, *op cit.*, p. 163.
49. Charles R. Lane, *Ask, Thank, Tell: Improving Stewardship Ministry in Your Congregation* (Minneapolis: Augsburg-Fortress, 2006).
50. *Ibid.*, pp. 67–92.
51. See also Larry Yonker, "Turning One-Time Donors into Lifetime Partners," Christian Stewardship Association phone seminar CD, January 2007.
52. Mark Vincent, *Teaching a Christian View of Money: Celebrating God's Generosity* (1997, Herald Press), p. 91.
53. Nathan Dungan, *www.sharesavespend.com.*
54. ———, *Money Sanity Solutions: Linking Money + Meaning* (Minneapolis: Share Save Spend, Minneapolis, 2010).
55. Rick Warren, *Discovering Spiritual Maturity* audiotapes, C.L.A.S.S. 201, Saddleback Valley Community Church, Orange County, California, cited by Herb Miller in *New Consecration Sunday Stewardship Program* (2007, Abingdon Press), p. 54.
56. Betsy Schwarzentraub, *Afire with God*, p. 91.
57. Lynn A. Miller, *Firstfruits Living: Giving God Our Best* (Scottdale, PA; Waterloo, ON: Herald Press, 1991), p. 88.
58. Robert C. Heerspink, *Firstfruits: A Stewardship Guide for Church Leaders* (Grand Rapids, MI: Barnabas Foundation and Faith Alive Christian Resources, 2008).
59. Lyle Ahrenholtz in "Stewardship Basics Part 2: Stories from Churches Like Yours," February 3, 2011, presented by the Barnabas Foundation.
60. Lynn Miller, *Firstfruits Living: Giving God Our Best*, p. 88.
61. Mark L. Vincent, *Money Mania*, p. 25.

62. ———, *The Whys and Hows of Money Leadership: A Workbook for Pastors and Lay Leaders* (Chicago: Evangelical Lutheran Church in America, 2003), ISBN 6-0001-9148-0, pp. 29–31; or Mark Vincent, *The Whys and Hows of Money Leadership*, Luther Seminary curriculum, at *archive.elca.org/stewardship/money_leadership/index.html*.

# The Church and Caring for Souls

**W**HEREVER WE GATHER with other Christians to worship and work to improve the world, we are not alone. As Jesus said, "For where two or three are gathered in my name, I am there among them." (Matthew 18:20)

Christian community does not have to be a traditional church with a permanent, official membership or even an official church building. Some of the most powerful faith communities I have participated in have been different: a gathering of college students sharing Communion with beer and pretzels, an intergenerational group of justice advocates staffing a Community House, a one-week Christian camp, two people in a spiritual discernment relationship, and an ecumenical Christian group that sponsored weekend retreats.

But authentic community can be hard to sustain when people hold privatistic views of their religion. For example, one myth people may tell themselves is that their life of faith is "just between me and God," as if a Christian's personal relationship with Jesus contains the entire scope of his or her spiritual life. But that couldn't be further from the truth. Yes, a faith-filled life involves a personal sense of connection with God, but that is just the beginning. That relationship needs to be renewed, challenged, and developed further in community. Such life-giving community may take a variety of forms, whether in small groups, whole congregations, or wider networks of people seeking to worship, learn, and serve.

From start to finish, the Bible describes people of faith primarily as part of a community, not as individuals. For example, in the early Old Testament it speaks about the whole of humanity in the times of Adam, Noah, and the twelve tribes of Israel. Likewise, God's promises relating to all nations appear throughout the Bible: in Isaiah, chapters 40 through 55; in the New Testament throughout the apostle Paul's writings; and in the Book of Revelation's vision of a worldwide "New Jerusalem."

But that's not all. Jesus said he has other sheep besides the New Testament "flock." (John 10:16) He offered the Good News to women from Samaria and Phoenicia and risked his life in his hometown by declaring his saving purpose for Gentiles as well as Jews. (John 4:1–15; Mark 7:24–30; Luke 4:24–27) His disciple Phillip shared the gospel with an Ethiopian court official, and Paul's entire ministry was sharing the Good News with Gentiles. (Acts 8:26–39; Acts 15:7–9) At Pentecost, considered the birth of the Church, Peter said the Good News of God's mercy and love is for all people of every class and station. (Acts 2:14–18)

In fact, at baptism, the very first statement of a person's Christian identity asserts, "There is no longer Jew or Greek; there is no longer slave or free; there is no longer male and female, for all of you are one in Christ Jesus."[1] (Galatians 3:28) These examples affirm the experience of Christians down the centuries: a person's faith can mature and strengthen in Christian community, benefitting both individuals and the world they seek to aid.

At the same time, a Christian congregation is not meant to be just any kind of community. As one writer puts it, God designed the church to be a "new family" with "an alternative value system" that makes itself known in giving to others.[2] When it comes to current congregations, "the last thing most people need in their lives is a committee job," says minister Paul Nixon. "They need community; they need to get beyond themselves and invest in the lives of others."[3]

# Shifting the Paradigm

We talked in Chapter One about how easy it is to fall into *doing* church—trying one program after another, becoming so focused on doing tasks and fulfilling roles that we lose touch with *being* in community together. In fact, *doing* church may have become our primary "paradigm:" that is, the model or pattern we follow, as well as the underlying ideas about how we should do it.[4]

Likewise, when we say "church," we can have different images in our minds, whether we are thinking of a traditional church a traditional church building for one congregation, church property shared by two denominations, a house church, or a group that meets in a library or park. For example, we might picture a "successful" church as one where new members keep coming in, the budget keeps growing, and activities take place every night of the week. Such paradigms may or may not fit our congregation's current reality, and uncritically adopting these assumptions can block us from growing into a healthy faith community where we receive and care for one another's souls.

How can we break out of what might be a restrictive conception of our faith community? The first step is to admit that we got stuck in our thinking and behavior somewhere along the way. Without blaming any present or previous leaders or circumstances, we can simply name our current obsession (with "busy-ness" and achievement, for example), noticing together how, even within the church, organizational demands can eat up people's spiritual reserves.

A second step is to acknowledge our unspoken expectations of ourselves and others as church leaders and participants. For example, many pastors and leaders want to strengthen the church's role as a "full-service church." Unfortunately, that phrase can imply a consumer mentality where people focus *only* on shopping for whatever services meet their personal needs.

There are at least two problems with the "full-service" expectation. First, it implies that it's possible to serve everyone's every need. But no matter what the size of the congregation or the number of staff, that's not possible. Second, "full service" implies that providing a smorgasbord of members' needs is the primary purpose of the church. But it is not. The church's purpose is to share the Good News; to make, equip, and encourage disciples of Jesus Christ; and to bring relief in a variety of ways to those—within the congregation and without—who are oppressed. (Matthew 28:19–20; Luke 4:18–19)

Once we have assessed our current paradigm and its unspoken expectations, we can take step three: trying out a different way of being a community.

This is what John Wesley did with the Methodist movement in eighteenth-century England. He created a network of midweek gatherings based on the *class meeting*, or small group. The purpose of these class meetings was to be a "school for growing souls,"[5] a space for individuals to be "consciously shaped in the faith."[6] First and foremost, the meetings provided opportunities to reach out to people with the gospel,[7] as a means of financial support and as a way to hold one another accountable in their Christian living.[8] The class-meeting participants, in turn, connected with other class meetings in a larger network called *Societies*. In this way, Wesley created a network of interdependent relationships that became the organizational principle of the United Methodist Church.[9]

Many things look different between our twenty-first-century cultural, social, and religious context, and the English setting of Wesley's day. But like thousands of people in his time, great numbers of people today are "longing for small, deep and creative community."[10] They want to meet vibrant spiritual people with whom they can grow in an open, caring faith community positively engaged with the world.

In addition, many people these days see themselves as "spiritual free agents, beholden to no church, practicing their Christian faith but willing to associate with organized churches only when they fit with their personal quests for meaning."[11] No longer does a denominational label, such as Roman Catholic, Baptist, or Episcopalian, form part of their core identity. Likewise, many people have lost connection with a congregation altogether. A recent study[12] shows that among U.S. religiously unaffiliated people (the so-called "nones" in census religious-preference statistics), a majority believe in God, but either have stopped believing in some aspects of religious teachings or have had negative experiences with a church.[13]

In a lot of congregations that follow restrictive models, elders expect prospective members to agree with the congregation's set of beliefs first, and later develop a sense of community through common worship or doing projects together. But thousands of people today come into a life of faith by experiencing community first (on a mission project, for example), and only then consider the congregation's beliefs.

"That [new order of community first] used to bother me," says one pastor. "Now I simply rejoice when the [person's] experience of loving community is transforming, evoking gratitude, faith, and hope."[14]

Viewing the church as a network of caring groups helps individuals reflect on what they know about God and themselves, about Scripture, tradition, and their personal experiences. This network understanding is part of how Stanley Hauerwas, Professor Emeritus of Divinity and Law at Duke Divinity School, defines "theology."[15] He cites world-changing examples such as Dorothy Day's justice-advocate Catholic Worker movement, and Jean Vanier's L'Arche supportive residential communities. "Holiness turns out to be the character of a community that can produce some very tough people," he says, where "Christians learn the basic grammar of the faith."[16] In the process, people nurture their relationships with one another as they work to apply their trust in God to everyday life.

One metaphor for such a community is that of a mosaic, fitting differently colored and uniquely shaped bits of stone into one vibrant image. "How might each of us become an artist helping to create the beautiful mosaic of a living, growing, and life-giving community?" ask the authors of *Companions in Christ*. Just as "great artists have many native skills, but their work is the result of disciplined effort and a willingness to try and try again," they recognize, "so we constantly invest our skills and gifts in the effort to create community that more and more reflects the divine image."[17]

In biblical times, Paul must have sensed this living process in the Thessalonian congregation, as he focused on growth in their life together. He thanked God for how they were developing as a community, "because your faith is growing abundantly, and the love of every one of you for one another is increasing." (2 Thessalonians 1:3)

While discussing contemporary small-group life in the church, the authors of *Companions in Christ* describe five basic elements of a Christian community that help its participants deepen spiritually:

- Faith in God, who as a gift of grace forms us into community;
- Personal authenticity, admitting our secrets and accepting each other;
- Shared goals, looking to the interests of one another;
- Mutual accountability to specific commitments as part of a covenant; and
- "Desire to experience the joy of mutual caring, sharing, and discovery in the Christian journey."18

However a group is formed, these dimensions can bring authentic Christian community to life.

Teams do the core work of any sustained Christian congregation. Whereas almost every congregation has committees, not all committees develop into teams. A *team* is a group in which the members work together as a unit to accomplish the group's goals. They develop a sense of group identity and belonging, where members know they are valued for who they are, not just for what they can do for the group. Team participants exchange ideas freely and clearly and are able to share leadership functions without hierarchical limits.[19]

Before undertaking work, a team forms a sense of group identity by spending sufficient time together to get to know and value one another. They go through a process of what psychologist Bruce Tuckman calls "forming, storming, norming, and performing."[20] A one-day Church Council retreat at the beginning of the year does this effectively. Committees can meet thereafter for monthly or quarterly meetings and still maintain their sense of being a team, caring for one another as persons in the process.

Team members not only cover the group's necessary content and decision-making, but also encourage, compromise, and harmonize with one another, paying attention to relationships as well as tasks.

Organizational development expert Rensis Likert identified six essential leadership skills in highly functioning teams:

- Support by leader;
- Receptivity both to seek and use ideas and to talk freely and openly;
- Team building;
- Performance expectation;
- Work facilitation; and
- Decision making.

Likert described the church as a living organism consisting of overlapping teams, and he created a systems theory based upon team life.[21] He also discovered that by consciously improving these same skills, a team could bring about positive change more effectively in its congregation.

One example of a team-based, permission-giving ministry is Christ Church in Fort Lauderdale, Florida, where the congregation's mission statement and written core values became the only criteria for supporting new ministries. In one instance, a church member wanted to start a ministry with homeless neighbors. When he asked the pastor about doing it, the minister said the proposed project fit the church's value of relieving suffering, so he could do it—if he found two or three others willing to join him. Eighteen months later, one hundred and fifty church members had established the second-largest homeless shelter in their county.[22] The Church Council never voted on the project—it didn't need to, since a team had gone forward with the idea.

Sometimes the hardest part about team-based ministry is getting rid of the church's outdated, permanent committees, each with its own budget line item and jurisdiction. Like unwanted clutter in our closets, excessive structure seems to multiply in the night. Eric Geiger, executive pastor of Christ Church Fellowship in Miami, helped his congregation delete most of its former structure and become (as his book says) a *Simple Church*.[23] Claiming that most churches drift away from their mission and into complexity, Geiger says that a "simple church" is a congregation designed around a strategic process that moves people through stages of spiritual growth. The essential (and tough) part is committing together "to abandon everything that falls outside the simple ministry process."[24]

Thinking as teams can help us see members of our congregation differently, as well. For example, Davis Community Church in Davis, California, facilitated periodic member meetings with other congregants in a similar vocation, such as teaching, or the health field. They met in public places, such as at a restaurant for lunch, to encourage one another's life of faith while dealing with the challenges their jobs can bring.

The Faith at Work Movement is another way to help people form vocational teams for the care of souls. Founded by David Miller, originally a senior executive in international banking, the Faith at Work Movement seeks to address "the Sunday/Monday gap"[25] to integrate faith and work. The Movement includes businesspeople, professionals, and workers of all types who gather in their communities to discuss questions of meaning, purpose, calling, ethics, character, spiritual identity, and expression in the workplace.[26] These gatherings provide a new framework to facilitate theological reflection and practical discourse about faith and work.[27]

When we dare to shift our models of church from that of providing services to caring for souls, we find plenty of creative alternatives to explore team-based ministries. In each unique instance, we are "practicing the presence of the whole community of faith, remembering that we move through the joys and difficulties, challenges and privileges of each day together rather than alone."[28] Being part of such a community reminds us we are not islands unto ourselves. Our interaction challenges us to grow spiritually, and encourages us to stay connected, caring for others.

# *Koinonia* Community

Faith is always personal, coming out of the core of our being, but it is never limited to a private affair. Our trust in God inevitably leaves visible traces in the ways we relate to other people.

Stories in the Gospels always put community at the center, where the faithful community brings new life. One situation involved Tabitha, also called Dorcas, a follower of Jesus. As the Bible puts it, her life overflowed with good works and acts of charity on behalf of people in need. (Acts 9:36) When she died of an illness, widows in her town asked Peter to come. They showed him the clothing she had made for them, as evidence of her lifelong care for them. Peter asked them to step outside, then prayed intensely to God. Next, he told Tabitha to get up. She sat up, fully alive. Then Peter presented her back to the widows, restoring her to her community.

Several people have been inspirational in my own life, for creating and strengthening communities. One amazing community builder was Mary Lou Spiess, who slept in an iron lung every night. A former teacher who had contracted polio just one week prior to being vaccinated, she held onto her activism to help others. Even while having to consciously take every breath, she was an advocate for those who are physically handicapped, humorously reminding the rest of us that we were "TABs," meaning those who are "temporarily able-bodied." With the help of a customized wheelchair her husband made, she used her right hand to address mailers every month to members of the California Association of Physically Handicapped, alerting us about state legislation. But that wasn't the end of it. She and her husband regularly traveled to the state capital so she could personally speak to the legislators about accessibility issues. Through the person she was and what she did, she brought thousands of differently abled people together on behalf of those often otherwise left on the margins.

These days, each time people get together for Bible study, they strengthen and invigorate their community. Jamie Clark-Soles is the New Testament editor for the *Covenant Bible Study* curriculum. "When we gather to study the scriptures," she says,

> we are simultaneously connected to the ancient communities that bequeathed the texts, our present community that is being shaped by these texts, and the community that will succeed us that we are helping to shape.[29]

From this viewpoint, studying together builds community across both time and space.

The Gathering United Methodist Church is a multi-site congregation in St. Louis, where small groups carry out its most important ministries. Visitors come mainly due to word of mouth. Begun in September 2006, The Gathering's average weekly attendance has grown to 1,200 people, but it has kept its interpersonal emphasis.

Newcomers to The Gathering are invited to attend one of the regular group coffees with the pastor. Next, church leaders steer them toward an introductory small group called "The Living Room," where they discuss the basics of their faith. After that, they get involved in one of the congregation's "core groups," and may also decide to join a volunteer team.[30] One important dimension of their ministry is called "Gathering Care," which provides Care Ministers to talk and pray with people confidentially when they are going through difficult life changes, such as spiritual, health, relational, or emotional challenges.

A healthy faith community shows vitality in at least two aspects: *koinonia* and *diakonia*.

The first dimension is *koinonia*. While this Greek word is sometimes translated as "fellowship" or "sharing," it points to something more intense and more intimate than that. The Bible uses the term to describe a particular relationship with Jesus, with the Good News

282

itself, with those who are poor, and even with members of the community outside the congregation.[31] (1 Corinthians 1:9; Philippians 1:3-5; Romans 15:26; 2 Corinthians 9:13)

There are at least three striking things about the Bible's use of this word:

1. It describes a partnership that includes all aspects of our life and witness as a community of faith. (Philippians 1:3-5)
2. It includes our economic lives, connecting a sense of unity with how we manage our possessions and give to people in need. (2 Corinthians 9:13; Acts 2:42–47)
3. It expresses mutuality in both giving and receiving. Somehow, we cannot give without receiving something in the process of giving, and we cannot receive without giving back gratitude and something of ourselves to the giver.[32]

The apostle Paul uses *koinonia* to talk about a certain quality of relationship when he writes to Philemon (in verse 6) about his runaway slave. Paul prays that the owner's "partnership in the faith" will become effective by understanding the bigger picture of his situation. This partnership is what we might call "Communion community," a bond we develop with one another as joint recipients of God's love and grace.

*Koinonia* also links to the distinctive identity of a Christian congregation. Loren Mead is an educator, consultant, author, and pioneer in congregational studies. He notes that while many people have had what they identify as direct experiences with God or a transcendent dimension, most of them "do not connect those experiences with the religious congregations to which they belong,"[33] separating their deep religious experiences from congregational life. "Congregations need to provide space for intimate storytelling that encourages members to share those deep experiences with one another," he says. They need to "let go of their preoccupation with programs and activities," to become "a home in which religious experience and religious yearning [are] welcomed and nurtured."[34]

In the Bible, Paul uses *koinonia* to describe his close relationship with the church in Philippi, when he says:

> I thank my God every time I remember you with joy in every one of my prayers for all of you, because of your sharing in the gospel from the first day until now. (Philippians 1:3-5)

"Koinonia" is the closest term a person could use for sharing in ministry: a kind of divine partnership, or stewardship, of the gospel. Because of the depth of this sharing, I have quoted this verse from Philippians when saying goodbye to the congregations I've served. Having gone through the ups and downs of life with one another merited my use of the term, as we had sought closer union with God and Communion ("union with") one another in the process.

## *Diakonia* Ministry

The second aspect of a healthy Christian community is *diakonia*, which means "service" or "ministry:" people giving and receiving practical care in everyday ways.

For example, at Christ United Methodist Church in Salt Lake City, people grow in their faith through hands-on ministries. In a program called Family Promise, they welcome homeless families into their facility. The church hosts Volunteers in Mission who come to their city to work at the denominational depot, which houses disaster-response supplies for the western United States. The congregation also gives foundational support for Crossroads Urban Center, which provides the poor with a food bank, thrift store, and advocacy services. Members of Crossroads give Angel Tree gifts for children of incarcerated parents, host lots of neighborhood children at their Vacation Bible School, offer financial scholarships for young people through the Alberta Henry Foundation, donate dental services and sandwiches for the St. Vincent de Paul Meal site, and more.[35]

*Diakonia* also refers to ministry in relation to the congregation's neighbors. The focus of community ministry is based not so much on the number of activities as on the quality of its community presence, in what Loren Mead calls "holding the center." This includes experiencing God's presence, centering in worship, reflecting on the church's heritage, and "building an interpersonal community within which each person can be nurtured and strengthened, as well as challenged and sent [into ministry]."[36]

In this section we have seen the importance of community life not only in biblical times but also for individuals and congregations today. Small-group life connects ancient and present communities and can provide the basic network for gathering as a people of faith. A healthy faith community shows its vitality in both *koinonia* and *diakonia*. *Koinonia* is a partnership and quality of relationship that reflects God's love for us, and our mutual giving and receiving from one another, linked to our distinctive identity. *Diakonia* is practical service or ministry toward one another and to the church's nearby and global neighbors. Such a presence reflects our identity and our activities.

## From Tasks to Relationships

What we do arises out of our sense of who we are. If we think of people as only worth the money they make, for example, it is difficult to honor ourselves and others as whole persons. But if we are constantly reminded that we are children of God, we tend to treat others as God's children: as brothers and sisters, part of our family.

The tasks we take on, and the commitments they require, are important whenever we interact as adults in organizations. But frequently our focus on the group's activity-oriented goals can overwhelm the time we give to relationships with our co-workers, drowning out a balanced point of view.

The same thing may happen in a congregation, as well. It can be arduous to counter the image of a "successful" church as a whirlwind of busyness. Excessive involvement in otherwise good activities can inundate people with bustling schedules, thus limiting opportunities just to *be* with each other. One minister puts it this way:

> If forty years of pastoral leadership has taught me anything, it is that a "busy parish" is not necessarily a spiritually healthy one. In fact, teaching people to say no to a variety of activities designed to raise money, create fellowship, or just generate social capital is a perennial challenge.[37]

While enthusiasm for exciting projects and services can involve us in subconscious resistance, it is just as important to help people have a peaceful experience of themselves and others as whole persons in God's presence. One way to encourage this is to strengthen relationships that draw out other people's gifts.

For example, Broadway Christian Parish United Methodist Church in South Bend, Indiana, is a small church that puts a priority on sharing stories to strengthen community between church participants and their neighbors. Located in a low-income part of town where drugs and gangs are prevalent, the congregation chooses to encourage abundant life for everyone in the community.

"We decided to treat people as if they are more than a sack of needs," says their minister, Mike Mather. "When people come to our food pantry, we...ask them about their gifts instead of about their need," getting people to talk positively about their own abilities and where they invest these gifts for the sake of others.[38]

Broadway Christian Parish also chose some non-traditional places to invest seed money and personal effort. For example, they hired Joe, a college student, to encourage the talents of Aaron, then twelve years old. Joe noticed Aaron's interest in computers and introduced him to the Boys and Girls Club. Aaron started giving his time after school repairing the club's computers and teaching younger children how to use them.[39]

Aaron's involvement led even further. After the death of a young boy in their neighborhood, Aaron noticed that several of the children had artistic abilities. So he and Joe asked them to draw pictures of their part of town. Then they invited the kids to gather up broken glass from the streets, keeping some of the colors, to make a mosaic depicting their part of the city. As he and Joe walked around the neighborhood, a growing crowd of children began to follow them, eventually numbering more than fifty. With spray paint provided by the church, they painted the rest of the glass red, yellow, and blue. After eight weeks of working together, the neighborhood children had created an eight-by-four-foot plywood mosaic titled, "You Are the Light of the World." Pastor Mather says,

> This mosaic now has a spot on the front wall of our sanctu-
> ary. It is a constant reminder to us of the creativity and the life
> and the perspective that is right there amidst the different story
> that the world will tell. It is a reminder to the children of the
> beauty of their neighborhood—beauty that they had a chance
> to name.[40]

While many specific things we do are unique, this relation-ship-building process inevitably begins with listening to people's stories, encountering each other individually, and building trust one person at a time.

Multiple ideas for encouraging a person's gifts come out of letting the congregation act more like an organism than a machine. Management consultant Margaret Wheatley identifies the difference between the two approaches and calls us to shift to a more organic perspective:

| Moving from: | Moving To: |
|---|---|
| Focus on structures | Focus on vision and mission |
| Seeing workers as cogs in the machine | Seeing workers as whole persons who long for community, meaning, dignity, and love |
| Having pre-fixed, definite destinations [goals] | Having potentials that will form into new ideas |
| Emphasizing boundaries where every piece knows its place   and lines of authority | Open to fuzziness, surprises, and patterns that connect people to   one another |
| Seeking progress by reversing decayas | Allowing living systems to renew  themselves while maintaining their   integrity and natural processes.[41] |

When we recognize ourselves as stewards of relationships, we can select our strategies, embracing a unique mixture of necessary structure and organic methods that encourage our growth together.

A key characteristic that helps us move in this direction is the ability to nurture others. Psychologist Erik Erikson first used the term generativity. "Generativity means nurturing others so that they are better able in turn to manifest their own gifts of love."[42] Since then, scientists have used it to refer to selfless giving to others, particularly for future generations.

In the outstanding book *Why Good Things Happen to Good People*, Stephen Post and Jill Neimark share some exciting scientific findings showing that generativity links to spirituality, leads to better health habits in middle age, and connects to social skills, empathy, and self-esteem.[43]

This is true in religious organizations, as well. In a 2016 survey of young adults, the Barna Group questioned 18- to-34-year-old

Americans who were not active churchgoers or committed to a congregation but showed interest in spiritual matters. It revealed that the strongest motivators for going to church include the chance for spiritual growth and authentic community. The respondents' top reasons to attend church were that the church: helps one's spiritual development; gives an opportunity to find out more about God; offers a chance to make friends and nurture friendships; assures them that anyone will be welcomed into the church community; and provides access to support during difficult times.[44] David Kinnaman, president of Barna, noted that although numerous young adults are connected to social media for much of their waking hours, four of the five listed motivations reveal a need for interpersonal community that virtual experiences cannot provide.[45]

"In the new community all members relate through their connection to God," says seminary professor, Dr. Thomas Thangaraj.[46] But such findings do not apply solely in modern settings. In the mid-300s A.D., the Christian philosopher, Augustine of Hippo, used the metaphor of a wheel, with God as the hub and people as the spokes. As in that image, he said, the closer we come to God, the closer we come to one another. When the love of Christ unites us, we experience the inner unity of our souls.[47] As we saw in Chapter Four, Augustine understood our souls as not divine, but rather "the place [we] go to see God" by turning "in, then up" to God.[48]

This wheel analogy fits with the apostle Paul's concept of our relationship with God and with one another, when he says the people of Macedonia first gave themselves to "the Lord" (Jesus Christ) and then to Paul, as he sought to raise funds to feed starving Jerusalem residents during a famine. (2 Corinthians 8:5) Catherine Malotky, Director of Development at Luther Seminary in St. Paul, Minnesota, says the way the Macedonians first gave themselves to the Lord was by ceasing quarrelling with one another. "For Paul, stewardship rests on relationships," she says, "not only individual relationships, but our communal relationships; what it means to be interdependent; what it means to live from and for others."[49]

Living from and for others tends to change us on the inside, as well, transforming our old social patterns. Psychologist David Benner says, "Christian spirituality involves a transformation of the self that occurs only when God and self are both deeply known."[50] This knowledge of God is not knowledge *about* God, but rather *knowing* God in the sense of a personal relationship: seeking to know God's heart, being grounded in relationship with the One who is both far beyond and also present deeply within us.

For millions of people around the world, this relationship is embodied in the act of Holy Communion, or the Eucharist. "We were created for communion with one another, not just with God," says theologian Miroslav Volf. "For the apostle Paul, the indwelling of Christ in the believer and the creation of the church as the body of Christ are intimately related." Volf asserts that when we receive from the bread and the cup, we are receiving Christ, "and with Christ, we receive ourselves as one body of Christ."[51] Both interdependence and mutual service are the life of Christ's people, in which we are members together. (Romans 12:4–5) So, "in giving himself to us, Christ gives us a community—ourselves."[52] It is a community in which we both give and receive, mutually encouraging each other's faith. (Philippians 4:5; Romans 1:12)

God's presence is even more interactive within us. In my own experience, the moments when I yield to God's grace are like a surprising breeze, a welcome zephyr. I let my life lean into my relationship with God, like a kite leaning with the wind. At the same time, such gusts bring a greater sense of freedom, to be lifted outside myself, more open and caring toward other people. Acknowledging God's incredible generosity, I try to align my actions toward others along the lines of God's love. When I reach out to strangers with a smile or a word, most often they are receptive and respond in kind. But fear can make me pull back, shocked that I really trusted the wind/breath/Spirit of God. I laugh at such moments of freedom when the divine Spirit is really there between us, holding me, as the poet Gerard Manley Hopkins puts it, "with ah! bright wings."[53]

In loving relationships with God and one another, even if just for a few moments, we become more the generous-hearted, grace-filled stewards God intended us to be. God has created us to live with one another in community, where our connection to neighbors, friends, and family affect our well-being. Wes Avram, Presbyterian pastor, goes even further. He says, "We *become* ourselves, and so become human, when we make and fulfill loving commitments, forgive broken intentions, and see ourselves by virtue of the life-giving promises"[54] we experience in community with one another.

Community Christian Church, just outside Chicago, emphasizes relationships as they strengthen a culture of generosity. Its leaders decided to operate the church on fifty-one weeks' worth of offerings, not fifty-two. Knowing that Easter and Christmas are the two highest-attended Sundays, they chose not just to specially invite visitors on one of those days each year, but to give their resources away to serve the surrounding community. They call this annual event "The Big Give," where all the money received in that day's offering is "given away to a short list of selected ministries that serve the community." That gathering has become so full of vision and celebration that church members invite their friends and neighbors to participate, as hundreds of thousands of dollars are given away to help their community. The congregation has been so inspired by this event that the money received that weekend is usually two or three times the church's normal weekly offering.[55]

In this section, as stewards of our relationships, we have noted the importance of balancing our *doing* with the quality of *being*, realigning how we live and do ministry to emphasize relationships as part of an organic process. We can prioritize listening to people's life experiences and sharing our stories with them. We can also demonstrate generosity in radical acts of giving. In these and other ways we encourage "generativity"—investing our efforts and resources to help people affirm and use their gifts to benefit others now and in the future. We are able to experience Communion, "union with" God, in a way that also offers us deeper community with one another and with our true selves, our "souls." In the process, both givers and receivers are transformed and deepened.

IN THIS CHAPTER we examined our churches as communities that care for people's souls. Acknowledging the community ideal that Jesus and the New Testament provide, we noted what steps we might take to shift the paradigm from *doing* church to *being* in community together. In other words, we can become a network of spiritual free agents centered in Jesus Christ, fostering first in newcomers a sense of belonging instead of conformity to right beliefs. Like a living mosaic, we can strengthen five basic elements of Christian community in our small-group life, empowering and reinforcing essential leadership behaviors to strengthen team-based ministry.

Considering healthy faith communities, we recalled the importance of both *koinonia* and *diakonia*: deep Communion community, and service alongside others. We saw examples of congregations that do their distinctive ministries based on their gifts and callings, moving to a more organic understanding of their involvement together. By focusing on persons in a "generative" way, churches encourage mutual care for one's self and others.

Like spokes on Augustine's wheel with God, the hub, the closer we draw to God, the closer we come to one another.

# Questions for Reflection

1. What strengths and weaknesses do I see in the *koinonia* and *diakonia* aspects of my primary faith community?
2. Given the five basic elements of Christian community named in *Companions in Christ*, which is the strongest where I worship and serve? Which is the one I would most like to strengthen?
3. What can I do now to experience more deeply community, generosity, and joy? How can I draw closer to my companions in faith, as I seek to live closer to God?

# Endnotes

1. In *Images of the Church in the New Testament,* Bible scholar Paul S. Minear identifies four such dominant images of the church in the New Testament: people of God, the new creation, fellowship in faith, and the body of Christ. See The Center for Parish Development, *Leadership Skills for Church Vitalization* (Chicago: Center for Parish Development, 1976), p. 9. John Driver's book, *Images of the Church in Mission* (Scottdale, PA: Herald Press, 1997) explores more metaphors, including family of God, a spiritual house, a city, a shepherd's flock, and a witnessing community.

2. J. R. Daniel Kirk, "Trusting God in the Land of Emptiness," *Upper Room Disciplines 2015* (Nashville: Upper Room Books, 2014), p. 297.

3. Paul Nixon, *I Refuse to Lead a Dying Church!* (Cleveland: The Pilgrim Press, 2006), p. 62.

4. *merriam-webster.com/dictionary/paradigm*

5. See Albert C. Outler's preface in *The Early Methodist Class Meeting,* by David Lowes Watson (Nashville: Discipleship Resources, 1985), p. ix.

6. F. Douglas Powe Jr., "Wesleyan Theology of Evangelism," *Circuit Rider,* November, December, January 2014–15, p. 19.

7. David Lowes Watson, *op cit.*, p. 5.

8. *Ibid.*, p. xi. A current adaptation of the class meeting is the system of Covenant Discipleship Groups. For a brief description of how Wesley's system developed, see Joe Iovino, "The method of early Methodism," *United Methodist Interpreter,* November-December 2016, pp. 56–57.

9. The United Methodist Council of Bishops, *Vital Congregations, Faithful Disciples: Vision for the Church* (Nashville: Graded Press, 1990), p. 62.

10. Carol Howard Merritt, "The grace of small things," *Christian Century,* April 27, 2016, p. 45.

11. Paul Nixon, *op cit.*, p. 10.

12. In *Christian Century,* October 26, 2016, pp. 16–17, Kimberly Winston cited a 2016 Public Religion Research Institute (PPRI) study, which found: "Most of the unaffiliated just 'stopped believing[.]'" The study, called *Exodus: Why Americans Are Leaving Religion and Why They Are Unlikely to Come Back,* surveyed 2,201 adults in the summer of 2016. For the full study, see *http://www.prri.org/research/prri-rns-2016-religiously-unaffiliated-americans.*

13. Katherine Ozment, author of *Grace without God: The Search for Meaning, Purpose, and Belonging in a Secular Age,* cited in Kimberly Winston, *op cit.* The desire for community has prompted the recent rise of so-called "atheist churches" such as Sunday Assembly and Oasis.

14. John Goodell of Vetal, New York, in a letter to *Christian Century*, March 18, 2015, p. 6.

15. Stanley Hauerwas, "Think Like a Wesleyan," *Circuit Rider*, November, December, January 2014–15, p. 7.

16. *Ibid.*

17. Gerrit Scott Dawson, Adele Gonzalez, E. Glenn Hinson, Rueben P. Job, Marjorie J. Thompson, Wendy M. Wright, *Companions in Christ: A Small-Group Experience in Spiritual Formation, Participant's Book* (Nashville: Upper Room Books, 2001), p. 62.

18. *Ibid.*, pp. 58–61.

19. Center for Parish Development, *Leadership Skills for Church Revitalization Resource Book* (Chicago: Center for Parish Development, 1976), p. 249.

20. Bruce Tuckman, "Forming, Storming, Norming, and Performing: Understanding the Stages of Team Formation," *mindtools.com*. *Forming* happens when people start to work together, getting to know their new colleagues. They may be anxious and excited, and unclear about the group's task and their responsibilities. *Storming* occurs when people push against the boundaries, noticing their different working styles, or jockeying for position until roles are clarified. When *Norming*, participants start to resolve their differences, appreciate colleagues' strengths, and respect the leader's authority. They develop a stronger commitment to the team goal and begin to see progress toward it. *Performing* takes place as hard work leads to achieving the team's goal. The leader can delegate many tasks, and people are able to join or leave without disrupting the group's quality of work together.

21. In the decades since its inception, Likert's church-related system theory continues to be used by the Ecumenical Center for Parish Development and helps bring about positive change in churches across North America as well as in Europe. For more about Likert's system theory of church organization, see Betsy Schwarzentraub, *Healing the Pastor as Legion: A Feminist Christian Ethics Contribution to Wholeness in Pastoral Management Styles*, Doctor of Ministry dissertation for San Francisco Theological Seminary, December 18, 1987, pp. 112–120.

22. Bill Easum, *Leadership on the Other Side* (Nashville: Abingdon Press, 2000), p. 136.

23. Thom S. Rainer and Eric Geiger, *Simple Church: Returning to God's Process for Making Disciples* (Nashville: B & H Publishing Group, 2006).

24. Eric Geiger, "Simple Church" workshop, February 4, 2010 at San Ramon Valley United Methodist Church, San Ramon, California.

25. *theologyofwork.org/the-high-calling/blog/faith-work-part-1*. Since 2008 David Miller has been the Director of the Princeton University Faith & Work Initiative as well as associate research scholar and lecturer at Princeton.

26. "The Faith at Work Movement," *Theology Today*, October 2003, pp. 301–310, at *http://ttj.sagepub.com/content/60/3/301.short?rss=1&ssource=mfc*.

27. *Ibid.*

28. Paul L. Escamilla, "Love Has Us Surrounded," *Upper Room Disciplines, 2015* (Nashville: Upper Room Books, 2014), p. 95.

29. Jaime Clark-Soles, "Teaching Bible Study Skills in a Seminary Setting: A Disciplined Knowledge for the Shared Life of Faith," *Circuit Rider*, May/June/July 2014, p. 16. Clark-Soles is also Associate Professor of New Testament at Perkins School of Theology in Dallas.

30. Heather Hahn, "What draws people to church? Poll has insights," July 5, 2016, at *umc.org/news-and-media/what-draws-people-to-church-poll-has-insights*. See also *gatheringnow.org*.

31. Betsy Schwarzentraub, *op cit.*, p. 45.

32. Romans 15:25–27 demonstrates this dynamic related to the Jerusalem offering (further described in 2 Corinthians 8 and 9), where both the Jerusalem Christians and the Christians in outlying regions received a blessing by giving to others. *Ibid.*, pp. 45–47.

33. Loren B. Mead, *Transforming Congregations for the Future* (New York City: The Alban Institute, 1994, 1995, and 1997), p. 53.

34. *Ibid.*

35. Rev. Jean Lofsvold Schwien, "Truly welcoming all people," *2015 United Methodist Program Calendar*; *christumcutah.net*.

36. Loren B. Mead, *op cit.*, p. 70.

37. Michael Tessman, Rhode Island, in *Christian Century*, January 7, 2015, p. 6.

38. Mike Mather, *Vital Ministry in the Small-Membership Church: Sharing Stories, Shaping Community*, p. 29.

39. *Ibid., pp. 26–27.*

40. *Ibid.*, p. 28.

41. Margaret J. Wheatley's book is *Leadership and the New Science: Discovering Order in a Chaotic World*, paperback (San Francisco: Berrett-Koehler, 2006). Notes from her previous edition were used in Faith Quest training led by Betsy Heavner, October 24–26, 2000, for the California-Nevada Annual Conference of the United Methodist Church.

42. Stephen Post and Jill Neimark, *op cit.*, p. 46.

43. Paul Wink of Wellesley College, in Stephen Post and Jill Neimark, *op cit.*, p. 50. Wink did a longitudinal study of 200 high school students from the 1920s to the present.

44. Heather Hahn, *op cit.*

45. *Ibid.*

46. M. Thomas Thangaraj, "New Venues of Obedience," *The Upper Room Disciplines 2015* (Nashville: Upper Room Books, 2014), p. 88. Dr. Thangaraj is Professor

Emeritus of World Christianity at Candler School of Theology, Emory University, Atlanta, Georgia.

47. Phillip Cary, Lecture 11: "The Development of Christian Platonism," *Philosophy and Religion in the West,* Compact Disk set (Chantilly, Virginia: The Teaching Company, 1999).

48. Phillip Cary, *Philosophy and Religion in the West, Course Guidebook,* p. 56. See Chapter Four for more about this "in, then up" process.

49. Catherine Malotky, ed. *op cit.*

50. David G. Benner, *op cit,* p. 20.

51. Miroslav Volf, *op cit.,* p. 86.

52. *Ibid.*

53. Gerard Manley Hopkins, "God's Grandeur," *Modern American & Modern British Poetry,* edited by Louis Untermeyer (New York: Harcourt, Brace and Company, 1955), p. 429.

54. Wes Avram, "Living By the Word," *Christian Century,* Dec. 10, 2014, p. 20.

55. Chris Willard and Jim Sheppard, *op cit.,* p. 170.

# A Renewed Sense of Mission

W E CAN DISCOVER community within the more usual circles of family, friends, neighbors, or with people around the globe. These four domains are what authors Post and Neimark call "the four spheres of love."[1] Often our involvement within one of these spheres has an impact on the other domains, like overlapping circles.

## Living in Our Wider Community

Most of us are familiar with the phrase, "Think globally, act locally." It encourages us to respond to big-picture issues by acting on them within our local network, letting the repercussions ripple out into the wider world. But to function effectively, first we need to listen to the people in our distinctive church and community before acting, then adapt our ministries and personal behaviors accordingly.

Meeli Tankler knows this firsthand. Living in Pamu, Estonia, she is not only the president of a seminary, but also a local preacher at the Agape United Methodist Church in that town.[2] Before developing outreach ministries, she says, the congregation needs to prove itself as trustworthy in the eyes of the local community by showing openness, acceptance, and a caring presence. Only then is it able to change ministry priorities or methods and embrace new challenges in a way that meets the strengths and needs of the people around them.

Listening and acting in this way involves making purposeful connections with others. Even within one's neighborhood, we can widen our circle of care. For example, Bethany United Methodist Church in Berwick, Pennsylvania is a church that connects in ever-widening circles. In 2012 its members began providing a free community dinner each Wednesday, serving more than 100 neighbors with money and food contributions, primarily from the church. Then they added a Bible study after the meal, with about thirty people in attendance as of 2015. They also continue to work with local Scout troops and have a van ministry. With a weekly Pioneer Club for children, a youth group, and Bethany Blessings Preschool, they encourage young people to gather, learn, and share.[3]

Partnerships offer a powerful way to serve a wider community. People from multiple churches in Michigan and beyond come together for an annual workday called "Hands4Detroit." On the Hands4Detroit Day in 2015, hundreds of volunteers from churches and college ministry groups cleaned up an entire city block, cleared out overgrown brush, and boarded up five abandoned homes. They also donated 2,200 pounds of canned goods, as part of an ongoing partnership with the Gleaners Community Food Bank of Southeastern Michigan. In 2016, St. Paul's United Methodist Church in Rochester, Michigan, celebrated its fifth annual participation in Hands4Detroit, joining volunteers from across metropolitan Detroit on the annual workday, to clear overgrowth, donate food, and build small, free neighborhood libraries.[4]

Another kind of partnership is what church leaders call a "flat model" for mission. In the previous two centuries, most local giving to far-off places required people from neighborhood churches to give "up" the chain of church hierarchy to their denominational offices or agencies, which in turn distributed resources "down" to selected recipients around the globe. But now, instant communication and access to technology have created a flat model, where people form direct lateral relationships, person-to-person and church-to-church around the world. For example, through personal connections one U.S. congregation rebuilt the water system for an entire village in the Sudan. Another church provided a new roof for a local hospital in Russia.

With the possibility of such direct relationships, top- or medium-level denominational administration could become a resource facilitator, instead of the coordinator and distributer of gifts and services. For example, 773 congregations in the Missouri Conference of the United Methodist Church have a long-standing partnership with churches in Mozambique, but that partnership takes on a different form for each church. The relationship "involves hundreds of church-to-church partnerships, pastor-to-pastor friendships, water-well projects, salary supports, mutual prayers, and educational and medical ministries," says the Missouri Bishop, Robert Schnase.[5] Congregations send video greetings to their partner congregations to show during worship, and ministers and other church leaders relate across the miles through video conferencing and social media.

There are at least three implications of this flat-mission approach. The first is that individuals, small groups, and petite churches can "act large" by developing a big online presence. Second, people with a passion for giving to a specific cause can find one another digitally across vast distances and support one another's giving, through such efforts as Giving Circles or crowdfunding. Third, faith communities of every kind can collaborate with financial foundations, universities, and other organizations, based on common values and concerns.

Whether such linkage is electronic or in-person, the overarching purpose of these connections is to care for one another.

I had the honor of serving a congregation in the Northern California delta. There, a thousand miles of interlaced waterways flow toward the Pacific Ocean, creating rural islands where people live as farmers, ranchers, and fisherfolk. Churches of different denominations, each representing a small cross-section of the population, dot the spread-out towns, but we tended not to know one another.

The flood of 1986 changed all that. It came as a combination of torrential rains and three dams upriver releasing water at the same time. Down in the delta, disaster resulted. Water covered 8,000 acres on one island alone. Protecting levees broke, and miles of homes were inundated. One day I had visited parishioners in their homes—the next day I was in a boat floating over the tops of their cars.

That was when we "widened the circle." Denominational labels no longer mattered, as the ministers from our scattered tiny congregations came together. We started meeting, forming what we tongue-in-cheek called the "CIA:" Community Interfaith Action. Each of us accessed what disaster-response funds we could find from our respective organizations. We brought our lay leaders into the group, and together decided to make grants of fifty dollars each to delta families. Then we went to residents' homes, bringing them not only the money, but also a few hours of volunteer labor: bailing water out of houses, pulling up rugs, shoveling debris, spreading out furniture to dry, helping the families save what they could.

The delta communities changed in a small but real way because of that person-to-person response. We had come alongside one another, becoming more of a caring community.

Seen on a larger scale, a flat approach to mission produces decentralized action with "higher levels of reciprocity, grassroots innovation, localized diversity,"[6] and potentially millions of technologically-linked participants engaged simultaneously. Instead of being coordinated by a larger structure, flat mission depends on networks of local groups interdependently collaborating, sharing resources, and acting with mutual accountability to support a specific mission. Such a process encourages diversification and adaptation, resulting in a greater variety of creative and dynamic engagement with the wider world.

One type of engagement and support is *crowdfunding*: the practice of financing a project or venture by raising money from many people, primarily online. In 2015, an estimated $34 billion was raised worldwide in this way.[7] The process involves three elements: the one who proposes the project idea, persons or groups who help fund it, and a moderating organization (the Internet "platform") that brings them together. In 2012 there were 450 crowdfunding platforms operating—but by 2016 that number had exploded to 2,000.[8] These channels let individuals browse through a list of small nonprofit projects without requiring donors to give large amounts of money.[9]

Global Giving is one of these platforms. Its giving opportunities include children, women, health, environment, disaster response, and technology. For example, donors may give as little as twenty dollars to complete artisan job training for women in the African country of Madagascar, where subsistence agriculture is the main livelihood for 300,000 rural residents. Families there earn less than one dollar a day. Through a wild silk program, families can increase their income by an average of 80 percent. Another project is to raise a total of $250 to provide a Learning Center and two new sewing machines to train Afghan women sewing and tailoring and help them start home-based businesses. Other projects range from tutoring and supporting nineteen village children in Romania, or feeding orphan cheetahs in Namibia, to improving education for 2,000 students in Kenya. The possibilities for flat-mission giving are endless.

Other crowdfunding platforms, such as Kiva, connect investors with individuals in developing countries, to receive microloans of as little as $25. An astounding 1.6 million people have made such loans in 82 countries, with an even more amazing repayment rate of 97 percent. Many of these investors follow Kiva's saying, "Fund a loan, get repaid, fund another."[10]

# People in Mission

Living in a wider circle empowers people to care for one another to an extent they could not have imagined before. For example, Roman Catholic Sister Mary Scullion has been helping homeless people for nearly forty years. In 1989 she co-founded Project HOME as a single emergency winter shelter for homeless men in Philadelphia. Over the years, the ministry grew. By 2016, Project HOME had a

30.5-million-dollar budget and offered a multipronged continuum of care aimed at root causes of homelessness."[11] "We learned that shelter wasn't enough," she said. "They need jobs, education, access to health care. They need community."[12] Now Project HOME provides long-term support including outreach teams, real-time data on all residences that are available throughout the city, and a housing placement resource for all agencies serving homeless people there.

In Long Beach, California, Grace First Presbyterian Church widened the circle of care in a different way. Their Session (leadership group) had decided to raise one million dollars to update their 1950s fellowship hall. But in 2006, when they saw the devastation Hurricane Katrina left on the U.S. Gulf Coast, they decided to live with the old fellowship hall, and raise one million dollars to give away instead. At that time Grace First Presbyterian was not a huge church. With 500 members, it had mostly school teachers, aerospace workers, and managers, along with some small-business owners. After discussing the opportunity, the congregation voted unanimously to go forward. They raised 1.1 million dollars—in just four months—and gave 110 percent of what they had pledged.[13]

In the ten years since initiating that mission campaign, Bill Saul and Tim Jackert, the campaign co-chairs, made forty-two trips to the Gulf, mostly at their own expense. The church's funds and involvement included multiple volunteer mission work trips. In addition, they:

- Paid one year of electric bills for a Louisiana church that was housing and feeding volunteers.
- Provided dumpsters for ten houses to be demolished and totally rebuilt.
- Installed an elevator for a disabled woman to access her new house, built on stilts above the flood plain.
- Paid the salary for a New Orleans church's part-time pastor for one year, then helped the congregation find a fulltime pastor, and paid that salary for two years.

- Bought a house and converted it into a mission center, used every day for five years by up to forty volunteers, then sold it and donated the proceeds.

This effort reshaped the life of the Grace First congregation. Their regular mission giving and hands-on support to their community increased. They even re-evaluated their building plans, and eventually completed the revised remodeling project.

These instances of ministry to a wider community remind us that we can help provide people with the capacity to live abundant lives in a global economy by: improving their health, nourishment, and shelter; assisting them to find meaningful labor and supportive relationships; and empowering them to contribute to society. We can do this to a far greater extent as communities than we can as individuals.

A key requirement for doing wider-based mission is persuading both recipients and coworkers to participate in the endeavor. In Milwaukee, Wisconsin, Common Ground formed a community consortium of congregations, nonprofits, small businesses, colleges, and labor unions. Certain Common Ground members spent months tracking foreclosure actions and documenting how specific banks had neglected upkeep on foreclosed properties. Then others attended shareholder meetings to confront the bank executives. As a result, they convinced the banks to contribute $34 million in cash and mortgage commitments "to revitalize Milwaukee neighborhoods that [had] been decimated by foreclosures."[14]

On the Canadian prairies, students of Canadian Mennonite University and alumni farmers formed the Metanoia Farmers Worker Cooperative. Together they use sustainable practices to provide food to urban consumers. They operate as a workers' cooperative, practicing consensus decision-making. "We hope to foster meaningful dialogue," says Winnipeg resident Dori Zerbe Cornelsen, "while joyfully stewarding God's gift of the land."[15]

The wider our outreach, the clearer we need to be about our distinctive identity as both individuals and a congregation. These days, faith communities are increasingly shifting to being more experiential and participatory, focusing more on what we do together, linked by common interests.[16]

One example is a network of churches organized around small groups, called "cell groups," by TOUCH Outreach Ministries in Houston, Texas.[17] Begun in 1972, By forming cell groups that meet in homes, it helps churches transition away from obsessing on programs and buildings. Its mission is to provide resources, training, and consulting to those who want to start a new church based on its group life. It also helps congregations shift from fixating on supporting programs or facilities, to establishing more small-group-based ministry.

Sometimes it takes an entire town to meet the challenge of caring for a wider community. In 2001, when terrorists attacked the U.S. World Trade Center and Pentagon on September 11, the air space was shut down, and hundreds of transatlantic airliners were rerouted. At that time the little fishing town of Gander in Newfoundland—with a total population of 10,000 people—found lining up on its small tarmac 38 international airlines, carrying 7,000 people!

"I was there on that morning," said Roger Janes, United Church of Canada minister. "[The people of Gander] opened up their communities, their homes, their restaurants, their businesses, their schools," he said.[18] The passengers came from more than 100 countries, so the Newfoundlanders gave them clothes to handle the Canadian coast's cold weather. Locals "took them on little trips to show them around."[19] They even found a way to care for the seventeen dogs and cats and the two great apes that also had been aboard the planes.[20]

Eighty-year-old Shirley Brooks-Jones was on Delta Flight 15, one of the planes diverted to Gander's nearby fishing village of Lewisporte. She and her fellow passengers spent the next three days in that town, where residents cooked them meals, let them use their showers, even loaned them their cars. As in Gander, none of the townspeople would accept money. So after the passengers finally re-boarded their plane, Brooks-Jones asked them to contribute to a scholarship fund for the local children. When they reached their final destination, $15,000 had been promised. A longtime professional fundraiser,

Brooks-Jones added to and invested the money. By September, 2016 it had grown to about $2,000,000. As of 2016, 228 graduates of Lewisporte Collegiate High School, including one-third of the 2016 graduating class, had received a scholarship from that fund over the past fifteen years.[21]

"I think the story is a human one," said Roger Janes. "It shows that generosity is contagious when you get that kind of thing going."

In this section we have seen people living and giving in widening circles, beginning by listening to the people around them, accepting those outside their usual boundaries, and becoming a caring presence in their midst. Entire communities have been transformed by partnerships with other congregations, nonprofit organizations, and individual volunteers.

Flat mission models create personally connected global partnerships between givers and receivers, often with positive consequences for all involved. Online options provide even farther-flung opportunities, as in crowdfunding. Some ministries have altered their expenditure of funds after perceiving deeper global needs. An entire town opened its doors to welcome strangers, nurturing a culture of a stronger commitment to generosity in the process. Whether urban or rural, people can discover vital ministry by sharing with people outside their places of worship. While doing so, they also gain greater awareness and understanding of one another.

## Communities of Gospel Stewards

As we noted in Chapter One, individual stewardship is the sum of all the decisions and actions we take to live out the Good News of God's love. This includes being stewards of the Good News itself: the message of God's love and grace given us in Jesus Christ, God's active presence with us in every moment, and God's gift of eternal life. One way to summarize this beautiful mystery is in John 3:16: "For God so loved the world that [God] gave [God's] only Son, so that everyone who believes in him may not perish but may have eternal life."

Christians are meant to be *stewards* of this Good News—that is, to receive, care for, and share this wonderful message—both when we gather together for worship and also when we scatter to individually serve the world. But I am *not* talking about the old-fashioned view of "evangelism," where people say what they think are "the right words" to magically convince a non-believer. Stewards of the Good News ("gospel" in Old English) are those who naturally demonstrate God's love by how they live alongside others.

Living as communities of people who steward the gospel with commitment and joy can be enriched by:

- Redefining the way we work together, moving from seeing ourselves as consumers of services, to stewards of God's wonderful news;
- Shaping the way we do ministry to facilitate the mutual flow of resources into and out of our congregation; and
- Teaching one another to be more generous as a community acting together.

In these ways, we can become more authentic stewards in how we receive, work with, and share God's Good News.

Redefining our "governance"—how we interact with one another and lead our faith community—challenges us as church leaders to quit trying to sell a raft of religious programs to our church constituents. As we've discussed earlier, a church is not necessarily more successful or more faithful in its stewardship because it has a lot of prayer and study groups or persons enrolled in the Sunday school program. While these in themselves are laudable activities, when made the predominant orientation of the church, it can fall prey to a consumerist expectation that "more is better." Rather, all of us as Christians are meant to encourage "a lifestyle of simplicity and trust" in God's generosity, where God redefines our needs.[22] We follow a Sovereign who serves, without lording his authority over others. (Matthew 20:25–28)

Whatever the size or shape of our Christian community, the center of all that we are is Jesus Christ. In 1 Corinthians 8:6, Paul states:

There is one God, the Father, from whom are all things and for whom we exist, and one Lord, Jesus Christ, through Whom are all things and through Whom we exist.

In this passage, says theologian N. T. Wright, Paul has rewritten the *Shema*, the daily repeated Jewish statement of faith, to put Jesus at the center as the one in whom God's identity is revealed.[23] Wright notes that the Greek word for "belong" gives multiple layers of meaning: we are meant to belong to Jesus Christ, to exist in relation to him, and to live toward him.

So the ways church leaders work together and interact with the congregation should reflect Jesus Christ more than anything or anyone else. This requires having a different-than-usual set of qualities as steward leaders. With that in mind, the Stewardship of Life Institute in Gettysburg, Pennsylvania, developed a list of core perspectives and practices needed for today's steward leader (see next page).[24]

These competencies or attributes are meant to be a guide to form steward leaders who mature in their "clear perspectives, sound personal habits and confident leadership skills in stewardship."[25]

Both in person and online, we can choose not only who will be in our network of mutual influence, but also what we will share through those connections. For example, an inspiring worship service that moves 100 people to do good in the community can potentially influence 500 people, assuming each person has five friends, and can multiply outward exponentially from there. When we post something online, it can touch thousands of people, or even "go viral," directly speaking to millions of persons around the globe.

As we shape our network of relationships for the inflow and outflow of resources, our interconnection can spread goodness and blessing.[26] Relationships with other individuals and groups are "currencies" in the sense that they are fluid, can be exchanged and grow, and can increase the flow of positive energy between persons and

| Core Perspectives: | Core Practices: |
|---|---|
| Trusts God's abundance | Embodies attitudes of abundance (instead of scarcity), generosity, and sustainability in making ongoing choices. |
| Grounds oneself in biblical and theological principles | Includes stewardship themes when listening to and interpreting all Scripture. Shows awareness of the history of stewardship in this church. |
| Holds a holistic perspective | Does not compartmentalize faith. Integrates care of the earth, family, money, self, and group relationships as part of stewardship. |
| Perceives connectedness | Acts responsibly toward all in one's personal stewardship practices. Is accountable for decisions, and collaborates with others about stewardship practice. |
| Engages and critiques culture | Understands economic systems and business realities. Reflects on one's consumer culture and its impact on the future. Shows concern about present injustice and future sustainability. |
| Embraces financial health as an expression of faith | Acts transparently with others in one's use of money. Manages and monitors one's own personal financial health. |

groups. We know from the story of Mary and Martha that relationship is important. (Luke 10:38–42) In the 1950s and 1960s a lot of people in the United States wanted to go to church, so each congregation strove to "'do church' better," says Holy Currencies consultant Eric Law. But since the late 1970s church has been one option among many. "Relationship is what is needed today," he says. Now people want to belong first, before they agree to common beliefs. "We need to use the early church model that built relationships first."[27]

Our external relationships, Law notes, encompass: people who are not currently church members; different racial, cultural, and ethnic groups in the neighborhood; individuals and groups who have resources, or who are in need; civic and community leaders and organizations; ecumenical and interfaith partners; local businesses; and the environment.

But while a church's external relationships are crucial, so are its internal relationships with church members, area congregations of the same affiliation, and the regional and national denominational organization.

For example, in New York, Hyde Park United Methodist Church is an active community of worship, friendship, Christian learning, and mission. One aspect of their ministries is called "Blessed Connections," a cluster of services that minister to the many needs of people in their Christian family.[28] Blessed Connection involvements range from their card ministry, College Connection, and visitation team, to Monday Night Lights (weekly meal and small groups), transportation, and Church Family Fellowship.

The internal care congregants receive from Hyde Park naturally spills over into their external relationships. For example, their Kairos Inside team joins with other Christians to go into a nearby prison for a three-day event presenting the gospel of Jesus Christ. They engage in ten weeks of training for it, learning to "go in with integrity, with love, and with respect for one another." Initially such oneness as a team is not easy, given the wide range of Christian beliefs of those who gather to do this ministry. But the skills learned in their Blessed Connections internal ministry give Hyde Park's participants the capacity to bridge any differences they may have had with one another.[29]

Modeling generosity as a community and teaching one another to be more generous is a lifelong challenge. As we have noted previously, generosity is our passion for giving of ourselves and what God has entrusted to us, out of gratitude for God's relationship of extravagant giving to us. It is a learned attitude and habitual action that focuses on the other's welfare, not only to do good but also to do no harm. It allows us to still have a degree of self-interest but extends our care to others in a way that vitalizes both giver and receiver.

We are called to learn with our hearts as well as our heads, so generous attitudes and actions can develop into a first-response habit in various situations. For example, one church becomes an evacuation center for flood evacuees; a second brings personally-written cards from its members to a mosque which was the victim of a hate crime. Yet another congregation gathers volunteers to care for people and their livestock forced out of their homes by a fire. One more helps Syrian refugees settle in their neighborhood and among their families.

"The best gift we can give to each other may be neither a thing (like a diamond ring) nor an act (like an embrace), but our own generosity," says theologian Miroslav Volf.

> It forges lasting bonds of reciprocal love. At the most basic level, generosity itself is exchanged in all our gift exchanges: My generosity is reciprocated by your generosity, and the circle of mutual love keeps turning.[30]

An amazing embodiment of generous community living came about in response to an event in 1995, when dozens of homeless families had moved into an abandoned Catholic church building in North Philadelphia.[31] The archdiocese told them they had forty-eight hours to move out, or they could be arrested. With nowhere to go, the mothers and children hung a banner on the front of the building that said, "How can we worship a homeless man on Sunday, and ignore one on

Monday?" They held their own press conference and announced that they had talked with the real "Owner" of the building, and that God said they could stay until they found somewhere else to go.

Over the span of three years, some of the students who had been part of that movement pooled their money and bought an old shoe repair store and made it their home. Over time, they bought and transformed other abandoned houses on that block. Now, more than twenty years later, their intentional community shares houses and gardens on about a dozen properties on the same block—and they are creating a park and greenspace where years earlier a fire had burned down part of their neighborhood.

Inspired by the Book of Acts, they share in their communal life, give freely to those in need, and challenge systems and structures that hold people down. "We paint murals, help kids with homework, share food, host neighborhood celebrations, and try to live as one big family," they say, "which means eating together, praying together, doing life together."[32] Founder Shane Claiborne brings it back to Acts 2 in the Bible, when the Spirit fell on Pentecost, and those early Christians immediately started sharing what they had with people in need. "Like those first Christians," he says, "generosity naturally happens in our lives when we are born again and realize that we are to love our neighbors as we love ourselves."[33]

In the midst of all our differences, Christ invites each person to reflect the gospel naturally by how we act as a community. We learn to do this by working together increasingly as managers of God's gifts instead of as consumers of services, by shaping our network for mutual resourcing, and by learning and modeling how to be more generous, both within and beyond our congregation.

## Loving God and Neighbor

Jesus calls us to love God with all our heart, soul, and mind, and to love our neighbor as we love ourselves. (Matthew 22:35–39) These two commandments are the interlaced foundation for all the

Scriptures and for our spiritual life together. This means that no matter how broken or compromised our relationships may be, God works toward healing "to create community. This is also *steward-ship*," says steward leader Glen Taibl. "Stewardship is relationship, as it unites God's action for others with our response."[34] When we receive our cues from our relationship with God, we can more effectively create families that are supportive of both parents and children. We can care for the land and manage our lives in a way that is life-giving for all.

"Loving" does not mean only a romantic kind of love, or even a particular feeling. Rather, its essence is caring for someone, being committed to that person's well-being. It is a commitment we are meant to act on, looking after the good of someone else.[35]

But just saying this does not make it easy. "Living in community is hard," says one pastor.[36] "It asks us to value right relationships over being right. It requires mutual forbearance, empathy, and humility. And inevitably it requires the ability to forgive."

MANY MINISTRIES have shown us ways to widen the circle of our care for one another, beginning with being open to listening for people's strengths and needs. Several flat-mission models encourage direct lateral relationships where, through the Internet and other channels, we can "act large" and collaborate with other organizations based on common values. Such a person-oriented process includes supporting one another and invites us to live in the context of a wider community, whether through in-person interactions, through technology, or in networked ministries around the world.

In any of the four "spheres of love," we can become more aware and interactive as gospel steward communities, valuing reciprocity, diversity, and innovation. Within this larger context, steward leaders are able to strengthen their key perspectives and practices, forging bonds to keep reshaping their service and modeling generosity alongside one another.

# Questions for Reflection

1. Which of the four areas of love—family, friends, neighbors, and people around the world—is most challenging for me to care for other people? In each of these spheres, where do I find the greatest support? In which do I take most for granted?
2. How might some new practices, such as the flat-mission model or crowdfunding, open more possibilities for my congregation to extend its mission?
3. How well does my faith community encourage the core perspectives and practices needed for steward leaders? What one could we work on to make the most difference?
4. In what ways might our local church reinforce or deepen our stewardship of relationships throughout our wider network?

# Endnotes

1. Stephen Post and Jill Neimark, *op cit.,* p. 302.
2. Meeli Tankler, "A Unique and Contextual Identity," *Circuit Rider*, May/June/July, 2016, p. 9.
3. Kathy Conway, "Learning and growing in the Lord," *2015 United Methodist Program Calendar.*
4. *http://rethinkchurch.org/impact-event/hands4dewtroit-2013; stpaulsrochester.org/ hands-4-detroit-2014; stpaulsrochester.org/hands-4-detroit-2015; https://events. rethinkchurch.org/hands-4-detroit; wmu.miwesley.org/event/hands-4-detroit.*
5. Robert Schnase, "Why Working Harder Isn't Working," *Circuit Rider*, February/ March/April, 2014, p. 7.
6. Dwight Zscheile, "Social Networking and Church Systems," *Word & World: Theology for Christian Ministry* (St. Paul, Minnesota: Luther Seminary), Summer 2010, p. 249.
7. *Wikipedia.com* crowdfunding.
8. *Ibid.*
9. *globalgiving.org.*
10. *kiva.org.*
11. Mary Beth McCauley, "Mary Scullion: Philadelphia's saint of the streets," *https:// www.christiancentury.org/article/2015-12/philadelphias-saint-streets.*

12. *Ibid.*
13. Rev. Steven E. Wirth, "Risking Generosity: Miracle at Grace First," *Chimes*, San Francisco Seminary, Spring, 2016, p. 23.
14. "Borrowers and lenders," *Christian Century*, April 4, 2012, p. 7.
15. Dori Zerbe Cornelsen, "We Are What We Eat," *stewardshipresources.org*.
16. Rev. Greg Bergquist, "Challenged to Re-think Our Vision for Ministry," *Instant Connection*, California-Nevada Conference of the United Methodist Church, November 1, 2012.
17. *touchusa.org.* "TOUCH" stands for "Transforming Others Under Christ's Hand."
18. Roger Janes in the January 21, 2017 conference call for the "Stewardship and Culture" online course taught by Betsy Schwarzentraub, at *transformingthechurch.org*, sponsored by the Ecumenical Stewardship Center.
19. *Ibid.*
20. Petula Dvorak, "On 9/11, a tiny Canadian town opened its runways and heart to 7,000 stranded travelers," *washingtonpost.com/local/on-sept-11-a-tiny-canadian-town-opened-its-runways-and-heart-to-7000-stranded-travelers/2016/09/08/89d875da-75e5-11e6-8149-b8d05321db62_story.html?utm_term=.535cfecf82a6*, Sept. 10, 2016.
21. Bill Anderton, "Follow-Up on 9/11 Gander Hospitality Story," January 21, 2017, in the "Stewardship and Culture" online course, Class Forum.
22. Marjorie Hewitt Suchoki, "Remembrance and Anticipation," *Upper Room Disciplines 2012* (Nashville: Upper Room Books, 2016), p. 342.
23. N. T. Wright, "One God, One Lord," *Christian Century*, November 27, 2013, pp. 22–27.
24. Catherine Malotky, ed. *op cit.*, pp. vi and 44. Paraphrases of their practice descriptions are mine.
25. *Ibid.*, p. 44.
26. Eric Law, *op cit.*, p. 19. Here he also refers to Nicholas Christakis and James Fowler's book, *Connected* (New York: Back Bay Books/Little, Brown and Company, 2009).
27. ——, speaking on the currency of relationship, at the California-Nevada Annual Conference of the United Methodist Church, Sacramento, June 20, 2013.
28. Dale Becker, "Blessed Connections Feature of the Month: 'Listen! Listen! Love! Love!'" Dec. 13, 2008, *hydepark-umc.org/home/node/18*. See also *umchp.com*.
29. Rev. Arlene Wilhelm, "Listen! Listen! Love! Love!" Ruminations & Reflections, *Hyde Park Messenger*, September, 2012.
30. Miroslav Volf, *op cit.*, p. 87.
31. *thesimpleway.org*.
32. *Ibid.*

33. "Generosity in Community: An Interview with Shane Claiborne," *Giving: Growing Joyful Stewards in Your Congregation* magazine, Live Simply issue (2016), p. 14.

34. Glen Taibl, "Stewardship: Creating Community," Center for Stewardship Leaders, Luther Seminary, May 6, 2014, *communic@luthersem.edu.*

35. Rev. Mike Harrell, "The Common Good," September 25, 2016, at Foothills United Methodist Church, Rescue, California.

36. Joann Haejong Lee, associate pastor of the House of Hope Presbyterian Church, St. Paul, Minnesota, "Reflections on the Lectionary," *Christian Century*, September 3, 2014, p. 19.

# Generosity as a Way of Living

G ENEROSITY IS A way of living based on gratitude, which includes listening with understanding, respect, and compassion. In this chapter we will investigate three ways to strengthen generosity as the essential pattern for our way of life. First, generous living can transform our care for the Earth and God's creatures. Second, while we give to others, we are also meant to honor ourselves, including managing our health and use of time. Third, as we deploy our talents and spiritual gifts for the community, we necessarily need to seek forgiveness from others and from ourselves.

## Amazing Grace

Ever since John Newton penned the lines for the hymn, "Amazing Grace," millions of people have claimed it as their own heart-warming favorite. But what exactly is *grace*?

The word for grace in the New Testament is *charis*. In secular Greek, it means a "favor" or "kindness" given, including the giver's feeling of graciousness, and the receiver's sense of gratitude.[1] This definition offers us a basic understanding, but in the Bible, *grace* takes on three even richer tones.

First, in the Christian Scriptures, *charis* refers to the power and presence of God, given and perceived both individually and collectively.

For example, Paul says God called him personally through grace (Galatians 1:15). He asserts that through the Corinthian church's ministries, grace extends to more and more persons (2 Corinthians 4:15). Likewise, in his warm words of thanks to the Christians in Philippi, he affirms how they "share in God's grace" with him in both the highs and the lows of proclaiming the Good News (Philippians 1:3–7). This means they share together in the actual presence and power of God.

We cannot undo our past failures, misdeeds, or betrayals, but God's grace offers us forgiveness, giving us the chance to start over. We no longer need to carry the weight of what we have done or have failed to do in our past relationships. So we are "saved" in both senses of the word: rescued from what might be a destructive situation, and offered the promise of wholeness, maturity, and completeness.

Perhaps the most famous Bible text about grace is Ephesians 2:8, where Paul says in part, "For by grace you have been saved through faith, and this is not your own doing; it is the gift of God." In other words, only God can initiate grace through Jesus Christ, and God offers it to us out of love, without our having to earn it.

This leads us to a second way of describing grace—as God's "unconditional love, acceptance and forgiveness—[as] a gift in the purest sense of the word."[2] It is entirely unmerited, offered equally to us all.

The Bible words for love do not depend only upon emotion, but rather on relationship and caring actions toward another. So God's "love" for us shows itself in God's mercy and compassion. We can see it both within and around us: God sustaining us in life and spirit and saving us from our own and others' worst devices. Nothing can place us outside of God's grace! (Romans 8:38–39)

So grace does not leave us where we are. It is God's presence with a purpose: "to create, heal, forgive, reconcile and transform human hearts, communities and the entire creation."[3]

This fact relates to a third dimension of grace in the Bible—as God actively working within us for the benefit of others as well as ourselves. It is "the power of God working in you to give [you] a transformed life,"[4] to reflect more fully the image of God, in which you were created.

As Christians, we want to live as instruments of this grace, but it is not an all-or-nothing kind of thing. It is a *process of growth* which extends throughout our lives, and even beyond. John Wesley describes three movements, or expressions, of this grace, which interweave throughout our lives:

- Prevenient—Grace which "comes before" our accepting God or Christ. It may include our love of family, natural conscience, yearning for God, and vision of goodness.
- Justifying—Grace which saves us or turns us around to look toward God, to accept the gift of a new beginning. It makes us aware of our identity as God's loved sons and daughters.
- Sanctifying—Grace that moves us beyond forgiveness and acceptance of who we are meant to be in God's eyes. It urges us to seek to become holy and whole, part of a restored creation.5

Given such a view of grace, is it possible to actually *steward* God's grace—to receive, manage, and share it with others? Stewarding is certainly different from controlling! There's no way we could possess, limit, or harness God's grace in our lives.

Stewardship is a way of living in response to God's grace, working with this gift of grace God has given us. In this case we can interact authentically with God's dynamic presence and power. What if we can work with God's grace as a partner in collaboration, in a creative, artistic way?

If so, God's grace remains an attribute and action of God, even as it works within us, using our human eccentricities, strengths, and limitations. At the same time, even with the most careful intentionality, whatever we do is an inevitably imperfect reflection of God's grace. We cannot manipulate its movement. But we can cooperate with it, catching glimpses of it at work in our lives and in the world. We can strive to open ourselves increasingly to God's grace, resist our initial wariness about being vulnerable, and practice deep trust that God is in charge of our lives with loving intention.

# Whole-Life Generosity

In the light of such overwhelming grace, how can we *not* seek to live generously in every dimension of our existence? We recall that "generosity" is both an attitude and a habit that seeks the well-being of others. It is a core value we hold, a spiritual discipline we practice, and a measure of deepening discipleship. Responding purposefully to God's generosity, we engage who we are as well as what we do, over time strengthening a generous character.

For the apostle Paul and for us, says pastor Douglass Key, generosity is not a self-rewarding calculation, and not merely a choice we make.

> It is a mark of our identity in Christ. When we are baptized into the one who is self-emptying we take on that self-emptying generosity for ourselves. It becomes who we are, not [merely] what we do.... It is a mark of our union to Christ, who himself laid down his divine glory and became poor for us so that we might know God's love and grace and redemption.[6]

In this way, generosity can become our basic orientation to life, including what we notice and focus on, where we put our priorities for involvement, and how we devote the full resources of what we have and are. All of these aspects are an unspoken "demonstration of God's love and a response to God's grace."[7]

There is more to generosity than money, says Bill Enright, Director Emeritus at the Lake Institute on Faith & Giving. Generosity has to do with how we use our skills, "share ideas, practice hospitality, offer encouragement, make connections and use our time to address the needs of others."[8] So while stewardship is our opportunity to live as witnesses to God's extraordinarily generous nature, generosity is the fullest expression of a steward's life, bringing glory to God.[9]

Examples of personal generosity abound. One is Mark Bustos, hair stylist in an upscale salon in Manhattan, New York. He gives free haircuts to homeless people every week on his one day off. He started the practice when he was on a trip to the Philippines in 2012 and finds that his homeless patrons are very thankful.[10]

Neighborly gestures can come through the Internet, as well. For example, David Perez saw his seventy-five-year-old neighbor up on his rickety roof trying to patch it all by himself. So David put a request on Facebook, saying he personally had no roofing skills, and asking if anyone could donate his or her time to help this neighbor finish the project. David set a time to meet in five days to see what they could do. When the day came, forty people converged on the site to offer their services, while others donated water, donuts, and pizza. "It took just four hours," David said, noting that his neighbor was in shock, grateful, and thankful to everyone for all their hard work.[11]

Likewise, congregations can affirm and celebrate their members' generosity. For example, Grand Junction First United Methodist Church, Colorado, printed in their newsletter some of the thank-you notes they had received after their volunteers served weekly lunches and gave Christmas gift cards to neighbors in poor circumstances. "We are a richly blessed people; let us 'walk worthy of the calling with which we are called,'" wrote their associate pastor. "This is what it means to be the Body of Christ."[12]

Each of us can have different reasons for acting generously. Researchers Stephen Post and Jill Neimark identified ten things that might motivate us to give. These are:

- Celebration—Engaging in fun rituals that well up out of gratitude for life, such as a thank-you card, gratitude journal, birthday party, anniversary, or graduation. It helps us savor the day, celebrate other people, and reframe our lives.

- <u>Compassion</u>—Responding to suffering with empathy, as the basis of one's morality. It calms us and connects us to others.
- <u>Courage</u>—Being willing to be a guiding influence, to confront harmful behavior, or to set a positive example. Courage often prompts the giver to reach a turning point, resulting in joy and connection.
- <u>Creativity</u>—Practicing the most joyful and spontaneous expression of life in any of various ways. It can include discovery, novel thinking, and openness to new experiences.
- <u>Forgiveness</u>—Gaining a sense of inner freedom or peace that releases us or others from the burden of guilt and/or pain. It's a process that preserves close relationships, improves one's mental and physical health, and shifts our perspective toward gratitude.
- <u>Generativity</u>—Nurturing others so they can pass on love to still others around them in unexpected ways. When linked with leadership and high self-esteem, it invests a sense of meaning to our days.
- <u>Humor</u>—Lifting a person out of emotional, physical, or spiritual pain, even if fleetingly, by offering a good joke or reframing situations in a lighter way. It helps us laugh at life and look at life's vicissitudes from a wider perspective.
- <u>Listening</u>—Being present and attentive to another's story in a reassuring way, hearing what is not said as well as what is said. It involves understanding and being deeply present to the other.
- <u>Loyalty</u>—Giving love and care to someone over time. Giving without expectation, finding compromises, soothing stress, and cultivating friendships.
- <u>Respect</u>—Offering tolerance and civility by accepting another person's life choices, even if they are different from our own. Offering kind words with buoyant courtesy.[13]

As individuals, we could consider the degree to which we are generous in each of these areas within the domains of family, friends, community, or the globe. Giving time periodically to do such self-examination might lead us in new directions. Church leaders might offer a six-week small-group experience on "Leading a Generous Life," by introducing the holistic definition of "generosity" and then pairing these ten dimensions, so participants can explore where they are thus far in their own generosity journey.

"Generosity is the sleeping giant of disciple-making," says the Thrivent Church Solutions Group. It states that there is an intimate link between how we deal with money and our spiritual growth.[14] While money is just one medium for potential generosity, the Thrivent leaders' recommendations can apply to any area of our personal lives.

Researchers in the Science of Generosity Initiative at the University of Notre Dame describe generosity as "an essential human value" and "the virtue of giving good things to others freely and abundantly."[15] The Initiative brings together scientists across countries and disciplines, and funds studies about the causes, manifestations, and consequences of generosity—all from the perspective of science instead of philosophy.[16] Their research affirms that generosity is a learned character trait, involves both attitudes and actions, and in its mature form becomes "a basic, personal, moral orientation to life."[17]

Acting generously toward others is part of natural human development. Research shows that children as young as two years old, without external reward or parental encouragement, begin to help others spontaneously in various contexts.[18] Parents can help their children internalize empathy for others and have regard for others' welfare. At the same time, children can influence their parents in this regard. For example, a child who cares for a hurt animal, or a teenager who gets involved in a neighborhood project can remind attentive parents about caring for others. This creates a "family cycle of kindness and generosity."[19]

Family is not the only context where one's generosity may grow and influence others. In the workplace, generous attitudes and behavior can spread across a social or professional network, rippling out from one person to the next, and affecting the giver and receiver, and the person who interacts with either of them.[20] For any of these people, generous behavior can promote better physical and mental health, creativity and productivity, more "prosocial" behavior (helping others), and stronger interpersonal relationships.

This contagious aspect of generosity takes place in the global domain, as well. For example, those who give to the Acumen Fund invest in entrepreneurs in India, Pakistan, and East Africa: countries where people make less than four dollars a day. Beginning in 2001, the fund began doing "impact investing" through microfinance, directly solving social problems by supporting micro-businesses. Since then, it has financed 192 projects. One such project in the state of Behar, India, is Husk, which creates energy from rice. Leaders of the Acumen Fund hope the effects of these loans will positively affect more than one million lives. They seek to bring together the best of philanthropy, government, and investment capital, to build new business models to serve the poor.[21]

# Stewards of the Earth

Whether church-goers or not, most people identify "stewardship" with stewardship of the Earth: how we care for other creatures, our planet, and its resources. Becoming *generous* stewards in this aspect of our lives can be both challenging and rewarding. In John Wesley's wording, before we can "do good," first we need to "do no harm."

The Bible overflows with affirmations of God's creation of the world and all that is within it. It asserts that the Earth is part of God's creation, waiting for redemption (Romans 8:21). Ultimately it will become part of "a new heaven and a new earth" (Isaiah 66:22) that God promises at the end of time.

Believing that God will ultimately transform this Earth does not give us an excuse to trash the planet on which we live. The Earth that God will eventually purify will be *this* Earth, and we are to care for every aspect of it now. Moreover, whether we are religious or not, despoiling the Earth itself betrays our fundamental humanity, since it is our home, and the biosphere for all creatures.

God made the world, producing every kind of plant life, and pronounced it good (Genesis 1:11ff.). All that God created makes melody to God, proclaiming God's handiwork (Psalm 19:1–4). The earth and all its inhabitants belong to God (Psalm 24:1), and God's act of creation prompts people to bless God with their whole being, or "soul" (Psalm 104:1). The belief that we belong to a loving God naturally leads us to praise.

Entire books continue to be written about faithful stewardship of our planet. Yet so much of the human way of life in recent centuries violates the Earth and its creatures. Often through heedless over-consumption, millions of us participate in the wasteful use of energy, land, and other resources, causing pollution and species extinction.

Nevertheless, the foundation of our Christian understanding of God and nature provides us with a strong platform of God's love for all that lives: God's creation. It also gives the basis for our calling to be faithful stewards of all living beings.

This Bible foundation could be expressed as:

- God made the entire cosmos, the Earth, and all living creatures. It is God's creation and belongs to God. Human beings are part of this web of living things. Ultimately, we find our source in God and our sustenance from God's gifts of life, energy, and abilities to develop, use, and share the resources God has made and entrusted to us.
- There is an inherent moral relationship between people and the creatures around us. We are meant to be responsible and accountable for how we conserve, consume, and share the soil, water, air, and other natural resources.
- Human beings are created to exercise stewardship and justice—dominion, not domination—guided by the mind that we have in Christ (Philippians 2:5), for wise and loving management of all that God has made, including animals, stones, and humans.[22]

Consequently, "as we become aware that our earth is one great household, we must face the challenge to live accordingly," says Benedictine Brother David Steindl-Rast. "This demands a new relationship to our environment based on reverence and frugality. . . ."[23]

The global organization called Creation Justice Ministries (CJM) takes this foundation seriously. It encourages action on policies about earth care and environmental justice made by the major Christian denominations throughout the United States. Working in cooperation with thirty-seven national faith bodies, CJM provides educational resources on a range of care-related topics including flora and fauna, drinking water, oceans, and air. It drafts policy statements on a wide array of subjects and encourages people to take action for God's creation by directly contacting decision-makers, getting research published, and organizing communities around environmental issues.[24]

Most action that changes minds and hearts takes place locally or interpersonally. For example, seminary professor Timothy Van Meter decided to advise local church youth groups on how they can make lifestyle changes to better care for the Earth. He has connected with existing ministries to help young people explore how to live on a finite planet with limited resources, and to discuss whether or not we will choose to limit our personal appetites in order to allow all life to thrive.[25] In these youth groups, participants re-read Scripture through the lens of stewarding God's creation, discuss their beliefs and practices, and learn about the diversity of life surrounding us. Then they partner with one another to reimagine and begin implementing sustainable, ethical communities.

While the topic of climate change is a moving target for political pundits, it is an increasingly crisis-level subject of research for global scientists, who say that the Earth has now reached a tipping point. In a consensus statement signed by more than 1,300 climate-change scientists in more than sixty countries, they agree the evidence that humans are damaging their ecological life-support systems is overwhelming.

They base a major consensus statement on five key concerns:
- Climate disruption—More, faster climate change since humans first became a species;
- Pollution—Record-level environmental contaminants in the air, water, and soil;
- Extinctions—Not since the dinosaurs died out have so many species and populations disappeared so fast, in the oceans and on land;
- Loss of diverse ecosystems—More than 40 percent of Earth's ice-free land has been plowed, paved, or otherwise transformed by humans, and no place on land or sea is free of human influence; and
- Population growth and consumption—Seven billion people are alive today, and this figure likely will grow to 9.5 billion by 2050, with consequent increased resource consumption, especially by the middle and wealthier classes in developed countries, proportionately increasing scarcity in less developed societies.[26]

This monumental issue faces us now, linking all stewardship-of-the-earth issues together. Climate change needs to become an immediate topic for us all.

An excellent Christian study resource on this subject is Sharon Delgado's book *Love in a Time of Climate Change*. It approaches both causes and consequences of global warming from the viewpoints of Scripture, tradition, reason, and experience, giving a theological basis as well as scientific resources. It includes nine specific actions for systemic change that governments could take right now to lessen the dangers of runaway climate change.[27]

Whether through local, regional or global-centered activities, Delgado's book invites readers to join a growing movement calling for systemic changes for the sake of everyone, but particularly the world's poor (who are most vulnerable), and for the interconnected web of life.[28]

Major sources of energy remain a giant concern. Fossil fuels, such as coal, oil, and natural gas, constitute the great majority of the world's commercial energy, resulting in pollution from fuel spills, greenhouse emissions, and acid rain. Hydroelectric power can result in flooding of animal habitat, mercury poisoning, and greenhouse emissions from decaying vegetation. Nuclear energy presents the dramatic question—how to store long-lasting radioactive waste—and the potential for a catastrophic meltdown.[29] Geothermal, solar, and wind power are alternative sources for energy. While all energy sources have benefits and costs, these are renewable on a global scale, and have a lower impact on the environment.

Those who engage these issues usually respond locally, seeking daily practices that can help move us in the right direction, even as they address the systemic issues. A few small-but-cumulatively-mighty, alternative-energy options include using a slow cooker as well as a solar oven and sharing those meals with friends, vacuuming refrigerator and freezer coils at least once a year, and turning off appliances when not in use.

Seemingly small actions can bring big rewards. For example, one congregation replaced fifty standard lightbulbs with Compact Fluorescent Lights (CFLs)—which eliminated 13,100 pounds of carbon dioxide each year and saved the local church $1,500 in electricity cost over the life of the bulbs.[30]

People can conserve energy in multiple ways, from shopping for energy-efficient appliances, to driving less and using more public transportation. Families and faith communities can engage in "green" building and remodeling: producing structures that are designed, built, renovated, operated, or reused in an ecological, resource-efficient manner. This can have a huge impact. For example, in the U.S. alone, traditionally constructed buildings account for more than 65 percent of total U.S. electricity consumption, 36 percent of total U.S. primary energy use, and 30 percent of total U.S. greenhouse gas emissions.[31]

Human activities are the cause of the great majority of our environmental woes.[32] In the year 2000, 20 percent of the global population had 85 percent of the world's wealth and income, used 88 percent of the world's natural resources, and generated 75 percent of the world's pollution and waste.[33] According to a 2004 study by the Redefining Progress organization, if the Earth's biologically productive land was divided among the world's population according to its use, each Canadian and each American would have 4.5 and 5 times, respectively, the amount of land per person than the rest of the world. This means if everyone around the world consumed at the same level as North Americans do, we would need an entire second planet and more to accommodate them![34]

Contrary to common assumptions, pollution of our soil, water, and air is not an unavoidable side effect of necessary human activity. Technological advances, recycling, and sustainable lifestyle choices can all reduce pollution—a task inextricably linked to the welfare of the Earth itself.

Congregations can encourage families to practice a "moral respect for nature."[35] For example, members of University Temple United Methodist Church in Seattle, Washington, went beyond just serving fair-trade coffee and switching from disposable to ceramic cups. They initiated a recycling and composting program. The congregation studied a book on simple living, hosted a DVD series called "Renewal," held various discussions about local food and farming, took their Sunday school children to a nearby biodynamic farm, and began a physical-health program led by their evangelism team. They provided inspirational stand-alone programs, drama in worship, and a film and discussion series on global warming. They continue to put monthly quotations in their worship bulletin, and post articles in "The Greening Corner" of their online newsletter.[36]

Family activities can make a difference. We can buy products in bulk or from recycled materials, and use refillable, reusable containers. Likewise, we can switch to cloth napkins and rechargeable batteries; plan a neighborhood garbage clean-up day; avoid over-packaged items; and rent, share, or borrow infrequently used items.[37]

Local churches can further encourage people through events such as an annual worship service with an Earth Day theme, a local park clean-up or other community service project, a church energy-use audit, or an organized hike in a local nature area.[38] In worship, they may read together an available Earthkeeping Liturgy or follow a five-week "Season of Creation" lectionary.[39]

Gloria Dei Lutheran Church, in Duluth, Minnesota, took one further step. A third grader in the church went to her pastor, dismayed at how much food was thrown away at her nearby school. So she and the pastor began talking with the school principal. As a result, the school started a Green Team composed of students and parents, reclaimed green space across the street, partnered with a local paper mill to raise school funds by collecting shiny paper, and implemented food waste composting at the school.[40]

Above all, our lives as stewards need to acknowledge the fact that our level of consuming is not aligned with a God-centered purpose for our lives. "Lack of restraint in consumption and production typical of the Western nations does not lead to increased happiness," says professor and author Loren Wilkinson. In fact, our records of divorce, suicide, and drug and alcohol abuse would suggest that the delusion that having more things brings more happiness leads to *decreased* happiness.[41]

"Biodiversity is one of the pillars upon which the natural world stands," says Mennonite author Joanne Moyer. "When one species disappears, the entire system is disrupted and other species are harmed as well. Biodiversity is as important as water to drink and air to breathe."[42] As the climate warms up, various species of plants and animals will face either migration (if possible) or extinction.[43] The cryosphere (areas of permafrost, snow, and ice) has begun to melt rapidly, releasing once-frozen greenhouse gases that make sea levels rise, and acidify and heat the oceans.[44]

Facing such momentous systemic changes, what can we do on a more local level to protect species' habitats and diversity, and to curb overfishing and the introduction of foreign species?

Depending upon a congregation's specific situation, it may encourage members to avoid eating threatened fish or other seafood, avoid buying drink containers with plastic rings in which animals can get entangled, or buy dolphin-friendly tuna. It may create a butterfly- or bird-friendly garden, use biodegradable cleaning products where available, become a member of a wildlife protection agency, or collaborate with neighboring communities to support parks and conservation areas. These are only a few possibilities.

One example of integrated local action comes from St. James Cathedral, in Seattle. The church established an Environmental Justice Group which has sponsored events where hundreds of neighbors participated. In addition to modifying and renovating their buildings, sponsoring Environmental Health Fairs and short-term courses about the relationship between faith and climate change, they have held educational tours of the Duwamish River (a Superfund Site) in collaboration with the ecumenical Earth Ministry group and the Duwamish River Cleanup Coalition.[45]

Ideas abound for creative action to help living things in our neighborhood environment, even as we are urged to address systemic changes using available local, regional, and global networks. As we seek to be good earth stewards, *generous* with our time, priorities, and involvement, we can acknowledge that "the natural world is the larger sacred community to which we belong."[46]

# Honoring Ourselves

So much is said in Christian circles about helping others, giving to others, and sharing God's love with others, that we may forget to receive God's love simply and joyfully for ourselves. But honoring ourselves as loved by God is just as important as honoring other people. As a popular phrase goes, "God don't make no junk"—and that includes us.

Jesus links the ideal of our all-out love for God and God's full-throttle love for us and for others when he says:

The first [commandment] is "Hear, O Israel: the Lord our God, the Lord is one; you shall love the Lord your God with all your heart, and with all your soul, and with all your mind, and with all your strength." The second is this, "You shall love your neighbor as yourself." There is no other commandment greater than these. (Mark 12:29–31)

In all three of the Synoptic Gospels (Matthew, Mark, and Luke), Jesus says these combined commandments are the most important of the entire body of God's Law. In Mark's version, Jesus goes on to say that these two commandments are even more important than the entire Old Testament Temple system of offerings and sacrifices. (Mark 12:33)

As we have said elsewhere, these two commandments (originally from Leviticus and Deuteronomy) are the interlaced foundation for the entire Bible, and for our spiritual life together. The fact is: we cannot know how to love other people if we do not "love"—that is, have positive regard and care for—ourselves, as well.

So how can we honor ourselves and give to ourselves in a healthy way? Writer Cathy MacHold lists some examples:

- Time for relaxation, quiet time, reading, and alone time;
- Wonderful friendships, which require nurturing and being selective about whom we hold close;
- The joy of savoring good food and beverage;
- Setting aside the rush of responsibilities in order to savor the moment;
- The ability to know and act on the difference between always saying yes to yet another task, and when to say no; and
- The gift of lifelong learning.[47]

No doubt you can think of other ways you can give to yourself, as well, as a reminder of God's amazing love for you.

Our *health* is a gift from God, and a gift we can give ourselves by taking good care of our bodies, getting proper nutrition, and balancing work and rest. In our world today, not all people have sufficient access to healthy alternatives and proper rest. But for a great number of people living above subsistence level in North America and Europe, choices do exist, and we can make the most of them.

But why should we care for our bodies at all? If, as some Christians believe, we will have risen bodies in eternal life, why bother to eat healthily and stay fit?

The apostle Paul wrote about this to gnostic Christians in his day. They mistakenly thought that what they did with their bodies did not matter, since God would give them new bodies in eternal life. So they either neglected or deprived their bodies or destroyed themselves with over-indulgent living. But Paul said:

> Or do you not know that your body is a temple of the Holy Spirit within you, which you have from God, and that you are not your own? For you were bought with a price; therefore glorify God in your body. (1 Corinthians 6:19f.)

In this way, Paul made the matter a clear issue of stewardship: how we care for ourselves on behalf of our Maker.

Later in the same letter, Paul explained to some of the Christians in Corinth, saying that our bodies are buried at death like a seed planted in soil, to be transformed in eternal life. (1 Corinthians 15:35–44)

Supportive relationships are crucial for any lifestyle change, and this can occur in the church, as well. For example, the Christian ministry called Run for God shares its curriculum with more than 450 churches in the U.S. and Canada. Other congregations have started running clubs as a way to encourage their members to care for their bodies.[48]

Under the name of Tobacco Trail Community in Durham, North Carolina, several congregations are embracing physical exercise as a key part of their ministries. Begun by American Baptist pastor George Linney, participants meet outdoors to run together as their worship experience.

Meantime, in Louisville, Kentucky, a church, called Sweaty Sheep, partners with three nonprofit organizations to hold fund-raising races for disabled athletes, children with Down's Syndrome, and others who are cognitively disabled. In April 2013, Sweaty Sheep led 300 runners in prayer as they ran in Louisville's Cherokee Park, praying for the victims of the Boston Marathon bombing.[49]

For many Christians, physical fitness choices are not directly addressed in their congregations but are left to individual decisions.

I'll never forget the phone call when my primary care doctor used the word "cancer." I had had additional diagnostic tests, but the call shocked me anyway. Thankfully, I took a proactive approach every step of the way. Anti-cancer techniques were an entirely new world of information for me, and I fought against a sense of powerlessness by learning all I could. My nurse sister confirmed that I could ask for the oncology doctors I preferred and choose what procedures to allow. Another cause for thanksgiving was that the doctors had caught the cancer very early.

The personal support from members of my congregation came as another surprise; I had not realized so many people were cancer survivors. One by one they came to me to share their experience and let me know they were praying for me. Their presence offered a palpable sense of community. At the same time, I started learning about naturopathic alternatives to traditional medical treatments and discovered a support group of people pursuing that path of long-term health. In the end I decided on an integrative approach, went off almost all my prescribed medicines, and substituted daily naturopathic supplements to strengthen my body for the rest of my life.

I now view that cancer episode as a wake-up call that got me off toxic medicines, increased some positive lifestyle habits, and set me on a much healthier, more fulfilling way of life. The journey goes on one step at a time. Within this lifetime it is never finished.

The United Methodist *Book of Resolutions* contains helpful, voluntary guidelines for people who want to get and stay healthy. In part, they recommend that congregations:

- Organize a Health and Wholeness Team to address health issues across the spectrum of the congregation's ministries;

- Educate and motivate members to follow a healthy lifestyle, reflecting our affirmation of life as God's gift;
- Get actively involved at all levels in support systems for health care in their community; and
- Become advocates for a healthy environment, affordable health care, and continued public support of health care for people unable to provide for themselves.[50]

Making personal resolutions can help us achieve and restore health, including exercise, proper nutrition, and reduction of food products that add toxins and excess weight to our frames while failing to provide appropriate nourishment. This recognizes that honoring our bodies is a lifelong process.

I have found these personal health dimensions to be paramount goals:

- Drinking half my weight in ounces of water each day;
- Reducing carbohydrates and making green, leafy vegetables half my daily food;
- Moving more each day with different activities; and
- Working at dropping those extra pounds.

I know: I am still working on it. Good health is a lifelong journey!

People have written and spoken for decades about the power of positive thinking. But in recent years, scientific studies have registered how a positive attitude is an important factor in improving and maintaining one's physical health.

For example, a 2013 research paper published in an online journal of the American Heart Association "shows that even for people dealing with heart disease—the number one killer of adults in [the United States]—a positive outlook means living longer and stronger..."[51] It found that patients with "higher levels of positive affect," measured by the Global Mood Scale, were more likely to exercise and had a lower risk of dying during the study's five-year follow-up.[52]

Likewise, the Women's Health Initiative Study, first reported in 2009 in an American Heart Association journal, "suggests that a positive mental outlook is associated with reduced evidence of coronary heart disease and total mortality in postmenopausal women."[53] By contrast, in 2000, Toshiko Maruta, M.D., a Mayo Clinic researcher, published a thirty-year study of 839 patients. The report showed that "a pessimistic view was a risk factor for early death, with a 19 percent increase in the risk of mortality" within the scope of the study.[54]

Physical therapist Dr. Katie Hohman says, "Choosing to be positive and being grateful for what has been accomplished throughout [one's] physical and emotional journey, is just that, a choice." She continues, "That choice overall can have an impact on how you maintain your overall health and recovery."[55]

# The Art of Forgiving

Thus far, this section has noted that we can show a positive self-regard by giving to ourselves in a variety of ways, taking good care of our physical health, and encouraging a positive, healthy attitude toward life. But there is another, equally vital way to live generously—with the act of forgiveness. As we have said, forgiveness can give us the gift of release from the debilitating weight of anger, guilt and suffering. With distinctions (discussed below), this applies both to forgiving others for doing wrongs against us and forgiving ourselves for the wrongs we have done against others.

However, before we can explore what forgiveness *is*, it is important to clarify what it is *not*. Forgiveness is *not*:

- Excusing what that person did or condoning their behavior;
- Giving away our personal power;
- Making only a gesture of forgiveness without meaningful commitment;
- Trusting the transgressor without reason;

- Allowing an injustice resulting in ongoing harm to continue to exist; or
- Reconciling in a way that endangers the victim's safety or health.

As these negative examples imply, true forgiveness is an intentional attitude, and often a work-in-progress.[56]

It may take years or even a lifetime to forgive another person: at first perhaps hesitantly and conditionally. But even though it may not be full-fledged forgiveness at this point, it can be a new start. Forgiveness takes place layer by layer, like peeling an onion, as specific memories, events, or locations trigger unfinished feelings, challenging us to take another step to distance ourselves emotionally from the original hurt. This is why, as the person wronged, we need to prepare psychologically to even consider taking steps toward forgiveness.

So what *is* forgiveness? One way psychologists define it is "a conscious, deliberate decision to release feelings of resentment or vengeance toward a person or group who has harmed you."[57] The process of forgiving can help us let go of any corrosive anger we may be feeling, as we decide not to be defined by that pain. Whatever the cause, forgiveness takes practice, especially when we struggle with the urge to "take back" our forgiveness when resentment resurfaces.

This is especially important because forgiving (or not) relates to how we *perceive* we have been wronged. In other words, it has to do with how we respond to something that has been done to us, not to the act itself. The same behavior may eventually be forgivable for one person, but not for another. There is no general recipe for how, to what degree, and over how long a time the forgiveness process takes—it all depends on the persons involved, the wrong, the aftermath, and the surrounding circumstances.

Forgiveness is more than just an emotional process. Psychologists have conducted hundreds of scientific studies of the topic. When forgiveness takes place, multiple benefits come to the forgiver. Research has shown that forgiving someone can:

- Reduce anger and boost a person's mood;
- Lower stress hormones and improve blood flow to the heart;
- Alleviate depression, even in the state of war; and
- Preserve close relationships, with mutual satisfaction and commitment.[58]

In addition, one study reveals that forgiving a person—regardless of the offender's response—improves one's well-being even more strongly than forgiving one who has shown contrition and has apologized.[59] Abundant scientific studies show forgiveness can bring a sense of inner freedom, serenity, and peace to the one who manages to forgive.

At the same time, forgiveness changes the relationship between the perpetrator and the one who feels violated. Miroslav Volf is a professor of theology at Yale Divinity School and Director of the Yale Center for Faith & Culture. In his book, *Free of Charge*, he says that forgiving a person does not "take them off the hook" for the damage they have done, but at the same time frees them of moral indebtedness against them, and eventually lets the wrongdoing slip into oblivion.[60]

But *how* is it possible for us to actually forgive another person? The act of forgiving someone is a process, and may follow a long, complex path. University of Wisconsin-Madison researcher Robert Enright suggests that it usually takes four stages:

- Uncovering the hurt, acknowledging fully what it has done to our life;
- Deciding what forgiveness might look like in terms of this situation and the one who has harmed us;
- Understanding what might have motivated the perpetrator, looking for what might be good about that person, and trying to see our shared humanity; and
- Reflecting more deeply, as we seek to apply this process of forgiving others and considering offering them compassion.[61]

There is no guarantee that we will fully arrive at forgiveness. But initiating the process may help us clarify the harm done, and bring some deeper, more satisfying reflection.

Forgiving can be harder than other forms of giving because of additional obstacles that may stand in our way. These might include the severity of the perpetrator's actions, the resultant injuries to us and possibly others, and the repentant or recalcitrant stance of the wrong-doer.[62] It also involves acknowledging any personal emotional benefit that we have been receiving by holding onto the hurt up to this time.

For Christians, our desire for forgiveness and our need to forgive others has its source in God's prior forgiveness of us all, through Jesus Christ. Forgiving those who hurt us offers them more than their offending actions deserve and can potentially release them from a debilitating sense of debt. But their acceptance of being forgiven depends on their willingness to admit the wrongdoing (in a sense confessing a sin), and so begin anew.

Throughout this book, we have explored the idea of being made in the "image of God." In *Forgiveness: Finding Peace Through Letting Go*, pastor Adam Hamilton says that being made in God's image has:

> nothing to do with our physical appearance, and everything to do with other ways in which we were created to reflect the character of God. We were created with the capacity to love, to reason, to create, to show compassion, to give, to sacrifice, and, yes, to forgive.[63]

Whenever we seek to forgive, we reflect more fully the God who created us in love.

The prayer Jesus taught us, known as The Lord's Prayer, says, "And forgive us our debts, as we also have forgiven our debtors." (Matthew 6:12) This is a courageous thing to say! When Christians are able to forgive from deep within, we are acknowledging that God is the source of any forgiveness toward us all.[64] In that case, "we forgive by echoing God's forgiveness to the best of our ability."[65] When consciously done in this manner, forgiving becomes a process of spiritual transformation.

Two examples, one personal and one collective, show how forgiveness can take place in stages, layer by layer:

- An unregistered car—Chuck Sandstrom was a seasoned organizational leader and motivational speaker. One day he was overseeing the removal of an unregistered car from a rental property he owned, when the car owner, Michael Ayers—drunk and angry—confronted him. Michael punched him, causing his head to snap back into a brick wall. Chuck's resultant traumatic brain injury sent him into a coma for six weeks; he lost his job, home, and social standing as collateral damage.

  By the time Chuck had begun to speak again, his wife had made contact with Michael's family. Chuck followed suit. They realized that Michael's family members were suffering greatly, too. An ex-convict and alcoholic, Michael had gone into hiding, and was taking huge risks to see his traumatized children. When Michael was finally arrested, Chuck and his wife realized that seeing him sentenced, though necessary, would not bring healing.

  During Michael's trial, Chuck and his wife joined the defense to petition for a reduced sentence and access to treatment, work, and school during Michael's jail time. Chuck and his wife continued to visit Michael's family. Then two years later, they started helping Michael Jr., who had been flunking the third grade.[66]

  "Forgiveness is first and foremost a way of seeing," says Chuck. While most people see his injury as a tragedy, he states, "for my wife and me it's created an opportunity to love more deeply."[67]

- An enemy nation—Enmity between Germany and Poland goes back centuries, and Hitler's multipronged invasion of Poland prompted the declaration of World War II in Europe.

Yet thanks to several initiatives over time, Poles and Germans have become friends and allies.[68]

The Second World War killed 6 million Poles, half of them Jews. Of all the countries mourning their losses after the war, Poland had the highest ratio of war deaths to total population. For decades after that war, many Poles were openly hostile to Germans. Yet even in the 1950s, former enemy nations France and Germany began to rethink their old roles. Influenced by that success, in 1965 the Catholic bishops in Germany and Poland risked calling for Polish-German reconciliation, saying, "We forgive, and we ask to be forgiven."

A generation later, when Poland was in crisis, West German people voluntarily donated and distributed food and clothes, as well as hundreds of thousands of aid packages, to Warsaw, Krakow, and Gdansk. By 1989, when the Berlin Wall was torn down, Poles and Germans were finally able to speak their own languages on the streets of the other country's cities without reprisal. Numerous Germans visited their confiscated family homes in Silesia (now mainly in southwestern Poland), not to challenge the current Polish owners, but to meet them. In thousands of cases, they formed lasting friendships. Then in 2004, Germany became Poland's strongest sponsor when Poland entered the European Union.

Forgiveness takes hard work to achieve when we have been harmed, and the process does not belong entirely to us. Citing the reformer Martin Luther, theologian Volf says that God never works in us without our (conscious or unconscious) participation in the work. He calls this mystery "God's indwelling."[69] In such moments God comes to live within a human being, prompting the forgiver to move from one stage to the next. Christ's action in and through us makes it more possible to offer forgiveness with sincerity.

The greatest challenge of forgiveness for many Christians is forgiving ourselves. In some ways it is harder than forgiving others, because it involves our deeply recognizing that God loves us no matter what good or bad deeds we have done.[70] Although the full depth of our own motivations can still be a mystery to us, nevertheless we know more about our own complexity, misgivings, and betrayals than we know about other people. As a result, we are more aware of what needs to be forgiven. When we have done something wrong (however we define that term), it registers in our nervous systems, and we tend to connect those feelings to a self-critical belief, such as "I'm always saying the wrong thing," or "I'll never be able to cover my bills."[71] But once we have forgiven ourselves for our human failings, it is easier to consider forgiving others for their wrongs.

At the same time, we have to admit that "all our forgiving is inescapably incomplete," because whether we're forgiving ourselves or others, we do not know the entire inner situation of the offender. "That's why it's so crucial to see our forgiving not simply as our own act," says Volf, "but as participation in God's forgiving."[72]

Psychologist Fred Luskin, Director of the Stanford University Forgiveness Project, has been conducting studies and workshops on the subject for years. His research shows that people find it particularly hard to forgive themselves when they have done one of four things:

- They did something they should not have done, harming others;
- They have hurt themselves by the self-destructive way they have led their lives;
- They did not do something they thought they should have, such as putting money away for their children, or intervening in a crucial family dispute; or
- They have failed at some major life task, such as making their marriage work.[73]

Researchers Stephen Post and Jill Neimark agree on how tough self-forgiveness can be, calling it the greatest challenge in life. Referring to theologian Paul Tillich's book *The Courage to Be*, they affirm that for Christians, our full self-acceptance can only come by recognizing that we are loved by God, despite whatever we have either done or failed to do.[74]

What can we do to move toward self-forgiveness in a way that is appropriate to the wrong we have done? As part of the healing process, we can use our awareness of our own feelings and thoughts to guide us in:

- Recognizing our unrealistic expectations for ourselves (those unconscious rules we may have absorbed in childhood, whether they fit with our adult lives or not);
- Realizing objectively that we may or may not have done the best we could at the time, given our perceptions, skills, and frame of mind, while accepting our responsibility for that act and its consequences;
- Stopping to refocus on more positive emotions, on the bigger picture, on lessons learned, on a person who loves us, or on a peaceful part of our lives;
- Starting to tell ourselves a new story, in which, despite our failings and frailties, we do everything we can to avoid a recurrence of our wrongdoing and become more forgiving toward others;
- Consciously replacing shame and guilt with intervals of gratitude, where we notice the small and large reasons for being thankful in our everyday living;[75] and
- Trusting that God knows us and offers us forgiveness.

In the process of becoming more intimately at home with ourselves, we can feel more intimately united with others, which helps us celebrate God's limitless presence.[76] In this way, we can come to better recognize the consequences of how we have taken advantage of a person or a situation. Our thanksgiving intertwines with forgiving ourselves and others, as we live from the core of who we are, loved by God.

Forgiveness requires a humble attitude, whether we are trying to forgive or hoping to be forgiven. Ultimately, the act of forgiving benefits the forgiver. We are able at last to let go of the burden of anger or resentment that has kept us back from being fully, joyfully alive to ourselves, to God, and to the world.

In this chapter we have explored generosity as a way of life based upon God's grace, evident in God's loving presence and offer of a transforming relationship with us. Ten qualities of generous living can motivate us to give, and by so doing live more fully among our family, friends, community, and the world. These qualities are: *celebration, compassion, courage, creativity, forgiveness, generativity, humor, listening, loyalty,* and *respect.*

We have noted how the Bible challenges us to become more generous stewards of the Earth—first by trying to "do no harm," and then to "do good." Establishing a healthier relationship with our environment and fellow creatures involves participating in individual and group action to reverse damaging pollution and limit climate change. At the same time, this challenge calls us to change wasteful habits and strengthen positive daily practices on a personal and congregational basis. It urges us to limit unchecked consumerism, and support biodiversity of the Earth's creatures.

An important part of whole-life generosity is honoring ourselves, which also empowers us to care better for other people. Such a lifestyle includes giving ourselves an appropriate quality of life in a variety of ways, such as nurturing friendships, savoring the moment, and taking good care of our health.

Another essential dimension of generous living is learning how to forgive other people when suitable, and how to forgive ourselves. Depending upon various factors, this is often a lifelong process. Both personal and communal forgiveness require us to work through layers of feelings, continuing to open ourselves to the immeasurable grace of God.

# Questions for Reflection

1.  Which one of the ten qualities listed above motivates me most strongly to try to live generously?
2.  How can I be a better steward, or manager, of my health? How might I be more "generous" toward my own well-being?
3.  What would it look like in my church and community if faithful stewardship of the earth became the key transforming part of my congregation's culture?
4.  How does my faith community support me in forgiving others, forgiving myself, and being forgiven?
5.  Which aspect of forgiveness has been harder for me: forgiving other people, or forgiving myself? Where might I start to forgive more deeply or more meaningfully?

# Endnotes

1.  Liddell and Scott, *An Intermediate Greek-English Lexicon*, Seventh Edition (Oxford: Clarendon Press, 1975), p. 882.
2.  Dan Dick, "Walking by Faith, Not by Sight," *Upper Room Disciplines 2017* (Nashville: Upper Room Books, 2016), p. 92.
3.  Kenneth L. Carder, "Wesleyan Understanding of Grace," *United Methodist Interpreter*, Nov.–Dec. 2016, p. 27.
4.  William Willimon, in "The Gift of Grace" by Cecile S. Holmes, *United Methodist Interpreter*, Nov.-Dec. 2016, p. 19.
5.  Kenneth L. Carder, *op cit.* The paraphrases are mine.
6.  Douglass Key, pastor of the Clover Presbyterian Church in Clover, South Carolina, "Living by the Word" (Bible study for Sunday, for July 1, 2012) in *Christian Century*, June 27, 2012. Here Key reflects on 2 Corinthians 8:9.
7.  Chris Willard and Jim Sheppard, *op cit.*, p. 18.
8.  Bill Enright, "A Theological Foundation for Generous Giving," *Giving: Growing Joyful Stewards in Your Congregation, Vol. 19: "Living Generously,"* pp. 3–5.
9.  Chris Willard and Jim Sheppard, *op cit.*, p. 19.
10. *The Week, Aug. 29, 2014*, in "On the Street," *Christian Century*, Sept. 17, 2014.
11. *https://gma.yahoo.com/california-strangers-repair-elderly-mans-roof-neighbor-heartwarming-151736606--abc-news-lifestyle.html*

12. Laura Cartwright, "Note from Rev. Laura," in Grand Junction First United Methodist Church's *The Messenger*, January 2013.
13. Stephen Post and Jill Neimark, *op cit.*, pp. 21–24. The authors use these categories in what they call "The Love and Longevity Scale."
14. *The Generosity Ladder*, pp. 1 ff. See their website, *generouschurch.com.*
15. Science of Generosity Initiative, University of Notre Dame, at *http://generosityresearch.nd.edu/more-about-the-initiative/what-is-generosity*
16. Christian Smith, Sociology, *Fighting for a More Generous World, https://www.youtube.com/watch?v=hK6xbsn1jfw,* based upon The Causes, Manifestations and Consequences of Generosity project of the Science of Generosity Initiative; *http://generosityresearch.nd.edu/current-research-projects/ndr*
17. *Ibid.*
18. Felix Warneken, Harvard University, The Development of Prosocial Behavior project of the Science of Generosity Initiative, *http://generosityresearch.nd.edu/current-research-projects/the-development-of-prosocial-behavior*
19. Ariel Knafo, Psychology, Hebrew University, The Family Cycle of Kindness and Generosity project of Science of the Generosity Initiative, *http://generosityresearch.nd.edu/current-research-projects/ndr*
20. Sonja Lyubomirsky, Sociology, The Causes and Effects of Workplace Generosity project of the Science of Generosity Initiative, *http://generosityresearch.nd.edu/current-research-projects/the-causes-and-effects-of-workplace-generosity*
21. Sasha Dichter, "The Generosity Experiment," *https://www.ted.com/talks/sasha_dichter*
22. This foundation statement is prompted by Loren Wilkinson, ed., *Earthkeeping: Christian Stewardship of Natural Resources* (Grand Rapids: William B. Eerdmans Publishing Co., 1980), pp. 256f.; and Joanne Moyer, *Earth Trek: Celebrating and Sustaining God's Creation* (Scottdale, PA and Waterloo, Ontario: Herald Press, 2004), pp. 20–22. I am indebted to Joanne Moyer for many of the positive action suggestions named in this section.
23. Brother David Steindl-Rast, OSB, in *Integral Yoga*, August, 1979, Vol. X #4, pp. 10–11.
24. *www.creationjustice.org/resources.* Creation Justice Ministries was formerly the National Council of Churches' Eco-Justice Program. Several of the local church examples that follow in this section come from *www.earthministry.org.* An excellent set of environmental theology resources is Richard Cartwright Austin's four books: *Baptized into Wilderness: A Christian Perspective on John Muir* (Atlanta: John Knox Press, 1987); *Beauty of the Lord: Awakening the Senses,* and *Hope for the Land: Nature in the Bible* (both Atlanta: John Knox Press, 1988); and *Reclaiming America: Restoring Nature to Culture* (Abingdon, VA: Creekside Press, 1990).
25. Timothy Van Meter, "Do Something in the World: Youth Ministry and Ecology," *Circuit Rider* Nov./Dec./Jan. 2015–16, pp. 15 f.

26. *Scientific Consensus on Maintaining Humanity's Life Support Systems in the 21st Century: Information for Policy Makers*, at *http://consensusforaction.stanford.edu.*)

27. Sharon Delgado, *Love in a Time of Climate Change: Honoring Creation, Establishing Justice* (Minneapolis: Fortress Press, 2017), pp. 154–156.

28. *Ibid.*, pp. 176, 179, 180.

29. Joanne Moyer, *op cit.*, p. 33.

30. Energy Star, U.S. Department of Energy, U.S. EPA, cited in Rhonda Parker and Daryl Riggins, "Environmental Stewardship: Practices That Matter;" United Methodist Foundation of North Carolina, *http://umf-nc.org.*

31. U.S. Green Building Council, cited in Rhonda Parker and Daryl Riggins, *op cit.*, p. 14.

32. Richard Cartwright Austin, *Hope for the Land: Nature in the Bible* (Atlanta: John Knox Press, 1988), p. 173.

33. Joanne Moyer, *op cit.*, p. 156.

34. Statistics from G. Tyler Miller, *Sustaining the Earth*, at *www.RedefiningProgress. org* give a fuller explanation, cited in Joanne Moyer, *op cit.*, p. 157.

35. Richard Cartwright Austin, *op cit.*, p. 174.

36. Judy LeBlanc, "University Temple United Methodist Church, Seattle, WA," Greening Congregation Colleague of the Month, Oct. 2012; *www.earthministry. org*

37. Joanne Moyer, *op cit.*, pp. 89f., 158f.

38. *www.creationjustice.org/educational-resources*; *https://umc-gbcs.org/ faith-in-action/celebrating-the-earth.*

39. Dakota Road developed the Earthkeeping Liturgy for Luther College in Regina, Saskatchewan, Canada. The Lutheran Church in Australia created the five-week "Season of Creation" alternative lectionary. Both are available for free as links in David Carlson, "Broadening Our Vision of Stewardship," p.3, at *communic@ luthersem.edu.*

40. David Carlson, *op cit.*, p. 2.

41. Loren Wilkinson, *op cit.*, p. 273.

42. Joanne Moyer, *op cit.*, p. 135.

43. *Climate Change 2014 Synthesis Report*, p. 6, cited in Sharon Delgado, *op cit.*, p. 20.

44. *Ibid.*

45. Patty Bowman, "St. James Cathedral, Seattle, WA," October 2011, *www. earthministry.com.*

46. Thomas Berry, *The Dream of the Earth*, p. 81, cited in Sharon Delgado, *op cit.*, p. 61.

47. Cathy MacHold, email to Betsy Schwarzentraub, dated March 26, 2016.

48. Jesse James DeConto, "Worship on the run," *Christian Century*, December 25, 2013, p. 20.

49. *Ibid.*, p. 23.

50. United Methodist Church, *The Book of Resolutions of The United Methodist Church, 2016* (Nashville: The United Methodist Publishing House, 2016), p. 253.

51. Dr. Oz and Dr. Roizen for *YouBeauty*, "Optimism and Health," in *http://www. huffingtonpost.com/2013/10/03/optimism-and-health_n_4031688.html*.

52. Madelein T. Hoogwegt, Henneke Versteeg, Tina B. Hansen, Lau C. Thygesen, Susanne S. Pedersen, Ann-Dorthe Zwisler, *Exercise Mediates the Association Between Positive Affect and 5-Year Mortality in Patients With Ischemic Heart Disease*; at *http://circoutcomes.ahajournals.org/content/6/5/559.short*.

53. *Chicago Tribune*, "A positive mental attitude benefits health, longevity and quality of life," August 28, 2017; at *www.chicago.tribune.com/classified/realestate/chi-primetime-pma-022611-story.html*.

54. Ken Budd, Executive Editor of *AARP The Magazine*, in *ibid*.

55. Hohman Rehab, "How a positive attitude impacts your recovery in Physical Therapy," April 17, 2014; at *www.hohmanrehab.com/how-a-positive-attitude-impacts-your-recovery-in-physical-therapy*.

56. Stephen Post and Jill Neimark, *op cit.*, pp. 80f.

57. The Greater Good Science Center, "What Is Forgiveness?" *https://greatergood. berkeley.edu/forgiveness/definition#why_practice*.

58. Stephen Post and Jill Neimark, *op cit.*, pp. 78–80. The authors name a number of studies and offer specific exercises to help readers shift their perspective. See also Miroslav Volf, *Free of Charge*, p. 195.

59. *Ibid.*, p. 79.

60. Lauren McGlynn, "Health Benefits of Forgiveness," *Guideposts*, March, 2001, p. 70.

61. Robert D. Enright of the University of Wisconsin-Madison, cited in Stephen Post and Jill Neimark, *op cit.*, pp. 83 f.

62. Miroslav Volf, *op cit.*, pp. 193 ff.

63. Adam Hamilton, *Forgiveness*, pp. 129f.

64. *Ibid.*, p. 86.

65. Miroslav Volf, *op cit.*, p. 220.

66. Katie Nielsen, "Eight incredible stories of forgiveness that will touch your heart;" *https://familyshare.com/22171/JustLetGo-8-incredible-stories-of-forgiveness-that-will-touch-your-heart*

67. *http://theforgivenessproject.com/stories/dr-chuck-sandstrom-usa*.

68. Elizabeth Pond, "Seventy years after World War II's start, old enemies take stock," *Christian Science Monitor*, September 1, 2009; *csmonitor.com/Commentary/Opinion/2009/0901/p09s01-coop.html*. The paraphrase is mine.

69. Miroslav Volf, *op cit.*, p. 51.

70. Adam Hamilton, *Forgiveness: Finding Peace Through Letting Go, op cit.*, p. 86.

71. Matt James, "How to Forgive Yourself and Move On From the Past,"
    October 22, 2014; *www.psychologytoday.com/blog/focus-forgiveness/201410/
    how-forgive-yourself-and-move-the-past.*
72. Miroslav Volf, *op cit.,* p. 220.
73. Ellen Michaud, "12 Ways to Forgive Yourself. No Matter What
    You've Done," August 31, 2015; www.prevention.com/mind-body/
    how-to-forgive-yourself-no-matter-what.
74. Stephen Post and Jill Neimark, *op cit.,* p. 86.
75. Ellen Michaud, *op cit.*
76. Brother David Steindl-Rast, *Gratefulness,* pp. 29, 35 ff., 200.

# Soul Making

T HE SPIRITUAL JOURNEY can be a thrilling, lifelong adventure, provided we keep surface preoccupations and religious logistics from sidetracking us. At best, our faith communities are like a house of precious jewels, each stone uniquely brilliant, reflecting God's light. (1 Peter 2:5) When founded on grace and gratitude, our leadership, teaching, and learning can radiate into our community and beyond. At any stage of our journey, we can reflect on some helpful questions and dare to act on them.

1. Developed countries, in particular, live in the midst of a culture that prizes productivity and unbridled work. In contrast, this book's holistic definitions of stewardship and generosity welcomed us to focus on being generous stewards of God's grace. God invites us to turn around: to make an about-face in our thinking and actions, to access God's internal rest and peace.

*In what ways have I felt driven to compulsive doing?*

2. Certain spiritually focused behaviors, such as Bible study and devotional reading, prayer, meditation, and contemplation, can shape us to be more attentive to God's presence and voice. These daily practices provide "spiritual whitespace," helping us move more fluidly into being and praise—the basic rhythm of our lives.

351

*What habits might I develop or refresh, to fortify my awareness of God's presence?*

3. A person's *soul* is the full expression of who we are in a loving relationship with God. Affirmed in both the Old and New Testaments, the soul includes mind, body, and intention, linking our breath with the Breath or Spirit of God. Outstanding philosophers and writers throughout the centuries have added a wealth of understanding to this sense of the soul.

*How have I experienced my own soul in relationship to God? In what ways might I lean more fully into a life-giving, trusting relationship with my Creator?*

4. Gratitude is a sense of wonder, thanksgiving, and appreciation for life. Like a muscle, our gratefulness becomes stronger the more we exercise it. Using any of a number of gratitude practices can more vividly bring out the lustrous colors of our life. Multiple scientific studies show that gratitude provides emotional, psychological, and physical benefits. We can also increase the depth of our gratitude, level by level, on a continuum ranging from a one-time *thank you* to a grace-filled way of life. Living gratefully prompts Christians to embrace God as the first, the infinite, and the utterly loving Giver. Despite multiple and sometimes intractable afflictions and conflicts that embroil humanity, we can find God showering this world with love, forgiveness, and eternal life.

*For what am I most deeply grateful? How have I expressed my gratitude at different times in my life? How could I share my gratefulness in the wider community?*

5. No matter where we live, we're constantly tempted by the lure of wanting more. Advertising encourages millions of people to confuse their wants with their needs. In opposition to these messages stands God's abundance and the Bible's concept of contentment.

These concepts prompt us to live by an ethic of enough with simple-living practices that can help us thrive with a sense of inner freedom.

*Are there ways, related to the things I have, that I can live more simply? To what extent do my attitudes toward my own and others' possessions reflect God's generosity and love?*

6. For those struggling to make ends meet, financial sufficiency is crucial. But beyond that point, true sufficiency can become a sense that, by God's grace, *we* are enough, as we experience the beauty and wholeness of life around and within us. Such freeing moments release energy for us to use our character, capabilities, relationships, and resources in life-giving ways. As we develop a healthier relationship with money, we can reduce some emotional dependence on it, thus separating our need for basic financial security from excessive consumption. We can give the first and the best of what we have to God's work in the world, seeking to manage that and the rest in accordance with God's generosity toward us.

*How do my money habits relate to my faith? How could I strengthen my own practice of First Fruits Living in more facets of my life?*

7. We have explored the steps necessary to focus less on frenetic *doing* in church, and more on *being* the people God calls us to be. We can help our congregations see themselves more as communities that care for people's souls, and as individuals acknowledging generosity as a core value of discipleship. Present-day examples and New Testament accounts of Communion community and service can inspire us to identify our congregation's distinctiveness, create networks for mutual resourcing, and invite recipients of our care to better care for others as well as themselves.

*How might I improve the quality of my faith community in caring for people as growing souls?*

8. The Bible encourages us to make generosity a basic stance in life, even as the world around us often distracts and thwarts us in this effort. We're urged to become generous stewards of the earth, participating in collaborative action to reverse damaging pollution and limit catastrophic climate change. We're also meant to honor ourselves in a variety of ways, including time for relaxation, and lifelong learning. Likewise, through nutrition, exercise, and a balance of work and rest, we are to take good care of our health as a gift from God. Generosity also grows stronger when we choose to forgive other people and ourselves. Often moving toward forgiveness is a lifelong yet rewarding and ultimately life-renewing process.

*When have I forgiven others, and where do I have unfinished work? In what ways can I forgive myself for what I have done or not done?*

9. We do not make souls; God does. But in our lives and in our ministries, we are invited to keep ourselves open and in alignment with God's ever-new work within and among us. Grace empowers us to imagine greater freedom and joy, and to embody it in the living of our days.

*In which dimensions of generous-hearted living have I been strong thus far? In what aspects do I hope to keep growing, by God's grace?*

I pray that the learnings, tools, examples, and questions in this book will prompt us to claim our true selves as made in God's image, ***growing generous souls: becoming grace-filled stewards***.

# Scripture Index

**Genesis** 1 ...............52, 115
Gen. 1:11ff. ...................325
Genesis 1:26...............97, 98
Gen. 2:26-27 .................53
Gen. 1:26-28 .............84, 92
Gen. 1:26-31 .............98, 99
Gen. 2:7 ....................53, 108
Gen. 9:16.....................184
Gen. 12:1-3 .................173
Gen. 12:2.......................261
Gen. 50:20......................140

**Exodus**...........................184
Ex. 3:1-4:20 ...............154
Ex. 3:14...................87, 105
Ex. 6:7...........................195
Ex. 14:2...........................22
Ex. 19:3-8 .....................195
Ex. 20:1-17 .............64, 195
Ex. 20:4-6 ......................99
Ex. 24:3-8 .....................195
Ex. 32.............................189

**Leviticus**......................332
Lev. 6:1-7 .......................237
Lev. 11:44 ......................150
Lev. 19:18 ......................103
Lev. 26:12 ......................195

**Deuteronomy**... 184, 195, 332
Dt. 6:5, ...........................80
Dt. 11:18-19 ...................80
Dt. 15:1-11 ....................236
Dt. 26............................262
Dt. 30:10..........................22

**Joshua** ..........................184
Josh. 24..........................195

**1 Samuel** 2:20f. ...............22

**2 Samuel** 22:38,...............22

**1 Kings** 8:33 ....................22
1 Ki. 22:19f......................98
1 Ki. 22:34 .......................22

**2 Kings** 17:13 ..................22

**2 Chronicles** 31:4-10....262

**Job** ...................................199
Job 1................................98

**Psalms**.................51, 57, 154
Ps. 8 ........................53, 199
Ps. 8:4 ...............................21

Ps. 19:1 .............................71
Ps. 19:1-4.........................325
Ps. 24:1 ...........................325
Ps. 24:1-2..................53, 84
Ps. 37:21 .........................233
Ps. 46:10 ...........................72
Ps. 62:8 ............................183
Ps. 95 ................................71
Ps. 104 ......................84, 199
Ps. 104:1 ..................80, 325
Ps. 119 .......................51, 52
Ps. 119:15-16....................52
Ps. 130:6 ...........................81
Ps. 143:8 ...........................81
Ps. 148 ..............................57

**Proverbs** .........................57
Prov. 1:19 ........................212
Prov. 3:18 ........................233
Prov. 11:25 ......................236
Prov. 19:17 ......................236
Prov. 22:26f.....................233
Prov. 22:7 ........................233

**Isaiah** .........................22, 29
Isa. 1-39............................29
Isa. 6 .................................98
Isa. 30:15 ..........................22

Isa. 40–55 ......................... 274
Isa. 43:1 .............................. 69
Isa. 49:15–16 ..................... 69
Isa. 55:1–3 ........................ 203
Isa. 65:17 .......................... 200
Is. 65:17ff ......................... 232
Isa. 66:22 ................. 200, 324

Jeremiah ..................... 8, 29
Jer. 2:4–13 ......................... 26
Jer. 30:22 .......................... 195

Amos ................................ 222
Amos 5:21–24 ................. 237
Amos 8:5 .......................... 222

Micah 6:6–8 ................... 237
Micah 6:8 ............... 211, 216

Zephaniah 3:17 ............. 200

Matthew .................. 81, 332
Mt. 2:16–18 ....................... 64
Mt. 4:4 .............................. 173
Mt. 5:41 ............................ 137
Mt. 6:9–13 .......................... 67
Mt. 6:12 ................... 200, 339
Mt. 6:25 ............................ 182
Mt. 6:25–34 ............. 204, 215
Mt. 6:31–33 ..................... 262
Mt. 13: 45f ................... 49, 96
Mt. 18:20 ......... 35, 148, 273
Mt. 20:25–28 ................... 306
Mt. 22:15–22 ............... 45, 53
Mt. 22:35–39 ................... 311
Mt. 22:34–40 ................... 103
Mt. 22:37–40 ..................... 64
Mt. 23:11 .......................... 100
Mt. 24:23–24 ................... 262
Mt. 25:14–30 ................... 231
Mt. 25:31–46 ............. 69, 236
Mt. 25:35–40 ................... 253
Mt. 28:5–10 ......... 19–20, 84
Mt. 28:19–20 ................... 276

Mark ......................... 81, 332
Mk. 6:30–44 ....................... 10
Mk. 7:24–30 ..................... 274
Mk. 8:35 ............................. 82
Mk. 10:42–45 ................... 100
Mk. 10:45 ........................... 81
Mk. 12:28–34 ................... 103
Mk. 12:29–31 ................... 332
Mk. 12:30–31 ................... 184
Mk. 12:33 .......................... 332
Mk. 14:36 ......................... 200

Luke ................. 81, 242, 332
Lk. 1:30 ............................ 176
Lk. 1:46 .............................. 82
Lk. 1:47–55 ...................... 192
Lk. 2:40 ............................ 176
Lk. 3:22 ............................... 36
Lk. 4:18–19 ............. 192, 276
Lk. 4:24–27 ...................... 274
Lk. 6:43–49 ........................ 38
Lk. 6:45 ............................... 38
Lk. 10:2 ............................... 23
Lk. 10:25–28 ................... 103
Lk. 10:29–37 ................... 184
Lk. 10:38–42 ................... 309
Lk. 11:42 ........................... 237
Lk. 12:13–21 .......... 186, 196
Lk. 12:15 ........................... 182
Lk. 12:15–21 ................... 128
Lk. 12:20 ........................... 103
Lk. 12:22–31 ................... 218
Lk. 12:22–34 ................... 233
Lk. 12:32–34 ................... 235
Lk. 16:1–13 ...................... 115
Lk. 16:19–31 ................... 256
Lk. 21:1–4 ........................ 115
Lk. 22:26–27 ................... 100
Lk. 24:39 .......................... 103

John ................................... 81
Jn. 1:14 ............................... 84
Jn. 1:18 ............................... 52
Jn. 3:16 ............. 84, 125, 305

Jn. 4:1–15 ........................ 274
Jn. 4:10 ............................. 174
Jn. 4:16 ............................. 173
Jn. 4:19 ..................... 125, 173
Jn. 6:1–13 ................. 213, 220
Jn. 6:1–14 ........................ 115
Jn. 10:10 ........................... 200
Jn. 10:16 ........................... 274
Jn. 12:24 ........................... 139
Jn. 13:12–15 ................... 100
Jn. 15:1–11 ........................ 84
Jn. 15:4–8 ........................... 83
Jn. 15:5 ......................... 12, 44
Jn. 15:12 ........................... 184
Jn. 17:1–11 ........................ 84
Jn. 20:19–22 ..................... 53

Acts ..................... 57, 81, 311
Acts 2 ................................ 311
Acts 2:14–18 ................... 274
Acts 2:42–47 ................... 283
Acts 7:46 .......................... 176
Acts 8:26–39 ................... 274
Acts 9:36 .......................... 281
Acts 10:43 ........................ 200
Acts 15:7–9 ...................... 274
Acts 17:24 ................... 28, 46
Acts 17:28 ................. 72, 89

Romans .......................... 104
Rom. 1:7 ............................. 11
Rom. 1:12 ......................... 290
Rom. 5:4–5 ........................ 35
Rom. 5:15–17 ................... 220
Rom. 5:20–21 ................... 156
Rom. 6:17 ......................... 176
Rom. 7:5 ............................. 81
Rom. 7:15 ........................... 34
Rom. 7:25 ......................... 176
Rom. 8:12 ........................... 81
Rom. 8:15f. ...................... 200
Rom. 8:21 ......................... 324
Rom. 8:25 ......................... 161
Rom. 8:26 ........................... 67

Rom. 8:29.........................46
Rom. 8:37–39 ..................28
Rom. 8:38–39 ..................318
Rom. 10:12b ..................127
Rom. 11:35......................173
Rom. 12..................202, 221
Rom. 12:2......................140
Rom. 12:4–5 ...................290
Rom. 13:7......................233
Rom. 14:8......................214
Rom. 15:25–27 .......206, 295
Rom. 15:26......................283
Rom. 15:27f. ..................206

1 Corinthians 1:2............11
1 Cor. 1:3–9 ..................177
1 Cor. 1:9......................283
1 Cor. 1:4–7 ..................161
1 Cor. 3:16........................46
1 Cor. 3:16–17 ................84
1 Cor. 6:19f. ..................333
1 Cor. 8:4–13 ..................211
1 Cor. 8:6......................307
1 Cor. 12:8–11 ................161
1 Cor. 12:31......................161
1 Cor. 13:1......................161
1 Cor. 13:11......................37
1 Cor. 15: 35–44.............333
1 Cor. 15:57....................176

2 Corinthians 3:2–6........52
2 Cor. 4:15......................318
2 Cor. 5:17........................46
2 Cor. 6:16......................195
2 Cor. 8............................295
2 Cor. 8:1–6 ..................126
2 Cor. 8:1–7 ..................266
2 Cor. 8:5......................289
2 Cor. 8:9......... 17, 127, 345
2 Cor. 8:16......................176
2 Cor. 9............................295
2 Cor. 9:6–12 ..................258
2 Cor. 9:8....... 172, 190, 201,
    207, 220, 258

2 Cor. 9:10......................201
2 Cor. 9:13......................283
2 Cor. 9:15......................176
2 Cor. 12:9......................209
2 Cor. 9:15......................176

Galatians 1:15................318
Gal. 3:2..........................103
Gal. 3:28 ........................274
Gal. 5 ............................103
Gal. 5:16 ................. 19ff., 81
Gal. 5:22f.........................233

Ephesians 1:1 ..................11
Eph. 1:7 ..........................200
Eph. 2:8 ..........................318
Eph. 3:16–19.... 10, 147, 149
Eph. 4:15 ........................35
Eph. 4:22–24....................99
Eph. 4:24 ........................97

Philippians ............180, 284
Phil. 1:3–5...............283, 284
Phil. 1:3–7......................318
Phil. 1:21 ......................219
Phil. 2:5 ..........................325
Phil. 2:5–11...............18, 109
Phil. 4:2–3......................11
Phil. 4:5 ..........................290
Phil. 4:8–10....................160
Phil. 4:11 ........................207
Phil. 4:11–13..................219

Colossians............150, 180
Col. 1:21 ..........................202
Col. 1:27 ..........................28
Col. 3:3–14......................150
Col. 4:5–17......................11

1 Thessalonians.............180
1 Thess. 5:16–19.....173, 174
1 Thess. 5:17 .............68, 176
1 Thess. 5:18 ..................208

2 Thessalonians............180
2 Thess. 1:3......................278

1 Timothy......................225
1 Tim. 6:10......................225
1 Tim. 6:17–19 ...............207

2 Timothy 3:16 ...............63

Philemon........................26
Phil. 6 .............................283

Hebrews 10:24 ...............259
Heb. 11 .............................36
Heb. 13:5 ........................207

James..............................263
James 1:17 .................15, 262
James 2:2–4....................263
James 2:16 ......................254
James 5:12 ........................35

1 Peter 1:15....................150
1 Peter 2:5 ......................351

1 John 4:10 ....................174
1 Jn. 4:16 ........................173
1 Jn. 4:19 .................125, 173

Revelation ......................274
Rev. 2 ..............................26
Rev. 3 ..............................26
Rev. 21:1 ..........................200
Rev. 21:1–22:5 ................232
Rev. 21:3 ..........................195
Rev. 22:13........................72

CPSIA information can be obtained
at www.ICGtesting.com
Printed in the USA
BVHW062151170220
572581BV00008B/716